Implementing Microsoft Dynamics NAV 2013

Discover all you need to know to implement Dynamics NAV 2013, from gathering the requirements to deployment

Laura Nicolàs Lorente

Cristina Nicolàs Lorente

BIRMINGHAM - MUMBAI

Implementing Microsoft Dynamics NAV 2013

First published: February 2013

Production Reference: 2180213

Published by Packt Publishing Ltd.
Livery Place
35 Livery Street
Birmingham B3 2PB, UK.

ISBN 978-1-849686-02-0

www.packtpub.com

Cover Image by Jarek Blaminsky (milak6@wp.pl)

Credits

Authors

Laura Nicolàs Lorente

Cristina Nicolàs Lorente

Reviewers

Dhan Raj Bansal

Steven Renders

Tony Hemy

Acquisition Editor

Mary Nadar

Lead Technical Editor

Ankita Shashi

Technical Editors

Jalasha D'costa

Veronica Fernandes

Soumya Kanti

Veena Pagare

Hardik Soni

Copy Editors

Brandt D'Mello

Insiya Morbiwala

Aditya Nair

Laxmi Subramanian

Ruta Waghmare

Project Coordinator

Leena Purkait

Proofreaders

Aaron Nash

Lindsey Thomas

Lauren Tobon

Jonathan Todd

Indexer

Hemangini Bari

Graphics

Aditi Gajjar

Valentina D'silva

Production Coordinators

Aparna Bhagat

Nitesh Thakur

Prachali Bhiwandkar

Aditi Gajjar

Cover Work

Aparna Bhagat

About the Authors

Laura Nicolàs Lorente had first started working with Dynamics NAV back in 2005 in the support department, mostly solving functional issues and doubts. She soon jumped to full deployment, that is, consultation, analysis, development, implementation, migration, training, and support.

Right from the beginning, she realized that it was very important for a Dynamics NAV consultant to have a deep knowledge of business workflows. Technical skills were just not enough. So she started to train herself in accounting, taxation, supply chain, logistics, and so on. She discovered a whole new world and she found it very interesting.

After having enough consultancy experience, she got to manage the first project on her own. It was then that she realized that technical and business knowledge was not enough; she also needed management skills. This is why, after reading different management books and trying different approaches with the projects she worked on, she decided to deepen her knowledge by doing a Master's in Project Management. She is now transitioning to Agile Management and Agile Development for better success in projects.

She continues her training in three areas — technology, business workflows, and management — whenever she gets the chance.

The Internet is a huge source of inspiration for her. She actively participates in group discussions, posts on forums and blogs, reads books, and so on. She also contributes by sharing her knowledge and experience with the Spanish Dynamics NAV community.

Acknowledgement

I would like to thank Rosa, my wife, for the patience she had while I was writing this book, and because she always believed I could do it. She encouraged me when times were hard and gave me the energy I needed to keep going.

I would also like to thank Cristina. She is my sister, my friend, and my colleague. We both wrote this book and had a great time together while writing and learning. I wish us many successful projects together, now and in the future.

Thanks to Josep Ma. I'm really grateful for all the talks and chats we have about projects, management, Agile methodology, and coaching. He helped me view projects with another perspective and pushed me to management.

I'm also grateful to those who encouraged me to start my own blog and get involved in the online community, and those who have read me during those years. The community helped me learn a lot and has given me great opportunities, such as writing this book.

I don't want to forget all my colleagues, managers, and customers who helped me grow, specially Mario, Núria, Germán, Noemi, Joan Carles, Genís and Ambre. Thanks to you all.

Cristina Nicolàs Lorente has been working with Dynamics NAV since 2005. She started in the ERP world as a developer but soon evolved into a complete Dynamics NAV professional, performing all the tasks involved in a Dynamics NAV implementation, such as consultancy, analysis, development, implementation, training, and support to end users.

When Cristina started developing solutions for Dynamics NAV, she had no idea about accounting or about any kind of business workflows. They don't teach that kind of thing in a technical university career. Soon, Cristina discovered that it is important to know the set of tools used but even more important to understand the meaning of whatever you develop. Without knowing the accounting rules, practices, and legal requirements, it is impossible to develop useful accounting functionalities even if you are the best developer. Only when you fully understand a company's process will you be able to do the appropriate developments.

With this in mind, Cristina has taken courses on accounting, warehouse management, and operations management. She is also willing to take courses on any other company-related topics.

Cristina thinks the best way to learn is to teach what you are learning to someone else. She has actually learned almost everything she knows about Dynamics NAV by responding to user questions on Internet forums, writing a blog about Dynamics NAV, and of course, writing the book you have in your hands. When you have to write about something, you have to experiment, try, investigate, and read. It definitely is a great way to learn.

Acknowledgement

I would like to thank Isabel, who supported me during this project. She has always believed in me and pushed me to find the time to invest in this book. Without her, this project would have been much more difficult than it turned out to be.

I would also like to thank Laura, my sister and colleague and the coauthor of this book, for always being positive about where you can reach with effort, discipline, and confidence in your own capabilities. She is the one who encouraged me to write this book.

A special thanks to Josep and Josep Maria. They have given me the opportunity to evolve professionally. They have always believed in me and given me the confidence needed to take my own steps and carry out my responsibilities.

The final thanks go to all my colleagues and customers, and also to all the people who helped me learn by posting questions on the forums. You have all contributed in developing me into the professional I am today.

About the Reviewers

Dhan Raj Bansal graduated in Electronics & Instrumentation Engineering from Kurukshetra University. After scoring an All India Rank 6 in the national-level entrance test called GATE (Graduate Aptitude Test in Engineering) in 2003, he got through the prestigious Indian Institute of Science, Bangalore (India), in the M.Tech (Instrumentation Engineering) stream. In 2005, he started his professional career as Navision Technical Consultant with PwC, India.

Currently, Dhan Raj works as a Sr. Techno-Functional Consultant with a Microsoft Implementation partner company in Delhi, India. He has worked for clients in the US, UK, Denmark, Australia, Dubai, Nigeria, and India.

Dhan Raj is an active member of the online communities for NAV, such as `dynamicsuser.net`, `mibuso.com`, and the online forums managed by Microsoft. For his contributions to these online communities, he received the Microsoft Most Valuable Professional (MVP) Award in July 2010 and renewed it in 2011 and 2012. The MVP Award is given out by Microsoft to independent members of technology communities around the world, and it recognizes people that share their knowledge with other members of the community.

Dhan Raj lives with his family in Delhi, India. He loves mathematics and solving puzzles.

Tony Hemy has been working with Dynamics NAV since 1998 and continues to be passionate about the product and what it brings to the market.

Tony's main focus is around designing and implementing robust, elegant, and well-engineered solutions to help drive value to businesses using the Dynamics platform. He also helps pursue R&D projects, develop relationships with customers, construct and fine-tune methodologies, and mentor other members of the team.

Having implemented Dynamics NAV in the UK, USA, and New Zealand, Tony now makes his home in Vancouver, Canada, where he can be found mountaineering, skiing, playing squash, and praying for a Stanley Cup win for the Vancouver Canucks.

Steven Renders is a Microsoft Certified Trainer and consultant with skills spanning business and technical domains. During the last few years, he has specialized in Microsoft Dynamics NAV and Microsoft SQL Server.

He has more than 15 years of business and technical experience. He provides training and consultancy focused on Microsoft Dynamics NAV, Microsoft SQL Server, business intelligence solutions, reporting, and database performance tuning.

Furthermore, he is also an expert in Microsoft Dynamics NAV, on which he has already delivered many training sessions. Steven was an author of the official Microsoft training material on Dynamics NAV reporting, development, upgrading, and SQL Server performance tuning.

Steven is the author of the books *Microsoft Dynamics NAV 2009: Professional Reporting* and was also a reviewer of the book *Programming Microsoft Dynamics NAV 2009* and *Programming Microsoft Dynamics NAV 2013*.

Steven has presented at various Microsoft MSDN and TechNet evenings, conferences, communities, events, and the MCT Summit.

In 2011, Steven started his own company, "think about IT," that is specialized in training and consultancy in Belgium and abroad, helping companies learn, implement, understand, and solve complex business requirements related to IT.

He specializes in Microsoft Dynamics NAV, Microsoft SQL Server, and business intelligence and reporting.

www.PacktPub.com

Support files, eBooks, discount offers and more

You might want to visit www.PacktPub.com for support files and downloads related to your book.

Did you know that Packt offers eBook versions of every book published, with PDF and ePub files available? You can upgrade to the eBook version at www.PacktPub.com and as a print book customer, you are entitled to a discount on the eBook copy. Get in touch with us at service@packtpub.com for more details.

At www.PacktPub.com, you can also read a collection of free technical articles, sign up for a range of free newsletters and receive exclusive discounts and offers on Packt books and eBooks.

http://PacktLib.PacktPub.com

Do you need instant solutions to your IT questions? PacktLib is Packt's online digital book library. Here, you can access, read and search across Packt's entire library of books.

Why Subscribe?
- Fully searchable across every book published by Packt
- Copy and paste, print and bookmark content
- On demand and accessible via web browser

Free Access for Packt account holders

If you have an account with Packt at www.PacktPub.com, you can use this to access PacktLib today and view nine entirely free books. Simply use your login credentials for immediate access.

Instant Updates on New Packt Books

Get notified! Find out when new books are published by following @PacktEnterprise on Twitter, or the *Packt Enterprise* Facebook page.

Table of Contents

Preface   **1**

Chapter 1: Introducing Microsoft Dynamics NAV 2013   **7**

Understanding Microsoft Dynamics NAV   **8**

History of Dynamics NAV   **10**

Functional areas   **12**

Financial Management   12
  Accountancy   13
  G/L budgets   14
  Account schedules   15
  Cash management   16
  Fixed Assets   17
  VAT reporting and intrastat   17
  Intercompany transactions   18
  Consolidation   19
  Multicurrency   19

Sales & Marketing   20
  Customers   21
  Order processing   21
  Approvals   22
  Pricing   24
  Marketing   24

Purchase   25
  Vendors   25
  Order processing   25
  Approvals   25
  Pricing   26
  Planning   26

Warehouse   27
  Items   28
  Locations   30
  Transfer orders   30
  Assembly   30

Pick and put-away	31
Inventory	31
Manufacturing	**33**
Product design	33
Capacities	35
Planning	37
Execution	38
Costing	39
Subcontracting	40
Job	**40**
Job card	41
Phases and tasks	42
Planning	42
Time sheet	44
Invoice jobs	44
Work in process (WIP)	44
Resource planning	**45**
Resource card	46
Pricing	47
Service	**47**
Service items	48
Contracts	49
Price management	49
Service orders	51
Service tasks	51
Fault reporting	52
Human resources	**52**
Employees	52
Absence registration	54
Country localizations	54
Vertical and horizontal solutions	**54**
Access Dynamics NAV	**55**
Windows client	**55**
Web client	**57**
SharePoint client	**59**
Web Services	**59**
Development environment	**61**
Summary	**62**
Chapter 2: What's New in NAV 2013	**63**
Application changes	**63**
Improvements to the Windows client	64
Ribbon	65
Select all	66
Copy/paste rows	67
Quick Entry	67
New keyboard shortcuts	70

Business Intelligence and KPIs   70
User collaboration tools   72
Application features   72
Financial Management   72
Assembly management   74
Warehouse management   75
Inventory   75
Supply planning   77
Jobs   78
Resources   79
RapidStart Services   79
CRM integration   80
Payment services   80
Development changes   **80**
Development Environment   80
Debugging   81
Page development   81
Page testing   83
Report development   84
Query development   85
XMLport development   86
Start ID Offset   86
Changes to C/AL functions, data types, properties, and triggers   87
.NET interoperability   92
Enhancements in RoleTailored client control add-ins   92
Standard C/AL code redesign   93
G/L Entry table locking redesign   93
Storing dimension entries   93
ADCS   95
IT changes   **95**
Installation   95
Dynamics NAV Server Administration   96
Windows PowerShell 2.0 cmdlets   97
Web client   98
Portal Framework for SharePoint 2010   100
User and credential types   100
NAS services   101
OData web services   102
Database changes   103
Unicode   103
ClickOnce   104
Deprecated features   **105**
Deprecated application features   105
Deprecated developer and IT features   105
Summary   **106**

Chapter 3: Dynamics NAV – General Considerations   107
The data model   108
Master data   108
Documents   109
Journals   113
Entries   118
    Creating ledger entries   120
Combining all concepts   126
No Save button   127
The main advantage   128
When is data checked   129
The main contra   130
The posting routines   130
Checking the posting routine with an example   131
Posted data cannot be modified (or deleted)   141
Navigating through your data   142
The Navigate functionality   142
Other ways to navigate   144
Filtering to find the data you need   146
Real-time data gathering – the SIFT technology   152
Everything leads to accounting   156
The Dynamics NAV database   158
The TableRelation property   158
Coded data rules   161
Summary   161

Chapter 4: The Implementation Process   163
What is an implementation   163
Methodology   165
The Waterfall approach   170
The Agile approach   171
Using the best of both   172
Microsoft Dynamics Sure Step   172
    Project types based on the Waterfall approach   173
    The Agile project type   177
Roles   179
Salesperson   180
Project manager   180
Business consultant   180
Key users   181
Analyst   182
Developer   182

Implementer	183
End users	183
Summarizing the roles	183
Phases	**185**
Presales	185
Getting the project requirements	186
Designing the solution	189
Configuration	189
Modifying standard Dynamics NAV functionality	191
New functionalities	192
Data migration	192
Development	192
Deployment	192
Software and hardware installation	193
Configuration	193
Data migration	194
User-acceptance test	194
End users' training	195
Go-live!	195
Support	195
Summary	**196**
Chapter 5: The Implementation Process on the Customer Side	**197**
Definition of goals	**198**
Defining the internal processes	**200**
Questions to be asked	200
Improve before automating	**204**
Getting the requirements	**204**
Change management	**206**
Get involved in testing the system	**207**
Involve end users	**208**
Summary	**209**
Chapter 6: Migrating Data	**211**
Tools to migrate data	**212**
RapidStart Services	212
Configuration wizard	215
Configuration packages	216
Configuration worksheet	219
Configuration templates	226
Configuration questionnaire	228
Summary of RapidStart Services	230
Using XMLports to migrate data	230
The XMLport structure	232
Running the XMLport	233
Writing code inside the XMLport	234

Writing your own tools	240
Converting data from the old system to suit Dynamics NAV's needs	**241**
Master data	**242**
Open entries	**243**
Customer entries	243
Vendor entries	249
Bank entries	249
Item entries	249
Fixed-asset entries	251
Accounting balances	253
Historical data	**254**
Open documents	**256**
Choosing a go-live date	**259**
Going live at the beginning of the fiscal year	259
Going live in the middle of a fiscal year	261
Summary	**262**
Chapter 7: Upgrading to Microsoft Dynamics NAV 2013	**263**
Upgrading philosophy	**264**
Upgrading process checklist	**266**
Preparing to upgrade	267
Upgrading from 2009, 2009 SP1 or 2009 R2	267
Upgrading the 2009 application code	268
Upgrading the 2009 data	268
Upgrading from 5.0 or 5.0 SP1	269
Upgrading the 5.0 application code	270
Upgrading the 5.0 data	271
Upgrading from 4.0, 4.0 SP1, 4.0 SP2, or 4.0 SP3	272
Upgrading the 4.0 application code	272
Upgrading the 4.0 data	273
Upgrading from 3.60 or 3.70	275
Upgrading the 3.60 or 3.70 application code	275
Upgrading the 3.60 or 3.70 data	276
Upgrading steps in detail	**278**
Preparing to upgrade	278
Migrating to SQL Server	278
Testing the database	279
Upgrading the application code	280
Getting object versions	280
Converting objects to the Dynamics NAV 2013 format	281
Carrying out customizations to the new version	281
Transforming forms to pages	282
Transforming reports	282
Revising and modifying customized code	283

Upgrading the data	283
Upgrading tools	**284**
Upgrade Toolkit	285
Text format upgrade	286
Form transformation	288
Report transformation	288
Upgrading Hybrid reports	289
Upgrading Classic reports	290
Comparing text tools	290
MergeTool	291
Downloading MergeTool	291
Installing MergeTool	291
Using MergeTool	292
Summary	**309**
Chapter 8: Development Considerations	**311**
Setup versus customization	**311**
Data model principles	**314**
Basic objects	314
Object elements	317
How tables are structured	320
Understanding table structures	321
The final picture	330
The structure of pages	331
Understanding page structures	332
The final picture	344
The posting process	**345**
The codeunit structure for sales posting	345
The codeunit structure for general journal posting	346
Where to write customized code	**347**
Validating fields	347
Checking data	348
Batch jobs	348
How to write customized code	**349**
Language	350
Spacing and alignment	350
Comments	351
Text constants	351
C/AL statements	351
Naming conventions	353
Naming objects	353
Using small functions	355
Summary	**355**

Chapter 9: Functional Changes on Existing Implementations	**357**
General guidelines	**357**
What is a functional change	**358**
The Requisition Worksheet	358
Fixed Assets	359
Item Tracking	359
Extending a customized functionality	360
Interactions with other functionalities	**360**
The Requisition Worksheet	360
Fixed Assets	361
Item Tracking	362
Creating a new item	364
Creating and posting a purchase order for the new item	365
Creating and posting a Sales Order for the new item	367
Turning on Item Tracking for the new item	368
Undoing the Sales Shipment posted for the new item	371
Extending a customized functionality	371
Writing a to-do list to implement a change	**373**
The Requisition Worksheet	373
Fixed Assets	375
Item Tracking	377
Extending a customized functionality	379
Choosing the right time	**380**
The Requisition Worksheet	380
Fixed Assets	380
Item Tracking	381
Extending a customized functionality	382
Planning the change	**382**
The Requisition Worksheet	383
Fixed Assets	385
Item Tracking	387
Extending a customized functionality	388
Summary	**390**
Chapter 10: Data Analysis and Reporting	**391**
Using filters and FlowFilters	**392**
Creating Views	**395**
Statistics	**397**
Charts	**398**
The Show as Chart option	398
Adding charts to the Role Center page	400
Creating and configuring charts	402

Using reports	**404**
Finding reports	404
Running reports	406
Types of reports	410
List reports	410
Test reports	410
Posting reports	410
Transaction reports	411
Document reports	411
Other reports	412
Account schedules	**413**
Analysis views	**416**
Understanding dimensions	416
Setting up new dimensions	417
Categorizing dimensions	418
Accessing dimensions	418
Creating an analysis view	420
Updating analysis views	423
Using analysis views	424
Analysis by Dimensions	424
Analysis views as a source for account schedules	425
Extracting data	**426**
Sending data to Microsoft Office applications	427
Sending data to Microsoft Word	428
Sending data to Microsoft Excel	428
Extracting data through web services	429
Other ways to extract Dynamics NAV data	429
Understanding report development	**429**
Reports anatomy	430
Defining the dataset	431
Designing the visual layout	433
Rules for flattening data	435
Report design guidelines	436
Summary	**440**
Chapter 11: Debugging	**441**
The art of debugging	**441**
Debugging in Dynamics NAV 2013	**442**
Starting the debugger	442
Break Rules	446
Placing breakpoints	447
From the Object Designer	448
In the current statement of the debugger	449
Conditional breakpoint	450
The debugger breakpoint list	451

Line-by-line execution	452
The Step Into option	452
The Step Over option	454
The Step Out option	454
The Continue option	455
The Call Stack FactBox	457
Watch variables	458
Adding variables from the Debugger Variables List window	458
Adding variables from the code viewer	460
Code Coverage	**461**
Importing the Code Coverage objects	461
How to use the Code Coverage feature	461
When to use the Code Coverage feature	466
Summary	**467**
Chapter 12: The Query Object	**469**
What is a query	**469**
Query Designer	**470**
Defining our first query	472
Adding complexity to the query	476
The DataItemLinkType property	478
Where to use queries	**481**
C/AL code	481
Charts	483
Web services	485
External applications	487
Excel and PowerPivot	487
Query performance	**489**
Summary	**491**
Chapter 13: Applications Included in Dynamics NAV	**493**
Jet Reports Express	**493**
Downloading Jet Reports Express	494
Installing Jet Reports Express	495
Installing Jet Reports Express on client machines	495
Installing Jet Reports Express on Dynamics NAV 2013	495
Configuring Jet Reports Express	497
Creating your first Jet Reports Express report	497
Adding filters	500
Analyzing the data	502
Using Jet Reports to retrieve data	503

Zetadocs Express   **504**
   Installing the Zetadocs client   505
   Adding Zetadocs SharePoint Extensions   505
   Importing NAV objects into Microsoft Dynamics NAV   506
   Configuring Zetadocs in Dynamics NAV   509
   Installing the Zetadocs help files   510
  Summary   **510**
Index   **511**

Preface

Implementing Dynamics NAV doesn't just mean installing the software. In the same manner, developing Dynamics NAV needs more than C/AL programming skills.

We first started working as Dynamics NAV programmers for a partner, but were assigned in-house work for one of our customers. We were lucky for many reasons. We gained experience due to being surrounded by end users, therefore getting to know their problems and the business needs behind each development. We were also very lucky with the customer's project leader with whom we had to work with. He is a person who likes to do things right. A working development was not enough, he also wanted everything to be easy to maintain, easy to scale, and easy to learn for end users.

In fact, all implementations and developments should follow these rules. But we all need mentoring to reach these goals. He gave us the mentoring we needed, and he also allowed us to take our time to learn how to do things right.

Soon we jumped to performing full implementations, such as consulting, analysis, development, migration, training, deployment, and support. When working on other areas, we went with the philosophy of doing things right as it was the only way to deliver true value on each implementation.

This book has been written to give you the mentoring everyone deserves.

Also, do not forget that for a Dynamics NAV consultant, it is not enough to have knowledge of the product and how to implement it. A Dynamics NAV consultant also needs deep knowledge of business workflows. We recommend you to train yourself in accounting, taxation, supply chain, logistics, manufacturing, or any other business area if you want to become a good Dynamics NAV consultant. This book is about Dynamics NAV 2013 and how to implement it, explained with the experience of several years of implementing Dynamics NAV.

What this book covers

Chapter 1, Introducing Microsoft Dynamics NAV 2013, introduces you to what an ERP (Enterprise Resource Planning) is and what you can expect from Dynamics NAV. It introduces all the functional areas found in Dynamics NAV 2013 and the different environments available, such as the Windows client, the web client, the SharePoint framework, or web services. For the nostalgic, we have also included details on the history of Dynamics NAV.

Chapter 2, What's New in NAV 2013, gives an overview of the changes made within the application. Dynamics NAV 2013 introduces quite a few new features, that is, new functionalities and tools available for the end user, such as the improvements that can be made on the Windows client or the assembly management feature. The chapter also covers development and IT changes.

Chapter 3, Dynamics NAV – General Considerations, is all about the Dynamics NAV structure, its data model, how information flows, how posting routines work, how users can navigate through their data, why everything leads to accounting, and how data integrity is approached.

Knowing the Dynamics NAV philosophy on how things are done is important for everyone. It is important for users because they need to know how to work with Dynamics NAV and also need to be aware of the consequences of what they do; it is also important for consultants, analysts, and developers because they need to use the same structures and the same way to make information flow when developing new functionalities.

Chapter 4, The Implementation Process, explains the meaning of implementation and covers different methodologies that can be applied while implementing Dynamics NAV. Several people may get involved in an implementation process, each one playing their own role and performing different jobs. This chapter also covers the phases and tasks needed to complete a Dynamics NAV implementation, from presales to deployment.

Chapter 5, Implementation Process at the Customer Side, explains what is expected from the company's team (users, key users, and project leader), and how to deal with the change that the new ERP will make for everyone in the company. For a really successful implementation of Dynamics NAV, the company that NAV has been implemented for has to actively participate on the project.

Chapter 6, Migrating Data, covers the tools that can be used to import data into Dynamics NAV, such as RapidStart services or XMLports. Companies may be new to Dynamics NAV, but they are usually not new companies. They have been working for a while and they have all kinds of data, such as their customers, vendors, items, and accounting information.

This chapter also explains which kind of data is commonly migrated to Dynamics NAV and the strategies used to migrate it. With a step by step example, the chapter conduces you to migrate master data, open entries, historical data, and open documents.

Chapter 7, Upgrading to Microsoft Dynamics NAV 2013, explains the migration process from Versions 3.xx, 4.xx, 5.xx, and 2009. Upgrading to a different version of Dynamics NAV is not a "Next-Next-Finish" process. It is the complete project that has to be planned and executed carefully.

We will explain the steps that have to be followed for all the versions and the tools that are out there to help us get through the whole process.

Chapter 8, Development Considerations, covers the main development considerations that should be taken into account when developing for Dynamics NAV. This includes a deep explanation of the data model principles in Dynamics NAV and how the posting processes are designed. It also includes explanations about where and how to write customized code.

Almost every Dynamics NAV implementation implies development. The customized code must fit inside the application's standard code and it should look as if it was part of the standard. This makes it easier for the user to understand how customized modules work and for partners to support them.

Chapter 9, Functional Changes on Existing Implementations, explains how to handle functional changes in existing implementations with a set of four examples. After working with Dynamics NAV for a while, companies may ask for functional changes on their implementations, such as adding some extra developments or starting to use an existing functionality. Some extra things have to be taken into account when dealing with such projects.

Chapter 10, Data Analysis and Reporting, provides an overview of the tools available to analyze Dynamics NAV data, both inside and outside the application, such as the use of filters and FlowFilters, statistics, charts, existing reports, analysis views, account schedules, or how to extract data from Dynamics NAV. Data analysis and reporting is an important part of the management of a company.

The chapter also includes a report development section that is meant to understand reports anatomy, to show how to define your dataset, and to show how the visual layout is designed.

Chapter 11, Debugging, covers debugging in Microsoft Dynamics NAV. Microsoft Dynamics NAV 2013 introduces a brand new debugger. Debugging will no longer be a painful task in Microsoft Dynamics NAV. Conditional breakpoints, debug other user sessions, and debug C/AL code in the RTC client instead of incomprehensible C# code. All these new features will convert the debugging experience into a happy experience.

Chapter 12, The Query Object, focuses on this new application object. Although not yet, queries are meant to be "The Microsoft Dynamics NAV reading data object" in the future (notice the capital letter in the word "The"), so you better get familiar with it as soon as possible.

In this chapter you will learn what queries are and what you can expect from them, how to define a query and where to use them.

Chapter 13, Applications Included in Dynamics NAV, will explain what Jet Reports Express and Zetadocs Express are meant for, and how to install and configure them to work together with Microsoft Dynamics NAV 2013. These are free versions of third-party applications recommended by Microsoft and compatible with standard versions of Microsoft Dynamics NAV.

What you need for this book

To successfully follow the examples in this book, you will need to install Microsoft Dynamics NAV 2013.

Who this book is for

This book is meant for Dynamics NAV implementation consultants, project managers, and developers who want to get a deeper view of what Dynamics NAV 2013 can offer.

It is also meant for Dynamics NAV developers who want to learn more about the whole application.

And finally, this book may be useful to IT managers of all kinds of companies that are considering the implementation of Dynamics NAV 2013 in their organizations, to fully understand what to expect and how to accomplish it.

Conventions

In this book, you will find a number of styles of text that distinguish between different kinds of information. Here are some examples of these styles, and an explanation of their meaning.

Code words in text are shown as follows: "The Customer table is the master data table for the Sales & Marketing area"

New terms and **important words** are shown in bold. Words that you see on the screen, in menus or dialog boxes for example, appear in the text like this: "not all items in the **Navigate** tab are secondary master data".

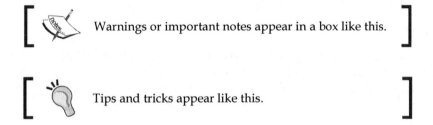

Warnings or important notes appear in a box like this.

Tips and tricks appear like this.

Reader feedback

Feedback from our readers is always welcome. Let us know what you think about this book—what you liked or may have disliked. Reader feedback is important for us to develop titles that you really get the most out of.

To send us general feedback, simply send an e-mail to feedback@packtpub.com, and mention the book title via the subject of your message.

If there is a topic that you have expertise in and you are interested in either writing or contributing to a book, see our author guide on www.packtpub.com/authors.

Customer support

Now that you are the proud owner of a Packt book, we have a number of things to help you to get the most from your purchase.

Errata

Although we have taken every care to ensure the accuracy of our content, mistakes do happen. If you find a mistake in one of our books—maybe a mistake in the text or the code—we would be grateful if you would report this to us. By doing so, you can save other readers from frustration and help us improve subsequent versions of this book. If you find any errata, please report them by visiting http://www.packtpub.com/submit-errata, selecting your book, clicking on the **errata submission form** link, and entering the details of your errata. Once your errata are verified, your submission will be accepted and the errata will be uploaded on our website, or added to any list of existing errata, under the Errata section of that title. Any existing errata can be viewed by selecting your title from http://www.packtpub.com/support.

Piracy

Piracy of copyright material on the Internet is an ongoing problem across all media. At Packt, we take the protection of our copyright and licenses very seriously. If you come across any illegal copies of our works, in any form, on the Internet, please provide us with the location address or website name immediately so that we can pursue a remedy.

Please contact us at copyright@packtpub.com with a link to the suspected pirated material.

We appreciate your help in protecting our authors and our ability to bring you valuable content.

Questions

You can contact us at questions@packtpub.com if you are having a problem with any aspect of the book, and we will do our best to address it.

1
Introducing Microsoft Dynamics NAV 2013

Microsoft Dynamics NAV 2013 is an **Enterprise Resource Planning (ERP)** system targeted at small and medium-sized companies.

An ERP is a system, a software, that integrates the internal and external management information across an entire organization. The purpose of an ERP is to facilitate the flow of information between all business functions inside the boundaries of the organizations. An ERP system is meant to handle all the organization areas on a single software system. This way, the output of an area can be used as input of another area, without the need to manually duplicate data.

This chapter gives you an idea of what Dynamics NAV is and what you can expect from it. The topics covered in this chapter are:

- What is an ERP
- Functional areas found on Microsoft Dynamics NAV 2013
- A bit of history of Dynamics NAV
- How to use Dynamics NAV on different environments (the Windows client, the Web client, the SharePoint framework, Web Services, and so on)

Understanding Microsoft Dynamics NAV

Microsoft Dynamics NAV 2013 is a **RoleTailored ERP**, : it is focused on roles. The system is based around the individuals within an organization, their roles, and the tasks they perform. When users first enter Dynamics NAV, they see the data needed for the daily tasks they do according to their role. Users belonging to different roles will have a different view of the system; each of them will see the functions they need to properly perform their daily tasks. Dynamics NAV 2013 covers the following functional areas inside an organization:

- **Financial Management**: The following functionalities are covered under financial management: accounting, G/L budgets, account schedules, financial reporting, cash management, receivables and payables, fixed assets, VAT reporting, intercompany transactions, cost accounting, consolidation, multicurrency, and intrastat

- **Sales & Marketing**: This area covers customers, order processing, pricing, contacts, marketing campaigns, and so on

- **Purchase**: This area includes vendors, order processing, approvals, planning, costing, and other such areas

- **Warehouse**: Under the warehouse area you will find inventory, shipping and receiving, locations, picking, assembly, and likewise

- **Manufacturing**: The manufacturing area includes product design, capacities, planning, execution, costing, subcontracting, and so on

- **Job**: Within the job area you can create projects, phases and tasks, planning, time sheets, work in process, and likewise

- **Resource Planning**: This area includes resources, capacity, and other such areas

- **Service**: Within the service area you can manage service items, contract management, order processing, planning & dispatching, service tasks, and so on

- **Human Resources**: It allows you to manage employees, absences, and so on

These areas are covered in more detail in the next section of this chapter.

A good thing about Dynamics NAV is that it can be customized. A brand new functional area can be created from scratch or new features can be added to an existing area. All the development is done with a proprietary programming language called C/AL.

When someone creates a new functional area, a vertical or horizontal solution, they usually create it as an add-on. An add-on can be registered and is now available to anyone who pays the corresponding fee. If some features are added to an existing area, usually it is a customization that will only be used on the database of the customer who asked for the feature.

A bad thing abut Dynamics NAV is that the code of the application is not on a multilayer architecture. All code is located on a single layer. Therefore, if you customize an area, you have to do it by modifying the standard code and adding code in the middle of the standard object definition. This makes it hard to upgrade to new versions of Dynamics NAV. Dynamics NAV 2013 uses a three-tier architecture:

- SQL Server is the data tier and is used to store the data into a database.
- Microsoft Dynamics NAV Server is the middle or server tier, managing all business logics and communication. It also provides an additional layer of security between clients and the database, and an additional layer for user authentication.
- On the client tier we find the RoleTailored clients, such as the Windows clients and the Web client. Dynamics NAV 2013 also supports other kind of clients, including Web Services (both SOAP and OData), a SharePoint client through Microsoft Dynamics NAV Portal Framework, and a NAS service.

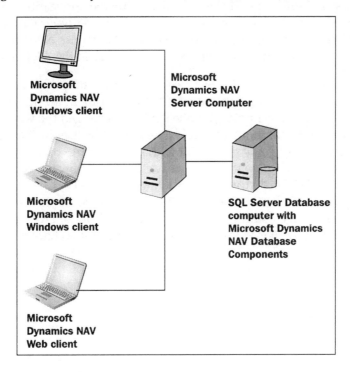

In the previous diagram you can see a simple installation. You can install Dynamics NAV in more complex scenarios, as you can have multiple instances of any of the core components.

History of Dynamics NAV

We are not historians, but we thought that it is important to know where we come from and where are we going. Some of the current restrictions or features can be better understood if we know a bit of the history of Dynamics NAV. This is why we have added this section.

Dynamics NAV was first eveloped by a Danish firm and the program was called Navision A/S. In 2002, Microsoft bought Navision A/S and included it on the Microsoft Business Solution division. The product has gone through several name changes. The names Navision Financials, Navision Attain, and Microsoft Business solutions Navision Edition have been used to refer to this product that is currently called Microsoft Dynamics NAV. Note that all the previous names included the word Navision. This is why many people keep calling it Navision instead of NAV.

In the early 90s, with the release of Navision 3.04, the AL programming language was introduced along with the designing tools for designing screens, tables, reports, imports, batches, and functions. This way of designing the application objects has persisted over the years. Major changes were made to the designer tools later on when Pages and RTC reports stepped in with the release of Dynamics NAV 2009. NAV 2009 also introduced the possibility to use the .NET framework in the AL language.

RTC reports brought in a big change because the layout of the report had to be designed in Visual Studio, outside Dynamics NAV, to bring in the advantages of SQL Server Reporting Services technology; while the Pages changed the way of developing the user interface. Until that moment, while developing the user interface, you could just see what the user was going to see. But with Pages report you could create an indented structure to determine the fields and actions, and how to group the demand; whereas the rendering of that structure was left to the RTC client. The reason was to make the design independent of the client who was going to run it. We can perceive the benefits of this change in the architecture with the release of Dynamics NAV 2013 that brought us two new clients. We will discuss it later in this chapter.

The release of Navision Financials 2.50 brought the SQL option for Navision with itself. From Navision Financials 2.50 to Dynamics NAV 2009, two database options coexisted: the native Server and the SQL Server. With the release of Dynamics NAV 2013, the only option possible is SQL. This really makes a difference, because we can get rid of the restrictions that were only there to assure compatibility between the two options. As an example, Dynamics NAV 2013 has bought the new Query object; with this new object we can now specify a set of data from multiple tables. The query gets converted to a single SQL statement, using the SQL JOIN clause. This is something that was not possible at all in the native option. Now that this option does not exist, the restriction is gone, and we can use multiple JOIN clauses within Dynamics NAV.

The release of Microsoft Business Solutions NAV 4.0 introduced the Menu Suite, which completely changed the menu structure of the product. This was the first step in making the menu role-orientated instead of functionality-oriented. The look and feel of the new menu was very similar to Outlook, bringing NAV closer to other Microsoft products.

The three-tier architecture appeared with the release of Dynamics NAV 2009, along with the RTC client, the new Page object, designing Report layouts on Visual Studio, and Web Services. The old client was renamed and called the Classic client. In Dynamics NAV 2013 the Classic client disappears, but this release includes the new Web client and the SharePoint client.

For existing customers, upgrading to NAV 2009 with the new RTC client was a huge effort. This is why many companies chose to do a technical upgrade – to take advantage of the new Web Services interface. But they used the Classic client and therefore did not move to the full three-tier architecture.

And finally Dynamics NAV 2013 has been released, and this is what the book is all about.

Functional areas

From a functional perspective, Dynamics NAV hasn't changed much over the years. Lately, no new functional areas have appeared and the existing one just like they worked in many previous versions. In the last version of NAV 2009, Microsoft was focused on changing the whole architecture (for good), and NAV 2013 is the consolidation of the new architecture. All those architectural changes were made to bring Dynamics NAV closer to the existing Microsoft technologies, namely, Microsoft Office, .NET, SQL Server, and so on; in the meantime, functionality has been left behind. Although NAV 2013 includes a few new minor features that will be covered later in the book, we are willing to see plenty of new feature in future versions.

Anyway this section is about the existing functionality and what can we expect from each area. As we have seen earlier in this chapter, Dynamics NAV 2013 covers all the following functional areas:

- Financial Management
- Sales & Marketing
- Purchase
- Warehouse
- Manufacturing
- Job
- Resource Planning
- Service
- Human Resources

In order to use Dynamics NAV, all organizations have to use the Financial Management area. It is the epicenter of the whole application. Any other area is optional and their usage depends on the organization's needs. The sales and the purchase areas are also used in almost any implementationDynamics NAV.

Now let's take a closer view of each area.

Financial Management

As we said, financial management is the epicenter of Dynamics NAV. Actually, accountancy is the epicenter, and the general ledger is included inside the Financial Management area. What else can be found? The following screenshot shows the main page of the **Financial Management** department:

Financial Management		
Choose by department		
General Ledger	Payables	
Cash Management	Fixed Assets	
Cost Accounting	Inventory	
Cash Flow	Periodic Activities	
	General Ledger	Consolidation
Receivables	VAT	Receivables
	Currency	Payables
	Fiscal Year	Cost Accounting

We'll give a few details about each of these areas.

Accountancy

Accountancy is the act of recording, classifying, and summarizing, in terms of money, the transactions and events that take place in the company. Accountancy is thousands of years old; the earliest accounting records, dating back to more than 7,000 years, were found in Mesopotamia. Of course, nowadays we don't use the same accounting system, but it is interesting that accounting is useful in every single company, no matter how different it is from any other company. Probably the fact that keeping accounting records is mandatory in almost all countries helps! You know you have to do it, so at least we have to have a benefit from it.

Hey, no, we are serious! Accountancy is useful. Sometimes it's too strict, most of the time completely illogical for techies like us, but it's useful.

Accountancy has its own language: accounts, credit amounts, and debit amounts. This language is managed through strict and clear rules. Dynamics NAV has implemented those rules using posting groups, so the system can translate everything to accounting language and post it to the general ledger entries on the fly.

An important difference between Dynamics NAV and the other accounting systems is that you don't need to open an individual account for each customer, each vendor, each bank, or each fixed asset. Dynamics NAV does not keep detailed information about them on the accountant system. Only one or a few accounts are needed for each group. This is something that shocks accountants when they use Dynamics NAV for the first time.

G/L budgets

The **General Ledger** part also contains G/L budgets. This feature allows you to create accounting budgets with different levels of detail. You can break down the budget by different periods (day, week, month, quarter, year, or any accounting period), by accounts (on single posting accounts or heading accounts), by business units, or by dimensions.

The budget can be edited inside Dynamics NAV or can be exported to Excel, edited there, and then imported back to Dynamics NAV. You can do multiple imports from Excel and the new entries can be added to the existing ones.

You can also create distinct budgets inside Dynamics NAV and then combine them in a single budget. The following screenshot shows the main **Budget** page:

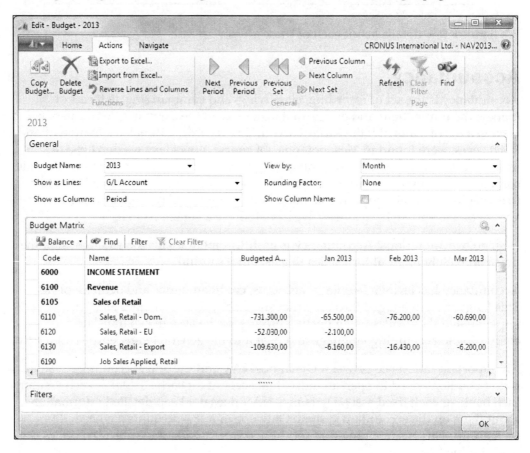

After presenting the budget, you can find different ways of tracking it. Either from the **G/L Balance/Budget** page, from Trial Balance/Budget report, or from the account schedules defined by you.

Account schedules

Account schedules are meant for reporting and analysis of financial statements. Dynamics NAV includes some standard statements, but the good thing about it is that you can modify the existing ones or you can create new ones in order to meet specific requirements of an organization. In the following screenshot you can see a list of the existing schedules:

Account schedules can be made of ledger entries, budget entries, or analysis view entries. Analysis view entries are used to summarize ledger entries by a period and a set of dimensions. You can also combine entries from these different sources into a single schedule.

You can also define what kind of information is shown in the rows and the columns. Each column can show data from different periods so you can compare amounts over the periods. Account schedules are therefore a powerful tool that end users can use to create their own customized financial reports. The **Acc. Schedule Overview** window has been displayed in the following screenshot:

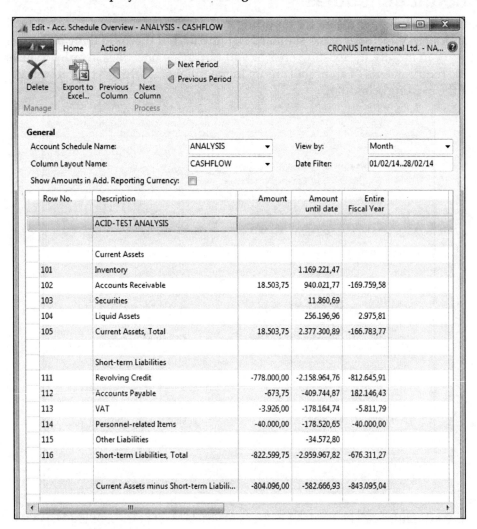

Cash management

The cash management feature is used to manage the company's bank accounts. You can process the payments received from customers, payments to vendors, and bank reconciliation.

You can create a bank account card for each account the company has in the banks. Whenever a transaction is made in Dynamics NAV using a bank account, the system will post an entry in the bank account entry, plus a related G/L entry according to the bank posting group. The posting of bank entries is done from the cash receipt journal or from the payment journal. Other journals, such as the general journals could also be used.

The payment journal includes a suggest vendor payments action to help you decide what is to be paid.

Fixed Assets

The Fixed Assets functionality is used to manage the company's assets, their cost and depreciation, and also its related maintenance and insurances.

Fixed Assets has unlimited depreciation books that track the depreciation expense reliably. All the ordinary methods of depreciation are available, plus the ability to create custom depreciation methods is also available.

Fixed Assets include two different journals: the FA G/L journal and the FA journal. The FA G/L journal is used to post entries on the FA ledger entry and also a corresponding entry on the G/L entry. The FA journal is used only to create entries on the FA ledger entry. This means that depending on your configuration, you may not be posting anything related to FA in the G/L entry. You therefore need to be careful and know exactly when to post on the G/L and when not to, but keep everything synchronized.

VAT reporting and intrastat

VAT is the acronym of Value Added Tax. It is a transaction that is paid by the end consumer and business. In Dynamics NAV you can find a table called `VAT Entry` where all VAT transactions are recorded, mainly through purchase and sale invoices. In addition, the corresponding amounts are also posted on the accounts determined by its posting groups.

As in many other areas, all VAT processes are mainly based on their own entries, not in the amounts found in the accounting areas.

A process named `Calculate and Post VAT Settlement` helps you to post the G/L transactions for the VAT Settlement. Dynamics NAV also includes VAT statements that are pretty similar to the Account Schedules we discussed before. Therefore you can define your own VAT statements that will help you submit it to the tax authorities.

The following screenshot shows how a **VAT Statement** definition looks like:

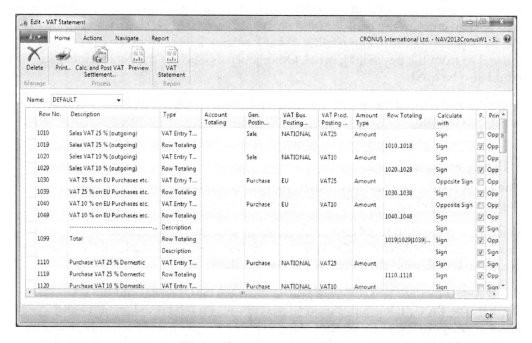

Intrastat is a required reporting process for all European Union (EU) companies that trade with other EU countries/regions. Each company within the EU is responsible for reporting the movement of goods to their statistics authorities every month and delivering the report to the tax authority. In Dynamics NAV, the intrastat journal is used to complete periodic intrastat reports.

The intrastat journal requires item entries to contain information related to tariff numbers, transaction types, and transport methods. The tariff numbers are assigned on each item card, while transaction types and transport methods are assigned on sales and purchase documents.

Intercompany transactions

Intercompany postings are used to transfer transactions electronically from one partner company to another. To be able to send and receive transactions, the companies involved need to agree on a common chart of accounts and a set of dimensions to use in the intercompany transactions. Therefore, a setup phase will be needed before you can start using this functionality. This setup phase will probably take longer than you expect.

When company A creates a document that needs to be sent to company B, the following flow occurs:

1. Company A creates the document and sends it to his IC outbox.
2. Company A sends all the transactions from his IC outbox.
3. Company B receives the transactions in his IC inbox.
4. Company B converts the IC inbox transactions to a document and processes it.

A transaction can be sent to the partner's inbox directly if both companies coexist on the same database, or you can also send transactions by e-mail or through XML files.

Consolidation

The **consolidation** is the process of adding up general ledger entries of two or more separate companies (subsidiaries) into a new company, called the consolidated company. Each individual company involved in a consolidation is called a business unit.

Note that we have only talked about adding up general ledger entries; no other entries on the system are used for consolidation purposes. In the chart of accounts of each business unit, you can indicate which accounts are to be included in the consolidation.

The consolidation process creates a summarized G/L entry on the consolidated company for the period you have selected while running the process, and for each account and combination of dimensions, if you choose to copy dimensions on the consolidated company. The consolidation functionality contains a process to help you register the consolidation eliminations.

Multicurrency

Multicurrency can be used if you buy or sell in other currencies besides your local currency. You can assign currency codes to bank accounts and also to customers and vendors. You can also use multicurrency to record general ledger transactions in an additional currency (besides your local currency). The additional currency feature is very useful for international companies that need to report in a currency different than the one they use in their daily transactions. You can register exchange rates for each foreign currency and specify from which dates the exchange rates are valid. Each time you post a transaction in a different currency, a conversion is made to translate that currency amount into the local currency amount. All entries in Dynamics NAV keep all the amounts in the transaction currency and in the local currency in separate fields.

The Adjust exchange rates process will help you to update the amounts of posted transactions to the new assigned rates. The following image shows how the currency exchange rates are defined for the USD currency:

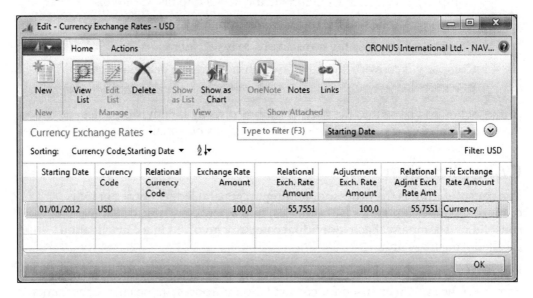

Sales & Marketing

The sales area can be used to manage all common sales processes information, such as quotes, orders, and returns. There are also tools to plan and manage different type of customers' information and transaction data. The following screenshot shows the main page of the **Sales & Marketing** area:

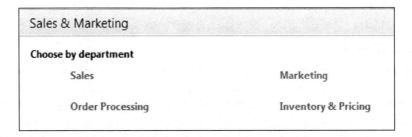

We'll give a few details about each of these areas later in the chapter.

Customers

In the **Sales & Marketing** area, everything revolves around customers. The customer card contains a lot of information, but only a few fields are mandatory in order to be used by the customer on transactions; they are the ones which corresponds to the posting groups. All other fields can be filled or not depending on how you want the sales area to work.

You can define a salesperson for the customer, to track the sales of each salesperson. You can set a credit limit for each customer, so that you get a warning when you try to create a new order for the customer and the credit is exceeded. You can group your customers by price and discounts groups to help you define prices. You can define different payment terms and methods. You can indicate how you are going to ship the goods to each customer, and you can also indicate a currency and a language for the customer. Besides that, you can also create multiple bank accounts and credit cards.

Many times, the company establishes a criteria for filling up all of this information. As an example, the company could have a norm that large customers will be part of a particular price group, will use specific posting groups, and will have particular payment terms. In this case you can create as many customer templates as the defined criteria, and apply a template each time a new customer is introduced to the system. In the following screenshot, you can see all the fields that can be included in a customer template:

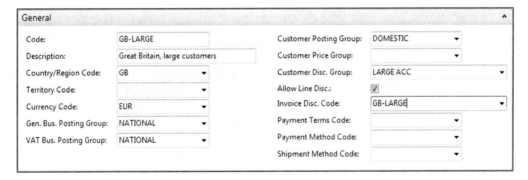

Order processing

The order processing part is all about documents. Dynamics NAV allows you to create quotes, blanket orders, orders, return orders, invoices, and credit memos.

The sales process can start with any of those documents, depending on the company's needs. In the following diagram you can see the information flow through the documents. The image documents with a gray background are the ones from where the process can start.

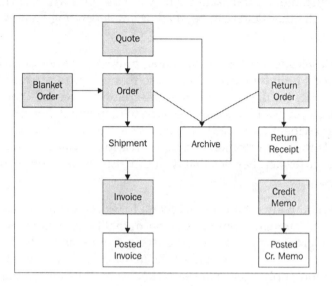

All the data from one document is carried forward to the next document. In addition, you can also create new documents by copying the data from any other sales document on the system.

In the previous diagram, the documents with the green background are passed to the documents with the white background through a posting process, but posting routines can take a while to process. Dynamics NAV 2013 has introduced a new feature, the background posting. If background posting is enabled, then the data is put in a queue and posted later in the background. This allows users to keep working while the system is posting their documents.

When you select a customer in a document, many fields from the customer card are copied to the document header. This is considered as default data from that customer. You can change most of that data on a particular document.

Approvals

The approval system allows the user to submit a document for approval according to a predefined hierarchy of approval managers with certain approval amount limits. The approval of a document can be initiated by an e-mail notification sent to the user. Similarly, reminders of overdue approvals are also sent. Pending approvals can also be viewed from the **Order Processing** menu.

The system allows you to create several approval templates where you can choose the document types to be included in the approval process and which approval and limit type is to be used for each document. Document amounts are the main criteria to include a document in the approval process. The different limit types that can be used are as follows:

- **No limits**: The document is included in the approval process, no matter how small or big the total amount is. It will then depend on the user setup.

- **Approval limits**: The document is included in the approval process if the total amount is greater than the amount limit.

- **Credit limits**: If a sales document that will put a customer over their credit limit is created, the document is sent for the credit limit approvals. After that, amount approvals may also have to approve the document.

The following screenshot shows how the **Approval Templates** page looks like:

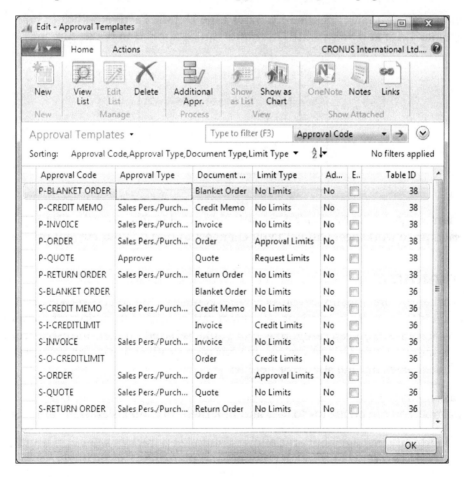

Pricing

The pricing option allows you to specify how you want to set up the sales prices agreements. You can specify prices and discounts. Both prices and discounts can be for an individual customer, a group of customers, all customers, and for a campaign. You need to specify one price for each item. If no price is found, the last sales price of the item is used. When a price agreement is created, you can specify if VAT is included in the price or not. Sales prices and sales discounts are introduced in separate tables.

Dynamics NAV always retrieves the best price. The best price is the lowest permissible price with the highest permissible line discount on a particular date.

In addition to specific item prices and discounts, you can also indicate invoice discounts or service charges. This can only be set up for individual customers, not for a group of customers or a campaign.

When you create a sales document, a **Sales Line Details** FactBox indicates how many **Sales Price** and **Sales Line Discounts** can be applied to the document.

Sales Line Details	^
Item No.:	1976-W
Availability:	-6
Substitutions:	0
Sales Prices:	0
Sales Line Discou...	1

You can see the details by clicking on each blue number found on the FactBox. The sales price worksheet will help you change and update your current prices.

Marketing

The marketing functionality revolves around contacts. You can create a contact and indicate his/her business relations. A contact can be related to customers, vendors, or bank accounts. You can categorize your contacts based on their industry groups or job responsibilities. Or you can create your own profile criteria, for example, educational level, marital status, or hobbies.

The task management feature allows you to create and organize marketing campaigns. You can create to-do lists and link them to contacts and/or campaigns.

The opportunity management area allows you to keep track of sales opportunities, have an overview of what is in the pipeline, and plan ahead accordingly.

Purchase

The purchase area can be used to manage all common purchase process' information, such as quotes, orders, and returns. There are also tools to plan your purchases according to your company's needs.

The main page of the **Purchase** area is shown in the following screenshot:

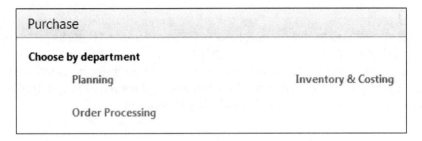

We'll give a few details about each of those areas, although most processes are similar to the ones we have discussed in the *Sales & Marketing* section.

Vendors

In the **Purchase** area, everything revolves around vendors. Vendors' cards are pretty similar to customers' cards. Please refer to the *Customer* section of this chapter to see what you can expect from vendors.

Order processing

The order processing part is all about documents. Dynamics NAV allows you to create quotes, blanket orders, orders, return orders, invoices, and credit memos.

Please refer to the *Order Processing* subsection of the *Sales & Marketing* section in this chapter to see what you can expect from order processing.

Approvals

The approval system allows the user to submit a document for approval according to a predefined hierarchy of approval managers with certain approval amount limits. The approval system works just as explained in the *Approvals* subsection of the *Sales & Marketing* section of this chapter.

Besides the different limits explained before, the purchase approval system includes a new type of limit:

- **Request Limits**: By using the request limit in combination with the request amount approval limit, a purchase request process can be set up for internal purchases in the company

Pricing

This option allows you to define purchase price agreements. It works just as the pricing model of the *Sales* section of this chapter, with one difference. In the *Sales* section, we said that both prices and discounts could be set for an individual customer, a group of customers, for all customers, and for a campaign. In the *Purchases* section it can only be set for individual vendors.

Planning

If you purchase goods, the requisition worksheet can help plan your purchases. You can manually enter items on the worksheet and fill in the relevant fields, or you can also run the `Calculate Plan` process. This calculates a replenishment plan for the items that have been set up with the replenishment system of purchase or transfer; for example, the program will automatically suggest an action you should take to replenish the item; it could be increasing the item quantity on an existing order or creating a new order.

You can also use the `Drop Shipment` function to fill in the requisition worksheet lines. This function retrieves the sales orders that you want to designate for a drop shipment. You use `Drop Shipment` when an item is shipped directly from your vendor to your customer. The system may sometimes suggest planning lines that need extra attention by the planner before they can be accepted.

The calculate plan batch job investigates the demand and supply situation of the item and calculates the projected available balance. The balance is defined as follows:

Inventory + Scheduled receipts + Planned receipts – Gross Requirements

It also respects the minimum order quantity, the maximum order quantity, and the order multiple of each item.

The following screenshot shows how the **Req. Worksheet** page looks like after you have run the calculate plan batch job:

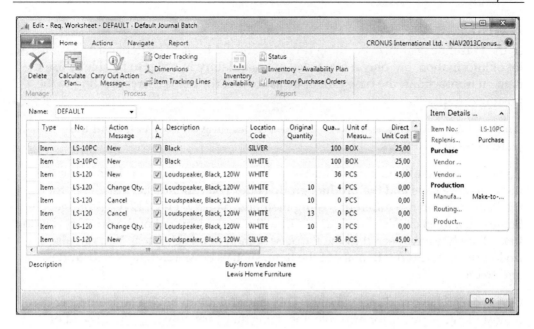

When you have finished reviewing the suggested purchases, you can use the **Carry Out Action Message** option to create new purchase orders and modify or cancel the existing ones.

Warehouse

After the goods have been received and before they are shipped, a series of internal warehouse activities take place to ensure the effective flow through the warehouse and to organize and maintain company inventories. Typical warehouse activities include putting items away, moving items inside or between warehouses, and picking items for assembly, production, or shipment. The following screenshot shows the main page of the **Warehouse** area:

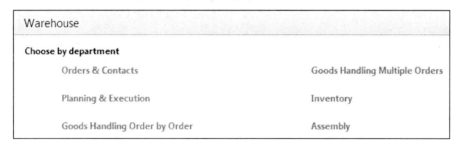

Items

In the **Warehouse** area, everything revolves around items. The item card contains a lot of information, but only a few fields are mandatory in order to be able to use the item on transactions: the base unit of measure and the fields corresponding to the posting groups.

All the other fields can be filled or unfilled depending on how you want the warehouse area to work.

You can create multiple units of measure. You can categorize your item using the item category code and the product group code. You can indicate a shelf no. for the item. You can use different costing methods, namely, FIFO, LIFO, Average, Standard, and so on. You can indicate how the replenishment of the product is going to be done (we have seen it in the *Purchase* section of this chapter). You can also set up lots of other information about the item, such as cross-references, substitutes, and so on.

One item can have multiple variants. This is useful if you have a large number of almost identical items, for example, the items that vary only in color. Instead of setting up each variant as a separate item, you can set up one item and then specify the various colors as variants of the item.

As part of your warehouse management you may need to use multiple locations. We will cover locations in the next section. If you use multiple locations, you can create stock-keeping units for your items. Stock-keeping units allow you to differentiate information about an item for a specific location. As an example, the replenishment system of an item may be different on different locations. Stock-keeping units also allow you to differentiate information between two variants of the same item. Information on the stock-keeping unit has priority over the item card.

One interesting feature about item is the item tracking. You can track an item by serial numbers, lot numbers, expiration dates, or a combination of all of them. You can create different tracking codes and set them up with the different tracking policies. The following screenshot shows an **Item Tracking Code Card**:

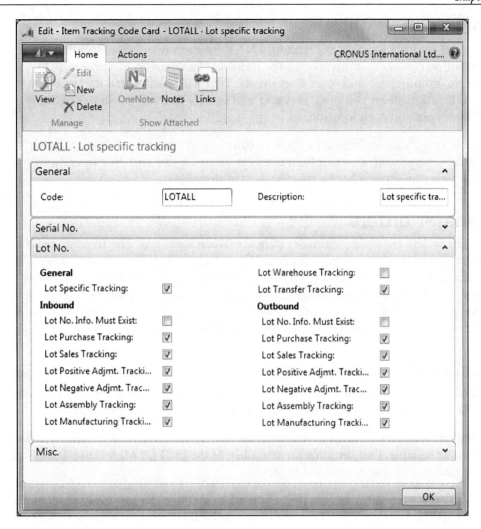

These policies reflect where it is mandatory to track the item, for example, you may only need to track lots on purchases but not on sales.

Locations

You must set up a location in Dynamics NAV for each warehouse location or distribution center. You can specify the location elsewhere in the program, for example, on purchase and sales documents. This will then record the transactions for the location when you post, and you will be able to track the item inventory and item value on each location.

You can specify an unlimited number of **bins** in each location. A bin denotes a physical storage unit. You can then use bins on put-away and pick operation, so that you can know where a specific item is stored.

Transfer orders

Transfer orders are used to transfer items between locations. The transfer order is a document similar to a sales order or a purchase order. The transfer order contains information about the origin location, the destination location, and the date connected to the shipping and receiving of the order. An intransit location must be used when working with transfer orders. The posting process of transfer orders is done in two separate steps, shipping and receiving.

Assembly

Assembly is used to create a new item, for example, a kit combining components in simple processes. This can be seen as a small manufacturing functionality.

To use this feature you need to define assembly items. An assembly item is an item defined as sellable, that contains an assembly **BOM (Bill Of Materials)**. Items can be assembled to order or assembled to stock.

You can create assembly orders that are used to manage the assembly process and to connect the sales requirements with the involved warehouse activities. Assembly orders differ from the other order types because they involve both output and consumption when posting.

As this is a new functionality that Microsoft Dynamics NAV 2013 introduce, it will be covered in more detail in *Chapter 2, What's New in NAV 2013*.

Pick and put-away

Inventory can be organized and handled on locations at the bin level. Multiple variables can be defined per bin as:

- Their type
- The type of actions that can be performed on the bin: pick, put-away, ship, and receive
- Their maximum capacity
- Their desired minimum capacity, and so on

With all this information, you can create pick and put-away documents that will tell you:

- Where to pick your inventory for shipment purposes
- Where to store your inventory when it is received

There are also documents to manage internal inventory movements, to move inventory from one bin to another, to calculate the replenishment of pick bins, and so on.

Inventory

Each single item card contains a field called Inventory that specifies how many units of the item are on inventory. Units are counted using the base unit of measure indicated on the item card. Dynamics NAV automatically calculates the content of the field using the `Quantity` field in the `Item Ledger Entry` table. This means that every time a new `Item Ledger Entry` record is created, for example, after posting a sales order, the inventory of the item is updated.

You can filter the `Inventory` field so that its contents are calculated only on the basis of one or any combination of global dimension values, locations, variants, lots, or serial numbers.

An inventory is used in combination with other fields to know the availability of an item. Item availability can be shown by event, by period, by variant, by location, by BOM level, and by timeline. The following screenshot shows the **Item Availability by Periods** page:

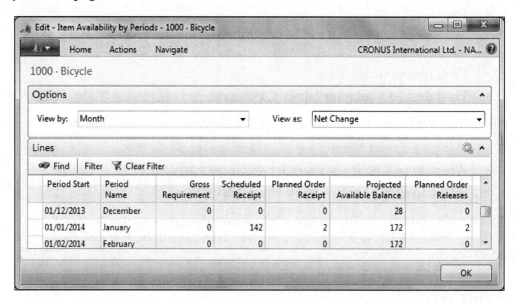

At least once in every fiscal year, you must take a physical inventory to see if the quantity registered is the same as the physical quantity in stock. The physical inventory journals designed to help you during such a task. But inventory is not only about units, it is also about the value of those units and their cost.

You can indicate different costing methods for an item. The choice determines the way the program calculates the unit cost. You can select any of the following costing methods: FIFO, LIFO, specific, average, and standard.

The system uses the value entries to keep track of each item ledger entry's cost. One or more value entries can exist per item ledger entry. Every time you post an order, invoice, credit memo, and so on, the program creates value entries because all of these operations affect the item value. In addition, you can use the revaluation journal to change any item ledger entry cost. Some other concepts, such as freight or handling charges, may also affect the item value. You can use item charges to assign those charges to item ledger entries.

Manufacturing

The manufacturing area is used to manage production. Starting with the design and engineering work that will specify how and when items are handled, the components and resources that go into creating an end item, and the routings that define the process requirements of a given produced item.

The manufacturing area also provides tools to schedule production activities, manually or automatically pull production components for consumption, record time consumption, post finished operations that do not qualify as finished output but as scrapped material, and so on.

The following screenshot shows the main page of the **Manufacturing** area:

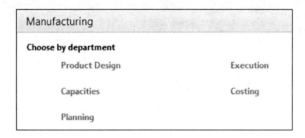

Product design

The product design starts on the item card. You need to create one item card for each end item that you want to produce, and also one item card for each component that you need to consume to obtain the end product.

For each component you have to specify whether you purchase it, assemble it, or produce it. You also need to specify if you need the component to stock or if you just need it when an order is made. You can specify all of this information on the **Replenishment** tab of the item card as shown in the following screenshot:

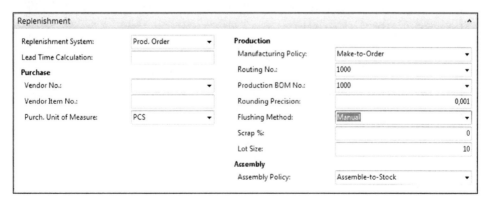

For items that need to be produced, you have to create a **BOM**. It is a listing of all the sub assemblies, intermediates, parts, and raw materials that go into a parent item and the quantities needed of each component.

Production BOMs may consist of several levels. You can use up to 50 levels. One production BOM always corresponds to one level. You have the possibility to copy the existing BOMs for creating a new BOM.

The following screenshot shows the production BOM for item no. 1000, Bicycle.

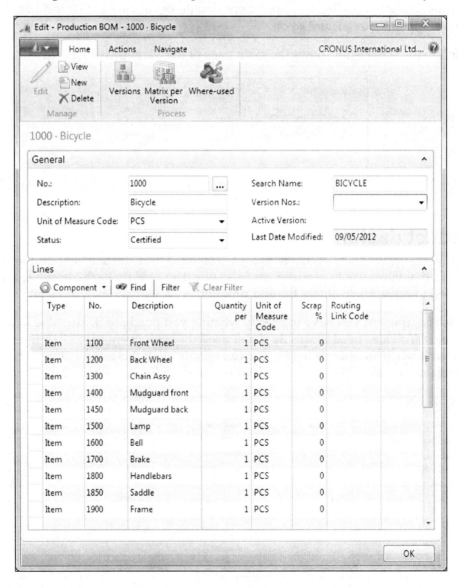

You also need to define routings to show the production process. The routings form the basis for production planning and control. Routings include detailed information about the method of manufacturing of a particular item. It includes the operations to be performed and sequenced. You can also include information about tools, resources, and personnel and quality measures.

Routing is the basis for process scheduling, capacity scheduling, material need scheduling, and the production documents.

The program also supports the production of parts families, that is, the same or similar item can be manufactured with a single routing. A production family is a group of individual items whose relationship is based on the similarity of their manufacturing processes. Forming production families can optimize material consumption.

Capacities

The program distinguishes between three types of capacities:

- Work centers
- Machine centers
- Resources

These are arranged hierarchically and each level contains subordinate levels. You can assign various machine centers to every work center. A machine center may only belong to one work center.

Planned capacity of a work center consists of the availability of the corresponding machine centers and the additional planned availability of the work center.

The planned availability of the work center group is thus the sum of all corresponding availabilities of the machine centers and work centers. The availability is stored in calendar entries. To work with capacities you need to create several calendars:

- **Shop calendar**: This calendar defines a standard work week according to the start and end time of each working day and the work-ship relation. It also defines fixed holidays during a year.
- **Work center calendar**: This calendar specifies the working days and hours, shifts, holidays, and absences that determine the work center's gross available capacity, measured in time, according to its defined efficiency and capacity values.

- **Machine center's availability**: In this calendar you can define the time periods when machine centers cannot be used. The machine centers are not assigned their own shop calendar; the shop calendar of the work center is used. The calendar for the machine center is calculated from the entries of the assigned shop calendar and the calendar absence entries of the machine center.

- **Resource Capacities**: Resources, such as technicians, have their own capacity. You can use work-hour templates that contain the typical working hours in your company; for example, you can create templates for full-time technicians and part-time technicians. You can use work-hour templates when you add capacity to resources.

The following screenshot shows the statistics of one **Work Center**. It shows the total capacity calculated from all the calendar entries that were set up.

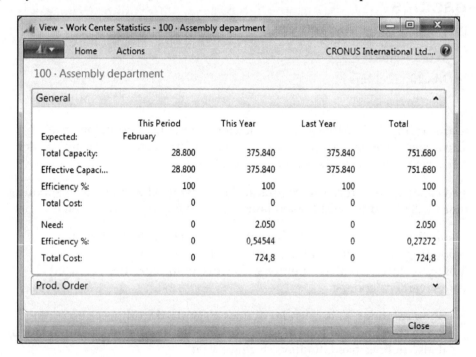

Planning

The planning system takes all demand and supply data into account, nets the results, and creates suggestions for balancing the supply to meet the demand. Another goal of the planning system is to ensure that the inventory does not grow unnecessarily.

The terms running the planning worksheet, or running MRP, refer to the calculation of the master production schedule and material requirements based on the actual and forecasted demand. The planning system can calculate either Master Planning Schedule (MPS) or Material Requirements Planning (MRP) on request, or it can calculate both at the same time.

- **MPS**: It is the calculation of a master production schedule based on the actual demand and the production forecast. The MPS calculation is used for end items that have a forecast or a sales order line. These items are called MPS items and are identified dynamically when the calculation starts.

- **MRP**: It is the calculation of material requirements based on the actual demand for components and the production forecast on the component level. MRP is calculated only for items that are not MPS items. The purpose of MRP is to provide time-phased formal plans, by item, to supply the appropriate item, at the appropriate time, in the appropriate location, and in the appropriate quantity.

Several planning parameters have to be filled in the item, or the stock-keeping unit and the manufacturing setup, in order to tell the system how you want to plan your supply. The planning parameters control when, how much, and how to replenish based on all the settings. Some of the planning parameters are: dampener period and quantity, quantity reorder policy and reorder point, maximum inventory, and manufacturing policy or combined MPS/MRP calculation.

Planning is affected by many additional factors, such as the planning horizon defined by the order and the ending dates specified when you run MPS/MRP from the **Planning Worksheet** or **Order Planning** page.

The forecasting functionality is used to create anticipated demand; it allows your company to create what-if scenarios to plan for and meet the demand. Accurate forecasting can make a critical difference in the custom levels with regard promised order dates and on-time delivery. The following screenshot shows the **Production Forecast** page:

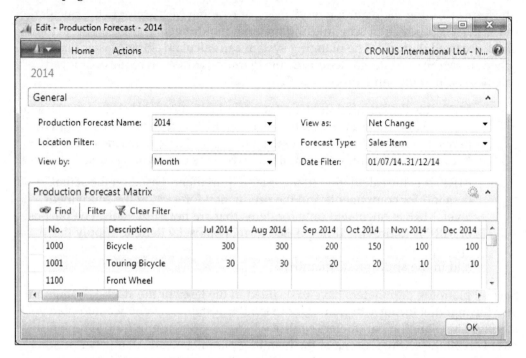

The sales forecast is the sales department's best guess at what will be sold in the future, and the production forecast is the production planner's projection of how many end items and derived sub-assemblies to produce in specific periods, to meet the forecasted sales.

Execution

When materials have been issued, the actual production operations can start and then be executed in the sequence defined by the production order routing.

An important part of executing production is to post the production output to report progress and to update inventory with the finished items. Output posting can be done manually, or it can be done automatically with the use of backward flushing. In that case, material consumption is automatically posted along with output when the production order changes to finished.

You also have to post the scrapped materials and consumed capacities that are not assigned to a production order, such as maintenance work. You can use the output journal and the capacity journal respectively, to perform those operations.

Finally, you need to put-away the output of the production. You will perform your put-away task according to how your warehouse is set up as a location. The inbound warehouse request will inform the warehouse that the production order is ready for put-away.

In basic warehousing where your warehouse location requires put-away processing, but not receive processing, you use the inventory put-away document to organize and record the put-away of output. In advanced warehousing where your location requires both put-away and receive processing, you create either an internal put-away document or a movement document to put away the output.

Costing

Many manufacturing companies select a valuation base of standard cost. This also applies to companies that perform light manufacturing, such as assembly and kitting. A standard cost system determines inventory unit cost based on some reasonable historical or expected cost. Studies of the past and estimated future cost data can then provide the basis for standard costs. These costs are frozen until a decision is made to change them. The actual cost to produce a product may differ from the estimated standard costs.

Standard costs of the manufactured item can consist of direct material cost, labor cost, subcontractor cost, and overhead cost. A batch job can be run to create suggestions to change item costs as well as standard cost on work center, machine center, or resource cards. After revising the suggested changes, another batch job will help you implement them.

Subcontracting

When a vendor performs one or more operational steps in production, subcontracting is a standard operational step in many manufacturing companies. Subcontracting can be a rare occurrence or can be an integral part of all production processes. Dynamics NAV provides several tools for managing subcontract work:

- **Subcontract work center**: This is a work center with an assigned vendor (subcontractor). The subcontract work center can be used on a routing operation, which allows you to process the subcontracted activity. In addition, the cost of the operation can be designated at the routing or the work center level.

- **Work center cost based on units or time**: This feature enables you to specify whether costs associated with the work center are based on the production time or a flat charge per unit. Although subcontractors commonly use a flat charge per unit to charge for their services, the program can handle both options, production time and flat charge per unit.

- **Subcontracting worksheet**: This feature allows you to find the production orders with material ready to send to a subcontractor, and to automatically create purchase orders for subcontract operations from the production order routings. Then the program automatically posts the purchase order charges to the production order during the posting of the purchase order. Only production orders with a released status can be accessed and used from a subcontracting worksheet.

Job

The **Jobs** area supports common project management tasks, such as configuring a job and scheduling a resource, as well as providing the information needed to manage budgets and monitor progress. The jobs feature is meant to manage long-term projects that involve the use of man hours, machine hours, inventory items, and other types of usage that you need to keep track of.

Job card

The Job card shows information about the job, such as the job number, job name, and information about job posting. There is one card for each job. The following screenshot shows a **Job Card** page:

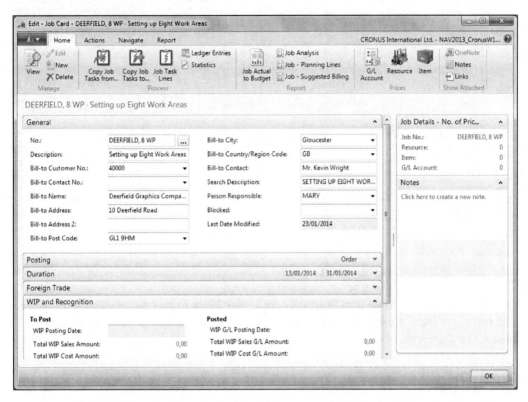

Phases and tasks

A key part of setting up a new job is to specify the various tasks involved in the job. Every job must have a minimum of one task. You create tasks by adding **Job Task Lines**, as shown in the following screenshot:

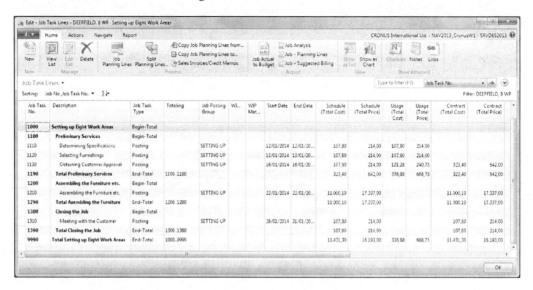

You have additional tools that help you copy task lines from one job task to another. You can copy from a job task in the job you are working with, or from a job task linked to a different job.

Planning

You can define each task that you have created for a job into planning lines. A planning line can be used to capture any information that you want to track for a job. You can use planning lines to add information such as which resources are required, or to capture which items are needed to fulfill the job.

For example, you may create a task to obtain customer approval. You can associate that task with planning lines for items such as meeting with the customer and creating a services contract.

For each planning line you must define a line type, which can be schedule, contract, or both, explained as follows:

- **Schedule**: This line type provides estimated usage and costs for the job, typically in a time and materials type contract. Planning lines of this type cannot be invoiced.

- **Contract**: This line type provides estimated invoicing to the customer, typically in a fixed price contract.

- **Both schedule and contract**: This line type provides scheduled usage equal to what you want to invoice.

In addition, you can specify an account type and fill in information such as quantity. As you add information, cost information is automatically filled in; for example, when you enter a new line, the cost, price, and discount for resources and items are initially based on the information that is defined on the resource and item cards.

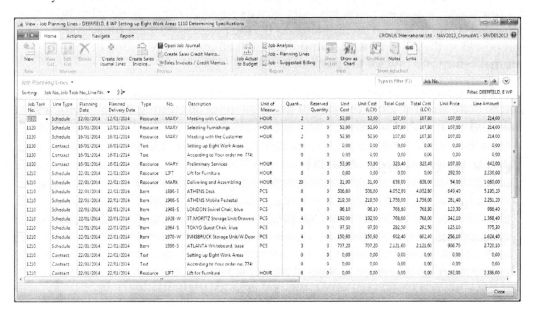

Time sheet

You can track machine and employee hours on the project by using time sheets. Using the jobs functionality will provide a good overview, not only of individual jobs, but also of the allocation of employees, machinery, and other resources being used in all projects. You can also use this functionality for many types of services and consultancy tasks.

Time sheets in Microsoft Dynamics NAV handle time registration in weekly increments of seven days. You use them to track the time used on job, service orders, and assembly orders. In addition, you can use them to record simple resource time registration and employee absences. Time sheets can be set up so an approval is required before you can post them to the relevant job journal.

Invoice jobs

During the job's development, job costs such as resource usage, materials, and job-related purchases can accumulate. As the job progresses, these transactions get posted to the job journal. It is important that all costs get recorded in the job journal before you invoice the customer.

You can invoice the whole job or only invoice the selected contract lines. Invoicing can be done after the job is finished or at certain intervals during the job's progress, based on an invoicing schedule.

Work in process (WIP)

If a job runs over a long period, you may want to transfer these costs to a **Work In Process** (**WIP**) account on the balance sheet while the job is being completed. You can then recognize the costs and sales in your income statement accounts when it is appropriate.

Dynamics NAV 2013 allows you to calculate the value of the WIP of your jobs. The calculation is based on the WIP method selected on individual jobs.

The WIP process creates WIP entries in connection with the jobs. This function only calculates WIP; it does not post it to the general ledger. To do so, another batch job must be run, the job posts WIP to G/L. There are several WIP methods that you can use on your jobs:

- **Cost value**: It starts by calculating the value of what has been provided by taking a proportion of the estimated total costs, based on the percentage of completion. Invoiced costs are subtracted by taking a proportion of the estimated total costs, based on the invoiced percentage.

- **Cost of sales**: It begins by calculating the recognized costs. Costs are recognized proportionally based on scheduled total costs.

- **Sales value**: It recognizes revenue proportionally based on the usage total costs and the expected cost recovery ratio.

- **Percentage of completion**: It recognizes revenue proportionally based on the percentage of completion, that is, the usage total costs against schedule costs.

- **Completed contract**: Completed contract does not recognize revenue and costs until the job is complete. You may want to do this when there is high uncertainty about the estimates of costs and revenue for the job.

The system also allows you to create your own job WIP method that reflects the needs of your organization.

Resource planning

Many companies use resource management to track the time and effort that is involved with performing and providing services, for example, an employee may visit a site to talk with a customer about a project. That time and effort can be charged to the customer on a sales order.

Resource planning is integrated with jobs, services, and assembly orders. When resources are used or sold in a job, for example, the prices and costs associated with them are retrieved from the information set up in the resource planning area.

But before you can start selling services and jobs, or assigning resources to assembly projects, you must set up information about policy and pricing, which can be used in resource transactions. All pricing information is adjustable.

Resource card

The resource card is used to specify resources, which can be employees, machinery, or other company resources. For most companies, an optimal assignment of resources is an important part of the planning and production process. The following screenshot shows the **Resource Card** page:

You can base production and project planning on the availability and capacity of resources. Resources can also be included in bills of materials, job planning, and job costing. Resources can be integrated with the general ledger. Resources can also be posted by using the documents in sales and receivables. Global dimensions can be used with resources.

You can invoice customers for sales that are composed of various resources. Resource costs can be calculated. You can use general ledger integration to post costs and revenues that are related to the sale of resources.

You can set up alternative costs for resources, for example, if you pay an employee a higher hourly rate for overtime, you can set up a resource cost for the overtime rate. The alternative cost that you set up for the resource will override the cost on the resource card when you use the resource in the resource journal.

Pricing

You can specify the default amount per hour when the resource is created. For example, if you use a specific machine on a job for 5 hours, the job would be calculated based on the amount per hour.

To correctly manage resource activities, you must set up your resources and the related costs and prices. The job-related prices, discounts, and cost factor rules are set up on the job card. You can specify the costs and prices for individual resources, resource groups, or all available resources of the company. For services, you can adjust pricing in the Service Item worksheet.

A few batch jobs allow you to get resource price suggestions based on standard prices or based on alternative prices. You can then implement the price changes.

Service

Providing ongoing service to customers is an important part of any business and that can be a source of customer satisfaction and loyalty, in addition to revenue. Managing and tracking service is not always easy, but Microsoft Dynamics NAV provide set of tools to help. These tools are designed to support repair shop and field service operations and can be used in business scenarios such as complex customer service distribution systems, industrial service environments with bills of materials, and high volume dispatching of service technicians with requirements for spare parts management. With these tools you can accomplish the following tasks:

- Schedule service calls and set up service orders
- Track repair parts and supplies
- Assign service personnel based on skill and availability
- Provide service estimates and service invoices

In addition, you can standardize coding, set up contracts, implement a discounting policy, and create route maps for service employees.

In general, there are two aspects to service management: configuring and setting up your system, and using it for pricing, contracts, orders, service personnel dispatch, and job scheduler. The following screenshot shows the main page of the **Service** area:

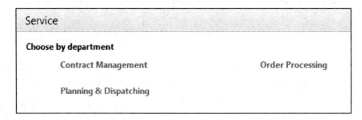

Service items

A service item is an item that has been sold to a customer and has been registered for service. A service item has a unique identification number and can be linked to an item. You can assign warranty to service items and specify the response time for their service. Service items can consist of many components.

Service items can be created automatically when you ship sold items, or you can create them manually. The following screenshot shows the **Service Item Card** page:

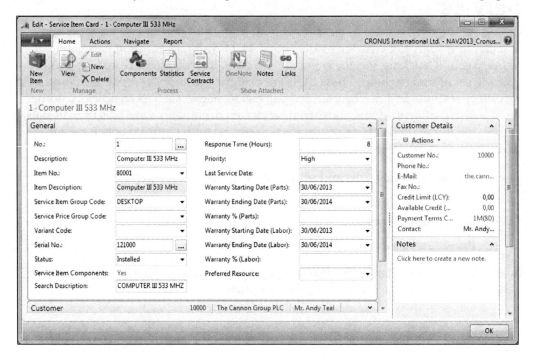

When you have set up service items, you can register them in service orders and service contracts.

Servicing some service items may require specific skills. If this is the case, you can assign skill codes to the items that these service items are linked to, or directly to these service items. This way, when a service is scheduled for the item, you will be able to assign the proper resource to do the job.

Sometimes, you cannot repair a service item, but you can choose to replace it instead. Dynamics NAV offers you the chance to replace it either temporarily or permanently.

Contracts

One way to set up a service management business is to have standard contractual agreements between you and your customers that describe the level of service and the service expectations. You can set up contract templates, which you can then use to create standardized contracts for your business. In addition, you can set up a system to create quotes for service and to turn those quotes into contracts.

After you have set up the template, you can customize the resulting contract to keep track of service hours, or other items that may vary from customer to customer.

Contracts specify the general information, which includes information about the serviced customer, the starting date of the contract, the service period, the response time, the bill-to customer, the invoice period, the annual amount, the prepaid and income accounts, price update specifications, and so on. A contract can include more than one service item.

You can also set up a system to keep track of contract status, and view how gain and loss information about your contracts is being posted.

Price management

This feature allows you to apply the best price to service orders and set up personalized service price agreements for customers. You can set up different service price groups, so you can consider the service item or service item group, in addition to the type of fault that the service task involves. You can set up these groups for a limited period of time, or for a specific customer or currency. You can use price calculation structures as templates to assign a specific price to a specific service task.

For instance, this makes it possible to assign specific items included in the service price, in addition to the type of work included. This also makes it possible to use different VAT and discount amounts for different service price groups. To make sure that the correct prices are applied, you can assign fixed, minimum, or maximum prices, depending on the agreements that you have with your customers.

Before adjusting the price of a service item on a service order, you are provided with an overview of what the results of the price adjustment will be. You can approve these results, or you can make additional changes if you want to have a different result. The whole adjustment is performed line-by-line, which means that there are no additional lines created.

The service price adjustment groups are also used to set up the different types of price adjustments. For example, you can set up a service price adjustment group that adjusts prices for spare parts, one that adjust prices for labor, one that adjusts prices for costs, and so on. You can also specify whether the service price adjustment should be applied to just one specific item or resource, or to all items or resources.

Each service price adjustment group holds the information about the adjustments that you want to make on the service lines, as you can see in the following screenshot:

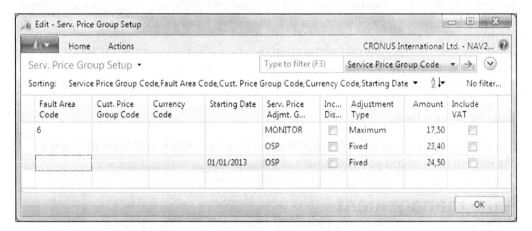

The service price adjustment function does not apply to service items that belong to service contracts. You can only adjust the service prices of items that are part of a service order. You cannot adjust the price of a service item if it has a warranty. You cannot adjust the price of a service item on a service order if the service line linked to it has been posted as an invoice, either completely or in part.

Service orders

Service orders are the documents in the Dynamics NAV Service Management application area in which you can enter information about services (repair and maintenance) on service items. Service orders are created in the following instances:

- When a customer requests a service.
- Automatically by the program at the time intervals defined in service contracts.
- When you convert a service quote to a service order. A service quote can be used as a preliminary draft for a service order.

Service orders and service quotes are composed of the following instances:

- **Service header**: It contains general information about the service, such as the customer, the contract related to the order, the service order status, or the start and finish dates
- **Service item lines**: They contain information related to the service item such as the service item number, its description, the serial number, or the response time
- **Service lines**: They contain information about the service costs, such as spare parts (items) used on the order, resource hours, G/L accounts payments, and general costs

You can lend customers loaner items to temporarily replace the service items that you have received for servicing.

Service tasks

After you have created a service order or service quote, registered service item lines, and allocated resources to the service items in the order or quote, you can start repairing and maintaining the service items.

The service task page can give you an overview of the service items that need servicing. You can update the information on the service items for each task, such as the repair status, or enter service lines for that service item.

Fault reporting

When the customer brings in a service item for repair, you can assign a fault code to indicate the nature of the fault. The fault code can be used with the resolution code to determine the possible repair method to use. In the following screenshot you can see an example of **Fault Codes** and **Resolution Codes**:

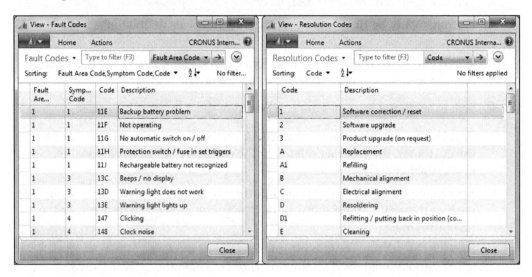

Depending on the level of fault reporting in a company, you might also need to register fault area codes symptom codes.

Human resources

The human resources feature lets you keep detailed records of your employees. You can register and maintain employee information, such as employment contracts, confidential information, qualifications, and employee contacts. You can also use the human resources feature to register employee absence.

Employees

To use the human resources feature, you need to create employee cards. From the employee card, you can enter basic information about the employee. The following screenshot shows the **Employee Card** page:

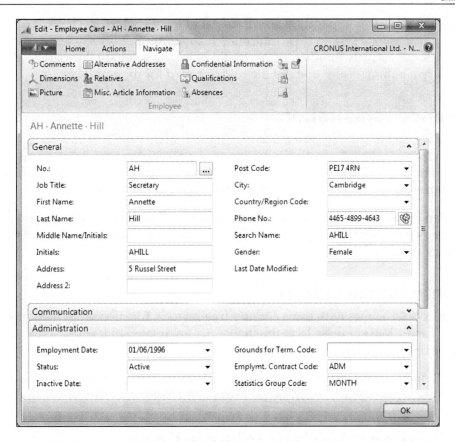

Linked to the employee card, you can set up alternative addresses, relatives, qualifications, and miscellaneous information where you can keep track of any information you want, for example, if the employee uses a company car. In the following screenshot you can see an example of miscellaneous articles. You can create as many miscellaneous articles as you need and link them to the employees.

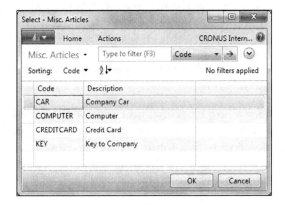

The human resources application area is linked to the resources application area. So when you update certain basic information about the employee (such as name, address, social security number, employment date, and so on) in the `Employee` table, the program automatically updates the resource card for the employee.

Absence registration

You can register employee absences and assign different causes of absences. You can then see the information in various ways throughout the program and analyze employee absences. For example, you can compare your company's rate of absenteeism to national or industry-related averages for absenteeism.

A sudden increase in an employee's absences may reflect personal problems on the employee's part. With the `Employee Absence` table, you can take notice of these problems at an early.

Country localizations

Dynamics NAV comes with some country/region local functionalities to address specific needs. Most of these local functionalities are related to tax registering and tax reporting, or are legal requirements for the country.

You will find a complete list of local functionalities on this website:
`http://msdn.microsoft.com/en-us/library/hh922908(v=nav.70).aspx`

Vertical and horizontal solutions

As we said earlier in this chapter, a good thing about Dynamics NAV is that it can be customized. A brand new functional area can be created from scratch or new features can be added to an existing area.

Many people and companies have developed new functional areas or have expanded the existing ones, and they have registered their solution as an add-on. This means that the standard functionality of Dynamics NAV is much more extended than the functional areas we have covered in this chapter.

Actually, you can find almost 2,000 registered add-on or third-party solutions that cover all kinds of functional areas.

If a customer asks you for a huge modification of their Dynamics NAV, the best solution will probably be to look for an existing add-on that already covers your customer's needs. Implementing this solution usually consists of configuration and some limited custom development. On the other hand, if you choose to develop it all from scratch, you might get a lengthy high-cost and high-risk project.

Access Dynamics NAV

In the past, Dynamics NAV had a single client access. But technology has changed, evolved, and so has Dynamics NAV. The release of Dynamics NAV 2009 already brought two new ways of accessing the application: the RoleTailored client and Web Services. Dynamics NAV 2013 also brings new accessibility options: the Web client and the SharePoint client. It has also removed an accessibility option, the Classic client, although it has been maintained and converted for development purposes.

In this section we will explain the different environments in which you can access your Microsoft Dynamics NAV 2013 application.

Windows client

The Windows client is also known as the RoleTailored client, or the RTC client. That was its name when the client was first released on Dynamics NAV 2009. But Dynamics NAV 2013 introduces a new client, the Web client, which is also a RoleTailored client. So, we cannot call it the RoleTailored client anymore.

The Windows client is based around the individuals within an organization, their roles, and the tasks they perform. When users first enter Dynamics NAV, they see the data needed for the daily tasks they do according to their role. Users belonging to different roles will have a different view of the system, each of them seeing only those functions they need to be able to perform their daily tasks.

For those of you who haven't used Dynamics NAV 2009 yet, but had the chance to work with Microsoft Dynamics NAV 4.0 or 5.0, you might remember how difficult it was sometimes to locate a specific feature in the jungle of the navigation pane. Switching back and forth between the specific menus in search of a menu item was a frustrating experience, especially for users performing tasks in several functional areas of the application. Unless you used shortcuts, accessing any feature required three of four clicks, provided you knew exactly where it was. The system also didn't do much to help users focus on what was needed to be done, and after you found the feature you needed, you typically had to spend extra time searching for documents or tasks that needed your attention. With the RoleTailored client, the feature jungle was gone.

The Windows client allows users to widely customize the data they see on each page. They have the ability to personalize the pages according to their requirements by hiding, moving, and configuring parts contained on pages, and also by saving queries, adding filters, and adding or removing fields. The ribbon can also be customized, you can add, remove, and rename actions, menus, and tabs.

The following screenshot shows how the **Role Center** of the Windows client looks like. The **Role Center** is the main page of the client, and it is the first page a user sees when entering Dynamics NAV.

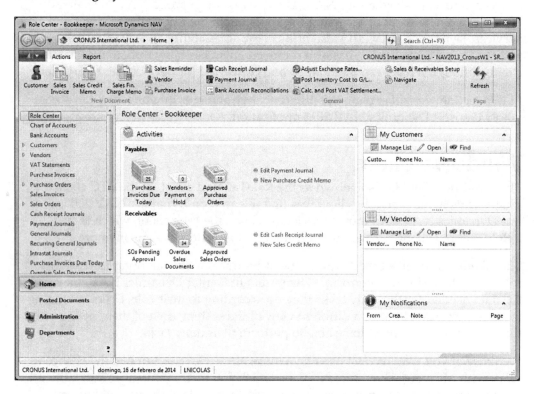

The Windows client supports three methods for authenticating users who try to access the Dynamics NAV Web client:

- **Windows**: This credential type authenticates users using their Windows credentials (Active Directory, local workgroup, or the local computer's users). Because they are authenticated through Windows, Windows users are not prompted for credentials when they start the Windows client.

- **Username**: This setting prompts the user for username/password credentials when starting the client. These credentials are then validated against Windows authentication by the Microsoft Dynamics NAV Server.

- **NavUserPassword**: This setting manages the authentication by Microsoft Dynamics NAV Server but is not based on Windows users or Active Directory. The user is prompted for username/password credentials when they start the client. The credentials are then validated by an external mechanism.

Web client

The Microsoft Dynamics NAV Web client gives users access to Microsoft Dynamics NAV data over a network, such a the Internet. From a web browser, users can view and modify data from a user-friendly interface that resembles the Windows client, where the starting point is the Role Center. The Role Center can be customized to the user's individual needs based on their role, company, and daily tasks. The Web client does not replace the Windows client but complements it by enabling scenarios that are not possible with the Windows client. The following screenshot shows how the **Role Center** of the Web client looks like:

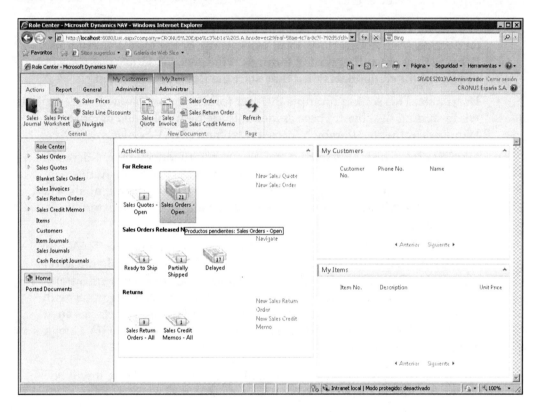

The Microsoft Dynamics NAV Web client supports most of the features that the Microsoft Dynamics NAV Windows client supports, but there are some exceptions and limitations:

- Chart parts are not supported
- The **Departments** button does not appear in the navigation pane of Role Center in the Web client

- The search feature is only partially supported

- Users cannot perform configuration and personalization tasks on the Web client

- Navigate page types are not shown on the Windows client

This is to name just a few limitations. There are some other limitations that will need to be taken into account while choosing to use the Web client.

The Web client supports four methods for authenticating users who try to access the Dynamics NAV Web client:

- **Windows**: This credential type authenticates the users to use their Windows credentials (Active Directory, local workgroup, or the local computer users). Because they are authenticated through Windows, Windows users are not prompted for credentials when they start the RoleTailored client.

- **Username**: This setting prompts the user for username/password credentials while starting the client. These credentials are then validated against Windows authentication by Microsoft Dynamics NAV Server.

- **NavUserPassword**: This setting manages the authentication by Microsoft Dynamics NAV Server but is not based on Windows users or Active Directory. The user is prompted for username/password credentials when they start the client. The credentials are then validated by an external mechanism.

- **AccessControlService**: This setting makes Microsoft Dynamics NAV rely on Windows Azure Access Control Service (ACS) for user authentication services. ACS is a cloud-based service that provides user authentication and authorization for web applications and services. ACS integrates with standards-based identity providers, including enterprise directories such as Active Directory, and web identities such as Windows Live ID, Google, Yahoo!, and Facebook.

As the Web client is a new feature released with Dynamics NAV 2013, it will be covered in more detail in *Chapter 2, What's New in NAV 2013*.

SharePoint client

Microsoft Dynamics NAV SharePoint client enables you to interact with Dynamics NAV data from a Microsoft SharePoint website. The Microsoft Dynamics NAV SharePoint client is built on the Microsoft Dynamics NAV Portal Framework for Microsoft SharePoint 2010, which is a web-based application framework that integrates Microsoft Dynamics NAV with the Microsoft SharePoint applications. By integrating with SharePoint, the Microsoft Dynamics NAV SharePoint client can use the business and administration features in Microsoft SharePoint, including workflows, business connectivity services, workspaces, SharePoint authentication, and scalability.

With Microsoft Dynamics NAV Portal Framework for Microsoft SharePoint 2010, you can also do the following:

- Display Microsoft Dynamics NAV pages and reports on SharePoint sites using an URL

- Add a page by using a Microsoft Dynamics NAV web part and connect the web part to other web parts on a SharePoint page

- Edit data on pages in web applications and update the changes in the Microsoft Dynamics NAV 2013 database by using the same metadata and business logic that is rendered in the Microsoft Dynamics NAV Windows client

Working with Microsoft Dynamics NAV pages and reports in the SharePoint client is very similar to working with the pages and reports in Microsoft Dynamics NAV Windows client or Microsoft Dynamics NAV Web client. The Microsoft Dynamics NAV SharePoint client is designed for occasional users who typically need an overview of their daily work status and perform relatively simple or light data entry.

As the Web client, some features are not supported or are partially supported on the SharePoint client. The SharePoint client will be covered in more detail in *Chapter 2, What's New in NAV 2013*.

Web Services

Microsoft Dynamics NAV 2013 provides Web Services, which makes it easy for other systems to integrate with Microsoft Dynamics NAV. Web Services allow you to expose the business logic of Dynamics NAV to the other environments.

Web Services are a lightweight, industry-standard way to make an application functionality available to a wide range of external systems and users. Microsoft Dynamics NAV 2013 supports creation and publishing of Microsoft Dynamics NAV functionality as Web Services. You can expose pages, codeunits, or queries as Web Services and even enhance a page Web service with an extension codeunit. When you publish Microsoft Dynamics NAV objects as Web Services, they are immediately available on the network.

Developers can publish two types of Web Services from Microsoft Dynamics NAV objects:

- **SOAP Web Services**: You can publish either Microsoft Dynamics NAV pages or codeunits as SOAP services.

- **OData Web Services**: You can publish either pages or queries as OData services. The OData protocol offers new and flexible opportunities for interacting with Microsoft Dynamics NAV data. For example, you can use OData Web Services to publish a refreshable link to Microsoft Dynamics NAV data that can be displayed in Microsoft Excel with Power Pivot or in SharePoint.

Three different objects can be exposed as Web Services:

- **Page Web Services**: When you expose a page as an OData Web service, you can query that data to return a service metadata (EDMX) document or an AtomPub document. When you expose a page as a SOAP Web Service, you expose a default set of operations that you can use to manage common operations such as create, read, update, and delete. For SOAP services, you can also use extension codeunits to extend the default set of operations that are available on a page.

- **Codeunit Web Services**: Currently available only for SOAP Web Services, codeunit Web Services provide you with maximum control and flexibility. When a codeunit is exposed as a web service, all functions defined in the codeunit are exposed as operations.

- **Query Web Services**: When you expose a Microsoft Dynamics NAV query as an OData Web Service, you can query that data to return a service metadata (EDMX) document or an AtomPub document.

OData Web Services are a new addition to Microsoft Dynamics NAV 2013 and they will be covered in detail in *Chapter 2, What's New in NAV 2013*.

Development environment

You use the Microsoft Dynamics NAV Development Environment to develop Microsoft Dynamics NAV applications. This component, which was also an end user client in the earlier versions of Microsoft Dynamics NAV, was formerly known as the Classic client.

When you open the development environment, the Object Designer opens, which gives you access to Microsoft Dynamics NAV objects. You use the Object Designer to modify the application or to create new application areas.

You can also use the development environment to create and manage Microsoft Dynamics NAV 2013 databases, to create and manage Microsoft Dynamics NAV companies, and to upload or change Microsoft Dynamics NAV licenses.

The following screenshot displays how the **Development Environment** looks like:

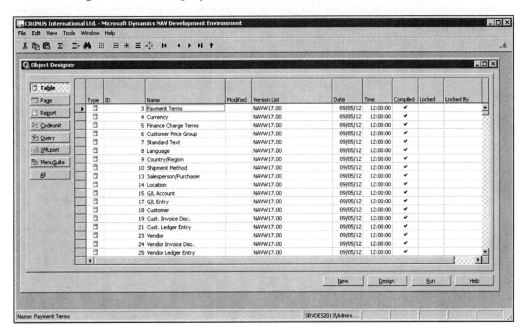

Summary

In this chapter we have seen that Dynamics NAV is an ERP system targeted at small and medium-sized companies.

Dynamics NAV is focused on roles and their daily tasks, and offers solutions in different functional areas, including financial management, sales and marketing, purchase, warehouse, manufacturing, job, resource planning, service, human resources, and add-ons created by partners. We have described each functional area so that you know what can be expected.

Dynamics NAV can be used on different environments such as the Windows client, the Web client, the SharePoint client, or an external application that connects to Dynamics NAV via the Web Services. The development environment is used to develop new features on top of Dynamics NAV.

In the next chapter we will cover the new features released with Microsoft Dynamics NAV 2013 in detail.

2
What's New in NAV 2013

There are quite a few new things in Microsoft Dynamics NAV 2013. Previous releases of Dynamics NAV mainly concentrated on application changes or on architectural changes. Dynamics NAV 2013 provides changes on both sides at the same time.

In this chapter we will get an overview of the new features included in Dynamics NAV 2013. We will first go through what end users will appreciate in Dynamics NAV 2013 (the application changes). After that, we will take a look at what developers and administrators will appreciate (the IT changes).

The main things we will see are:

- Application changes
- Development changes
- IT changes
- Deprecated features

Application changes

There are many things that have changed in this new release of Microsoft Dynamics NAV. Some things have disappeared, some others have changed, and a bunch of new functionalities and improvements have been added.

The first thing that users will see is the new look and feel of Dynamics NAV. It has changed a lot over the years. This new look and feel for the Windows client is not all that different from its predecessor, the **RoleTailored** client of Microsoft Dynamics NAV 2009, but you will see the differences anyway.

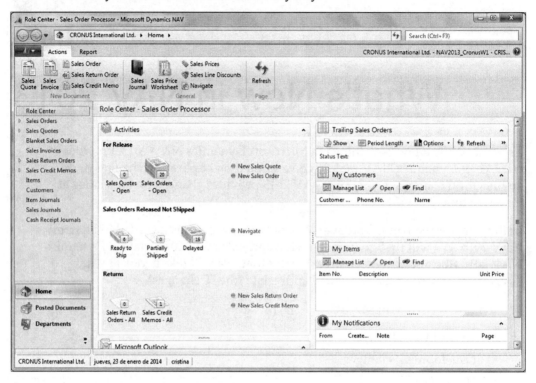

Improvements to the Windows client

Several improvements have been made to the Windows client to improve user productivity. Let's see them in detail.

Ribbon

The Actions pane has been redesigned and is now referred to as the **ribbon**.

The following screenshot shows the former Actions pane on the RoleTailored client for Microsoft Dynamics NAV 2009. The Actions pane shown corresponds to the item list page.

The Actions pane contained only actions that were supposed to be more relevant to the user. The rest of the actions and processes could be found under the **Actions**, **Related Information**, and **Reports** menus.

And now, the new ribbon on the Windows client for Microsoft Dynamics NAV 2013 for the item list page looks as shown in the following screenshot:

The redesign is meant to optimize the use of the actions and commands by providing easier access to them. The ribbon is organized into tabs and groups and contains commands that are important to the user in a given context. All the actions and processes are in the ribbon; there aren't other menus.

The user can customize the ribbon by choosing the **Customize Ribbon** option in **Application Menu | Customize**. To customize the ribbon, the following tasks can be performed:

- Adding, renaming, or removing tabs, groups, actions, and menus
- Changing the order of actions
- Restoring the ribbon to its default setting

The ribbon has changed not only for pages but also for subpages. The following screenshot highlights the ribbon for the subpage of the **Sales Order** page:

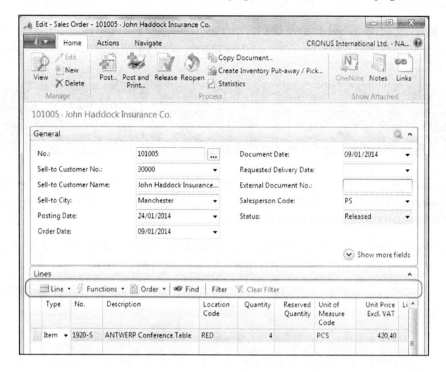

It is a small ribbon, but it offers a lot more than the subpage's Actions pane in Dynamics NAV 2009, which only contained the functions associated with the subpage; there was no easy way for users to find and filter items.

Select all

The ability to select all lines in a grid by clicking on the upper-left corner of the grid is back. It existed in the classic client of Dynamics NAV 2009 and in previous versions of the product, but it was not possible on the RoleTailored client of Dynamics NAV 2009, in which you had to select them all one by one.

Copy/paste rows

The ability to copy all selected rows from Dynamics NAV and paste them into any other application, such as Excel, has been available for a long time. But, there is something new in Dynamics NAV 2013. You can do the copy and paste action the other way around as well. That is, one can copy rows from Excel and paste them into Dynamics NAV 2013.

A lot of users prefer to do some things in Excel because it is easy to use and they can write their own formulas to apply to their data to obtain new data.

We can now copy a complete grid in Dynamics NAV, paste it into Excel, add new rows in Excel or change the value of a column by using Excel formulas, and copy the grid back to Dynamics NAV. This is simply amazing and will surely save tons of time for many Dynamics NAV users.

Quick Entry

For those users who mainly perform data entry tasks on the system, there is a new property in Dynamics NAV 2013 called **Quick Entry**, which will make their lives easier.

Dynamics NAV has a bunch of fields in all pages. Depending on our business processes, we may only have to enter a few ones and leave the rest blank or to their default values.

With Quick Entry, a user can now select those controls he wants the system to focus on as he presses the *Enter* key. This makes data entry much faster. Fewer keystrokes are needed, and you can even avoid the use of the mouse.

Imagine Susan, a sales processor who mainly enters sales orders in the system. The **Sales Order** page has a lot of fields both on the **General** and **Lines** headers. Because of the business rules in Susan's company, she actually only has to enter values into the fields **No., Sell-to Customer No., Order Date**, and **Requested Delivery Date** for the **General** header, and the fields **Type, No.**, and **Quantity** for the **Lines** header. The rest of the fields are left blank (for example, **Responsibility Center**) because the company does not use the functionality associated with that field or at their default values (for example, **Unit Price**, which gets automatically informed in the sales line) because the company has sales prices and discounts defined on all items.

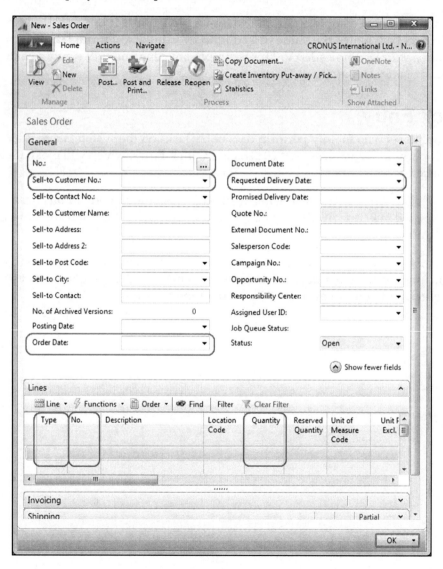

Susan's main task on the **Sales Order** page is to correctly populate eight fields. Wouldn't it be great if she could do that with only eight keystrokes?

At the moment, when she successfully informs a field and presses the *Enter* key, the system moves to a field that Susan probably doesn't want to inform or change. She has to repeatedly press the *Enter* key until she reaches the desired control or has to use the mouse to move directly to that control.

She will now use the **Quick Entry** property. This will allow her to concentrate on what's important and will result in faster and better sales order entries.

She will open the **Sales Order** page by choosing the **Fast Tabs** option in **Application Menu | Customize | Customize This Page**. She will select the **General** FastTab and then will click on the **Customize** FastTab button.

She will go through all fields on the **General** tab, and she will check or uncheck the **Quick Entry** mark. She wants **Quick Entry** checked for those fields that she usually has to inform and unchecked for the rest of the fields.

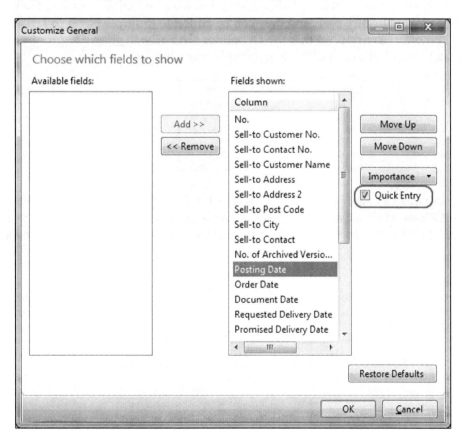

New keyboard shortcuts

With the ribbon, new keyboard shortcuts are available:

Keyboard shortcut	Functionality
Ctrl + F1	Toggles between hiding and showing the ribbon
Alt	Displays access keys on the screen
Alt + F2	Toggles between hiding and showingFactBoxes
F12	Moves to the main Dynamics NAV window
Shift + F12	Moves to the user's **Role Center** page
Alt + F12	Optimizes space on the current page

Business Intelligence and KPIs

Dynamics NAV 2013 now includes generic and specific charts.

Generic charts can be built by taking information from any table or query. They can easily be created by any user, and they can be added to multiple pages in Dynamics NAV. You may have noticed that the Dynamics NAV ribbon shows two icons called **Show as List** and **Show as Chart** when displaying a list type of page.

You can display a chart with data from any list in Dynamics NAV. You just have to select **Show as Chart**, select a measure, and select a couple of dimensions for the chart, and you will get something like the chart shown in the following screenshot:

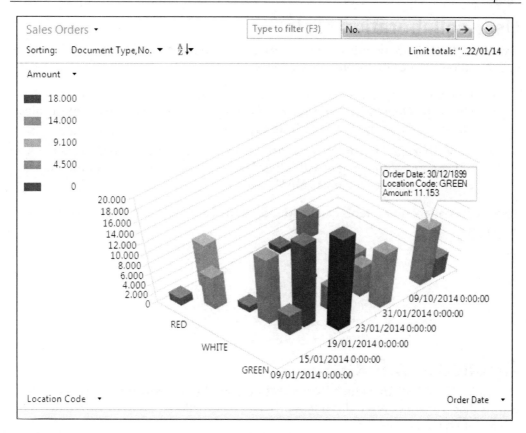

Specific charts are built using advanced data from a concrete application area. They can only be created or edited by advanced users, and they can be only added to the **Role Center** page.

Dynamics NAV 2013 also includes a new way of integration with Excel to produce Excel-based reports that use Dynamics NAV pages as data sources.

As part of the installation process for the Dynamics NAV client components, a complement for Microsoft Excel can be installed. This component will add a new tab on the Excel ribbon specific to Dynamics NAV. This tab consists of only an option to refresh data.

You can send data to Excel by selecting the **Microsoft Excel** option in **Application | Print & Send**. Once data is exported to Excel, you can build Excel reports, including PivotTables. You can use the **Refresh** button in the Dynamics NAV tab in Excel to refresh the Excel report with the most recent data from Dynamics NAV.

User collaboration tools

Dynamics NAV 2013 includes some enhancements to improve opportunities for user collaboration. Those enhancements are listed as follows:

- **OneNote Integration**: Dynamics NAV 2013 includes integration with OneNote. OneNote integration can be enabled on a per-role basis in profiles. Notes can be set up for records and pages.
- **Link Sharing**: Dynamics NAV 2013 includes the ability to share direct links of Dynamics NAV pages with other Dynamics NAV users. The link will open the specific Dynamics NAV page.

Those user collaboration tools can be found on the Dynamics NAV ribbon for all pages.

Application features

Dynamics NAV 2009 introduced several IT changes but no new functionalities. That means that Dynamics NAV did not evolve from a functional point of view since the release of Dynamics NAV 5.0.

Dynamics NAV 2013 still introduces plenty of IT changes but also some new application functionalities, such as assembly management, and improvements in existing functionalities.

Financial Management

The Financial Management area in Dynamics NAV 2013 includes some new features and improvements, such as the cash flow feature, the cost accounting feature, VAT Rate Change Tool, and VAT Reports.

Cash flow

The cash flow feature can be used to create short-term forecasts to predict how and when money is expected to be received and paid out. Periodic forecasts, such as for salary payments, can be set up. With the result of the cash flow calculation, the company will know whether there will be cash surplus or cash deficit in a concrete period of time and decide to either reduce their credits if they have a cash surplus or borrow extra money if they have a cash deficit.

Cost accounting

The cost accounting functionality is not new to Dynamics NAV 2013, but it has been restructured and improved in the current release of the application.

This functionality is used to allocate budgeted and real costs of operations, departments, products, and projects to analyze the overall profitability of the company.

VAT Rate Change Tool

VAT Rate Change Tool was released for previous versions of Dynamics NAV after some countries raised their VAT rates. The tool was available as a separate download. With Dynamics NAV 2013, VAT Rate Change Tool is now part of the standard application.

VAT Rate Change Tool is used to perform VAT and general posting group conversions. Changes in VAT rates and general postings groups are implemented in general ledger accounts, customers, vendors, open documents, journal lines, and so on.

You can configure all kinds of data so that:

- VAT product posting groups are updated
- General product posting groups are updated
- Both posting groups are updated
- No conversion is done

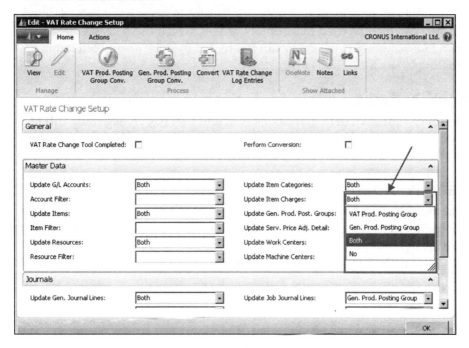

VAT Reports

VAT statements are periodically submitted to the appropriate tax authorities. In addition to that, your local tax authority may require you to submit other reports of transactions that include VAT. Those reports can be defined in Dynamics NAV by using the VAT Report window, in which reports are defined just like creating documents such as orders or invoices. The defined reports can then be exported in different formats.

Assembly management

Assembly management is a new functionality in Dynamics NAV 2013. It is based on a functionality called **kitting**, which existed in previous versions but only on certain localized versions of Dynamics NAV.

Assembly management can be seen as a light manufacturing and is integrated with the sales, planning, and warehousing functionalities of Dynamics NAV.

The assembly management functionality is useful in the following business scenarios:

- **Light manufacturing**: Simple manufacturing processes that assemble items to stock and can be performed in the warehouse or shop floor
- **Kitting**: Packing of different items that are sold together as a kit, such as a gift basket

In the assembly management functionality, assembly items have to be defined so that they can then be used in assembly orders, which can be associated with a demand (assembling to order) or can be created to stock assembled items (assembling to stock).

Assembly items

An assembly item is an item that can be sold and that has an assembly **bill of materials (BOM)**. On the assembly item, the assembly procedure for the item (assembling to order or assembling to stock) is defined.

Assembly orders

Just like a production order, an assembly order is an internal order that is used to manage the assembly process and that connects the sales requirement with the involved warehouse activities. Assembly orders can be created to respond to sales requirements (assemble to order) or to respond to stock requirements (assemble to stock).

Warehouse management

Warehouse management in Dynamics NAV now includes:

- **Inventory movements**: This is a new warehouse activity that can be used to move items to and from internal departments without the need of a source document

- **Dedicated bins**: Bins can be set to `Dedicated`, which means that the inventory on the bin will not be available for any other resource than the one specified on the dedicated bin

- **Integration to service orders**: Service lines, just like any other outbound document lines, can now function as a source document for picking the shipment

Inventory

Enhancements in inventory features have been introduced in Dynamics NAV 2013. The enhancements refer to the item availability views, which now include a total of six views. Three of them already existed in previous versions of Dynamics NAV, and the other three have been newly introduced in Dynamics NAV 2013:

- **Item Availability by Event**: This shows projected inventory by demand or supply event. It can also include planning suggestions.

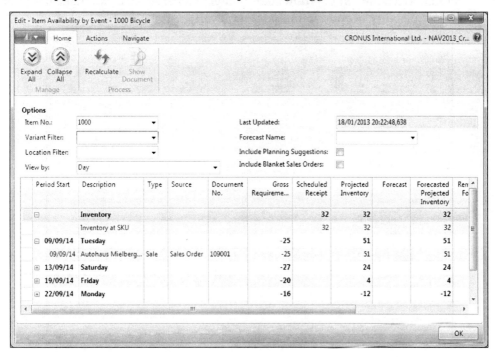

- **Item Availability by Timeline**: This provides a graphical view of an item's inventory based on future supply and demand events. This view includes drag-and-drop editing on the graphical view to modify Planning Worksheet.

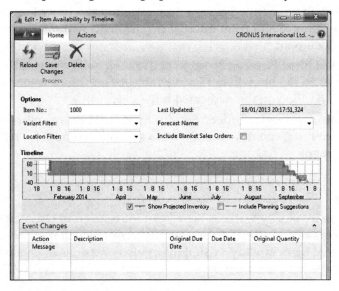

- **Item Availability by BOM Level**: This provides availability figures for bills of materials that tell you how many units of a parent you can make based on the availability of child items at lower levels.

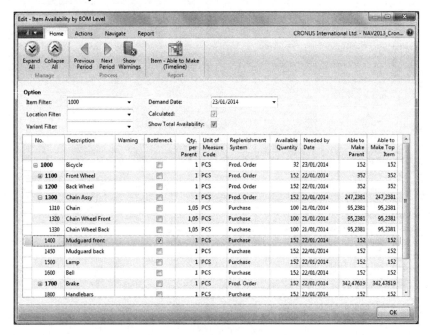

Supply planning

The supply planning feature of Dynamics NAV 2013 is now better than in previous releases of the application:

- It includes new planning parameters
- It includes default planning parameters to apply if they are not explicitly defined on items
- One now has the option of making order modifiers apply even if exception warnings exist
- Demand overview can now be seen from many application areas
- A new help topic has been introduced to allow us to better setup the supply planning functionality. It is called **Setup Best Practices**

New planning parameters

The following screenshot shows the **Planning** tab on the **Item Card** page. The planning parameters are now better organized, and some new parameters are now included to help us better define how to plan the replenishment of our items.

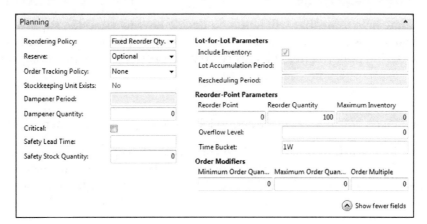

The new reordering parameters are:

- **Time Bucket**
- **Rescheduling Period**
- **Lot Accumulation Period**
- **Dampener Period**
- **Overflow Level**
- **Dampener Quantity**

On the **Manufacturing Setup** page, we can now specify the default dampener period and default dampener quantity that will apply if they are not specified on the items.

Order modifiers

With the new organization of the replenishment parameters on items cards, we now have a clear picture of the order modifiers. No matter what quantity we really need, if we have any restriction on a minimum or a maximum quantity(or on multiples of quantities) to order, these parameters will apply on the supply planning calculation.

In the previous versions of Dynamics NAV, those parameters applied for regular orders but did not apply for orders that were triggered by an exception (for instance, when the actual inventory of an item is below the safety stock quantity).

When calculating the reordering of our items, we can now check an option called **Respect Planning Parameters for Supply Triggered by Safety Stock** in Requisition Worksheet and **Respect Planning Parameters for Exception Warnings** in Planning Worksheet. The name of the options defines exactly what they do when they are checked.

Setup best practices

There is a new help topic that will help you decide how to setup the supply planning for your items. This topic explains the meaning of every planning parameter and also which reordering policy better suits every item according to an ABC classification.

Jobs

Several enhancements have been added to jobs and project management features.

- Tracking **work in process (WIP)** is now easier and can better suit any company's needs because WIP methods can be defined by the users and a default WIP method for all jobs can be specified in the job setup. There is also a new page named **Job View Cockpit** from which all WIP jobs can be managed and tracked.

- Tracking usage versus planning for a job is now easier with a new feature called **Job Usage Tracking**. This feature allows us to link usage entries with planning entries so that we can have a clear view of what work remains to be done to complete a job.

Resources

Dynamics NAV 2013 includes a new feature regarding resources called **Time Sheets**. Time Sheets manages time collection in weekly increments of seven days. It can be used to plan and record resource usage on jobs, service orders, or assembly orders.

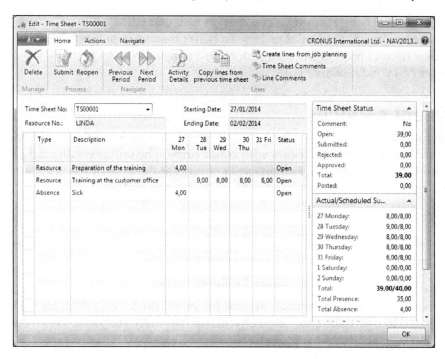

RapidStart Services

RapidStart Services is a new feature of Microsoft Dynamics NAV 2013. It allows you to configure your company using out of the box configurations. Microsoft Dynamics NAV 2013 also allows streamlined importing of opening balances into journals and active documents with dimensions.

The following components can be used to setup a new company:

- **Configuration Wizard**
- **Configuration Packages**
- **Configuration Worksheet**
- **Configuration Templates**
- **Configuration Questionnaire**

RapidStart Services is covered in detail in *Chapter 6, Migrating Data*.

CRM integration

Dynamics NAV 2013 enables integration with the customer relationship solution Microsoft Dynamics CRM in its versions 4.0 and 2011, both for the on-premise and online versions.

The integration synchronizes data common to ERP and CRM software, such as customers, contacts, and sales orders. To help preserve data integrity, the synchronization of most of the data is done in a single direction (usually from Dynamics NAV to Dynamics CRM).

Payment services

Payment services is an Internet-based payment solution. It is used to enable your customers to pay their sales orders with credit cards. The online credit card payment feature automates authorizing credit card amounts at the time of the order and processing the actual charge when the order is shipped and invoiced.

These are the tasks in the preferred order in a typical credit card payment process:

1. Enter setup data for the customer, such as the customer payment terms and setting up the credit card payment method code.

2. Create a sales order or invoice for the customer.

3. Authorize the total amount against the credit card. The authorization can be setup to occur automatically, or you can manually authorize the amount.

4. When the shipment is ready, post the sales order or invoice and send the actual payment to the payment service.

Development changes

Dynamics NAV 2013 introduces several development changes. There are changes regarding the development environment, with new features and object properties, and changes in the standard C/AL code, which has been redesigned in some areas.

Development Environment

Development Environment is the former Dynamics NAV classic client. In previous versions, the classic client was used both as an application client for end users and for development purposes. With Dynamics NAV 2013, the classic client is no longer available as an application client but has remained as the development environment. That is why it has been renamed to **Microsoft Dynamics NAV Development Environment**.

The development environment in Dynamics NAV 2013 introduces several improvements, including:

- New object types
- Enhancements on the development of object types that existed on previous versions
- New features
- New object properties
- Better .NET interoperability

Debugging

Microsoft Dynamics NAV 2013 introduces a brand new debugger. Debugging will no longer be a painful task in Microsoft Dynamics NAV. Conditional breakpoints, debug other user sessions, and debug C/AL code in the Windows client instead of incomprehensible C# code are the new features, which will convert the debugging experience into a happy experience.

With the new debugger, you can now debug the following sessions:

- Microsoft Dynamics NAV Windows client sessions
- Microsoft Dynamics NAV SharePoint client sessions
- Microsoft Dynamics NAV Web client sessions
- OData web services sessions
- SOAP web services sessions
- NAS services sessions
- Background sessions that you start by using the STARTSESSION function

You will find more information about the new debugger in *Chapter 11, Debugging*.

Page development

Page development is easier with Dynamics NAV 2013 than it was with Dynamics NAV 2009. Several enhancements have been added to the **Page Designer** page, as follows:

- **Page Preview in Page Designer**: Dynamics NAV 2013 introduces **Page Preview**. A page can be previewed without having to run the page in the client. It is an interactive preview. As we move through the page controls and page actions on the **Page Designer** page, the corresponding element on the rendered page will be highlighted in a blue rectangle. To preview a page, click on the **Preview** button available on the **Page Designer** page.

- **Page Field arrangement in a Grid**: There is a new page control in Dynamics NAV 2013 called **GridLayout**. With this control, fields can be laid out in rows and columns. The following screenshot shows **GridLayout** page control defined on the **Page Designer** page and what it looks like on the corresponding page:

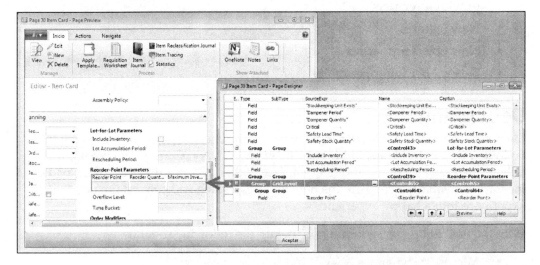

- **Standard Dialog page type**:This is a new page type that can be used to create simple pages for entering data. The **Standard Dialog** page does not include a ribbon and cannot be customized on the Windows client.

- **Page wizard**: Dynamics NAV 2013 includes a page wizard to easily create pages. With the page wizard, we can select fields on a table to be displayed on the page, we can create tabs to arrange the fields, and we can add subpages, FactBoxes, and charts.

- **Action and Activity button icon selection**: We can now select an icon for an action or an activity from a list instead of manually entering the icon's name.

- **Default control names and captions**: By default, the name and caption on a field control use the source field's name in the database.

- **Quick Entry property**: We have explained what the Quick Entry property is and what it can be used for, in the *Improvements to the Windows client* section. This property can be set by a developer on the **Page Designer** page.

Page testing

Testing options were introduced with Dynamics NAV 2009 SP1. Dynamics NAV 2013 has gone further in testing and introduces the ability to test pages.

On a test codeunit, we can now create a new type of variable, `TestPage`.

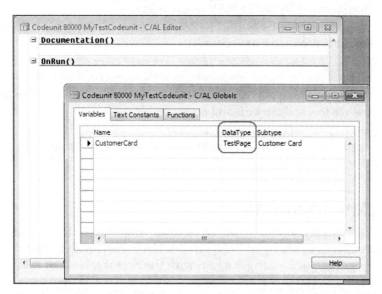

With this type of variable, we will be able to do with code almost the same things a user can do in a page. We will be able to:

- View or modify the value of a field on a test page
- View the data on page parts
- View or modify the value of a field on a subpage
- Filter the data
- Perform any actions that are available on the page
- Navigate to different records

A set of tests that use this new feature is available for Dynamics NAV 2013: **Application Test Toolset**. With this tool, you will be able to do testing on most of the standard functionalities provided with Dynamics NAV. It is important to run those tests when developing for Dynamics NAV as we want to make sure our developments do not introduce bugs into standard Dynamics NAV functionality.

Application Test Toolset can be downloaded from the following link (requires access to PartnerSource):

```
https://mbs.microsoft.com/partnersource/deployment/
resources/supplements/msdnav2013applicationtoolset.htm
```

A blog post from the Dynamics NAV development team explains how to use the tool and can be found at:

```
http://blogs.msdn.com/b/nav/archive/2012/11/07/
application-test-toolset-for-microsoft-dynamics-
nav-2013.aspx
```

Report development

Report development is completely different from what it used to be. The report development experience changed in Dynamics NAV 2009, with the introduction of RLDC-based reports, but it changes again with the actual release of the application.

With Dynamics NAV 2009, RLDC-based reports were introduced, but reports were still compatible with the classic definition of reports in Dynamics NAV. RLDC reports were actually based on the classic definition of the report.

With Dynamics NAV 2013, the classic definition for reports has disappeared and only RLDC-based reports are now available. But RLDC reports cannot now be based on the classic definition of reports. That is why the report development experience has changed again.

The report development experience in Dynamics NAV Development Environment now resembles the development experience of pages, queries, or XMLports. We now include, in the report designer, not only data items but also columns (fields) that will be displayed on the report.

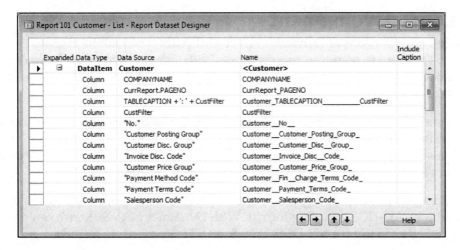

The second part of report development, the development of the layout of the report, has to be done in Visual Studio 2010 (Dynamics NAV 2009 used Visual Studio 2008).

Reports in Dynamics NAV 2013 include a new function, SAVEASWORD, that enables you to save a report on the computer that is running Dynamics NAV Server as a Microsoft Word (.doc) document.

Reports in Dynamics NAV 2013 include three new properties to specify the printer tray from which pages of a report are printed. Those properties are as follows:

- The PaperSourceFirstPage property
- The PaperSourceLastPage property
- The PaperSourceDefaultPage property

Query development

Microsoft Dynamics NAV 2013 introduces a new application object, the Query.

A Query is a read-only object that allows us to combine data from multiple tables into a single dataset using several SQL join types. Results in a query can easily be filtered, sorted, and grouped, and totals can easily be calculated using methods such as sum, average, or count.

You will find more information about this new application object in *Chapter 12, The Query Object*.

XMLport development

In the previous versions of Dynamics NAV, XMLports could not be executed directly. They had to be run from a codeunit. With Dynamics NAV 2013, we can now run XMLports directly from **Object Designer**. The XMLport will run on the Dynamics NAV server.

In previous versions, when using XMLports with the **Import** option, new records could be inserted but existing records could not be modified. XMLports now have a set of new properties, called `AutoSave`, `AutoReplace`, and `AutoUpdate`, to determine whether records are automatically inserted, replaced, or updated.

In the previous versions, XMLports could only import and export data in text format encoded with MS-DOS encoding format. With Dynamics NAV 2013, we can now specify whether to use the MS-DOS, UTF-8, or UTF-16 encoding formats.

Start ID Offset

When you add new elements to a Dynamics NAV object, such as new global or local variables, new functions and new controls in pages, you are automatically given an ID for that new element that always starts with the same ID.

When developing in Dynamics NAV, we usually identify changes for a specific solution using the object's version list and also using object and field numbering. However, we cannot use element numbering in standard objects to identify developments done for a specific solution. In Dynamics NAV 2013, that is now possible with **Start ID Offset**.

When we specify a Start ID Offset, for example 1000, all elements that we create will have an ID starting with 1000 and then incremented by 1. That is, the first element created on an object will have 1000 as ID, the second element will have 1001 as ID, and so on.

To specify a Start ID Offset, the following steps have to be performed:

1. Open Dynamics NAV Development Environment.
2. Click on **File** | **Database** | **Alter**.
3. Select the **Advanced** tab.

4. Specify the desired offset value in the **Start ID (UidOffset)** field.

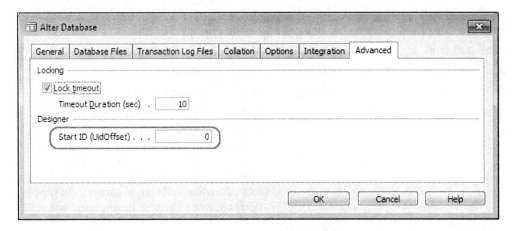

Changes to C/AL functions, data types, properties, and triggers

Dynamics NAV 2013 introduces new data types, functions, properties, and triggers. There are also some data types, functions, properties, and triggers that have changed or that have been removed.

The following table provides an overview of all the changed properties and their replacements:

Property	Type of change	Description of the change
AutoReplace	New	New property in XMLports
AutoSave	New	New property in XMLports
AutoUpdate	New	New property in XMLports
PaperSourceDefaultPage	New	New report property
PaperSourceFirstPage	New	New report property
PaperSourceLastPage	New	New report property
DrillDownFormID	Changed	Name changed to DrillDownPageID
CardFormID	Changed	Name changed to CardPageID
LookupFormID	Changed	Name changed to LookupPageID
RunFormLink	Changed	Name changed to RunPageLink
RunFormOnRec	Changed	Name changed to RunPageOnRec

Property	Type of change	Description of the change
RunFormView	Changed	Name changed to RunPageView
SubFormLink	Changed	Name changed to SubPageLink
SubFormView	Changed	Name changed to SubPageView
UseReqForm	Changed	Name changed to UseRequestPage
TransactionType	Changed	In Microsoft Dynamics NAV 2013, the default transaction isolation level is REPEATABLE READ. In earlier versions of Microsoft Dynamics NAV, it was SERIALIZABLE. This affects FIND and NEXT function calls when transaction type is Update, Snapshot or UpdateNoLocks.
BottomMargin	Removed	-
PaperSourceOtherPages	Removed	-
SaveTableView	Removed	-

The following table provides an overview of all the changed triggers and their replacements:

Trigger	Type of change	Description of the change
OnAfterModifyRecord	New	New XMLport trigger
OnBeforeModifyRecord	New	New XMLport trigger
OnCreateHyperlink	Removed	-
OnHyperlink	Removed	-
OnPreSection	Removed	-
OnPostSection	Removed	-

The following table provides an overview of all the changed data types and their replacements:

Data type	Type of change	Description of the change
BLOB	Changed	If you call the CALCFIELDS function (Record) on a BLOB field, you get the value of BLOB that is in the database, not the value that you wrote to BLOB OutStream.
Code	Changed	The Code data type supports Unicode. Limits are not enforced on the length of a Code variable.

Data type	Type of change	Description of the change
Text	Changed	Text supports Unicode in Microsoft Dynamics NAV 2013. Limits are not enforced on the length of a Text variable. You can specify a maximum length in the C/AL Globals or C/AL Locals window when you create the variable, but it is not required.
Binary	Removed	Binary was used to store fixed lengths of binary data in a record. BLOB should now be used for this purpose.

The following table provides an overview of all the changed functions and their replacements:

Function	Type of change	Description of the change
SETAUTOCALCFIELDS(Record)	New	New function to calculate FlowFields at the same time that you retrieve them from the database
CURRENTEXECUTIONMODE	New	New function
STARTSESSION	New	New function
STOPSESSION	New	New function
CALCFIELDS (Record)	Changed	CALCFIELDS execution is decoupled from Microsoft Dynamics NAV SIFT index definitions
CALCSUM (FieldRef)	Changed	CALCFIELDS execution is decoupled from Microsoft Dynamics NAV SIFT index definitions
CALCSUMS (Record)	Changed	CALCFIELDS execution is decoupled from Microsoft Dynamics NAV SIFT index definitions
COUNT (Record)	Changed	The COUNT function does not always ignore security filters. It adheres to the SecurityFiltering property
COUNT (RecordRef)	Changed	The COUNT function does not always ignore security filters. It adheres to the SecurityFiltering property
CREATETOTALS	Changed	Redundant in Microsoft Dynamics NAV 2013 reports. We recommend that you use the SUM function in Visual Studio instead.

Function	Type of change	Description of the change
Debugger functions	Changed	New functions have been introduced
INSERT (Record) and INSERT (RecordRef)	Changed	You cannot call the INSERT function on a record for table 2000000001, the object table or table 2000000006, the company table
MODIFY (Record) and MODIFY (RecordRef)	Changed	Microsoft Dynamics NAV 2013 does not let you modify the database by using an old copy of a record. You cannot call the MODIFY function on a record for table 2000000001, the object table or table 2000000006, the company table.
DELETE (Record) and DELETE(RecordRef)	Changed	You cannot call the DELETE function on a record for table 2000000001, the object table or table 2000000006, the company table.
RENAME	Changed	Microsoft Dynamics NAV 2013 does not let you modify the database by using an old copy of a record.
FormHandler	Changed	Name changed to PageHandler
ModalFormHandler	Changed	Name changed to ModalPageHandler
ISSERVICETIER	Changed	Obsolete in Microsoft Dynamics NAV 2013, but still supported. This function always returns true.
RECORDLEVELLOCKING (Record and RecordRef)	Changed	Not used in Microsoft Dynamics NAV 2013. The function is still available and compiles, but always returns true.
READCONSISTENCY (Record and RecordRef)	Changed	Not used in Microsoft Dynamics NAV 2013. The function is still available and compiles but because Microsoft Dynamics NAV 2013 uses SQL Server's locking mechanisms and does not use snapshots like earlier versions of Microsoft Dynamics NAV did, the return value is always false.
SETCURRENTKEY (Record)	Changed	In Microsoft Dynamics NAV 2013, you do not have to define keys only for SIFT indexes. Fewer SIFT indices and fewer Microsoft Dynamics NAV keys can improve performance.

Function	Type of change	Description of the change
BEEP	Removed	-
COMMANDLINE	Removed	-
COUNTAPPROX	Removed	-
ENVIRON	Removed	-
EXPORT (BLOB)	Removed	-
EXPORTOBJECTS	Removed	Not supported in Microsoft Dynamics NAV 2013. Use the finsql.exe executable with the ExportObjects command instead.
IMPORT (BLOB)	Removed	-
IMPORTOBJECTS	Removed	Not supported in Microsoft Dynamics NAV 2013. Use the finsql.exe executable with the ImportObjects command instead.
LANGUAGE	Removed	-
NEWPAGE	Removed	-
NEWPAGEPERRECORD	Removed	-
OBJECTID	Removed	-
OSVERSION	Removed	-
PAGENO	Removed	-
PAPERSOURCE	Removed	-
SAVEASHTML	Removed	-
SAVEASXML	Removed	-
SETPERMISSIONFILTER (Record)	Removed	Not supported in Microsoft Dynamics NAV 2013. Instead, you change the SecurityFiltering property from Validated to Filtered.
SETPERMISSIONFILTER (RecordRef)	Removed	Not supported in Microsoft Dynamics NAV 2013. Instead, you change the SecurityFiltering property from Validated to Filtered.
SHELL	Removed	-
SHOWOUTPUT	Removed	-
SYNCHRONIZEALLLOGINS	Removed	-
SYNCHRONIZESINGLELOGIN	Removed	-

Function	Type of change	Description of the change
TOTALSCAUSEDBY	Removed	–
URL	Removed	–
VARIABLEACTIVE	Removed	–
YIELD	Removed	–

The following table provides an overview of all the changed objects and their replacements:

Objects	Type of change	Description of the change
The Query object	New	New object type
Test Pages	New	New objects and functions
Dataports	Removed	–
Forms	Removed	–
The RequestOptionsForm system variable	Removed	–

.NET interoperability

Dynamics NAV can be extended with the .NET Framework assemblies. We can reference assemblies and call types directly from C/AL code of Dynamics NAV objects, such as pages and codeunits. Dynamics NAV objects can also subscribe to events that are published by .NET Framework types.

Enhancements in RoleTailored client control add-ins

Control add-ins has been enhanced with the following features:

- **Additional data types are supported with database binding**: Dynamics NAV 2013 now supports data types, such as DateTime, Boolean, Char, Decimal, Int32, Int64, and Guid. Data binding and firing of the OnControlAddIn C/AL trigger is enabled by implementing respective interfaces.

- **Methods and properties can be exposed to C/AL code**: To extend user interface controls on a page, methods and properties can be exposed in a control add-in assembly so that they can be called by C/AL code on page triggers.

- **Control add-ins can be sized**: We can now specify an area of a page that a control add-in occupies both with a fixed size or by setting the control add-in to resize as the page window resizes in the Dynamics NAV Windows client.

Standard C/AL code redesign

Standard Dynamics NAV C/AL code has been redesigned in Dynamics NAV 2013 to use some new development functions introduced with this release of the application and to make the application faster.

G/L Entry table locking redesign

The sales, purchase, and service posting routines of Dynamics NAV 2013 have been redesigned to lock differently from how previous versions of Dynamics NAV locked.

In previous versions, posting routines used to lock the G/L Entry table at the very beginning of the transaction. That meant that a user could not initiate a posting transaction while another posting transaction was being executed. This was a huge performance issue in multiuser environments.

Dynamics NAV 2013 sales, purchase, and service posting routines have been redesigned to lock the G/L Entry table later on, when the lock is really needed. Thus, the time for which this table remains locked is shorter than in previous versions, letting multiple users execute a posting routine at the same time and thus improving performance in multiuser environments.

Storing dimension entries

With Dynamics NAV 2013, the dimension feature has been redesigned. From the user's point of view nothing has changed; dimensions still work as they used to, and they are used for the same purposes.

But the way dimensions are stored in the database has been completely redesigned. Instead of explicitly storing each dimension value in the database, a dimension set ID is used, and all the tables that use dimensions (documents, journals, entries, and so on) now refer to the same dimension set ID. This way, a dimension set is stored only once in the database, reducing the database space required to store dimensions and improving the application's overall performance. A new table called `Dimension Set Entry` has been created. Dimension set IDs are then assigned to journal lines, documents headers, and document lines.

Dimension sets

A dimension set is a unique combination of dimension values. It is stored as dimension set entries in the database. Each `Dimension Set Entry` table represents a single dimension value. The dimension set is identified by a common dimension set ID that is assigned to each `Dimension Set Entry` table that belongs to the dimension set.

Dimension set entries

Dimension sets are stored in the `Dimension Set Entry` table as dimension set entries with the same dimension set ID.

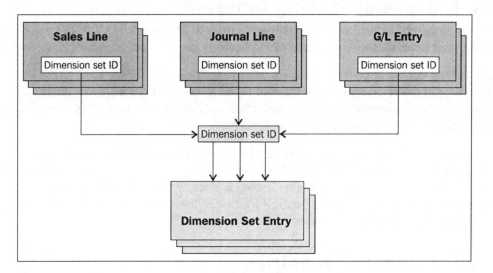

When you create a new journal line, document header, or document line, you can specify a combination of dimension values. Instead of explicitly storing each dimension value in the database, a dimension set ID is assigned to the journal line, document header, or document line to specify the dimension set.

When you edit and close the **Edit Dimension Set Entries** window, a check is performed to see whether the combination of dimension values exists as a dimension set in the table. If the combination occurs in the table, the corresponding dimension set ID is assigned to the journal line, document header, or document line. Otherwise, a new dimension set is added to the table, and the new dimension set ID is assigned to the journal line, document header, or document line.

Performance improvement

By storing dimension sets once in the database, database space is preserved and overall performance is improved.

ADCS

The implementation of **Automated Data Capture System**, known as ADCS, was implemented in previous versions of Dynamics NAV using NAS services. In Dynamics NAV 2013, the implementation of ADCS is now based on web services. The user experience remains the same.

IT changes

Several changes regarding IT have been introduced with the release of Dynamics NAV 2013, including:

- Easier installation and deployment
- Easier administration
- New clients
- New services

Installation

The Microsoft Dynamics NAV setup program has been enhanced and redesigned. There are now four setup options instead of six. The classic database server is no longer available.

When you install Microsoft Dynamics NAV in a production environment with the client, server, and database tiers each installed on a separate computer, you are no longer required to manually configure delegation or to manually create SPNs to enable the Microsoft Dynamics NAV Windows client to communicate with SQL Server.

Microsoft Dynamics NAV Server now only runs on 64-bit editions of Windows operating systems. Microsoft Dynamics NAV 2013 also now requires a 64-bit edition of SQL Server. If a supported version of SQL Server is not found on the computer, setup installs the 64-bit edition of SQL Server 2012 Express.

Microsoft Dynamics NAV 2013 now requires Microsoft .NET framework 4.0 as a prerequisite. If it is not found on the target computer, setup installs Microsoft .NET Framework 4.

Dynamics NAV Server Administration

Dynamics NAV 2013 includes a new server administration tool for administering Dynamics NAV Server.

It is a snap-in for the Microsoft Management Console. When installing the server option, the server administration tool is a default feature.

Once it is installed, you will find it on your Windows **Start** menu with all the other Dynamics NAV components installed on the same machine.

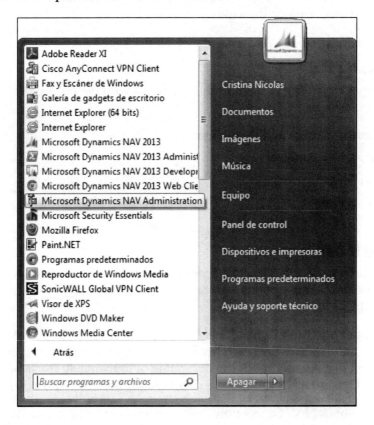

From the server administration tool, we will have a clear picture of all Dynamics NAV instances running on the machine, their version, status, and configuration (name, database to which the instance connects, ports for the different types of services, and so on).

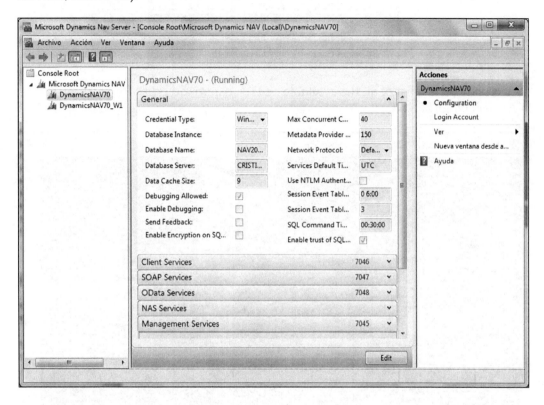

From the server administration tool, we can add or remove instances (we can even add instances running on a different server), edit their settings, start or stop the services, and so on.

Windows PowerShell 2.0 cmdlets

Dynamics NAV 2013 comes with a set of PowerShell 2.0 cmdlets that allow us to perform administering tasks on our Dynamics NAV installation.

You will also find it on your Windows **Start** menu with all the other Dynamics NAV components installed on the same machine.

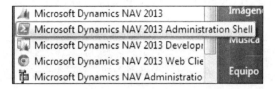

When you run it, a list of all the available `cmdlet` command types for Dynamics NAV will be displayed.

Web client

Dynamics NAV 2013 introduces a new user client, the Web client. This new client enables users to access Dynamics NAV data over the Internet using a browser.

The Web client resembles the Dynamics NAV Window client; thus, it is an easy-to-use user interface for users who are already used to the Dynamics NAV Windows client.

The Web client can be accessed via browsers such as Internet Explorer, Mozilla Firefox, Google Chrome, and Safari, and also via browsers on various mobile platforms, such as Windows Phone 7.5, Android, and iOS for iPhone and iPad.

The Dynamics NAV Web client can be accessed by just typing `http://<servername>:8080` in the address bar of the browser and providing the user credentials when required by the browser. Note that for this URL to work, your computer has to be on the same network that the server hosting Dynamics NAV is on (either physically or through VPN), or the server has to be visible on the Internet. Otherwise, you will not be able to use the Dynamics NAV Web client.

The following screenshot shows the start page of the Dynamics NAV Web client:

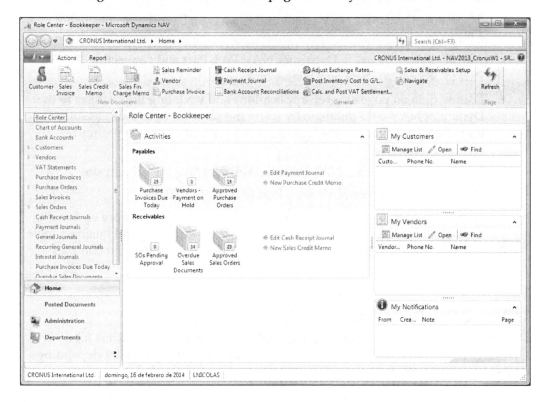

The deployment of the Dynamics NAV Web client is easy since it has to be only deployed on a web server. Nothing has to be installed or configured on the client machines since client machines already have browsers installed.

The solutions for the Dynamics NAV Web client are developed on Dynamics NAV Development Environment the same way they are developed for the Dynamics NAV Windows client. But the development doesn't have to be developed twice for the different clients. Actually, the same objects used by the Windows client are also used by the Web client, so a change made in any objects will be seen from the different clients.

Portal Framework for SharePoint 2010

Dynamics NAV Portal Framework for SharePoint 2010 is a web-based application framework for developing Dynamics NAV solutions for SharePoint 2010 applications. Dynamics NAV Portal Framework can be used to give users access to data in Dynamics NAV 2013 from SharePoint websites by displaying pages and reports.

With Dynamics NAV Portal Framework, the following can be done:

- Displaying Dynamics NAV pages and reports on SharePoint sites using a URL.

- Adding a page by using Dynamics NAV Web Part and connecting the Web Part to other Web Parts on a SharePoint page.

- Editing data on pages in web applications and updating the changes to the Dynamics NAV 2013 database by using the same metadata and business logic that is rendered in the Dynamics NAV Windows client without complex setup steps.

- Displaying a Dynamics NAV page in Web Part on a SharePoint site.

- Connecting Dynamics NAV Web Part to other Web Parts.

- Editing Dynamics NAV pages on a SharePoint site. Changes are updated in the Dynamics NAV database by using the same metadata and business logic that is rendered in the Dynamics NAV Windows client without complex setup steps.

User and credential types

Dynamics NAV 2013 supports four credential authorization mechanisms for Dynamics NAV users. Different information about the user is provided depending on the credential type used.

The supported credential mechanisms are:

- **Windows**: With this credential type, users are authenticated using their Windows credentials (Active Directory, local workgroup, or the local computer's users). Before a Windows user can be created in the Windows client, there must already be a corresponding user in Windows. In Dynamics NAV 2009, all Windows client users were Windows users. Because they are authenticated through Windows, Windows users are not prompted for credentials when they start the Windows client.

- **Username**: With this setting, the user is prompted for username-password credentials when starting the Windows client. These credentials are then validated against Windows authentication by Microsoft Dynamics NAV Server. There must already be a corresponding user in Windows. Security certificates are required to protect the passing of credentials across a wide area network. This setting should typically be used when the Microsoft Dynamics NAV Server computer is part of an authenticating Active Directory domain but the computer where the Microsoft Dynamics NAV Windows client is installed is not part of the domain.

- **NavUserPassword**: With this setting, authentication is managed by Microsoft Dynamics NAV Server but is not based on Windows users or Active Directory. The user is prompted for username-password credentials when they start the client. The credentials are then validated by an external mechanism. Security certificates are required to protect the passing of credentials. This mode is intended for hosted environments; for example, where Microsoft Dynamics NAV is implemented in Azure.

- **AccessControlService**: With this setting, Microsoft Dynamics NAV relies on Windows Azure Access Control Service (ACS) for user authentication services. ACS is a cloud-based service that provides user authentication and authorization for web applications and services. ACS integrates with standards-based identity providers, including enterprise directories such as Active Directory and web identities such as Windows Live ID, Google, Yahoo!, and Facebook.

NAS services

Dynamics NAV Application Server, known as NAS, has been redesigned in Dynamics NAV 2013. NAS is no longer a separated and dedicated Dynamics NAV service. It is now a part of the unique Dynamics NAV service. A single service manages client services, NAS services, and the different types of web services.

NAS services, just like other Dynamics NAV services, can be managed with the Dynamics NAV Server Administration tool.

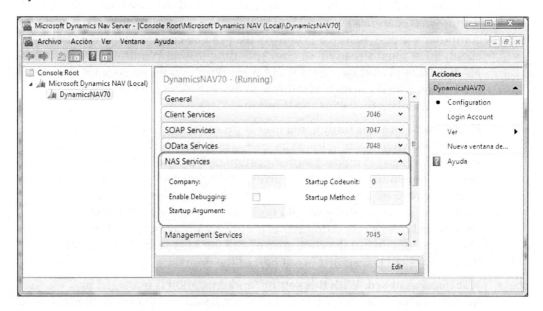

OData web services

Dynamics NAV 2009 already introduced the ability to publish web services. They were SOAP web services. With Dynamics NAV 2013, we can now also publish OData web services.

OData stands for **Open Data protocol**. It is a web protocol designed for querying tabular data. You will find more information about this protocol at http://www.odata.org/.

OData web services can be published in Dynamics NAV the same way that SOAP web services are published.

To publish a web service, follow these steps:

1. Open the Windows Client for Microsoft Dynamics NAV 2013.
2. Navigate to **Departments/Administration/IT Administration/General**.
3. Select web services.
4. Select **New** on the ribbon bar to publish a new web service.
5. The **New – Web Services** page opens.
6. Select **Query** or **Page** as the object type.

7. Select a query or a page in the **Object ID** field.
8. Populate a name for the web service in the **Service Name** field.
9. Check the **Published** field.
10. Close the Windows client.

The URL to the OData web services published in Dynamics NAV is:

```
http://<ServerName>:<ODataPort>/<ServerInstance>/Odata
```

In a typical installation, `<ODataPort>` will be `7048`. `<ServerName>` will be the name of the server on which you have installed the server options of Microsoft Dynamics NAV 2013, and `<ServerInstance>` will be the name given to the Dynamics NAV service.

If you are accessing the published web service in the server where Dynamics NAV is installed and you haven't changed the default port at which OData web services are published, you can use the following URL:

```
http://localhost:7048/DynamicsNAV70/Odata
```

To access a concrete web service, enter its name at the end of the URL as shown in the following URL:

```
http://localhost:7048/DynamicsNAV70/Odata/MyServiceName
```

In *Chapter 12, The Query Object*, we have included an example of consuming a Query OData web service using Excel.

Database changes

The SQL Server interface from Microsoft Dynamics NAV Server has been rewritten for Microsoft Dynamics NAV 2013 to use ADO.NET instead of ODBC.

This results in a simplified deployment of Dynamics NAV 2013, a decrease in resource consumption, an improved cache system, and improvements in performance.

Unicode

Dynamics NAV 2013 data can be stored in the database in any language because Unicode is now supported. Because of Unicode support, the following limits have changed:

- No limit is enforced on the length of `Text` and `Code` variables
- The size of a Dynamics NAV table key has increased to 900 bytes

- The maximum length of a security filter expression has increased to 504 bytes
- The size of a record ID has increased to 900 bytes

Unicode is not supported for metadata such as captions and object names. However, if you want to enter and view metadata in a language that requires Unicode, you set the format and language to the desired language on both the computer that is running the Microsoft Dynamics NAV Development Environment and the computer that is running Microsoft Dynamics NAV Server.

Additionally, Unicode is not supported for text constants in code. However, you can import Unicode constants into the database by using an XMLport and then reference records in the database that contain Unicode constants.

ClickOnce

ClickOnce is a component of the Microsoft .NET Framework that lets you deploy web applications by choosing a link on a web page.

Dynamics NAV 2013 can now be deployed using the ClickOnce technology, which makes deployment easier and faster with centralized configuration, easy deployment of languages and add-ins, and so on.

There are some limitations, though. If the deployment of Dynamics NAV 2013 is done using the ClickOnce deployment technology, users will not be able to run the Windows client with command-line arguments or run hyperlinks. The following is a list of things that will not be possible with a ClickOnce deployment:

- An end user will not be able to specify a home page
- An end user will not be able to specify a profile
- An end user will not be able to disable personalization
- An end user will not be able to disable the navigation pane
- An end user will not be able to send or open a link to a Dynamics NAV page or report
- An end user will be able to send data to Excel but will not be able to refresh the data from Excel
- A developer will not be able to run the debugger
- Third-party applications will not be able to start the Dynamics NAV Windows client

Deprecated features

Dynamics NAV 2013 offers several new features. We have seen them all in this chapter. But there are also some features that disappear with this release of Dynamics NAV. In this section, we will go through the deprecated features and their replacement if a replacement actually exists.

Deprecated application features

Some application features are no longer available in Dynamics NAV 2013. Here is a list of the Deprecated application features and their replacement technology (if it exists):

Feature	Replacement
Business Analytics	–
Business Notifications	–
Demand Planner	–
Production Schedule (Gantt Chart)	–
Microsoft Dynamics Mobile	–
Microsoft Dynamics NAV Employee Portal	Microsoft Dynamics NAV Portal Framework for Microsoft SharePoint 2010
Rapid Implementation Methodology Toolkit	RapidStart Services

Deprecated developer and IT features

Some developer and IT features are no longer available in Dynamics NAV 2013. Here is a list of the deprecated developer and IT features and their replacement technology (if it exists):

Feature	Replacement
Dynamics NAV Classic Client	Windows client, Web client, and SharePoint client
Dynamics NAV Classic Database	SQL Database
Dynamics NAV Classic Application Server (NAS)	Dynamics NAV NAS Services
Software Development Kit: C/FRONT and Communication Components	.NET Framework Interoperability SOAP web services OData web services

Feature	Replacement
Dataports	XMLports
Forms	Pages
Server-side COM	.NET Framework Interoperability
Client Monitor	SQL Server Profiler

Summary

Dynamics NAV 2013 introduces several changes compared to the previous version of the application. Those changes apply to all the application areas; there are changes in the client to access the application, on the functionality, on the way to develop, and also changes related to IT.

In this chapter we have gone through all the changes introduced in Dynamics NAV 2013.

In the next chapter, we will see some general considerations about Dynamics NAV, such as the data model used in the application, the way posting routines are developed, and the SIFT technology.

3
Dynamics NAV – General Considerations

Knowing the Dynamics NAV philosophy of how things are done is important for everyone.

It is important for users and people working in a company that uses or will use Dynamics NAV as their ERP. They have to know how to do things and, especially, be aware of the consequences of what they do.

It is also important for consultants, analysts, developers, people working in a company that implements Dynamics NAV, and for partners. They have to fully understand the way NAV works, not only because they are the people responsible for transmitting that knowledge to users, but also because they will probably be designing and developing new functionalities or modifying existing ones. For this, it is important to use the same structures, way to present data, way to make information flow, and, in the end, the same philosophy Dynamics NAV uses in all its standard functionalities. Completely different behaviors may confuse your end users.

In this chapter we will cover:

- The structure of Microsoft Dynamics NAV 2013 in the section *The data model*
- The way information flows in Microsoft Dynamics NAV 2013 in the sections *The posting routines*, *Navigating through your data*, and *Real-time data gathering – The SIFT technology*
- Other general considerations in the sections *No save button*, *Posted data cannot be modified (nor deleted)*, and *Everything leads to accounting*

The data model

If you have never worked with Microsoft Dynamics NAV and start playing around with it, there are a few words you will see over and over, including setup, journal, posting group, post, document, entry, dimension, and so on. You may not have a clue of what all of this means or what it is used for. But don't worry, we will explain it all!

Dynamics NAV is structured into different functional areas, namely Financial Management, Sales & Marketing, Purchase, Warehouse, Manufacturing, Jobs, Resource Planning, Service, and Human Resources.

Each of the functional areas has its own setup, where the behavior of each of the areas is defined. A general setup also exists on the **Administration** menu.

Master data

Each of the functional areas has a master data table. The `Customer` table is the master data table for the Sales & Marketing area. The `G/L account` table is the master data table for the Financial Management area. There are also other master tables, secondary master tables, that relate to the main master table in a functional area. For instance, the `Customer` table has quite a few secondary master data tables, such as `Contacts`, `Bank Accounts`, `Ship-to Addresses`, or `Cross-References`. They are defined in this way because a single customer may have multiple contacts, bank accounts, ship-to addresses, or cross-references.

The secondary master data of a main master data register can be found in the **Navigate** tab (although not all items in the **Navigate** tab are secondary master data):

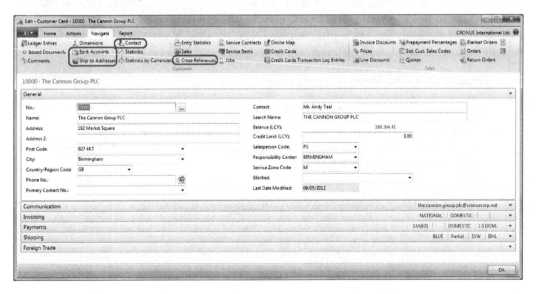

So far we've seen what we could call core master data tables, which hold the basic information in a functional area, and we've seen that those tables may have some secondary master data tables associated.

A different kind of master data also exists in Dynamics NAV. We could call it information helper master data tables. Examples of this kind of information are locations, currencies, payment terms, payment methods, units of measure, item-tracking codes, and so on.

Some helper master data may have its own secondary master data. Locations have zones and bins, and currencies have exchange rates.

Documents

Several documents exist in Dynamics NAV, such as sales documents (quotes, orders, invoices, return orders, and credit memos), purchase documents (quotes, orders, invoices, return orders, and credit memos), warehouse documents (transfer orders, receipts, put-aways, shipments, and picks), and manufacturing documents (production orders).

A document combines information from different master data tables and is one of the entry points to a transaction.

For example, a `Sales Order` document combines information from the `Customer` table (the customer that buys), the `Item` table (the items that are being sold), the `Resources` table (the resources that will provide the services the company offers), and so on.

When the sales order is processed, it will lead to one or more transactions, such as `Item` transactions (the stock of the item will be reduced with the quantity being sold) and `General Ledger` transactions (accounting entries will be created when the sales invoice is posted).

A document always has a header-lines structure presented in a single screen. In the header section, we will find general information that applies to the whole document, such as `Sell-to Customer No.` In a `Sales Order` document, the status of the document, or the shipment date. In the lines section, we will find detailed information about the document, such as the list of all items being sold in a sales order or the list of all items being produced in a production order.

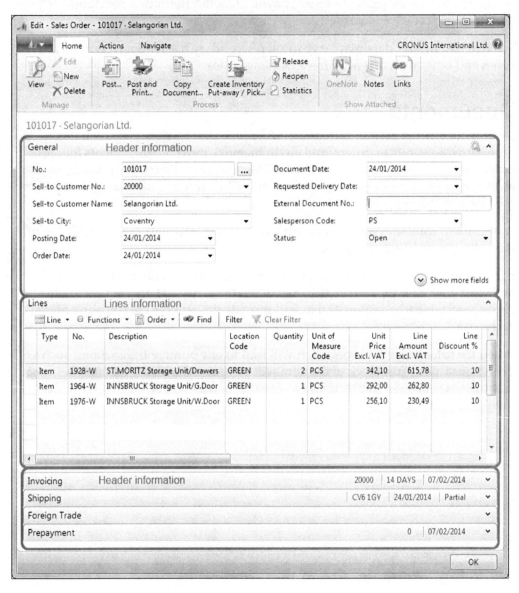

Under the **Actions** tab, you will always find one or more printing options to print the currently selected document. A printed document in Dynamics NAV looks somewhat like the following screenshot:

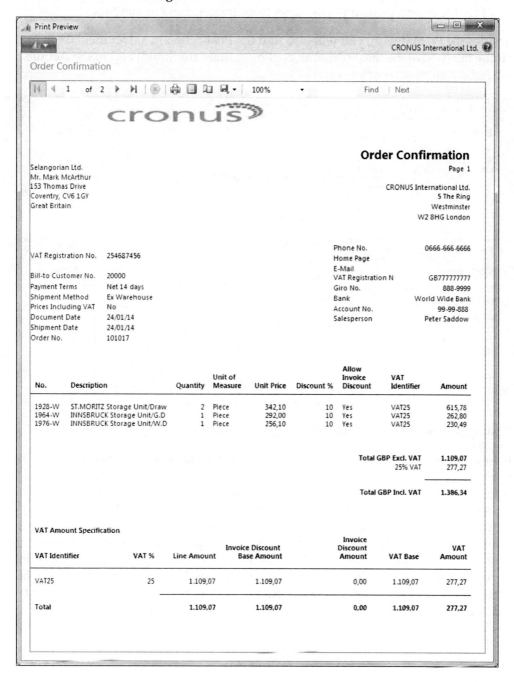

Printed documents in Dynamics NAV have all the common information that is needed. Most companies that implement Dynamics NAV ask their partners to modify the layout of the printed documents, at least those that are sent (either as a PDF file or as a printed paper copy) to their customers or vendors.

Besides the **Print** option, you will also find the **Post** action in a document, both in the **Home** tab (where the most common posting actions are found) and in the **Actions** tab (where all posting actions can be found).

Posting options in the Home tab

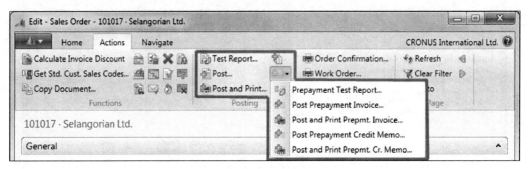

Posting options in the Actions tab

Posting is the most important action in Dynamics NAV.

Before a document has been posted, it is a document for which the action that is supposed to be done is still undone. That is, a non-posted `Sales Order` table is an order for which the items that were ordered have not yet been shipped or the services that had to be provided have still not been provided. You could see non-posted documents as a work area in which the user can enter the required information and post it when it is ready. When you post a document, you are telling Dynamics NAV that the action that had to be completed for the document has been completed (a sales order has been shipped, the items of a production order have been produced, a purchase order has been received, a sales invoice has been accounted for, and so on).

The posting action modifies the original document (to state that it has been posted) and creates new documents, that is, posted documents. For example, when a `Sales Order` is posted with the **Ship** option selected, `Posted Sales Shipment` is created, and when a sales invoice is posted, `Posted Sales Invoice` is created.

You will find posted documents from a Dynamics NAV functional area under the **History** category of the corresponding area.

```
Sales & Marketing, History

History
Sales Quote Archives
Sales Order Archives
Sales Return Order Archives
Posted Sales Invoices
Posted Sales Shipments
Posted Sales Credit Memos
Posted Return Receipts
G/L Registers
```

Journals

In Dynamics NAV, you will see journals all over the place, in every single functional area. Just to name a few, if you move around on the **Departments** menu, you will find:

- General Journals
- Recurring General Journals
- IC General Journals
- Intrastat Journals
- Cash Receipt Journals
- Payments Journals
- Sales Journals
- Purchase Journals
- FA G/L Journals
- FA Journals
- FA Reclass. Journals
- Insurance Journals
- Recurring Fixed Asset Journals

- `Item Journals`

- `BOM Journals`

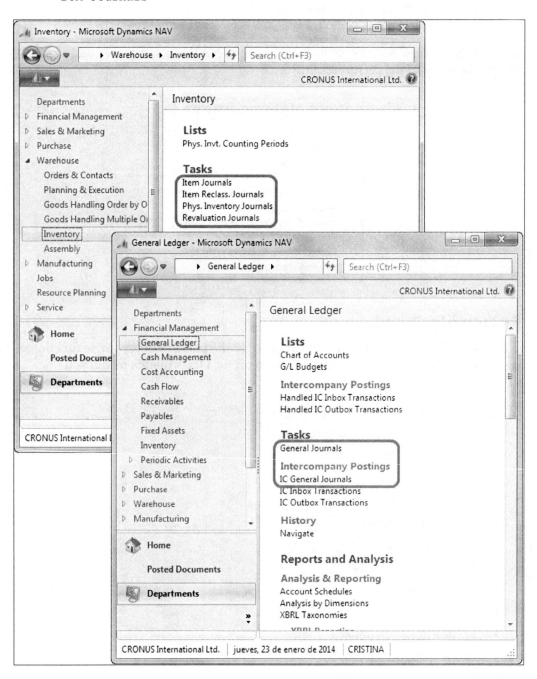

We may have skipped some journals, but we counted 27 different journals. That's quite a lot. Such a large amount of journals can make you think that this is something important. And yes, you are right, journals are very important in Dynamics NAV. They are just as important as the posting actions on documents because, when posting, Dynamics NAV internally uses journals to do the job.

Journals are where all kinds of transactions in Dynamics NAV, such as accounting transactions, sales transactions, item transactions, and so on, take place.

You could actually write down all the company transactions in journals and post them there (journals also have a posting action) without using any kind of document. In fact, some companies follow this method, although we would not recommend it.

Imagine you want to post a sales invoice in which you have sold an item, a resource, and a fixed asset. Using the appropriate G/L accounts, you could post all transactions by going to **Item Journal** and posting the necessary movements to reduce the stock there, then going to **Resource Journal** and posting the necessary movements associated with the resource there, then going to **FA Journal** and posting the movements associated with the fixed asset there, and finally going to **General Journal** and posting the accounting transaction of a sales invoice there, without using a `Sales Invoice` document.

It's a lot of work. It is actually what Dynamics NAV does when posting a document. It goes to the appropriate journals, depending on the document and on the concepts used in the document, creates the necessary journal lines, and posts the different journals.

You may be wondering why journals are available to users if they are something Dynamics NAV uses internally and users should not care about. They are actually there because even if a high percentage of the company transactions can be done using a document, there are some other transactions that do not have a document, so a journal will have to be used.

Among the journals, the one that is the most used in Dynamics NAV is probably General Journal. General Journal is mainly used to post accounting transactions. There are many accounting transactions, such as salary payment to employees and many others, that a company has to make, and the company does not have a document to make them (not in Dynamics NAV at least).

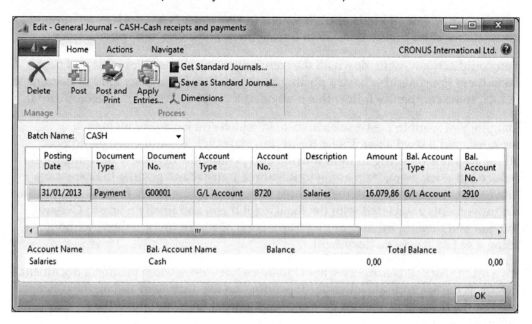

Another journal that is commonly used is Item Journal, where stock increases and decreases not associated with a document can be registered. What happens if an item is broken and thrown away? There is no document in Dynamics NAV to enter such a transaction. Well, the place to actually do that is Item Journal, where the user can post a stock decrease for the item that broke.

Did we say 27 journals? Actually just a few journals exist in Dynamics NAV, namely General Journal, Item Journal, BOM Journal, Resource Journal, Job Journal, FA Journal, and Warehouse Journal. There are a few more, but these are the most important ones.

Many journals we've seen on the Dynamics NAV menu are actually the same journals, but they show and let the user enter different information and have preselected options and built-in functionality depending on what the journal is meant for. For example, Item Journal, Phys. Inventory journal, and Output Journal actually rely on the same real journal, that is, Item Journal.

`Phys. Inventory Journal` is meant to register the system inventory differences when a physical inventory is completed. It is an item transaction; that's why it's built on top of `Item Journal` but has some peculiarities. In a physical inventory, we count how many units we have in the inventory. We know how many units we've counted, but we do not know how many units are registered in Dynamics NAV; so when coming to `Phys. Inventory Journal`, we do not know whether the transaction will have to be a positive or a negative adjustment, nor do we know the amount of times the transaction will have to be posted. That's why in the `Phys. Inventory Journal`, we inform the real quantity we've counted (field **Qty. (Phys. Inventory)**), and the functionality of the journal decides the rest, comparing the real stock that was counted with the stock registered in the system.

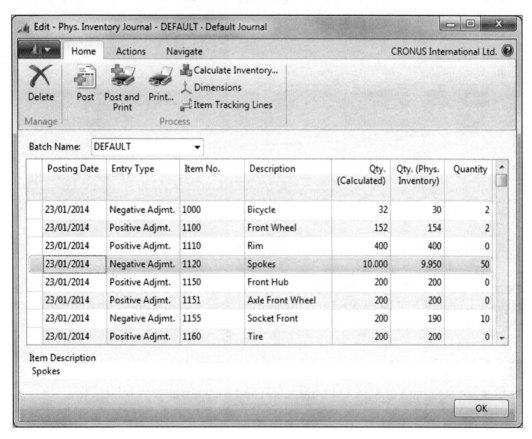

`Output Journal` is meant to register the stock increase of a manufactured item in the system, when a production order is finished. It is again an item transaction and that's why it is built on top of `Item Journal`. However, the user will have to provide some extra information that is not usually entered in other kinds of item transactions, such as the `Production Order` that is being posted, the `Operation` in the `Production Order`, or the `Scrap Quantity`. The `Output Journal` line shows the user the fields that he/she has to fill in to post this transaction. These fields are not shown in other item journals.

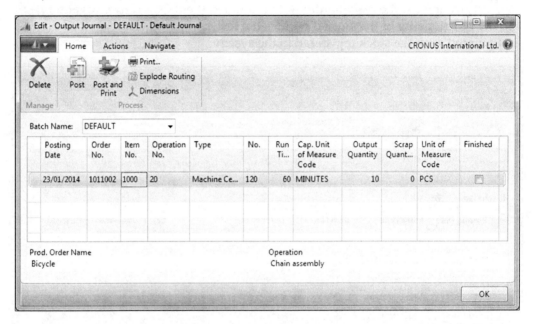

Once a journal is filled in with all the needed transactions, it has to be posted. Once it is posted, entries will be created and the journal lines will disappear (except for those that belong to `Recurring Journal`).

Entries

Entries are the result of a posted transaction and they are always related to a master record.

In the following table, you will find the most important entries in Dynamics NAV. You will also see the master tables they are related to.

Entry table	Related master table
G/L Entry	G/L Account
Cust. Ledger Entry	Customer
Vendor Ledger Entry	Vendor
Item Ledger Entry	Item
Res. Ledger Entry	Resource
Bank Account Ledger Entry	Bank Account
VAT Entry	Customer or Vendor
Job Ledger Entry	Job. Also Resource, Item, or G/L Account

Entries are created by a journal. G/L Entries are created by General Journal, which can also create Cust. Ledger Entries, Vendor Ledger Entries, Bank Account Ledger Entries, or VAT Entries. Item Ledger Entries are created by Item Journal.

In the following diagram you can see which journal is responsible for creating which entry:

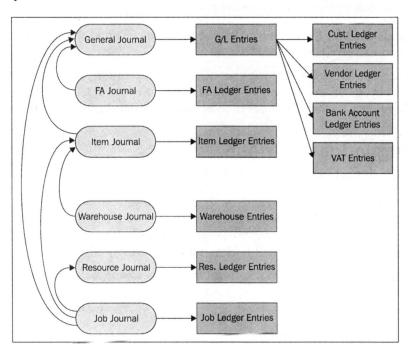

The image also shows that some journals, if needed, may call some other journals. So, the final result of the transaction will not only be the corresponding ledger entries for the journal that is being posted but also ledger entries corresponding to a different journal.

For example, when posting an Item Journal transaction, if Dynamics NAV has been configured to automatically post costs to the Inventory account, the Adjustment account, and the COGS account, a General Journal line will be created and its posting route will be called from Item Journal.

Entries in Dynamics NAV are the result of a transaction. They are the final stage of the transaction. Once an entry has been created, it cannot be modified.

You are probably thinking, Hey! There is some information that must change on an entry! For instance, after you post a sales invoice, at some point the invoice will be paid. Therefore, Cust. Ledger Entry will have to be updated to reflect the new remaining amount for the invoice. Definitely, you are right. This is managed in Dynamics NAV using detailed ledger entries. Most entry tables in Dynamics NAV have a related detailed entry. Some information in the entry table is actually a calculation of the related detailed entries. So, there is no need to modify the original entry or even the related detailed entry. Changes are resolved adding new detailed ledger entries.

You will find only two exceptions to the norm:

- Fields used for the system's internal purposes (such as the open field found on some entry tables).
- Some specific fields that the user can modify manually, such as the Due Date field in customer and vendor entries or the Shipment Agent Code field in the shipments' header. Changes in these fields are handled in special codeunits.

Creating ledger entries

Let's see how this actually works step by step:

1. Using the CRONUS International Ltd. demonstration company, create a new Sales Invoice for customer number 10000, The Cannon Group PLC. Create a line on the invoice for Item, 1000, and Bicycle. The quantity of the line will be 1 PCS. You will find it in the following path:

   Departments/Sales & Marketing/Order Processing/Sales Invoices

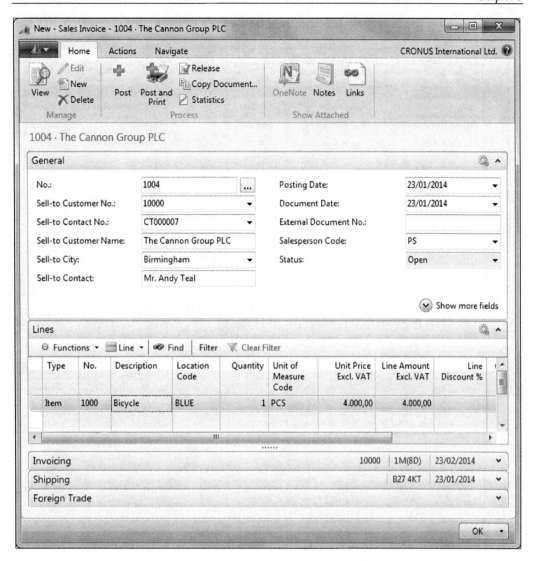

2. Post Sales Invoice.

3. Open Customer Card for customer number 10000, The Cannon Group PLC.

4. Click on the **Navigate** tab and then on **Ledger Entries** (or press *Ctrl + F7*).

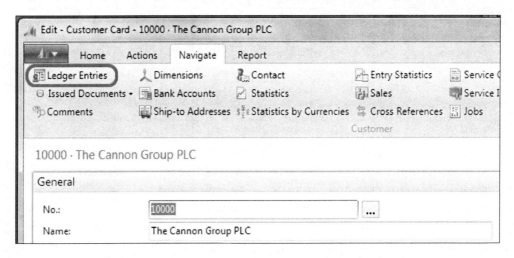

5. Locate the Cust. Ledger Entry value that corresponds to the invoice that has been posted. In this example, it is Entry No. 2768. Original Amount for this entry is 5.000,00, same as the actual Remaining Amount.

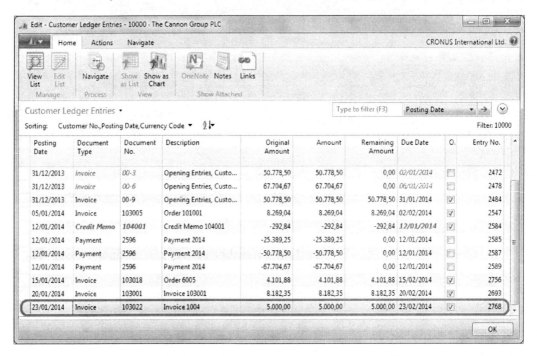

6. Open `Cash Receipt Journal`. You will find it in the following path:

Departments/Financial Management/Cash Management/Cash Receipt Journals

Create a line in the invoice to indicate the partial payment of 2000 that was on the date of February 16, 2014, using the following steps:.

- ° Select **Payment** as **Document Type**
- ° Select **Customer** as **Account Type**
- ° Select customer number **10000** as **Account No**
- ° Select **Invoice** as **Applies-to Doc. Type**
- ° Select the invoice that has been posted on field **Applies-to Doc. No.**

In this example, it is invoice **103022**.

Note that since the amount of the original invoice is `5.000`, the system has automatically set up the **Amount** field of the payment to `-5.000`. Change it to `-2.000` to partially pay the invoice. The **Amount** value in the **Cash Receipt Journal** field is negative because the payment of a sales invoice is, in accounting language, a credit amount and is translated in Dynamics NAV as a negative amount.

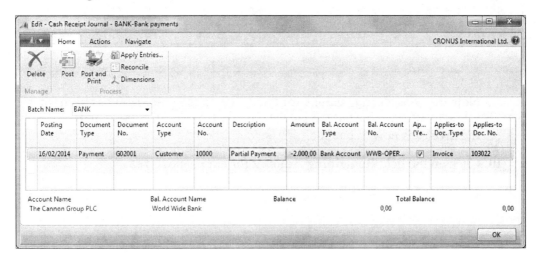

7. Post `Cash Receipt Journal`.

8. Again, open `Customer Card` for customer number `10000`, `The Cannon Group PLC`.

9. Click on the **Navigate** tab and then on **Ledger Entries** (or press *Ctrl + F7*).

   Locate the `Cust. Ledger Entry` value that corresponds to the invoice that has been posted in the previous steps. You will also see `Cust. Ledger Entry` that corresponds to `Payment` we have just posted.

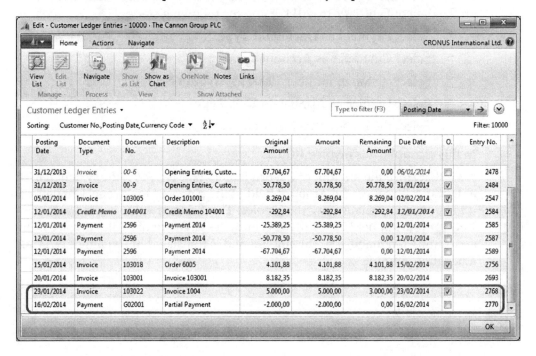

Note that `Remaining Amount` for `Entry No. 2768 (Invoice)` has been updated after we posted the partial payment. `Remaining Amount` for the invoice is now `3.000,00`.

10. Click on the field **Remaining Amount** for `Entry No. 2768`.

11. The **View – Detailed Cust. Ledger Entries** page is opened.

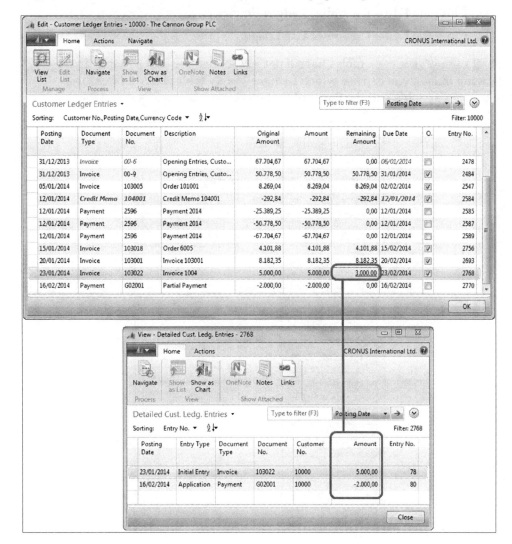

There are two detailed entries for `Entry No. 2768`:

- º The first one is the initial entry that corresponds to the `Invoice` entry with `Document No. 103022`

- º The second one is the entry that corresponds to the `Payment` entry which has `Document No. G02001`, which has been applied to the invoice

`Remaining Amount` for `Entry No. 2768` is the sum of these two detailed entries: `5.000 + (-2.000) = 3.000`.

12. Close the **View – Detailed Cust. Ledger Entries** page.

13. Close the **Edit – Customer Ledger Entries** page.

14. Close the **Edit – Customer Card** page.

Not all `Ledger Entries` tables have a `Detailed Ledger Entry` table. In the following image, you can see which `Ledger Entry` tables have a `Detailed Ledger Entry` table and the name of that `Detailed Ledger Entry` table:

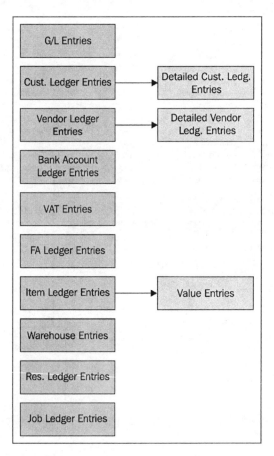

Combining all concepts

We've talked about master data, documents, journals, and entries. As we talked about each of these concepts, we explained a little bit how they were connected to each other. Now we will see the general model combining all four concepts.

The general data model looks somewhat like the following diagram:

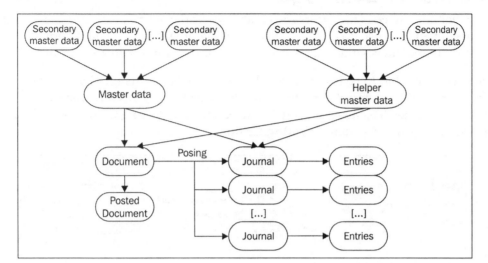

Master Data and **Helper master data** are combined in **Document**. When **Document** is posted, its corresponding **Posted Document** is created. Also, journal lines are created and posted. The journal lines will end up in different **Entries**.

Master Data and **Helper master data** can also be combined directly on **Journal** without using any document. These journal lines will also end up in different **Entries**.

No Save button

Dynamics NAV does not have any kind of save button anywhere in the application. So, data is saved into the database while it is being introduced.

Usually, a record is inserted in its table right after the field (or fields) of the primary key is (or are) filled. Some pages have the DelayedInsert property set to Yes, which means that the record won't be inserted until the user leaves the record, moving the cursor to the next line or to the next card. But the user can leave the record at any point without filling all the fields, so it doesn't make a big difference.

Once the record is inserted, new data is saved right after the user leaves the field, and an undo functionality is not available.

This way of work has one major advantage and one major contra. There's nothing you can do with it, but it is important that you know it and that you transmit it to your users so they don't get frustrated when working with Dynamics NAV.

The main advantage

The major advantage is that users can create any card (for instance, `Customer card`), any document (for instance, `Sales Order`), or any other kind of data without knowing all the information that is needed. Let us explain it with an example:

A new customer has to be inserted into the database. For Dynamics NAV, it is mandatory to fill in some information to actually be able to post any transaction with the customer. The mandatory fields are **Gen. Bus. Posting Group**, **VAT Bus. Posting Group**, and **Customer Posting Group**.

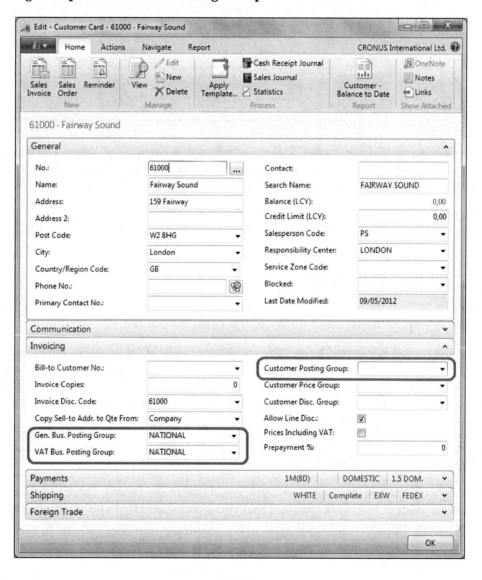

As you can see in the previous image, the **Customer Posting Group** field has not been filled for this customer. It doesn't matter right now; you can leave the card without losing the rest of the information that was introduced, and come back to the card when you have figured out the **Customer Posting Group** group that has to be used with this customer. The not-losing-the-rest-of-the-information part is important.

Imagine that there actually was a **Save** button; you spend a few minutes filling in all the information and, at the end, hit the **Save** button. At that moment the system carries out some checks and finds out that one field is missing. It throws you a message saying that the customer card cannot be saved. So you basically have two options:

1. To lose the information introduced until that moment, find out the posting group for the customer, and start all over again.

2. To cheat. Fill the field with some wrong value so that the system actually lets you save the data. Of course, you can come back to the card and change the data once you've found out the right one.

Nothing will prevent any other user to post a transaction with the customer in the meantime.

When is data checked

How does Dynamics NAV work then? When is the data checked? It is checked when it is needed. In most cases, information in the master tables is needed when selecting the record either in a document or in a journal line, or when the posting routines are run.

Since customer number `61000` has a relevant field missing on its card, if you try to select this customer in `Sales Order`, you will get a runtime error that will say **Customer Posting Group must have a value in Customer No.=61000. It cannot be zero or empty.**.

Some other data, such as the posting dates, will be checked when posting the transaction. You can set up your Dynamics NAV solution so that you only allow your user to post transactions using a specific range of dates. Posting dates can be restricted for the whole company or only to certain users.

Posting dates are an example of data that the system checks while posting the transaction. If posting dates are not allowed, an error message will be thrown saying **Posting Date is not within your range of allowed posting dates.**.

The main contra

There is one main contra of this way of checking data, that is, that all the problems come at the end. It is like when we have to post the shipment, the shipping agent is waiting with his truck, we are already late, and Dynamics NAV throws an error message and doesn't allow the shipment to be posted. So the shipping agent cannot leave yet, and the person responsible for the missing data is not in the office to solve the problem.

The person who posts the documents is the person who gets most of the errors and is usually the one with less responsibility. There is no way to restrict the person from creating Customer or Item to leave the card if data is missing.

Of course, even if Dynamics NAV allows it, the company must have business rules that people have to follow, they must be responsible for their work anyway. This means that people working with Dynamics NAV should know what to do, what not to do, and the consequences of both. You need thinking people.

If the company needs non-thinking people, who are just allowed to do a couple of things in Dynamics NAV, and you need the system to lead them through all the process, then Dynamics NAV is probably not the system that the company needs. In some special cases, a new functionality can be developed to guide users in one specific area, but don't try to do it everywhere in the application.

The posting routines

Dynamics NAV has one big key word (among others), called **post**. If you read the word post anywhere in the application or see the following icon, it means that if you click on the button, a routine will be run and this will lead to posted documents and posted entries that are on their last stage. It is the trusted data that won't change anymore.

As explained in *The data model* section of this chapter, Dynamics NAV has some tables called Entries (G/L Entries, Cust. Ledger Entries, Vendor Ledger Entries, Item Ledger Entries, and so on) that correspond to transactions related to master data. The only way to insert data into entry tables is through the posting routines. A bunch of validations are carried out during the posting routines as the system has to check if all the data is correct and that no inconsistencies exist.

One unique posting process usually creates multiple entries, and all of the entries are related and consistent to each other. For instance, when you post a sales invoice, the system needs to create the following entries (depending on what the invoice includes):

- **Customer Entries**: It is used to track all the transactions related to the customer.

- **Item Entries**: It is used if the invoice contains the items that you need to reduce the stock of, plus if in the future you need to track all the transactions related to one particular item.

- **VAT Entries**: You will need to report to the tax authorities, all VAT charged to your customers. Therefore, the VAT amount charged on every invoice has to be tracked.

- **General Ledger Entries**: Accounting rules say that when you issue an invoice, you have to record the related amounts on certain accounts. Dynamics NAV does it for you by creating G/L entries.

As explained in *The data model* section of this chapter, entries are created by reading information from a journal line. Therefore, if you choose to post a document, the first step that the process must follow is to create all the related journal lines. Then all the related entries have to be created. The next diagram shows the general schema:

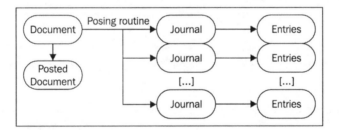

Checking the posting routine with an example

The best way to understand the posting routines is to create an example and dive into the code. We'll create a sales invoice document and turn on the debugger to follow the whole posting process. You'll get a pretty clear idea on what it does and when. You don't need to turn the debugger on right now; we have already selected the most relevant pieces of code for you. If you want to use the debugger anyway, we would recommend you to read *Chapter 11, Debugging,* and then come back to follow this example.

Create the new `Sales Invoice` table for customer number `10000`. Insert two item lines, one for item number `1000` and another one for item number `1160`. We'll sell one unit for each item. Leave the default values for the rest of the options.

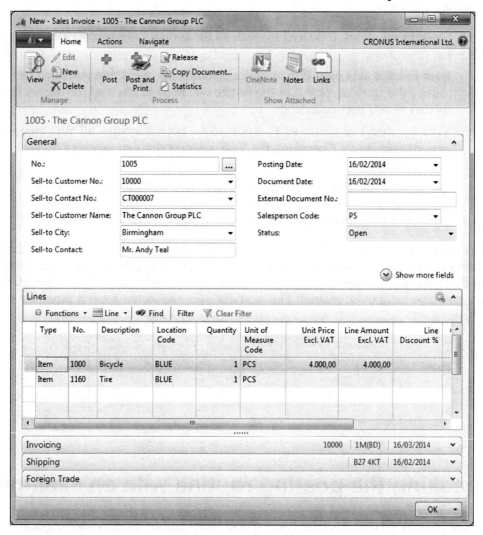

The posting process for this `Sales Invoice` will go through all the steps shown in the following diagram. The main steps are to:

- Insert posted document headers
- Create item journal lines and post them
- Insert posted document lines
- Create general journal lines and post them

You'll find the steps that insert data into the database with a grey background. These are the posted documents and posted entries that the user will see after the posting process is completed:

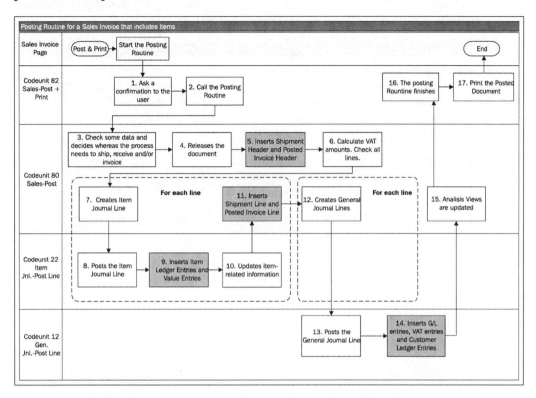

To see the exact code that corresponds with each step, turn the debugger on and click on the **Post and Print** button found on the ribbon bar on top of the page.

Following are the steps for posting routine for a sales invoice that includes items:

1. **Ask a confirmation to the user**: The confirmation question asked to the user corresponds with the following code. The [...] icon shows that the functions include code, which is not shown in the following screenshot:

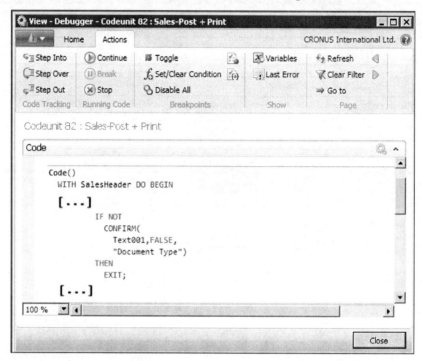

2. **Call the Posting Routine**.

3. **Check some data and decide if the process needs to ship, receive and/or invoice**: The TESTFIELD lines of code correspond to some basic checks related to the invoice. TESTFIELD statements are there to ensure that there is a value in the field and that it is not blank or null. The next basic step is to check if posting dates are allowed. After this, the system decides if the process needs to ship, receive, and/or invoice and keeps the result in global variables.

```
Codeunit 80 : Sales-Post

Code                                                          🔧 ▲

    OnRun(VAR Rec : Record "Sales Header")
    [ ... ]
      WITH SalesHeader DO BEGIN
        TESTFIELD("Document Type");
        TESTFIELD("Sell-to Customer No.");
        TESTFIELD("Bill-to Customer No.");
 ⇨    | TESTFIELD("Posting Date");
        TESTFIELD("Document Date");
        IF GenJnlCheckLine.DateNotAllowed("Posting Date") THEN
          FIELDERROR("Posting Date",Text045);

        CASE "Document Type" OF
          "Document Type"::Order:
            Receive := FALSE;
          "Document Type"::Invoice:
            BEGIN
              Ship := TRUE;
              Invoice := TRUE;
              Receive := FALSE;
            END;
          "Document Type"::"Return Order":
            Ship := FALSE;
          "Document Type"::"Credit Memo":
            BEGIN
              Ship := FALSE;
              Invoice := TRUE;
              Receive := TRUE;
            END;
          END;
        END;
```

4. **Releases the document**: If the document has not yet been released, the code to release it is run.

```
        [ ... ]
        IF (Status = Status::Open) OR (Status = Status::"Pending Prepayment") THEN BEGIN
          TempInvoice := Invoice;
          TempShpt := Ship;
 ⇨      TempReturn := Receive;
          GetOpenLinkedATOs(TempAsmHeader);
          CODEUNIT.RUN(CODEUNIT::"Release Sales Document",SalesHeader);
          TESTFIELD(Status,Status::Released);
          Status := Status::Open;
          Invoice := TempInvoice;
          Ship := TempShpt;
          Receive := TempReturn;
          ReopenAsmOrders(TempAsmHeader);
          MODIFY;
          COMMIT;
          Status := Status::Released;
        END;
        [ ... ]
```

5. **Insert Shipment Header and Posted Invoice Header**: When the first data is inserted into the database, the system must assure that while the transaction is being processed, no other process modifies or deletes the information that the process is taking into account. This is why the LOCKTABLE instruction is placed in the following part of the code:

```
[...]
// Insert shipment header
IF Ship THEN BEGIN
  IF ("Document Type" = "Document Type"::Order) OR
     (("Document Type" = "Document Type"::Invoice) AND SalesSetup."Shipment on Invoice")
  THEN BEGIN
    IF DropShipOrder THEN BEGIN
      PurchRcptHeader.LOCKTABLE;
      PurchRcptLine.LOCKTABLE;
      SalesShptHeader.LOCKTABLE;
      SalesShptLine.LOCKTABLE;
    END;
    SalesShptHeader.INIT;
    SalesShptHeader.TRANSFERFIELDS(SalesHeader);
[...]
// Insert invoice header or credit memo header
IF Invoice THEN
  IF "Document Type" IN ["Document Type"::Order,"Document Type"::Invoice] THEN BEGIN
    SalesInvHeader.INIT;
    SalesInvHeader.TRANSFERFIELDS(SalesHeader);
[...]
```

6. **Calculate VAT amounts. Check all lines**: Even if each invoice line contains information related to the VAT tax, all the amounts need to be calculated again to solve rounding issues.

```
[...]
TempVATAmountLineRemainder.DELETEALL;
SalesLine.CalcVATAmountLines(1,SalesHeader,CombinedSalesLineTemp,TempVATAmountLine);
[...]
```

7. **Creates Item Journal Line**.

```
PostItemJnlLine(SalesLine : Record "Sales Line";QtyToBeShipped : Decimal;QtyToBeShippedBase : Decimal;QtyToE
  IF NOT ItemJnlRollRndg THEN BEGIN
    RemAmt := 0;
    RemDiscAmt := 0;
  END;
  WITH SalesLine DO BEGIN
    ItemJnlLine.INIT;
    ItemJnlLine."Posting Date" := SalesHeader."Posting Date";
    ItemJnlLine."Document Date" := SalesHeader."Document Date";
    ItemJnlLine."Source Posting Group" := SalesHeader."Customer Posting Group";
    ItemJnlLine."Salespers./Purch. Code" := SalesHeader."Salesperson Code";
  [...]
```

8. **Posts the Item Ledger Entry**.

```
[...]
OriginalItemJnlLine := ItemJnlLine;
ItemJnlPostLine.RunWithCheck(ItemJnlLine);
[...]
```

9. **Inserts Item Ledger Entries and Value Entries**.

```
InitItemLedgEntry(VAR ItemLedgEntry : Record "Item Ledger Entry")
  ItemLedgEntryNo := ItemLedgEntryNo + 1;

  WITH ItemJnlLine DO BEGIN
    ItemLedgEntry.INIT;
    ItemLedgEntry."Entry No." := ItemLedgEntryNo;
    ItemLedgEntry."Item No." := "Item No.";
    ItemLedgEntry."Posting Date" := "Posting Date";
    ItemLedgEntry."Document Date" := "Document Date";
    ItemLedgEntry."Entry Type" := "Entry Type";
    [...]
InitValueEntry(VAR ValueEntry : Record "Value Entry";ItemLedgEntry : Record "Item Ledger Entry")
  ValueEntryNo := ValueEntryNo + 1;

  WITH ItemJnlLine DO BEGIN
    ValueEntry.INIT;
    ValueEntry."Entry No." := ValueEntryNo;
    IF "Value Entry Type" = "Value Entry Type"::Variance THEN
      ValueEntry."Variance Type" := "Variance Type";
    ValueEntry."Item Ledger Entry No." := ItemLedgEntry."Entry No.";
    ValueEntry."Item No." := "Item No.";
    [...]
```

10. **Updates item-related information**: Some item-related information, such as the average cost, gets updated after posting any item journal line.

11. Inserts Shipment Line and Posted Invoice Line.

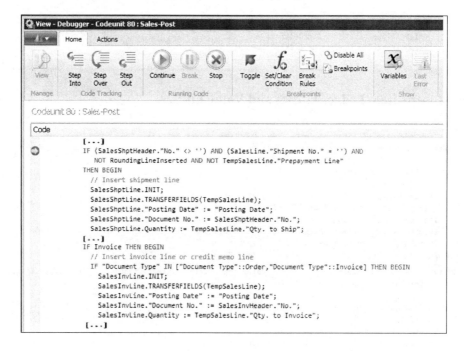

12. Creates General Journal Lines.

```
Codeunit 80 : Sales-Post

Code

      [...]
      IF Invoice THEN BEGIN
          // Post sales and VAT to G/L entries from posting buffer
          LineCount := 0;
          IF InvPostingBuffer[1].FIND('+') THEN
            REPEAT
               LineCount := LineCount + 1;
               Window.UPDATE(3,LineCount);


               GenJnlLine.INIT;
               GenJnlLine."Posting Date" := "Posting Date";
               GenJnlLine."Document Date" := "Document Date";
               GenJnlLine.Description := "Posting Description";
            [...]
```

13. **Posts the General Journal Line.**

```
Codeunit 80 : Sales-Post
```
```
Code

        [...]
          GLEntryNo := RunGenJnlPostLine(GenJnlLine);
        [...]
```

14. **Inserts G/L Entries, VAT entries and Customer Ledger Entries.**

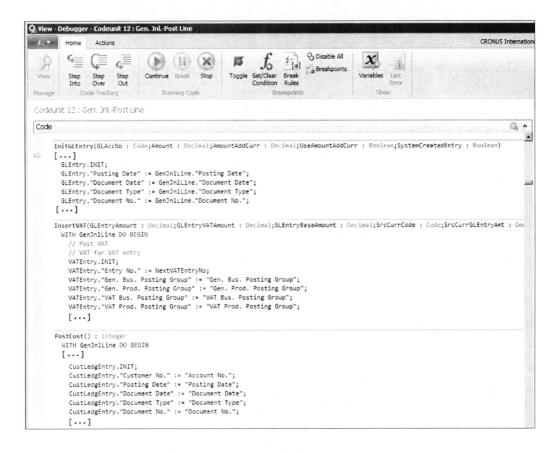

15. **The posting routines finishes**: At the end of the OnRun function there is a COMMIT instruction. When the system finds a COMMIT instruction, it saves all the data into the database. If an error occurs after this instruction, all changes will only be rolled back until this point. In this case, Posted Invoice and all its entries will still be posted.

```
Codeunit 80 : Sales-Post
  Code
        [...]
        IF NOT InvtPickPutaway THEN BEGIN
          COMMIT;
        [...]
```

16. **Analysis views are updated**.

```
Codeunit 80 : Sales-Post
  Code
        [...]
          UpdateAnalysisView.UpdateAll(0,TRUE);
          UpdateItemAnalysisView.UpdateAll(0,TRUE);
        END;
        [...]
```

17. **Print the Posted document**.

```
Codeunit 82 : Sales-Post + Print
  Code
        [...]
        GetReport(SalesHeader);
        [...]
```

If you have reached the end of this section, we applaud you since it's been a tough one. The posting routines are the core of the application, so all the time you invest to know them is worth it.

We've only seen a small example with the sales posting routine that involved the general journal posting routine and the Item Journal posting routine. Other posting routines that can be found on the system are:

- The BOM posting routine
- The Purchase posting routine

- The `Resource` posting routine
- The `Job` posting routine
- The `Fixed Asset` posting routine
- The `Transfer Document` posting routine
- The `Warehouse` posting routine
- The `Service` posting routine

Posted data cannot be modified (or deleted)

One of the first things an end user faces when he/she starts to work with Dynamics NAV is the inability to modify what has been posted, whether it's a posted sales invoice, a shipment document, a general ledger entry, or any other posted data. Any posted document or entry is unchangeable. This causes frustration for new Dynamics NAV users, especially if they are used to other systems that allow them to modify data. However, this Dynamics NAV feature is a great advantage since it ensures data integrity.

There are a few exceptions where posted documents can be deleted or fields changed; they are as follows:

- Posted documents can be deleted after they are printed. This feature cannot be used as a way to undo the document, as only the document is deleted but the corresponding entries remain in the database.

  Anyway, we do not recommend that you delete any document, especially sales documents. If you delete them, you will have to consider keeping a hard copy of the documents as you will not be able to print them again. Some countries require you to keep a copy of the documents for a certain period of time.

- Fields used for the system's internal purposes (such as the `Open` field found on some entry tables).

- Some specific fields can be modified by the user manually, such as the `Due Date` field in customer and vendor entries or `Shipment Agent Code` in the shipments header. Changes on these fields are handled by special codeunits.

As we have seen in earlier sections of this chapter, when one document is posted, the output consists of several entries that are all consistent to each other and to the rest of the application data.

If one single piece of information has to be changed, this single piece of information will probably be replicated many times. For instance, the posting date is replicated in all the entries the posting routine creates. As you can imagine, changing one single date without changing the rest of the dates of the same transaction could be a disaster.

If data cannot be changed, how can users correct a mistake in the data? The only way is to post the reversed documents or entries so that their sum voids the transaction. Now the user can post the correct document or entry and the mistake will be resolved.

Navigating through your data

In Dynamics NAV, it is extremely easy to navigate through the data and remove default filters set by the system, and set your own ones to find or analyze your own data.

The Navigate functionality

You have probably seen the following **Navigate** button in many places in Dynamics NAV:

You can actually see it on every single page that shows posted transactions, either in `Posted Documents` and/or in all kinds of entries.

If you hit the **Navigate** button, no matter where you are, the **Navigate** page will open, showing all the posted documents and entries that were created and those that are related to the document or entry from which you hit the **Navigate** button.

Earlier in this chapter, we created and posted `Sales Invoice`. If we open `Posted Sales Invoice` and hit **Navigate**, the following navigation page will be opened:

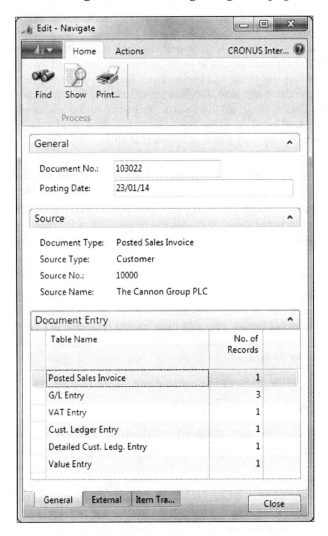

The navigation page is telling us that we can find a **Posted Sales Invoice** document, three **G/L Entry** records, one **VAT Entry**, one **Cust. Ledger Entry**, one **Detailed Cust. Ledg. Entry**, and one **Value Entry** table related to the **Document No.** field with the value **103022** on the **Posting Date** field with the value **23/01/2014**.

When posting the invoice, all these documents and entries have been created.

If we want to take a look at any of the documents or entries, we have to select the information we want to look at and click on the **Show** button.

 The Navigate feature is used within Document No. and Posting Date. The Navigate feature will show all the posted documents and entries that have used the same Document No. and Posting Date. If you use the same numbering rules for, let's say, sales invoices and purchase invoices, the Navigate functionality may show you information about all the Sales Invoice and Purchase Invoice tables that have the same Document No. and Posting Date, although they may have no relation at all.

Note that in the lower part of the **Document Entry** tab, there are three different sub tabs, namely **General**, **External**, and **Item Tracking**. By default, the selected tab is the **General** tab, which navigates using internal document numbers. You can use the **External** tab to navigate using External Document No. (the Order No. value of your customers, for example) or use the **Item Tracking** tab to navigate using serial or lot numbers.

 If you develop customized ledger entries or documents, do not forget to modify the Navigate functionality so that it also considers customized tables. You will have to add code in the FindRecords and ShowRecords functions found on the Page object that has the number 344.

Other ways to navigate

The Navigate functionality is extremely useful and is extended all over the application, but there are other ways to navigate through your data.

You can navigate to Customer Card from Posted Sales Invoice, for example. Imagine you are looking at Posted Sales Invoice and you want to go to that customer's card to check some information. There is no need to close Posted Sales Invoice; go back to the main menu, find the menu entry point for customers, locate the customer in the list of customers, and finally look at its card.

Once you get to the customer list, you may have forgotten the Customer No. value or you may have mistyped it, or chances are that you have to open Posted Sales Invoice again and perform all the steps to get to Customer Card.

Well, you actually don't need to do all this, because if a relation exists between the information of a field and some other information in some other table, it will be shown as a hyperlink on the page you are looking at. By clicking on the hyperlink, you will be directed to the right place.

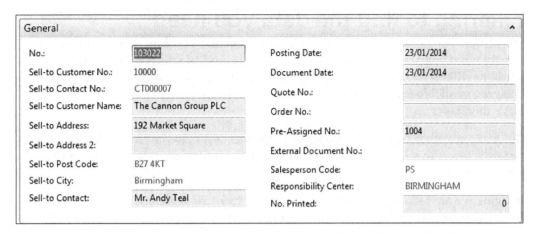

Take a look at the **General** tab of a posted sales invoice. The value of the **Sell-to Customer No.** field is showed as a hyperlink.

If you click on the hyperlink, a drop-down list is shown with the customer list, as follows:

Clicking on the **Advanced** link in the lower-right part of the drop-down list will actually take you to the **Customer List** page, and from there you can access Customer Card. You can achieve all of this by using Customer Card without having to remember or write down the Customer No. value for which you wanted to check some information.

Hyperlinks are also shown when a value in a field is the result of a calculation. In that case, clicking on the hyperlink will open a page where the records taken into account during the calculation are shown. This will be discussed in the next section.

Filtering to find the data you need

Sometimes you need to look for some information and you find no report to show exactly what you want with the grouping of data, and to which data you can apply the filters you need. Dynamics NAV doesn't (unfortunately) have a report designer available for end users. Reports have to be developed by a Dynamics NAV developer.

But there are other ways to find data in Dynamics NAV. Removing and applying our own filters in a page that is displaying a list of information is a powerful tool for end users.

Imagine we are talking to a customer and need to know which items have been sold to him between a certain period of time, on which dates, and for what quantities. We begin looking around the system and find a report called Customer/Item Sales, but that is not quite what we need because it summarizes values per item, giving the total quantity that was invoiced. We need to know exact dates and shipped quantities rather than the invoiced quantities.

You may examine all the reports that exist in Dynamics NAV and end up finding the one you need. But if you don't find it, don't worry; following are the steps to do so:

1. Open the **Items** page (**Departments/Warehouse/Planning & Execution/Items**).

2. Select an item (it doesn't matter which one you select).

3. Go to the **Navigate** tab and click on **Entries | Ledger Entries** (or press *Ctrl + F7*).

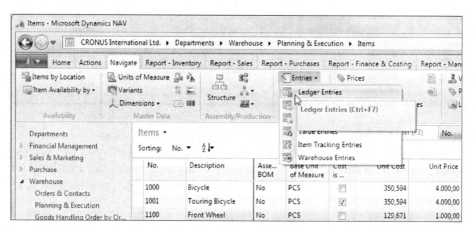

4. **View - Item Ledger Entries** is shown with a predefined filter that only shows the Item Ledger Entries values for the item you selected in step 2. You can see that a filter is applied because the word **Filter** and the filter applied are both displayed on the screen, on the filtering bar.

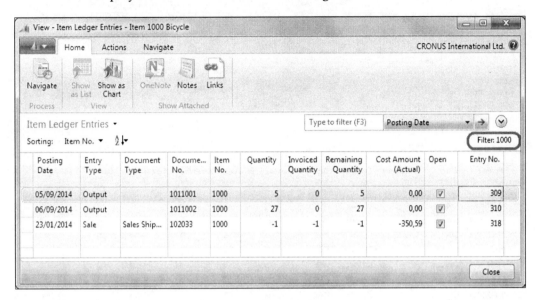

5. Expand the filter bar by hitting the down arrow button located to the right of the bar.

6. The extended filtering bar is shown as follows:

7. Hit the red cross shown at the left of the current filter to remove it.

8. The filter is removed and you are now looking at the **Item Ledger Entries** page:

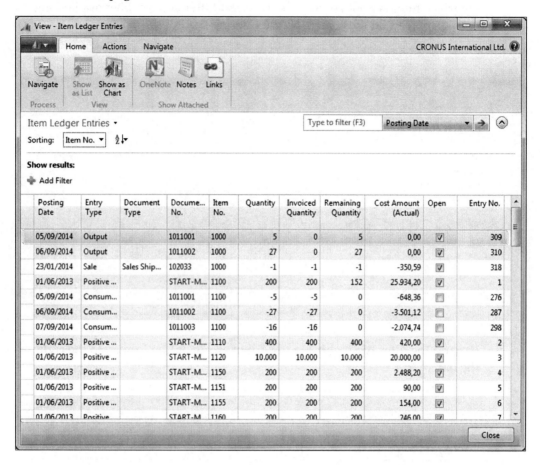

9. Click on **Add Filter** to add your own filters. A **Where** line is shown.

10. Select the field for which you want to apply a filter.

To do so, click on the down arrow that appears to the right of the preselected field name and choose a field among **Visible Columns**, or open the list of **All** columns to select a different field.

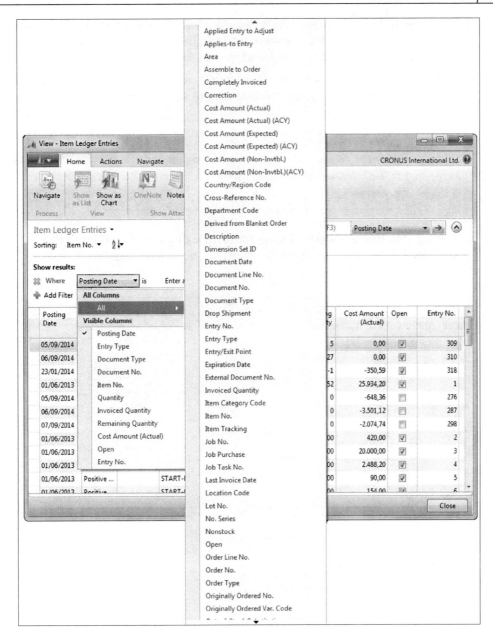

11. Select the field **Entry Type** and select **Sale** in the **Enter a value** field.

12. Click on **Add Filter** to add a new filter.

13. Select the field **Posting Date** and enter `01/01/2014..31/12/2014`.

14. Click on **Add Filter** to add a new filter.

15. Select the field **Source No.** and write `10000`. (`10000` is **Customer No.** of the customer whose sales we are searching for. In the `Item Ledger Entry` table, `Customer No.` in a `Sales` entry is stored in the field `Source No.`)

The `Source No.` field is a generic field that can either contain `Customer No.`, `Vendor No.`, or `Item No.` depending on the `Source Type` of the entry.

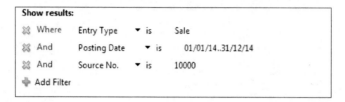

16. The information we were looking for is now displayed, that is, all the sales that were made to customer number `10000` from January 1, 2014 to December 31, 2014.

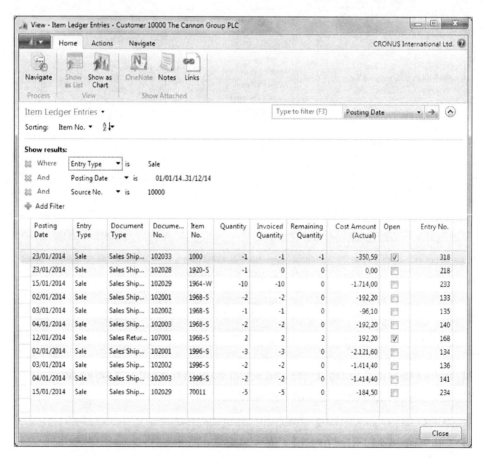

17. Export this data to Microsoft Excel by clicking on the Dynamics NAV logo in the upper-left corner of the screen, and then click on **Print & Send | Microsoft Excel** or press *Ctrl + E*.

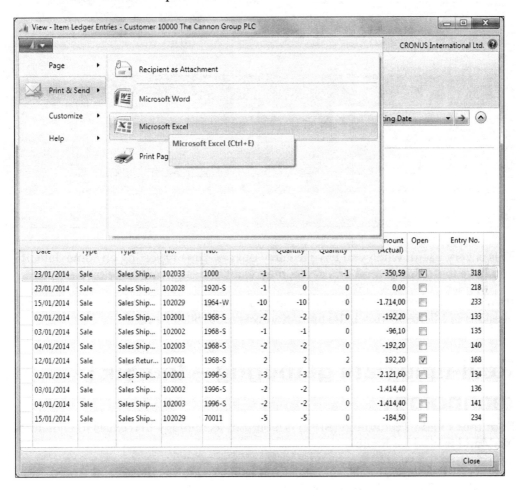

18. The filtered data is exported to Microsoft Excel.

This is very useful when you have to carry out one-time reporting on some data. If you have to do this several times, you may want to design and develop a report.

If you use Microsoft Excel 2007 or higher, you can export up to 65000 rows. In earlier versions of Microsoft Excel, the limitation was set to 5000 rows.

Real-time data gathering – the SIFT technology

Sum Index Field Technology(SIFT) is a built-in technology that exists in Dynamics NAV and is used for totaling.

In other ERP systems, totals, subtotals, and balances are calculated and stored somewhere. This calculation has to be redone over and over so that numbers are up-to-date.

In Dynamics NAV, as a developer you don't have to worry about that as it is done by the SIFT technology. Creating a new subtotals field is as easy as indicating in the field properties that the field is a `Flowfield` and specifying the formula that is going to be used to calculate the subtotal. After this you will not have to worry about keeping it up-to-date.

As a user, you know that balances for your G/L accounts, customers, vendors, or bank accounts are always up-to-date, just like many other calculations done using the SIFT technology, such as the inventory of an item or all the customer statistics that are shown on the right-hand side of the screen when looking for or creating sales orders.

Do you remember when we explained a few sections ago, in the *Creating ledger entries* section of this chapter, that some ledger entries had detailed ledger entries and that some information shown at the ledger entry level was actually a calculation done over its detailed ledger entries? Well, this is actually managed by the SIFT technology.

In that example, we talked about the remaining amount of Cust. Ledger Entry field that was a sum of the field Remaining Amount of its Detailed Cust. Ledger Entry field. Let's see how this is defined:

1. Open the Dynamics NAV development environment.
2. Locate the table **21 Cust. Ledger Entry**.
3. Click on **Design** to open the table designer for the table **21 Cust. Ledger Entry**.
4. Locate the field **14 Remaining Amount**.
5. Click on **View | Properties** or press *Shift + F4* to open the **Properties** window for the field **14 Remaining Amount**.
6. The **Properties** window is opened.

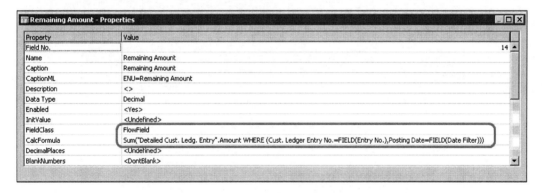

There are two key properties called FieldClass and CalcFormula that define that the SIFT technology will be used.

   °   FieldClass: By setting its value to FlowField, we are telling the system that this field will not be stored in the database; it will be calculated every single time it is needed

    °   `CalcFormula`: This is the formula that will be used to calculate the value of the field

In this example, the value of the field `Remaining Amount` will be the result of totaling the field `Amount` from the table `Detailed Cust. Ledg. Entry`, by applying the following conditions:

    °   The value in the field `Cust. Ledger Entry No.` in the table `Detailed Cust. Ledg. Entry` has to match the value in the field `Entry No.` in the table `Cust. Ledger Entry`

    °   `Posting Date` in the table `Detailed Cust. Ledg. Entry` has to match the date filter specified in the field `Date Filter` in the table `Cust. Ledger Entry`

 Using a date filter in the calculation will allow us to know not just the actual remaining amount for `Cust. Ledger Entry` but we will also know the remaining amount for that particular time.

7. Close the **Properties** window for the field **14 Remaining Amount**.

8. Close the table designer for the table **21 Cust. Ledger Entry**.

In prior versions of Dynamics NAV, defining a field that was going to be calculated and the formula that had to be used was not enough for the SIFT technology to act. If nothing else was done and `FlowField` was used somewhere in the application, the user encountered a runtime error like the one shown in the following screenshot:

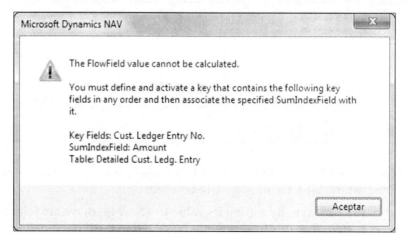

The first part of the error message stated that the `FlowField` value could not be calculated.

The second part of the error message actually told the user what had to be done to be able to calculate the value of `FlowField`. A key had to be defined (in the table for which its records were filtered and the sum was calculated) and the field that would be the base of the calculation had to be associated to the key as `SumIndexField`. The key had to contain all the fields that were part of the condition that was set to calculate the value of the field.

> This was a runtime error. Only the conditions applied at the moment when the error occurred were taken into account. In the example, the conditions were set for the fields `Cust. Ledger Entry No.` and `Date Filter`. The error message only mentioned the field `Cust. Ledger Entry No.` because when it occurred, we had no date filter set, so the condition over the `Posting Date` field in the table `Detailed Cust. Ledg. Entry` was not applied.

The following steps show how all of this was done in Dynamics NAV:

1. Open the Dynamics NAV development environment.

2. Locate the table **379 Detailed Cust. Ledger Entry**.

3. Click on **Design** to open the table designer for the table **379 Detailed Cust. Ledg. Entry**.

4. Click on **View | Keys** to open the **Keys** window.

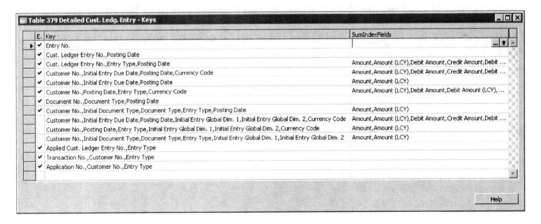

As you can see in the preceding screenshot, there are a bunch of keys defined for the table **379 Detailed Cust. Ledg. Entry** and some of them have one or more fields associated with them called **SumIndexFields**.

To calculate `Remaining Amount` in the table `Cust. Ledger Entry`, a key had to exist that included the fields `Cust. Ledger Entry No.` and `Posting Date` (the fields for which conditions could be stated), and this key had to have the field `Amount` (the field that was being summed in the calculation) as `SumIndexField`.

The third key you can see in the screenshot complies with all the conditions.

5. Close the **Keys** window.

6. Close the table designer.

Having `SumIndexField` associated with a key actually tells Dynamics NAV that we want to maintain the totals and subtotals of the field specified for all the values of the key.

These totals and subtotals are maintained in Microsoft SQL as a view.

`SumIndexField` calculations and their conversion to Microsoft SQL views still exists in Dynamics NAV 2013, but they are not a mandatory requirement anymore for the SIFT technology to act.

Everything leads to accounting

Accounting rules teach how to translate everything that happens in a company to accounting language, that is, accounts, credit amounts, and debit amounts.

Dynamics NAV has implemented these rules using posting groups, so the system can translate everything to accounting language and post it to general ledger entries on the fly.

Posting groups are related to master data. When you create a new record in the master data (for instance, you create a new customer), you need to say which posting group it belongs to.

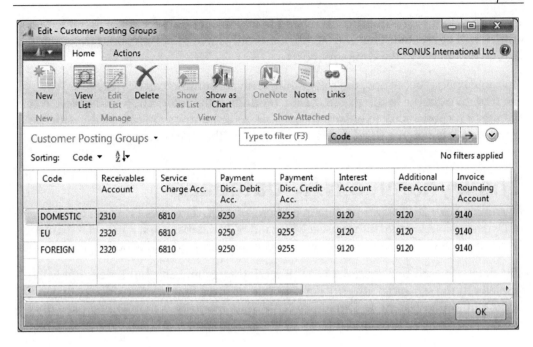

In the previous image, you can see the existing posting groups for customers. For each posting group, all the columns are filled with an account value. Dynamics NAV uses these accounts to post the general ledger entries anytime a transaction is made with a customer.

You need to create as many posting groups as the amount of detailed information you need. In Europe, for example, you have to separate domestic customers, customers from the European Union, and foreign customers. This is why three customer posting groups exist on the CRONUS International demo company.

The following posting groups exist, and each master data is related to at least one of these:

- Customer Posting Group
- Vendor Posting Group
- Job Posting Group
- General Posting Setup
- Bank Account Posting Group
- VAT Posting Setup
- FA Posting Group
- Inventory Posting Setup
- Service Contract Account Group

Every time you post a transaction related to any master data record, general ledger entries will be created. This way accountants only have to bother about transactions that no other area in the company posts.

On some special occasions, the integration with accounting can be disabled. We can find an example in the `Fixed Asset` module. If the integration is disabled, it is the user's responsibility to ensure that `Fixed Asset` entries are consistent with the amounts posted on the fixed assets accounts from the charts of accounts.

The Dynamics NAV database

Dynamics NAV 2013 stores its data in a Microsoft SQL database. Previous versions of Dynamics NAV could either use a Microsoft SQL database or a native database for Dynamics NAV. The native database has been discontinued and is no longer available.

The database used by Dynamics NAV is a relational database, but it does not fully implement the *referential integrity* concept that ensures that relationships between tables remain consistent. In Dynamics NAV, data integrity is maintained partially by the database engine itself and mainly by code. Sometimes, it is not even maintained.

 When developing new Dynamics NAV functionalities, consider data integrity inside your analysis and design work.

The TableRelation property

The **NAV Service Tier (NST)** uses the `TableRelation` property of fields in tables to maintain data integrity.

There are plenty of fields in Dynamics NAV tables that are related to other tables. In a sales invoice, for instance, the field `Sell-to Customer No.` is related to the table `Customer`.

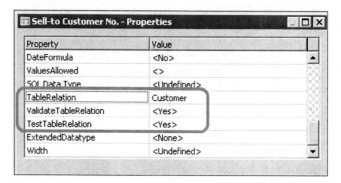

The relation is stated in the `TableRelation` property of the field. `Sell-to Customer No.` is related to the primary key field of the table `Customer`.

A relation is established for three important purposes, and two of them are related to data integrity:

- To establish data integrity: If `TableRelation` is defined, only values existing on the related table will be allowed to be written in the field. That is, you cannot create a sales invoice for a customer that does not exist.

  This rule can be omitted if `ValidateTableRelation` is set to `No`.

- To maintain data integrity: If a value is changed in the primary key fields of a related table, the change will be propagated to all tables that have `TableRelation` with the first table. This means that if you rename a customer, all existing sales invoices will change its `Sell-to Customer No.` field value so that the sales invoice points to the renamed customer (and not to the old value of `Customer No.`).

- To enable the lookup functionality: If `TableRelation` is defined for a field in a table whenever you are editing the value of that field, the system will allow you to pick up one of the possible values by showing a drop-down list.

`TableRelation` properties may be as simple as the one shown for the field `Sell-to Customer No.` in the table `Sales Header`, but they can also be more complicated. Conditional `TableRelation` properties can be defined, or you can apply filters to the relation.

`TableRelation` of the field `No.` in the table `Sales Line` is an example of a conditional `TableRelation`.

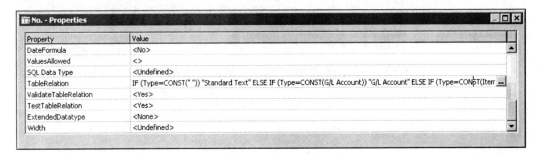

It's such a long `TableRelation` value that it is even difficult to read and understand in the `TableRelation` property. To take a better look at it, click on the Assist Edit button that appears at the rightmost part of the Value column for the property `TableRelation`.

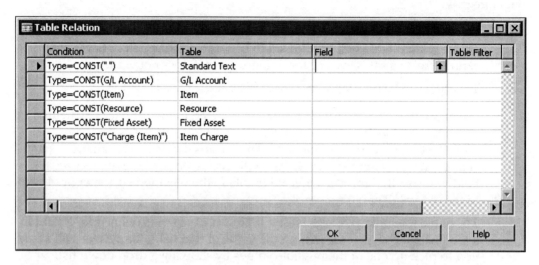

Now we can clearly see that the field `No.` in the table `Sales Line` is related to several different tables depending on the value of the `Type` field.

An example of `TableRelation` with a filter can be found in the field `Ship-to Code` from the `Sales Header` table.

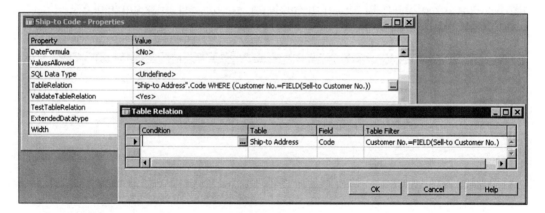

In this **Table Relation** table, a filter is applied so we can only select **Ship-to Addresses** belonging to the customer for whom the sales document is created.

Coded data rules

Coded data rules are written in table and field triggers. They are used to enforce data integrity when it cannot be obtained with simple mechanisms, such as field types or table relations.

One of these data rules that you can see all over the application can be found on the `OnDelete()` trigger of most tables. In this trigger, conditions are usually checked to prevent the user from deleting certain information.

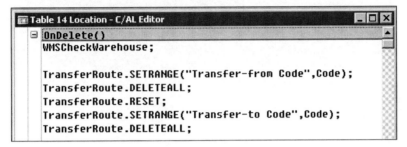

On the `OnDelete()` trigger of the table `Location`, some conditions are checked using the function `WMSCheckWarehouse`. If some conditions make it impossible to delete the location, an error message will be shown and the action will not be taken.

In the `OnDelete()` trigger of tables, code also exists to ensure that related information is deleted as well. In the example, transfer routes for the location that is being deleted are deleted as well. The `WMSCheckWarehouse` function has also deleted the zones, bins, and bin contents of the location that was deleted.

Summary

In this chapter, we've seen general considerations about Dynamics NAV and learned about its philosophy. It is important for everybody to understand it since every part of Dynamics NAV uses the same philosophy. So once you get it, you will find it extremely easy to understand new parts of the application.

If this is your first contact with Dynamics NAV, we encourage you to come back and read this chapter again a few months from now. It is important.

So far we have introduced Microsoft Dynamics NAV 2013 in *Chapter 1, Introducing Microsoft Dynamics NAV 2013*, we have talked about the new features that the current version introduced in *Chapter 2, What's New in NAV 2013*, and now we have talked about the general philosophy of Microsoft Dynamics.

In the following chapters, we will talk about how we can implement this ERP in a company.

4

The Implementation Process

In this chapter we will learn about the Dynamics NAV 2013 implementation process. We will explain the meaning of implementation and see that there are different methodologies that you can apply.

In an implementation process, several people may get involved, each one playing his/her own role. We will learn what kind of roles can be found in a Dynamics NAV implementation and the job that can be expected from each role.

We will also see that the implementation process can be broken down into phases, and we will learn about the tasks included in each phase.

The main topics discussed in this chapter are:

- Defining what an implementation is
- Using methodology
- Roles involved in an implementation project
- The phases of the project

What is an implementation

If you pick up a dictionary and look for the definition of implementation, you will end up with something like this:

"Implementation is the carrying out, execution, or practice of a plan, a method, or any design for doing something. As such, implementation is the action that must follow any preliminary thinking in order for something to actually happen. In an information technology context, implementation encompasses all the processes involved in getting new software or hardware operating properly in its environment, including installation, configuration, running, testing, and making necessary changes. The word deployment is sometimes used to mean the same thing."

This definition has been taken from the following website:
`http://searchcrm.techtarget.com/definition/implementation`

I especially like the part where it says: *getting new software operating properly in its environment.*

That is what needs to be done in a Dynamics NAV implementation process. Get the software (Dynamics NAV) to operate properly in its environment (the company that will use Dynamics NAV as their business management software).

Don't get us wrong. That doesn't mean that Dynamics NAV doesn't work properly. It actually does. But companies are completely different from one another. They work completely different as they have different processes and ways of doing business. Dynamics NAV, just as companies, can work in many different ways. Each company has to find its own way. And that is actually what will be done in the implementation process where you choose the way in which you want Dynamics NAV to work.

Dynamics NAV is not a software product that you can just install and start working with. There are many things that have to be configured, many others that have to be decided, master data that has to be introduced in the system, and a large etcetera of things that has to be done before a company can actually start using Dynamics NAV as their business software.

Dynamics NAV, as many other business software products, provides a large stack of what is called *horizontal functionality* that may be useful for any company using Dynamics NAV, regardless of the business sector in which they work, and it also provides the needed flexibility to adapt to any specific vertical requirement.

Vertical and horizontal solutions

A vertical solution is a stack of functionalities thought and developed to cover industry-specific requirements of a business sector. Manufacturing companies need software solutions different from what a health care company needs, for example.

A horizontal solution is a stack of functionalities that every single company needs or can use, such as word processing or spreadsheet applications. In Dynamics NAV, application modules like `Financial Management` are part of the horizontal solution, as it is useful and needed for every single company.

Apart from a bunch of horizontal functionalities, Dynamics NAV offers some out of the box vertical application modules, such as the `Manufacturing` module, that will probably be used by manufacturing companies but not by retail companies, for instance.

All the out of the box application modules and functionalities that Dynamics NAV offers can be put together in what is called the **Standard Solution** or **standard software**. Don't take the word standard as something standardized by an international standards authority. That is not what standard means in this context. It actually refers to how the company that has developed Dynamics NAV has decided that this software solution will behave.

If standard Dynamics NAV does not meet the specific requirements a company needs, a large channel of Dynamics NAV partners exists, which may have developed a vertical solution. The solution probably complies with many of the requirements of what your company needs.

You will find vertical solutions for as many business sectors as you may think of: retail, real estate, education, or health care, just to name a few.

If that is not enough, development can be done for a specific company to modify or extend Dynamics NAV functionality to meet any kind of requirement, automate functionalities that may have to be performed manually out of the box, or any other thing you may think of.

In an implementation process of Dynamics NAV, you have to choose whether you will implement standard Dynamics NAV or a vertical solution offered by yourself or by any other company. You will have to choose which functionalities will be used and how they will be used, you have to know if development will be required, and then you have to implement all of this by installing the product, develop what needs to be developed, and configure the whole system. But that's not it. You also need to load the initial data the company needs to start working with (primarily their master data, such as their customers, vendors, or items). Finally, you have to train the end users who will use Dynamics NAV, as they have to know how everything works and which tasks they are expected to perform in the system.

Methodology

Every implementation of Dynamics NAV is completely different from another one. The company that is going to use the ERP software (usually called *the customer*) is different, the requirements are different, the scope is different, and even the team implementing it might be different. This brings a lot of uncertainty to the process and is the main reason why methodology has to be used.

Implementing Dynamics NAV is considered as working in a project environment. By definition, a project is a temporary endeavor undertaken to meet unique goals. The company implementing Dynamics NAV (usually called *the consultant*) is probably used to this kind of environments. On the other hand, the customer is probably used to working on an operational environment, where the same processes are repeated over and over. For the customer, implementing a new ERP system might be like running in the jungle with dozens of options to take at each step and no idea of where to go. Therefore, methodology is not only going to help the consultant, but also the customer.

Methodology is not only applicable to the development and the implementation, but also to stuff like how the project is going to be billed or how the project team is going to transfer the knowledge to the support department at the end of the project. You have to define some aspects before starting any project:

- **Billing**: A Dynamics NAV project means time and work investment before the go-live date. Usually projects do not show results until the end. Even on Agile methodologies, you will need several iterations before go-live. Both the partner and the customer must be balanced in order to have the best relation possible. This can only be achieved by billing the project as it moves forward.

- **Estimating time and cost**: At the beginning of the project you will have to estimate the project, either in cost or time. Use templates to help you estimate and ensure that you don't forget any task.

  It is normal to think about the development time of a certain requirement, but forget the time it takes to design it or implement it. It is also normal to forget the tasks related to managing the project, and it is time consuming.

  For each requirement you can use a template like the following one:

	Analysis	Development	Test	Implementation
Requirement 1	3h	10h	2h	2h
Requirement 2	1h	4h	1h	0.5h

  Use this template to estimate all the requirements, even the ones that are going to be accomplished with standard functionality, because they will consume implementation time. Also use this template (or a similar one) to estimate migration requirements.

  Use another template for the rest of the tasks of an implementation. Write down all the tasks needed for an implementation and make sure to check them all for estimating a new project.

Some tasks that you should not forget are project management, software installation, training, support, and so on. To estimate the project management tasks, we use a percentage of the whole project estimation. It is up to you to fix this percentage, but it could be something like 10 percent. In a complex implementation you can also break down this task and perform the estimation from there.

- **Planning**: Determine how you will plan the project, both planning the phases and the everyday work. Visibility is important, therefore the whole team and other people in your company have to be aware of the project plan.

  We recommend you to use visible planning methods, like kanban boards. The following is an example of a kanban board we use; we call it the "iPad":

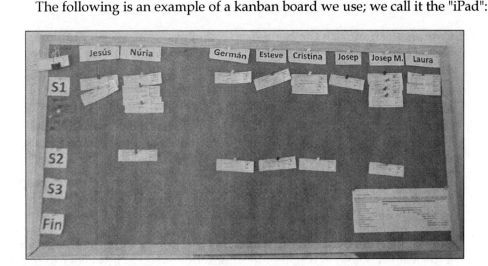

On the left column, **S1**, **S2**, and **S3** mean week 1, 2, and 3, while **Fin** means done. Every week we update the board. When people finish a task, they move the corresponding task to the done area. In the figure, there are no tasks on the done area, because the picture was taken just after a planning meeting and all the performed tasks were removed.

You might also need to use a tool like Microsoft Project to plan the whole project, as kanban boards only work for short periods. We print the plan of the whole project and attach it on the bottom-right corner of the board so that everyone can know when each phase has to be ready.

You could also share the Microsoft Project file with the rest of the organization on your intranet or somewhere else, but the reality is that usually no one but the project manager watches it. Kanban boards, however, are located in a conspicuous place at the office, so that everyone sees it even if they are not looking for it. We've placed our kanban board next to the coffee machine.

- **Purchases**: Your project will, at least, involve the purchase of the customer's Dynamics NAV license. In some projects you will also have to buy other things, such as hardware if you are in charge of providing it.

  Determine when and how are you going to do all your purchasing and do it the same way in all your implementations.

- **Communication with the customer**: Communication is a very important part of any project. Determinate how, who, and when you are going to communicate with your customers.

  It can be with meetings, through e-mails, phone calls, or with shared documents. But it is important to always use the same method to communicate the same kind of things. Also decide the person from the partner side who is going to talk to the customer, and the person from the customer side who is going to be the interlocutor.

  If too many people from the partner side are talking with too many people from the customer side, it can be a chaos and you will probably end up with inconsistencies.

- **Communication between the team**: This is also very important, especially if the team is placed at different locations. In this sense, it is better to put the team together in the same room, whenever possible.

  If someone has talked to the customer and has accorded something, the rest of the team must be aware of it. It also works the other way around. If people use different ways to communicate the same things, there is a huge probability of loss of information.

- **Development & testing**: Determine the strategy the company is going to use when developing and testing: how the code will be written and marked, where the development environment will be placed, and so on.

  If you have not defined this, you can end up with everybody developing on a local machine, marking their code in a completely different way, and having to invest a lot of time to put everything together.

- **Acceptance of the developments**: This is usually the Achilles' heel. Your methodology has to ensure that the customer accepts the developments as they move forward. Don't wait to show everything on the last week before go-live. If you do so, prepare yourself for a tough support phase with an unhappy customer.

- **Documentation**: Determinate what has to be documented, the structure each document will have, how will it be named, where will it be archived, and to whom is it going to be distributed.

  It may seem that this is a very bureaucratic process, but it can really be as simple as you want. By documentation we don't mean that each project has to generate a thousand pages of documentation, but that the few documents that are generated follow the same structure and are archived at the same place.

  Even on smaller projects, where only one person is involved, you have to think that you are not alone.

- **Reporting and control**: Think about what kinds of reports you will have to generate and the kind of control that the project will have. You may want to control the project advance, the time, cost consumption, and so on. Invest time of your project to this area, even if the project seems to be ok, or you won't see the diversions until it's too late.

  To control the project advance we recommend you to plan demo sessions, so that each developer can show his/her work to the rest of the team. These demo sessions have two purposes. On one hand, the project gains visibility and is part of the communication between the team members that we talked about before. On the other hand, it prevents the 99 percent done effect.

There are different kinds of methodologies. The main ones are Waterfall and Agile. The Waterfall approach is the most used approach while implementing Dynamics NAV, but Agile gives better results, especially on software requirements. This is why Agile approaches have been gaining ground from the past few years.

In the next sections we will cover both approaches and learn how to use the best of both.

The Waterfall approach

The Waterfall model is a sequential design process in which progress is seen as flowing steadily downwards (like a waterfall) through the phases. The Waterfall development model originates in the manufacturing and construction industries, that is, highly structured physical environments in which after the fact changes are prohibitively costly, if not impossible. Since no formal software development methodologies existed at the time, this hardware-oriented model was simply adapted for software development.

The following diagram shows the typical representation of a Waterfall approach:

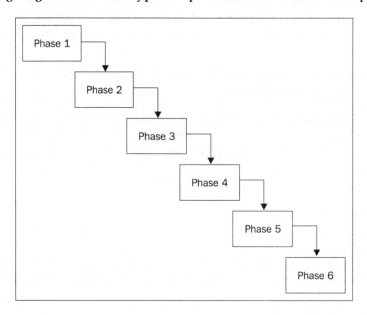

As you can see in the diagram, one phase does not start until the last one has finished. In the next section of this chapter, we'll talk about the phases of a Dynamics NAV implementation, which are presales, getting the requirements, analysis, development, deployment, and support. In our case, the analysis phase cannot start until all the requirements have been taken care of, and the development cannot start until all the requirements have been analyzed.

Companies have chosen this approach because it is the one that, theoretically, brings more certainty. Using this approach, the whole scope of the project is defined after getting the requirements, so it is easy to fix a cost for the project and fix an ending date. But, as we said, it is just theoretical. In real life the requirements you've taken are wrong, because in earlier stages the customer does not know Dynamics NAV well enough to think on all the requirements possible.

Also in real life, the design of the solution is wrong because the partner does not exactly know how the customer works, even if they spend several days taking the requirements and covering all the customer business processes.

The Agile approach

On the other hand, the Agile approach is based on iterative and incremental development. It is typically represented like the following diagram:.

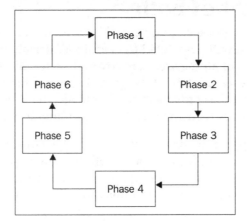

In this approach, you perform several iterations through all the phases before you reach the end of the project. With this approach, the customer needs to be more involved in the project and work closer with the partner team.

The Agile approach is best to meet the requirements and to perfectly fit into the customers' needs. It is the approach that adds more value. But it is hard to estimate times and costs at an early stage. And for a company implementing Dynamics NAV, not to exceed their budget may also be very important, in some cases more important than the value added.

This is usually solved by establishing a win-win / lose-lose relation between the customer and the partner. Both parties agree with a desired cost. If the project ends up with less cost than expected then both sides should win. If the project ends up costing more than expected, then both sides should lose.

We have worked for many years on projects implemented by following the Waterfall approach. The cost of the project was set up at the beginning of the project, and it was not possible to change it.

With the cost already fixed, the customer always tries to get more value for the same price and the partner ends up lowering the quality for the same price. Fights between both arrive when one party says that this is not what we agreed upon the first place, and the other party argues that this was implicit on the requirement.

The win-win / lose-lose relation balances the equation between the value added and the final cost.

Using the best of both

To use the best of both approaches, you could have an initial getting the requirements phase, but with less detail than in the Waterfall approach. In this first phase, the requirements of all the areas are covered, so it will help the partner team to make an approximate estimation of the project cost and time. This will help the customer identify if the project fits their needs and also their budget. After that you loop through all the phases focusing on a few requirements at a time.

Of course, using this approach, the cost of the project is only an approximation, it may cost less or more. Yes, we know, you are all thinking that it will always cost more than planned and the risk of ending up with an unaffordable project still exists. The trick is to keep everyone focused and this can only be achieved by a win-win and lose-lose relation.

If the project is finished with less cost than estimated, both the customer and the partner win, because they share the benefits of the savings. On the other hand, if the project costs more than expected, both have to share the overrun. This can be achieved by returning to the customer part of the savings, and also offering a lower price for the overrun hours.

This kind of relation between the customer and the partner is new in the Dynamics NAV world and several cultural aspects must change inside organizations, but we are sure that the results will be worth it.

Microsoft Dynamics Sure Step

Microsoft Dynamics Sure Step is a methodology designed by Microsoft focused specifically on the implementation of all the stacks of Microsoft Dynamics ERP and CRM products in which Microsoft Dynamics NAV is included.

This methodology is not just a set of methods and a knowledge base about implementation projects. It consists of:

- Best practices that let the consultant know how an implementation task or a set of tasks should be performed to achieve the best possible result, or to avoid mistakes that have already been made by someone in the past.

- Tools that make it easier to perform tasks by automating or streamlining time-consuming and error-prone tasks, such as organization and business process mapping.

- Templates that boost productivity by providing a documentation framework. Preparing documentation using these templates ensures that every important aspect of the documentation has been touched, and that nothing important has been missed.

The Sure Step methodology provides the two distinct implementation approaches we have been discussing, namely, the Waterfall approach and the Agile approach. We will define them in the following sections.

Project types based on the Waterfall approach

To address the scale and complexity of the customer's implementation, Sure Step offers the users the choice of three Waterfall-based implementation project types and one Waterfall-based upgrade project type. These are as follows:

- The Rapid project type
- The Standard project type
- The Enterprise project type
- The Upgrade project type

The Rapid project type

It represents the simplest delivery approach. The Rapid project type is designed for out of the box implementations of Microsoft Dynamics solutions, which essentially entail zero or minimal customizations of the standard solutions. It prescribes 14 activities from solution to "go-live".

The following is a screenshot of the Rapid project type, including the activities shown in the left navigation tree:

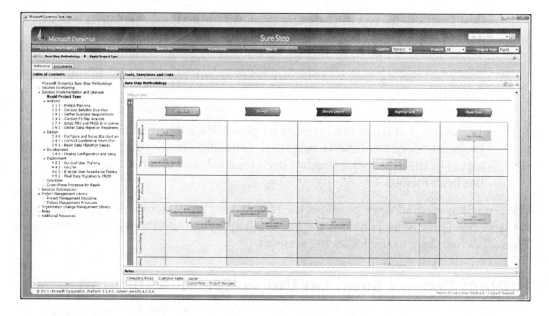

The Standard project type

It is suitable for a majority of Microsoft Dynamics projects, and hence the most widely used. This project type includes activities in all nine cross faces, to support customizations, integrations, and interfaces, as well as business process analysis.

The next screenshot is of the Standard project type in Sure Step. Included in the screenshot is a partial view of the activities shown in the left-hand side navigation tree, indicating additional severity in each of the cross phases:

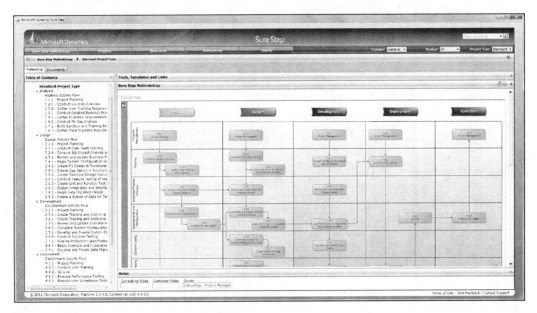

The Enterprise project type

It is the most rigorous of all the Sure Step project types. Designed for large complex scenarios, the Enterprise project type is characterized by deep program management activities, requiring focus and discipline from the customer and service provider throughout the length of the engagement.

The following is a screenshot of the Enterprise project type in Sure Step. Included in the left-hand side navigation tree view in the screenshot is a partial view of the activities in the **Analysis** phase, which highlights the depth and diligence that is prescribed for project governance alone.

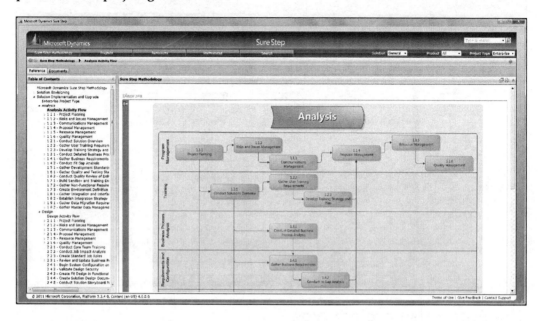

The Upgrade project type

It is a project type specially designed to address upgrade projects. It differentiates between technical upgrades and functional upgrades. A technical upgrade is meant to port an existing solution to a new product version. A functional upgrade is meant to not only port an existing solution to a new product version, but also to add new functionalities to the new product version.

The following is a screenshot of the Upgrade project type in Sure Step:

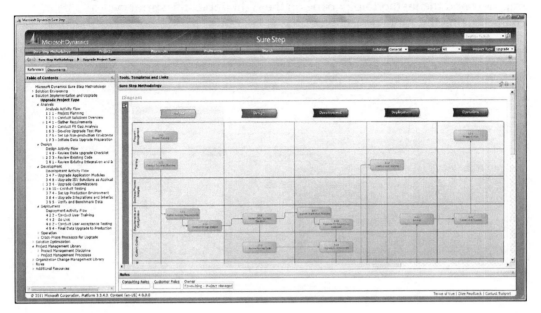

The Agile project type

We now turn to the Agile approach in Sure Step. The *Agile project type* was introduced in the Sure Step 2010 release, primarily to facilitate the development and rollout of the solution to those customers who expect to use Microsoft Dynamics as a platform and customize the solution to their specific needs. In doing so, these customers tend to involve their requirements during the course of the development process, necessitating a flexible and iterative approach to development, which is where the Agile project type is ideally suited.

The next screenshot shows the Agile project type in Sure Step. The left navigation tree view and the methodology pane on the right depict the sprint cycles characterizing the Agile project type.

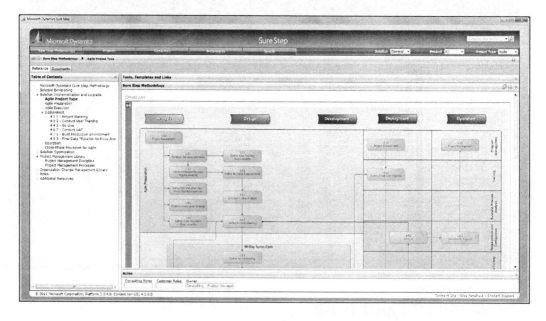

While the Sure Step Waterfall approaches have activities flowing across five phases, the Sure Step Agile project type has Sprint cycles to encompass the **Analysis**, **Design**, and **Development** phases.

A Sprint cycle is a set period of time during which specific work has to be completed and made ready for review. At the end of each sprint, you are adding value to the project by adding finished portions of the product. Usually sprints last from one week to one month.

The Agile project type does have two phases, **Deployment** and **Operation**, at the culmination of the Sprint cycles. So, in this context, the Agile project type deviates from a strict Agile approach, and is fashioned as a blended approach for ERP/CRM deployments. If you want to learn more about Microsoft Dynamics Sure Step, we recommend that you read the book *Microsoft Dynamics Sure Step 2010, written by Chandru Shankar and Vincent Bellefroid, and published in January 2011 by Packt Publishing.*

Roles

Implementing an ERP solution such as Microsoft Dynamics NAV 2013 in a company is not a trivial task. A lot of things have to be taken into account and a lot of things have to be done. That's why a lot of people have to get involved in the project, both in the company implementing Dynamics NAV, that is, the partner, and in the company that will use Dynamics NAV as their management software, that is, the customer.

Everyone will have a different and well-defined role in the project. In this section, we will try to explain who should get involved in the project and what are the tasks that they will be performing.

In the partner team, the following roles exist:

- Salesperson
- Project manager
- Business consultant
- Analyst
- Developer
- Implementer

In the customer team, we will find the following roles:

- Project manager
- Key users
- End users

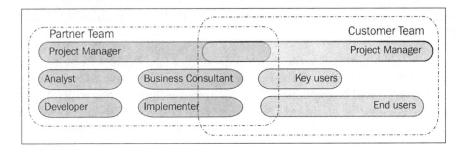

Salesperson

The salesperson acts before the implementation project itself begins, but it is an important role as he or she is the one who defines the big lines of the project requirements and who creates expectations in the customer about what Dynamics NAV is and will be for them. We will discuss this in detail later on in this chapter.

Project manager

The most important role in the project is the project manager. Two project managers exist in an implementation project, one at the partner side and another one at the customer side. They have maximum responsibility of the whole process of implementing Dynamics NAV 2013.

The project managers define the scope of the project, the functionalities that will be implemented, and the timeline.

Business consultant

The first roles that come into play in the project are the business consultants from the partner's team and the key users from the customer's team. These two roles define the business processes used by the customer, which of these processes will be done in Dynamics NAV, and how the system should behave.

While defining the business processes, the business consultant explains to the customer's key users whether these processes can be done in standard Dynamics NAV, if the processes exist in Dynamics NAV but are slightly different from those done by the customer (in which case the customer may change its process to adapt to Dynamics NAV process, or Dynamics NAV process may be changed to adapt to the customer's process), or if the process doesn't exist at all in Dynamics NAV and will have to be developed.

The business consultant will write down a document (the **Project Requirements Documents (PRD)**) in which all the business processes that have to be included in Dynamics NAV will be explained. The document will point out which business processes are covered by standard Dynamics NAV and which require development. When development is needed, the document will have to explain the expected behavior of the development.

The PRD is the main document of the project. Once the business consultant has written it, the key users that defined the processes will have to read it and make sure everything important in their business is covered in the document.

The business consultant and the key users, with the aid of their respective project managers, have to agree on a final PRD as this is the document that describes the project and that will be used later on by the analyst and the implementer to get to a final solution.

The business consultant should be someone who knows about business, as he or she must be able to understand the customer's business processes and needs. The business consultant should also be someone who knows standard Dynamics NAV 2013 behavior and capabilities, as he or she must be able to distinguish whether a specific business process is covered by Dynamics NAV 2013 or not.

Often there are specialized business consultants in a specific area or functionality. For example, we can find financial business consultants and warehouse business consultants. Financial business consultants know about business processes related to Financial Management and how the Financial Management functionality works in Dynamics NAV 2013, but they know nothing (or not too much) about warehouse management or any other business area. Warehouse business consultants know about business processes related to warehouse management and how the warehouse is handled in Dynamics NAV 2013 but they know nothing (or not too much) about Financial Management or any other business area.

Several business consultants may be involved in a Dynamics NAV implementation project when several and completely different business areas are implemented.

Key users

The key user from the customer's side should be someone who knows the processes currently being done in the company, is aware of the problems or inefficiencies the current processes have, and is willing to actively participate in the project. The same way several business consultants may get involved in the project, each one handling a specific business area, several key users may also participate in the definition of the project requirements, each one also handling a specific business area.

A common error regarding key users is to point out head of departments as key users without analyzing whether they are the right person to play this role. Having good key users, just as having good business consultants, is vital to the deployment of the project, as they are the ones who will define the project, the needs, and the processes.

Key users have to be good communicators and should know their own processes. Head of departments probably know the *theory* of their own processes, but since they are not the ones doing them on a daily basis, they may not know the real processes (which may differ from the *theoretical* processes) and the bunch of exceptions the processes may have.

Head of departments may or may not be good key users. We will discuss this in more detail in the next chapter, which will be dedicated to the implementation process at the customer's side.

Once the PRD is written and the project requirements are clear, both the analysts and the business consultant continue with the deployment of the project.

The business consultant will focus on all the standard functionalities of Dynamics NAV 2013 that the customer will use. The analyst will focus on all the functionalities of Dynamics NAV 2013 that have to be modified somehow or developed from scratch.

Some functionalities in Dynamics NAV 2013 can behave in multiple ways depending on how they have been configured. The business consultant is the person who defines the way in which the system has to be configured to meet the business process requirements reflected in the PRD.

Analyst

The analyst is the person who defines the way in which standard functionalities of Dynamics NAV 2013 will be modified to meet the business process requirements defined in the PRD. The analyst also defines the way in which new functionalities will be developed and the way the customer's data will be migrated into the system.

To achieve this task, the analyst must be someone who knows the standard design of Dynamics NAV 2013 and the development capabilities of the system. Modifications have to be carefully designed because a wrong modification in an area or functionality may cause inconsistencies in other areas or functionalities, or may disable the future use of a standard functionality. In addition, new functionalities should be implemented using the same design philosophy behind Dynamics NAV 2013.

Developer

When the developments required to be done in the project are defined, the developer comes into the scene. The developer is the person who will develop the modifications and new functionalities defined by the analyst.

Once the developments are finished, the business consultant should test them to validate that they certainly meet the business process requirements defined in the PRD.

Implementer

At this point everything is ready for the implementer to start working on the project. The implementer will configure the system as defined by the business consultant and will perform the data migration processes in test environments, using standard Dynamics NAV 2013 tools defined later on in this book or using tools defined by the analyst and developed by the developer.

Before going live, the implementer will validate all the business processes that will be done inside the system with the customer's key users, namely, the standard Dynamics NAV processes that have been configured, the processes that have been modified to meet the customer's requirements, and the processes that have been completely developed.

The implementer will be in charge of training the customer's end users for the usage of the system before the chosen go-live date.

The day the customer goes live, the implementer is the one who performs the data migration processes and supports the customer's end users the day they begin using Dynamics NAV for a defined period of time.

End users

The end user uses, on a daily basis, the final solution defined by the key users and the business consultants, developed by the developers, and implemented by the implementer.

The entire system is designed so that end users can do their job using Dynamics NAV as their main tool. Usually end users get involved when the project is almost ending, but they are the ones who get more affected because of the project, since it will affect their daily work.

Summarizing the roles

To summarize, the roles that play the implementer's game and the tasks they perform are:

- In the partner's team:
  - **The project manager**: Defines the scope of the project and the timeline. The project manager has the maximum responsibility of implementing the project.

- ° **The business consultant**: Defines the business processes, gets the project requirements, and writes the main document of the project, the PRD, in which the customer's business processes that have to be covered by Dynamics NAV are explained, especially those that will require development. It also defines the way in which standard functionality has to be configured to meet the customer's business process requirements and validates the developments done by the developer.

- ° **The analyst**: Defines the way in which standard Dynamics NAV functionality will be modified, the way new functionalities will be developed, and the way the customer's data will be migrated into the system.

- ° **The developer**: Develops the modifications and new functionalities defined by the analyst.

- ° **The implementer**: Configures the system, validates data migration processes, validates all processes with the customer's key users, trains end users on the usage of the system, performs data migration tasks on the go-live date, and supports end users for a defined period of time when the system is live.

- In the customer's team:

  - ° **The project manager**: Defines the scope of the project and the timeline. The project manager has the maximum responsibility of implementing the project.

  - ° **The key users**: Define the business processes, define the project requirements, and read the PRD document written by the business consultant.

  - ° **The users**: Use on a daily basis the final solution defined by the key users and the business consultants, developed by the developers, and implemented by the implementer.

As we have defined, different roles exist both at the partner's side and at the customer's side. Each role performs a specific set of tasks. The same person, though, may play different roles in the same project. The business consultant in the partner's team may also be the implementer, for example.

Phases

The following section of this chapter will describe each phase in a Microsoft Dynamics NAV implementation, and the tasks each one includes. In a Waterfall environment, you could do one thing after another. In an Agile environment don't forget to loop through all of them, especially the phases called getting the project requirements, analysis, development, and part of the task from the deployment phase.

It's especially important to define how information will flow through all the phases to ensure that important information does not get lost.

Presales

This is the first contact between the partner and the customer. The big lines on which the project will be, are drawn.

This phase is usually executed by the sales or marketing people, with the help of a business consultant. Many companies think that at this stage the project hasn't started yet, so they don't think that this job is part of the project. But it actually is.

Selling a project like a Dynamics NAV implementation is not just selling Dynamics NAV, the product. So, it is not enough to be aware of what the product can or cannot do.

Selling a Dynamics NAV implementation is all about confidence. Real confidence, do not oversell it saying that there will be no problems.

Therefore, sales people need to sell not only the product, but also the methodology the company is using, the amount of work the customer will face in the next months, and how the partner will help them face this work.

As sales people are part of the project, they have to identify fundamental aspects that will help other members to do their job. A salesperson can help by identifying some of the risks of the project. For instance, the department that asked for a new ERP system, or someone from the customers who is not convinced of the need to change the ERP, also if the customer processes are mature enough or need to be rethought, or if there is someone in the customer's side capable of doing this rethinking or are they expecting the partner to do it for them.

This may completely change how the project will be approached. So it is important to identify it at earlier stages. At the end of this stage, a first cost and duration estimation must be done. It is important to be as close to reality as possible.

Getting the project requirements

It's time to talk and talk a lot. The business consultants and the key users will do a series of meetings in which the key users will explain to the business consultants the way they do business, the information they have to handle through their business processes, the users that are involved in the different stages of each process, the problems they have with their actual business processes, how they expect to solve them in Dynamics NAV 2013, and so on.

The business consultants will listen carefully to the key users, trying to understand and interiorize the customer's business processes. Only if they really understand the customer's needs, they will be able to design the right solution for the customer. And to do that, they not only have to be passive listeners, but should also actively participate in the definition of the processes by asking all kinds of questions to the key users, namely, periodicity of the process, volume, amount of people involved, how automated it should be, how to handle exceptions to the process, how strict the process is, how important it is, and any other questions you may think of.

As they listen to the customer's processes' explanations, they should point out how this process is handled in Dynamics NAV 2013 to identify and evidence to everyone the differences between the actual customer's business process and the way it is handled in Dynamics NAV. That way, the customer may decide to change or reengineer its own processes or may ask to modify behavior of Dynamics NAV to adapt to their predefined process.

With all the information gathered in the project requirements meetings, the business consultants should write a document in which the processes are explained and defined in as much detail as possible. This document should be reviewed by the key users so that everyone agrees that what was explained is what has been understood, and that all the decisions made in the project requirements meetings are reflected in the document.

As part of the project requirements, data migrations will also have to be handled and will include questions such as which kind of data will be migrated into Dynamics NAV 2013, which volume of information this means, from where the data will be extracted and in which format, and so on.

To make sure everything has been talked through and defined, it is important for business consultants to have a checklist of things to ask to the customer and use it in the project requirements meetings.

In this checklist, all Dynamics NAV functional areas should appear and have their own questions. Let's see an example of a checklist:

- Financial Management:
    - Which are the tasks of the financial department?
    - Which chart of accounts is used? Is it sector specific?
    - How are posting accounts created?
    - Which kinds of transactions are posted? Can they be predefined or established as recurring transactions?
    - Which kinds of analytical information will have to be reported?
    - Does the company create accounting budgets? How often? Are they created over the chart of accounts or over analytical concepts?
    - Which legal reporting does the company have to do? How often?
    - Does the company consolidate accounting information with some other company in the same group?
    - Are additional currencies used?
    - How are banks managed?
    - Are fixed assets managed in the ERP system?
    - How many fixed assets the company has?
    - Which depreciation method is used?
    - Do you keep maintenance track of your fixed assets?
    - Will fixed assets have to be automatically imported in Dynamics NAV?

- Marketing and Sales:
    - Do you create your contacts in the ERP system?
    - Do you use a CRM system?

- Customers and sales processes:
    - How many customers do you have?
    - Is extra information about customers needed in the customer card?
    - Do your customers have different shipment directions?
    - How do you classify your customers?
    - What is your sales process?

- ○ Do you invoice your customers per sales order they make or do you make a single invoice with multiple sales orders?
- ○ When do you invoice your customers?
- ○ Which documents are sent to customers?
- ○ How are sales prices established?
- ○ Are discounts applied to customers?
- ○ Who introduces new sales orders in the system?
- ○ Do sales orders require some kind of approval?
- ○ Which payment terms are applied to customers?
- ○ Which payment methods are used to get the payments from the customers?
- ○ Do you ask your customers for prepayments of sales orders?

- Vendors and purchase processes
- Items and stock management
- Warehouse management
- Jobs and resources
- Manufacturing
- Service
- Human resources
- Others:
  - ○ Will Dynamics NAV receive information from some external application? A website, maybe?
  - ○ Will Dynamics NAV have to send information to some external application?
  - ○ In how many different devices will Dynamics NAV be used?

We have just written the functional areas of Dynamics NAV 2013 and a few examples of questions that can be asked for some of them. You get the idea, right? A complete checklist should be written for all the functional areas, and all those questions should be answered in the project requirements meetings.

Designing the solution

The solution design includes the configuration needed in standard Dynamics NAV 2013 functionality for it to behave in a way in which the customer's requirements are met. It also includes the technical analysis and design of modifications, the development of new functionalities, and the data migration tools that will be used to get data into the system. Different things have to be taken into account for each type of design.

Configuration

All kinds of configurations have to be established in a Dynamics NAV 2013 implementation process:

- Posting groups will determine how documents and transactions will end up in an accounting transaction. There are several posting groups that have to be configured such as:
    - General Posting Setup
    - Customer Posting Group
    - Vendor Posting Group
    - Fixed Assets Posting Group
    - Bank Account Posting Group
    - Inventory Posting Group
    - Inventory Posting Setup
    - VAT Posting Setup
    - Currencies
    - Job Posting Group
- Series of numbers to be used in all documents and master data registers.
- The dimensions that will be used for analytical purposes.
- The allowed dimensions' combinations and the dimension priorities.
- The default dimension values for G/L accounts, customers, vendors, items, and so on.
- Setup of all functional areas:
    - General ledger setup:
        - Allowed posting dates
        - The way addresses appear in printouts
        - The invoice rounding precision
        - The global and shortcut dimension codes
        - The payment tolerance

- ° Sales & Receivables setup:
  - ° The series of numbers to be used in customers and sales documents
  - ° Whether it is mandatory to inform about an external document number in sales documents
  - ° Whether stock out and customer credit warnings should be prompted to the user
  - ° Whether posted invoices and credit memos should also create shipments and return receipts

- ° Purchases & Payables setup:
  - ° The series of numbers to be used in vendors and purchase documents
  - ° Whether it is mandatory to include an external document number in purchase documents
  - ° Whether posted invoices and credit memos should also create receipts and return shipments

- ° Inventory setup:
  - ° The series of numbers to be used in items and item documents, such as transfer orders
  - ° Whether cost and expected cost should automatically be posted to the general ledger
  - ° Whether it is mandatory to use locations in item movements

- ° Warehouse setup:
  - ° The series of numbers to be used in warehouse documents
  - ° Whether receipt, put-away, shipment, and pick documents are required

- ° Manufacturing setup:
  - ° The series of numbers to be used in manufacturing documents and resources, such as work centers

- ° Jobs setup:
  - ° The series of numbers to be used in jobs
  - ° Whether job item costs should automatically be updated

  ° Resources setup:
    ° The series of numbers to be used in resources
    ° Work types
    ° Resource units of measure

- Item tracking codes if they are required.

- Payment terms for customers and vendors.

- Payment methods for customers and vendors.

- Configurations that will be used at customer or vendor level such as whether prices for a certain customer or vendor are VAT included or not.

- Configurations that will be used at item level like the costing method to be used or replenishment parameters.

- Approval workflows for sales and purchases documents.

This is a list of typical and common configurations that have to be established in Dynamics NAV. But that's not all. There is a bunch of things that can be achieved in Dynamics NAV through configuration. Not only those configurations have to be established on the implementation, but they also have to be documented so that users apply the same configurations to items, customers, vendors, and so on, created in the future.

Modifying standard Dynamics NAV functionality

The modification of standard Dynamics NAV functionality may be as simple as showing extra existing fields in some pages or as complex as altering the way in which item costs are managed.

All modifications have to be designed carefully so that they do not cause inconsistencies in other areas or functionalities and they do not disable the future use of a standard functionality.

For example, if a modification is done regarding items, even if item variants are not used, make sure you take them into account to not disable the item variant functionality.

We will discuss development in depth in *Chapter 8, Development Considerations*.

New functionalities

New functionalities should be designed complying with the design philosophy behind Dynamics NAV 2013, as explained in *Chapter 3, General Considerations*.

These functionalities include using a master data table, using series of numbers to number your master data registers and your documents, writing a posting routine for your functionality, using non-modifiable ledger entry tables, and using posting groups if the new functionality has to end up in accounting transactions.

Data migration

For each kind of data that will be migrated into the system, we will have to define the tool to be used to achieve this task. In *Chapter 6, Migrating Data*, all kinds of details regarding data migration are explained.

Development

Once the analyst has defined the developments that have to be done, it's time for the developer to do his/her job.

The development should follow the standard way of development in Dynamics NAV, using the appropriate name convention for tables, captions, fields, pages, and all other Dynamics NAV objects.

All kinds of developments should be clearly identified using the `Documentation` trigger than can be found in every single Dynamics NAV object and also by using comment lines in the code itself to identify where the developed code begins and where it ends.

Don't wait until the development has finished to validate it and show it to the customer. Use prototypes for complex functionality development and show it to the customer as it gets developed. That way design and development misunderstandings or mistakes can be identified in early stages and can be corrected so that no one's time is lost.

Deployment

The deployment phase ends with the go-live day. A lot of work must be done before the system is ready to start using it, and it is time to synchronize the entire job done in previous phases. The best way to face this synchronization is to actually have some of the tasks done in previous stages as provisional work. This way major inconsistences can be found and fixed.

The deployment phase includes the following tasks:

- Software and hardware installation
- Configuration
- Data migration
- User acceptance testing
- End users training
- Go live!

Software and hardware installation

This task is all about installing the Dynamics NAV components on the server side, and installing the Dynamics NAV client on the required machines. Also make sure that Dynamics NAV is accessible from all the required devices.

In big implementations with lots of users using Dynamics NAV from different locations, a load test must be performed. A load test simulates the amount of transactional operations and concurrency pressure that the system will face. The load test will help you determinate whether the hardware was properly sized and configured or not.

We recommend you to install the Dynamics NAV test environment at an earlier time in the project, so that you can release functionality to the customer as it gets developed. It will help you with the final user acceptance test and will allow you to improve your development.

Configuration

Dynamics NAV includes many tables that include the word "setup" on their name. They are the base to define how each module will behave, so they need to be properly configured. There are also all sort of supplementary setups, including posting groups, payment methods, dimensions, security roles, and so on.

If you are going to release your developments to the customer periodically, not just at the end of the project, then you will have to execute the configuration task at the beginning of the project. This way the customer can see and test the development with an environment that is similar to the one they will find once they start using the system. If you do so, you will also help the people doing the development. It's easier to develop using a development environment similar to the production one.

Don't think that if you do it at the beginning of the project, you will have to do the same job twice. The company you set up at the beginning cannot be used for production, since test transactions and documents will be posted during development and testing. However, you can always copy all the tables, except entries, posted documents, and master data. There are more than 200 tables that can be considered as part of the Dynamics NAV configuration.

We've done this dozens of times and it's something that really helped us on our implementation, so we encourage you to try it.

Data migration

Chapter 6, Data Migration, explains in detail what has to be taken into account to perform data migration. In many cases, data will have to be transformed or adapted in order to use it in Dynamics NAV.

The data migration task should be performed twice. The first time in the test environment, so that the user acceptance test can be performed using real data. The second data migration will be done the day before the go-live day. You can also do the first data migration at the beginning of the project, this way you will help developers do their job with real data, that will help them understand the company they are developing for.

Since data migration requires the partner to work closely with the customer, an early data migration will help both the partner and the customer to get used to working together. It will also help the customer to get more involved with the project right from the beginning.

User-acceptance test

All the work is done and the system is ready to go live. During development each individual functionality has been tested several times, also on every release the users test the system. One more test is required, the one that tests the whole system. All processes have to be tested, from the initial input, going through all the stages, to the last output. You also need to test if the data generated during each process fits their analysis and reporting requirements.

This test is the last chance to find out if something is wrong and needs to be adjusted. Detecting an issue during the acceptance test and fixing it before going live may save a lot of money.

It's after this test that both the partner and the customer have to agree that everything is ready to go in production. Do not go live if anyone is not feeling comfortable after the test.

End users' training

Last but not least, end users have to be trained. They are the ones who are actually going to use the system, so they need to know how it works. Many of them will see Dynamics NAV for the first time during the training. If possible, make them practice with the system during the training.

The training shouldn't be taken too early, or they will easily forget what has been told.

Go-live!

Finally, the go-live is here. We need to perform the final data migration, validate this data, and start working!

Support

The support phase starts on the go-live day. Dynamics NAV is ready and all users start to intensively use the system.

No matter how hard you try during the training (try it hard anyway), users will have a lot of doubts and they need someone by their side, solving doubts on the fly. So for the first couple of weeks, depending on the size of the implementation, someone from the partner side is going to be at the customer's office helping them.

But this is not only about functional doubts. It would be easy if it was only doubts. Actually, the support phase is the hardest one! During this phase you will also have to handle the following issues:

- **Old tasks from previous phases**: You will be carrying over a few tasks from previous phases that weren't important enough to stop the go-live. But the day you start, those tasks become very important all of a sudden. Those tasks become important because users don't feel comfortable with the program yet. They are having a hard time trying to get familiar with the new environment, and you are telling them that by now this process works like this, but that it's only provisional and it will be different in a couple of weeks. The reaction of the users is always similar. They don't want to learn something completely new that will be different in a couple of weeks. So, they start to say how important the process is for them.

  Our recommendation is to try to avoid leaving too many tasks open, even if they don't seem to be important at the moment.

- **System stabilization**: Even if testing has been done before the "go-live", you can expect users to find bugs in your developments once they intensively start using the system. Some setups may be wrong as well. You will have to handle and fix all these kinds of issues.

- **Data stabilization**: A massive data migration has been done right before the go-live and a lot of other data has been configured or entered by hand.

  Although data has been checked before going live, issues with the data will also appear. For the next few weeks you will have to spend time to stabilize that data.

Summary

In this chapter we have seen that an implementation is a process to get the software to operate properly in a company. To do so, we need to use a methodology that will take us from the beginning to the end of the project, not only on the technical part of the project, but also on other aspects such as billing the project, effort estimating, planning, and communication.

We have seen different methodology approaches, such as the Waterfall approach and the Agile approach, and how they are addressed in Microsoft Dynamics Sure Step.

We have also seen the phases and the activities included in a typical Dynamics NAV implementation project.

In the next chapter, we will learn some tips about the implementation process on the customer side.

5
The Implementation Process on the Customer Side

For a really successful implementation of Microsoft Dynamics NAV, the company for which NAV is implemented has to actively participate on the project.

In this chapter we will cover the following aspects of the work a company should do to implement an ERP system like Microsoft Dynamics NAV:

- Define goals
- Define internal processes
- Define requirements for the new ERP system
- Involve end users
- Follow up the whole process of implementation

We will explain the theory of all these points, but we will also follow up the whole process with a very specific example from a real implementation.

Definition of goals

Implementing Dynamics NAV as your ERP system is not a turnkey kind of project. It is not a product that you can order to a Dynamics NAV implementer, pay the bill, and just wait for the go-live day expecting everything to work perfectly. Several people within your organization have to get actively involved during all the phases. The quality of their job will affect the final result of the implementation.

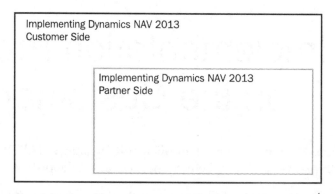

In the previous diagram you can see that implementing Dynamics NAV 2013 on the partner side is a project that can be framed within a larger project—the implementation of Dynamics NAV 2013 at the customer's side. Depending on the scope of the project, the amount of work on each side may differ.

As in any project, the definition of goals is essential to measure whether the project succeeds or not. Goals have to be clearly defined at the beginning of the project and all parties must agree on them. If you don't define clear goals, you may find yourself working as hard as you possibly can, and still never satisfy your boss or end users. During the project you may face several issues that you will have to solve. Do not let your project be defined as a failure just because some issues were experienced along the way. If you reach your goals, your project succeeds. Also, do not let your project be defined as a failure because your goals are not measurable. It is usual to define goals such as "improve the sales process" but by how much does it have to be improved, how are you going to measure it, and when are you going to measure it?

There are technics that help you define good goals. Remember this mnemonic: goals have to be SMART.

Specific
Measurable
Achievable
Relevant
Time bound

Define different goals for your company and for the partner that is going to implement your Dynamics NAV. Each party will be responsible for different parts of the projects and their goals must be specific to the area they are responsible for. If the definition of the goals is clear enough, it will help everybody to focus on the tasks that will help to accomplish them. This is something that will benefit both the customer and the partner.

Let's now take a specific example from a real Microsoft Dynamics NAV implementation. The example is from a company that provides public and private health care services. This company uses a specific health care software and an accounting software. They want to replace the accounting software, which only keeps track of accounting information. Their new accounting software will be Microsoft Dynamics NAV. However Dynamics NAV is not just an accounting application, it is actually an ERP system that can do several other things.

The main goal that this company wants to accomplish with Dynamics NAV is to make their departments stick to a budget. This budget will be established at the beginning of the year for each service that the departments offer. Nowadays, they do not have a detailed budget per service and they do not keep track of costs per service.

Making the departments stick to a budget is not actually a goal. It's not something specific or time bound; it is a general vision of where to go. To accomplish that vision, several goals that point in the same direction will have to be accomplished, one at a time.

The goals to accomplish that vision could be:

- Being able to define budgets per service
- Determine the service to which every cost applies
- Being able to compare budget and real costs
- Get a report of costs for a specific service

Let's take that last goal, to get a report of costs of a specific service. It is still a goal but it is not a SMART goal. It is specific, measurable, achievable, and relevant, but there is no timing for the goal. Let's write down the goal in a different way: get a report of costs for a specific service at the end of each month. That is definitely a much a better goal.

Defining the internal processes

Once the goals of the project are clear, and when the company knows what they want to accomplish with their brand new ERP, it's time to go into details and write down, one by one, all the company processes that will have to be done or supported by Microsoft Dynamics NAV.

When you think about your processes, don't just expose what they should *theoretically* be. Ask the people who are actually carrying out those processes about what they really do. Also ask about the exceptions to the processes, as handling exceptions usually requires more time. So, you probably also want to manage those and try to reduce the required time. Finally, ask whether the process may change in the future and how.

For instance, you have probably been told that Dynamics NAV handles sales orders, sales shipments, and sales invoices documents. Of course, that is true but those three documents can be created, revised, accepted, executed, and posted in several different ways. You have to find the way (with the aid of the Dynamics NAV partner providing the implementation services) in which you want your Dynamics NAV to work, and for that, you need to know what you require.

Questions to be asked

For each process, at least the following questions have to be answered:

- What is the desired outcome of the process?
- What are the start and end points?
- What activities are performed?
- What is the order of the activities?
- Who performs the activities?
- What information is required (documents)?
- How often is this process done?
- What is the importance of the process?

What is the start point for your sales orders? Customers pick up the phone, call you and tell you exactly which items they want in what quantities. Or maybe you receive the orders by e-mail, or customers submit them in a website, or maybe your salesperson visits your customers and gets the sales order, or customers asks you for sales quotes which finally get accepted (and thus converted into a sales order) or rejected, or you have blanket sales orders for a certain period of time and you do not receive any further sales orders.

In reality, it is a combination of all of this and many other ways to get sales orders that have not been exposed here as an example. Anyway, you have to think of all (and all means all!) the ways in which you receive sales orders and write them down.

After sales orders are received, you probably check them for the following: do you have a minimum sales order amount, do you sell your items per unit or per box, if you sell per box, you probably have to check whether the quantities asked by customers are multiple of quantities per box, and do you establish a credit limit for your customers? If so, before serving the order you may want to check if the credit limit has been exceeded. You may also want to check the *requested delivery date*. Is it possible to serve the customer in time or should you talk to them and negotiate a different delivery date?

Once the sales order has been revised and accepted, it has to be executed. What does that mean? How do you prepare your shipments? Do you group orders per customer so that multiple orders get prepared and served together? Do you pick up items of all the orders of the day together and then pack them separately per order or per customer in the preparation area? Do you attach the sales shipment document to the pack?

And finally in the sales invoice document, how do you do your invoices, do you do an invoice per sales shipment at the same time the sales shipment is done, a sales invoice per sales order, or a single sales invoice per customer, at the end of the month, including all sales orders served in the current month?

Now that we have a bunch of questions and their answers, it is time to write it all down. While writing down your processes, you may find new questions that have to be asked and answered. For example, you may know that your process has two sequential activities, but you may not have a clear picture of what triggers the beginning of the second activity. That is probably a good question to ask to the people involved in the process.

Writing your processes in a structured way — preferably using any kind of business process modeling diagrams or workflows — will help you and other people to understand them, and will also allow you to rapidly measure how simple or complex a process is, identify bottlenecks, redundant work and, basically, where the weakness of the process lies so that it can be improved.

Let's go back to our example of getting a report of costs for a specific service. This process was done in the company before the implementation of Microsoft Dynamics NAV. It wasn't done monthly, though, as it took too long and it was done manually. By asking the people involved in the process, we found out the following:

- **Desired outcome** – The cost amount of a specific service in a specific year.
- **Start point** – The service contract has reached its end.

- **End point** – The cost amount of a specific service in a specific year.
- **Activities and their order** – The following is the list of activities performed:
    1. Prepare a list of the vendors that provide goods to this service.
    2. Go through all the purchase invoices of the vendors in the list prepared in the first activity.
    3. Determine whether the purchase invoice is complete or in a high percentage, attributable to the service that is being analyzed.
    4. If it is attributable to the service that is being analyzed, write down the purchase invoice amount in a spreadsheet.
    5. Ask the head of the department providing the service, who and in what percentage of their time, works for the service.
    6. Calculate the costs of human resources attributable to the service. Write down the calculated amount in a spreadsheet.
    7. Get the total purchase invoice amount corresponding to general supplies or costs (water supply, energy supply, phone, general insurances, and so on). Because of the actual accounting practices, this amount can be found in a specific general ledger account.
    8. Attribute to the service being analyzed a percentage of the total amount obtained in previous activity. The percentage attributable to the service will be calculated based on the human resources that work on it and the surface the service uses from the whole company's surface.
    9. Sum up all the amounts on the spreadsheet.
- **People who perform the activities** – All the activities are performed by a person in the administration department.
- **How often is it done** – It is done four or five times per year, each time for a different service.
- **Importance** – It is a very important process, as this report will be used when negotiating with the public authorities the income that the company will receive to perform this public service for the following years.

We can write down the activities, their order, and the relations with other activities using a flow chart. It will look similar to the following diagram:

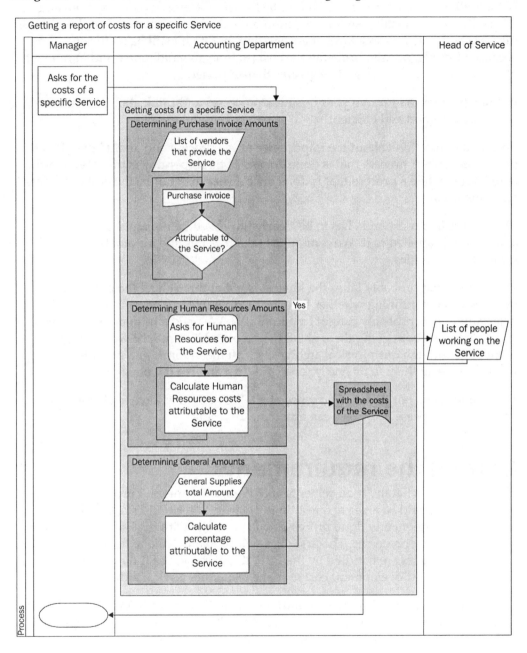

Improve before automating

IT tools allow us to automate all kind of tasks with the aim of reducing time and errors. But not everything should be automated. An inefficient and complex process can be sped up using some kind of automation, but it will still be inefficient, and because of its complexity, probably the cost (in time, in validations, and in money) of automating the process will be greater than expected.

It is much better to improve your business processes and think about automation once they are good and efficient.

You should also think about the importance of the process and about how often that process is done. A process that is done dozens of times per day is probably worth automating, while a process that is done once a year may not be the best candidate for automation.

The process in our example has to be clearly improved before any kind of automation is applied to it. We cannot just take it as it is and automate only some of the activities.

The activity that probably takes the longest is going through all the purchase invoices and determining whether they are attributable to a specific service. The determining part probably cannot be automated. We need a human to take this decision. What about going through all the invoices? Yes, maybe we could get a robot to go through our physical archives, get all the invoices of a provided list of vendors, present them to us one by one, and then archive the paper again.

This sounds cool, but it makes no sense at all. We definitely have to change and improve this process before we can automate anything.

Getting the requirements

How do I know what my requirements are? Well, if the internal processes have been defined, that should be an easy question to answer. You should start by the most important and frequently done processes and continue with the least important or infrequently done processes. The first ones will probably have to be handled by the ERP. If the last ones are handled by the ERP, it will be ok; but if they are not, maybe it is not worth the development cost to make Dynamics NAV handle it.

Talk to the consultants who will be implementing Dynamics NAV 2013. Tell them how your process looks like, who is involved in it, what information is required, and so on. They will tell you how this specific process is handled by Dynamics NAV 2013.

If the way Dynamics NAV 2013 handles the process meets the way you handle the process, eureka! You will be able to keep on doing it the same way you did before without any kind of modification in the behavior of the application. This is a requirement that may not need any work at all or at the most, may need some configuration work.

If the way Dynamics NAV 2013 handles the process does not meet the way you handle the process, two possible options exist: modify the behavior of the system to meet your requirements or change the way you handle your process to meet the Dynamics NAV 2013 way of doing things. Both the options have to be taken into account, or you can even consider a combination of both.

Is it ok to switch to the way Dynamics NAV handles the process? What will this involve? Will a different kind of information be needed? Who will have to do the process? Will it be the same people or different people? Will the steps or activities of the process be done in the same order or in a different order than before? Will all of this fit with the other processes? What will be the cost of changing the way we handle a specific business process?

On the other hand, is it possible to modify Dynamics NAV 2013 to handle the process in a different way? What would such a modification imply? How much development work will be needed to modify the behavior of the system? What will be the cost of changing the way Dynamics NAV 2013 handles a specific business process?

There is a third option, actually. Dynamics NAV 2013 doesn't handle your business process at all. If this is the case, development work will have to be done in Dynamics NAV so that the system can handle your process.

By doing this with all your processes, one by one, you will end up with your list of requirements.

Back to our example. If you ask any Dynamics NAV business consultant what is the goal of the example and the current process, they will tell you that there is something in Dynamics NAV called **dimensions**. Dimensions are actually meant to be able to analyze any information in Dynamics NAV according to a specific value of a dimension. That could definitely be useful in the example.

Any Dynamics NAV business consultant will tell the company that they have to set up a dimension that will be called *service*. The values of this dimension will be all the different services the company provides.

The service dimension can then be set up as mandatory in all the general ledger accounts that are used to post expenses. This means that before an expense is posted whether it is a purchase invoice or any other expense like salaries, insurances, and so on, someone has to determine the service to which the expense is attributable. If this is not determined prior to the posting of the expense, it will not be posted. That is, you will not be able to account your expense if you do not attribute it to a service.

This completely changes the process. At the moment, attributions to services are determined a while after the expense has been accounted or are never determined if no one asks for the costs of a specific service. But, having all this information can automate the process of getting an amount for a specific service in a specific period of time. The information is already in the system. A report can be automated using the appropriated reporting tools.

Once you have the whole explanation of the standard functionality provided in Microsoft Dynamics NAV, the best option in the example is to change the way the process is handled and use the Dynamics NAV way.

Two requirements will come up:

- Set up a dimension called *service* and make it mandatory in all general ledger accounts that are used to post expenses

- Develop a report to get the total expenses amount for a specific dimension value in a specific period of time

The first requirement will only require configuration work. The second one can be addressed through configuration (setting up the appropriate analysis view, a feature in Dynamics NAV to report the general ledger amounts based on the dimension values) or a concrete report could be developed.

Change management

Implementing a brand new ERP means a lot of changes within an organization. The first change is the software the company is using. This will affect the people that use the ERP intensively and they are probably worried about the project and how it will affect their daily task.

But this is not the only change that the company will face. While changing the ERP, you will probably change some processes, or you could even change who is responsible for doing certain tasks. Usually those changes are not easy to make. You will have to take some actions in order to reassure people, help them during the change process, and ensure that they don't boycott the project.

For example, a few years ago we worked on an implementation project. The company had an employee whose major task was to register all the sales invoices in the system. With the implementation of Dynamics NAV, it was decided that the warehouse staff were going to register the invoice while registering the shipment. Now, that particular employee will probably feel that he was going to lose his job, so he may start to boycott the project instead of helping the warehouse staff with their new task.

The first thing you need to do to face the change in management, is to identify all the stakeholders of the project. After that, you need to analyze their needs and their expectations from the project. You will also have to determine whether they support the project or not, and what actions you can take to change their position.

Usually communication is the easier way to face changes. Keep all the stakeholders informed on what the project is all about, why the company has decided to implement Dynamics NAV, how will it affect them, and how the project is advancing.

If communication is not enough for some stakeholders, you will need to take other actions. Getting them involved is usually a good way to change their vision on the project. Think carefully about how you are going to handle all those changes, since people are the most valuable asset you have to make the project a success.

Get involved in testing the system

When the project starts, a consultant will take all the requirements needed to implement Dynamics NAV. The consultant will determine which of those requirements will be covered with the standard application and which ones will be developed for you.

Implementing Dynamics NAV for a company is a unique process since it is going to cover specific needs of the company. Even for similar companies, there will be many differences in the processes that will make this implementation unique. No matter how much experience the implementer has in companies of your sector, you and the people in your company are the best testers to check that everything works as defined.

Usually, the implementer will install a second Dynamics NAV server for you, so that you can test the system before it goes in to production. The consultants and developers will conduct their own test before delivering the solution, but it is also important that you invest time in conducting a test too. Any issue found before the go-live day is much easier to solve than in a production environment.

Ask different people with different tasks within your organization to test the system. This way, all the areas will be covered by different people and more people can usually find more issues than just one person testing all the areas.

Testing with real data is one of the best tests you could do. Before going live, you could ask your users to perform the same activities using the old and the new system at the same time. This requires double work for a while, but testing with real data will bring you real issues.

Involve end users

The end users are actually the people that will be using Dynamics NAV 2013 on a daily basis. The project will truly succeed if they really use the system. And they will only use it if they think it is reliable and find that it makes their job easier.

For all of this to happen, it is important that they get involved in all the steps of the project from the very beginning. They may not have a responsible position in the company, they may not have the power to take certain decisions, but they definitely have a lot to say.

When we talked about the definition of the internal processes, we said that you had to ask yourself and your people, what were your processes, the activities inside each process, the information used by the process, and so on. We also said that the real processes should be considered and not just the *theoretical* processes. The ones who actually know the real processes and activities are the end users. If you don't ask them, if you do not involve them, you will not be working with the complete information and thus, you will not be able to define your real requirements.

Even if the final solution really meets all the requirements defined in the project, if those are not well-defined requirements, the project will fail as the end users will not find it useful. Instead, they will keep doing their extra processes, keeping their own information in spreadsheet files, and so on.

The definition of the processes and the requirements is the most important part in which the end users should get involved. If they get involved in defining how they work and how the system should behave, they will really find the system useful and actually use it. But that's not the only part of the implementation process in which they should get involved. It is also important that they participate in the testing process, especially in those functionalities that have either been modified or that have been completely developed. If they participate in this process, they might find errors or any other kind of improvement that could be done to make everything easier. If they bring it to your attention, the Dynamics NAV implementers will be able to fix or to improve the process. If they do not get involved in this process, they may find errors or improvements once the functionalities are live, but they might never tell you. Instead, they will find workarounds to their daily job that will make everything less efficient and more chaotic.

Summary

In this chapter we've seen how to handle the implementation of Dynamics NAV from a customer's perspective. We've covered a few areas, but the whole idea is that you, as a customer, have to manage the implementation as a project. The implementer cannot do all the work for you. People within your organization will have tasks and responsibilities assigned, and you will have to monitor and control all those tasks.

Do get involved with the project management and with the project's progress in order to make the project successful.

In the following chapter we will see how the data a company may have in the other applications (their old ERP System, spreadsheet files, and so on) and how it can be massively imported into Microsoft Dynamics NAV 2013.

6
Migrating Data

Microsoft Dynamics NAV 2013 is now completely configured and tuned. A range of brand new functionalities have been programmed and everything is ready for us to go live. But, data is needed for it to start working!

Companies may now start working with Dynamics NAV, but they are not new companies; they have been working for a while, and they already have all kinds of data: their customers, vendors, items, accounting information, and so on.

In this chapter we will see which tools can be used in Dynamics NAV to migrate data into the system and how to convert data to meet NAV requirements. We will look at tools such as:

- RapidStart Services
- XMLport
- User defined tools

We will also see what kind of data is commonly migrated to Dynamics NAV and which strategies can be used to migrate it. The kind of data and strategies are listed as follows:

- Master data
- Open entries
- Historical data
- Open documents

Tools to migrate data

There are several ways to migrate data into Microsoft Dynamics NAV 2013. You will choose the method depending on what is to be migrated and whether any additional processes need to be carried out on the provided data to meet Dynamics NAV requirements.

We'll go through the different tools available in Dynamics NAV to migrate data. We'll also explain how to write our own tools if the ones provided out of the box do not meet our requirement or expectation.

RapidStart Services

RapidStart Services is a new feature of Microsoft Dynamics NAV 2013. It allows you to configure your company using out of the box configurations. Microsoft Dynamics NAV 2013 also allows streamlined importing of opening balances into journals and active documents with dimensions.

Typically, a Dynamics NAV implementation project can go on for a great length of time. With RapidStart Services, Dynamics NAV 2013 delivers a new way for partners and customers to speed up implementations. RapidStart Services is a tool designed not only to shorten deployment time but also to improve quality, to introduce a repeatable approach to implementations, and to automate and simplify recurring tasks.

With RapidStart Services, you can set up the tables often involved in the configuration process of new companies. You can create a questionnaire to guide your customers through the collection of setup information. Your customers have the option of using the questionnaire to set up application areas, or they can open the setup page directly and complete the setup there. Most importantly, RapidStart Services helps you, as a customer, prepare the company with default setup data that you can fine-tune and customize. Lastly, when you use RapidStart Services, you can configure and migrate existing customer data, such as a list of customers or items, into the new company.

The RapidStart Services tools can be found under the **Department** menu, **Departments/Administration/Application Setup/RapidStart Services for Microsoft Dynamics NAV**.

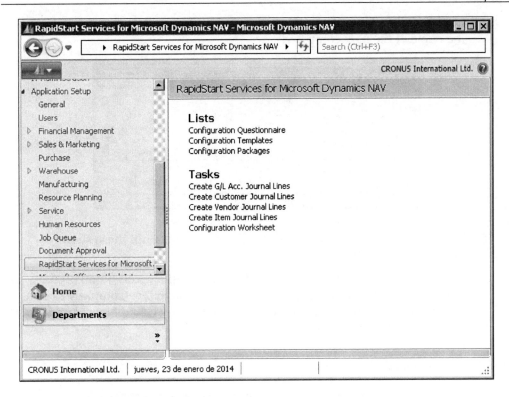

The following components can be used to set up a new company:

- Configuration wizard
- Configuration packages
- Configuration worksheet
- Configuration templates
- Configuration questionnaire

We will explain how these components work by following a step-by-step example of each of them. Before starting with the example, you need to create a new company, and we also recommend that you change your role to that of the RapidStart Services implementer. Follow these steps to do both these things:

1. Open Microsoft Dynamics NAV Development Environment.

2. Click on **File | Company | New**. A window opens; in it, you can enter the name of the new company.

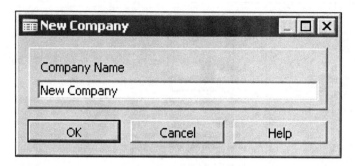

3. Click on the **OK** button and wait for a few seconds until the system finishes creating the company.

4. Open the Windows client. Click on the the Dynamics icon found on the upper-right corner of the page. Then, click on the **Select Company** option. On the **Select Company** page, choose the company called **New Company**. Then click on the **OK** button.

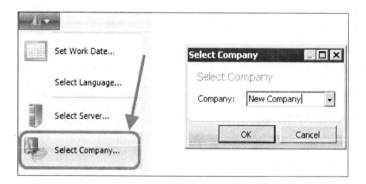

You have now entered in the New Company section. Follow the ensuing steps to change your role.

5. Open the **User Personalization** page, found via **Departments/ Administration/Application Setup/RoleTailored Client/ User personalization**.

6. Select your user ID and click on the **Edit** option.

7. In the **Profile ID** field, select **RAPIDSTART SERVICES**.

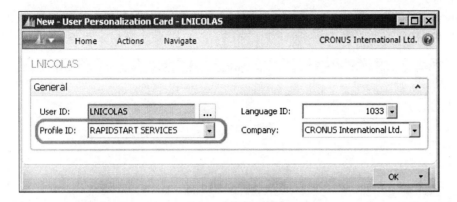

8. Close the Windows client and open it again. Your Role Center now looks like the following screenshot:

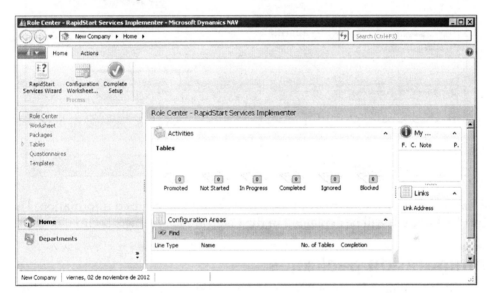

Now that we have a new company and we have selected the RapidStart Services implementer role, we are ready to use all the components of the RapidStart Services tool to set up our company.

Configuration wizard

The configuration wizard is used to quickly configure a new company. Click on the **RapidStart Services Wizard** option found on the ribbon bar.

A new page will open where you will be able to enter basic information about the new company.

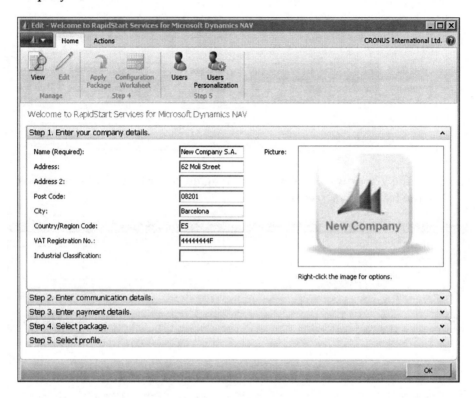

You can go through all the tabs of the page entering the required information. The **Select Package** tab will be explained in the *Configuration packages* section, next.

Configuration packages

There are more than 200 tables that could be considered configuration tables. You will need to fill them in when you create a new company.

First of all, you will find almost 50 tables with the word *setup* as their description, but there are many other tables that could also be considered as setup tables. Here you can see a list of some setup tables:

- **Posting groups**: There are 10 tables located here
- **Journal batch tables and journal template tables**: More than 20 tables are located here
- **G/L accounts, account schedules and VAT statements**: Almost 10 tables are present here.

- Payment terms, payment methods, currencies, languages, countries and regions, post codes, series, and so on are the other setup tables without the word *setup* in their description.

Having to edit all those tables manually on each implementation could take forever. Many companies can use Dynamics NAV with the same data or almost the same data on those configuration tables.

The best approach will be to create a configuration package for the data on the configuration tables and then apply it on each new implementation, like a template.

You can create one configuration package per functional area, for example, you can create one package for the manufacturing functionality. Another approach would be to create one package for each type of data, for example, you could create one package with data related to all the posting groups found in the application.

In this section we will see how to create a configuration package and also how to apply it to a new company.

Creating a configuration package

In this section we are going to create a new configuration package with all posting groups tables found on the application. Since posting groups refer to general ledger accounts, we are also going to include the chart of accounts in our package.

Follow these steps to create the new configuration package:

1. Select a company containing the data that you want to include in your configuration package, for example, we have selected the demonstration company CRONUS International Ltd.

2. From the RapidStart Services implementer Role Center, click on the **Packages** option.

3. Click on the **New** button on the ribbon bar. The **Config. Package Card** page opens. Fill in the fields in the **General** tab, as shown in the following screenshot:

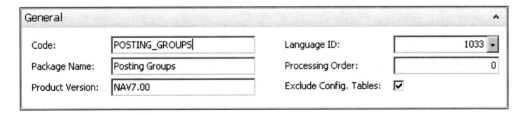

4. Add tables to the packages by creating new lines on the **Tables** tab, as shown in the following screenshot. You will only have to fill in the `Table ID` column.

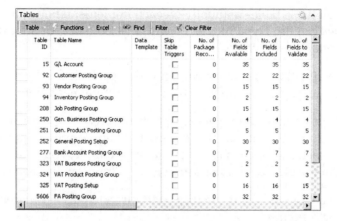

5. When you insert a table on the package, all table fields are included by default. In some cases, you may want to exclude certain fields from the package. Select the `G/L Account` table and click on **Table | Fields**. On the **Config. Package Fields** page, uncheck the `Include Field` column for the `Global Dimension 1 Code` field and the `Global Dimension 2 Code` field.

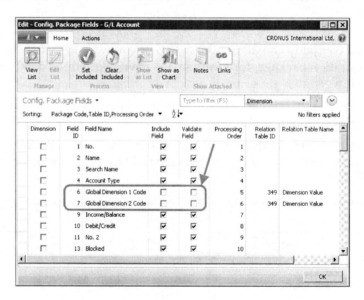

6. Click on the **Export Package** option on the ribbon bar. This will create a `RAPIDSTART` file that you can save.

Applying a configuration package

In the previous section we created a new configuration package. In this section we are going to apply this package to the company New Company, that we created earlier in this chapter.

Follow these steps to apply the configuration package:

1. On the Windows client, open the company New Company.

2. From the RapidStart Services implementer's role center, click on the **RapidStart Services Wizard** option.

3. On the **Select package** tab, select the configuration package that you created in the previous section.

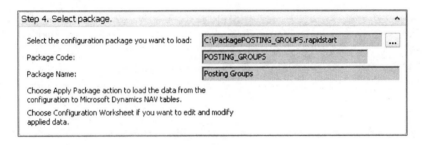

4. Click on the **Apply Package** option found on the ribbon bar.

5. Click on the **Configuration Worksheet** option if you want to edit the applied data check errors found during the importation. The configuration worksheet is explained in the next section.

The data contained in the configuration data has been imported to the new company. You can also import packages from the packages page we saw while creating the configuration package.

Configuration worksheet

The configuration worksheet is the central location in which you can plan, track, and perform your configuration work. For those of you that have used previous versions of Dynamics NAV, the configuration worksheet is the old migration tool with some new features.

You use the configuration worksheet to create the structure of tables that need to be imported with the company data. You will be able to export this structure to Microsoft Office Excel, fill in the data, and then import it back to Dynamics NAV. This makes it easy for companies to copy and paste information from another ERP system.

We'll explain how the configuration worksheet works by creating a migration structure for the sales area and then importing some demo data into the customer's table.

Creating the migration structure

To create a migration structure, you need to use a company that is already configured. We will use the demo company CRONUS International Ltd.

Follow the steps described in this section:

1. Open the configuration worksheet.

2. Create a line for table 18, Customer. You only need to fill in the Line Type field and the Table ID field.

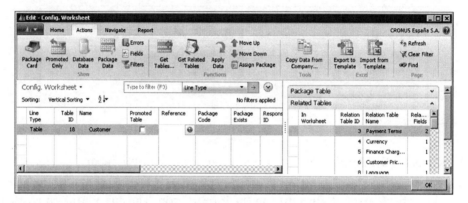

3. Now, we have to put the tables into a configuration package. Click on the **Assign Package** option from the ribbon bar.

4. The **Config. Packages** page opens. Create a new package and call it **Customer**. Then, click on the **OK** button.

5. Now we have to define which fields will be included in the migration process. Click on the **Fields** option on the **Actions** tab of the ribbon bar.

6. The **Config. Package Fields** page will open, showing all fields available in the table. In this list, we will have to place checkmarks on the **Include Field** column for all the fields we want to be part of the migration process. By default, all fields are checked. Click on the **Clear Included** option to uncheck all the fields.

 All primary key fields must be included in the migration process. The **Include Fields** checkmark cannot be unchecked for these fields.

7. Select the following fields to be included. Then, click on the **OK** button.

When importing the data into the table, fields will be validated according to their processing order. You can use the **Move Up** and **Move Down** options to change the default validation order.

You can also uncheck the **Validate Field** column for a field if you don't want to run the OnValidate trigger of the field. If you do so, you will have to validate the data consistency on your own.

8. We will now add a filter to determinate which records will be included in the template we are going to create later on. Click on the **Filters** option on the **Actions** tab of the ribbon bar. We will add a filter to the No. field to only include customers with a blank No. field. Since this is the primary key of the table, all customers should have filled up this field. No records will match the filter, so no records will be included while exporting the template. Add the filter as shown in the following screenshot:

9. Back at the configuration worksheet; the **Related Tables** FactBox shows the tables that are related to the Customer table.

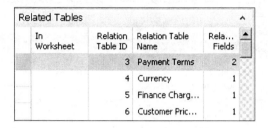

The first related table is Payment Terms. We will not be able to fill in the payment terms code for a customer unless it exists on the Payment Terms table. Therefore, we need to include related tables in the configuration worksheet. Use the **Get Related Tables** option found on the **Actions** tab of the ribbon bar to add new tables to the worksheet.

10. The system has included all the related tables. However for this example, delete all tables, except the ones shown in the following screenshot:

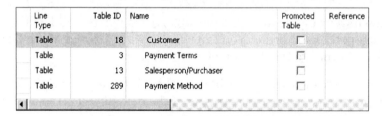

11. We are now going to group the tables by adding areas and groups. Create a new line and select the **Area** option on the Line Type field. Write Sales Area in the Name field. Use the **Move Up** option from the **Actions** tab of the ribbon bar to move the new line to the first position.

12. Create three new lines for the Master Data, Secondary Data, and General Settings groups. Use the **Move Up** and **Move Down** options to rearrange the tables as shown in the following screenshot:

Line Type	Table ID	Name	Promoted Table	Reference	Package Code	Package Exists	Responsible ID	Status	Page ID	Page Name
Area		**Sales Area**	☐		CUSTOMER	Yes				
Group		**Master Data**	☐		CUSTOMER	Yes				
Table	18	Customer	☐		CUSTOMER	Yes			22	Customer List
Group		**Secondary Data**	☐		CUSTOMER	Yes				
Table	13	Salesperson/Purchaser	☐		CUSTOMER	Yes			14	Salespeople/Purchasers
Group		**General Settings**	☐		CUSTOMER	Yes				
Table	3	Payment Terms	☐		CUSTOMER	Yes			4	Payment Terms
Table	289	Payment Method	☐		CUSTOMER	Yes			427	Payment Methods

13. Now, we have to put the tables into a configuration package. Click on the **Assign Package** option from the ribbon bar.

14. The **Config. Packages** page opens. Create a new package and call it `Customer`. Then, click on the **OK** button.

15. Back at the configuration worksheet page; you can see that the **Package Code** field is now filled for all the rows.

16. Click on **Package Card**, and then click on the **Export Package** option to save the package file for the migration structure we have defined.

Now that you, as a partner, have defined the migration structure, it's time for the users to complete the migration by providing their data.

Migrating your data

The partners are responsible for creating the migration structure according to company's needs. We have done that in the previous section. Then, the rest of the work can be done by the end users. Therefore, you will need to train the end users on the steps explained in this section.

To provide data for the new company, you can follow the ensuing steps:

1. Open the company named `New Company` that we created earlier in this chapter.

2. Open the package page and click on the **Import Package** option. Select the file created in the previous section. The data included in the package is stored in special tables. It will not be applied to the database yet.

3. Open the **Configuration Worksheet** page. The system has created the configuration structure of the new company while importing the package file.

4. Select the line for the table with the table-ID 3, `Payment Terms`. The **Package Table** FactBox shows us some information, as shown in the following screenshot:

For instance, we can see that 6 records were included in the package.

5. Click on the **Package Data** option on the ribbon bar. A page opens showing all the data included in the package.

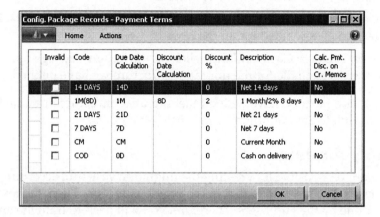

Before applying it to the database, you can delete or insert lines or modify the existing ones.

6. Go back to the **Config. Worksheet** page and click on the **Apply Data** option. Now the payment terms are created on the database. You can repeat this action for the `Payment Method` table.

7. Change the `Status` column for both tables and select the option **Completed**.

8. On your Role Center page, you will be able to see the level of completion of the migration tasks.

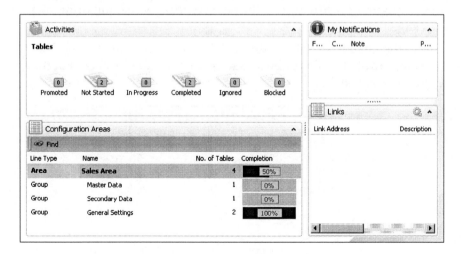

9. To migrate data for the `Customer` table, open the **Config. Worksheet** page and select the line for the `Customer` table. Click on the **Export to Template** option on the ribbon bar. The system will export the template, and will open the Excel file.

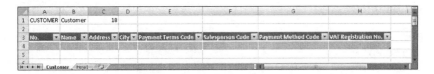

10. We will use the information extracted from the old system to fill in our Excel template. We are going to import the customers shown in the following screenshot:

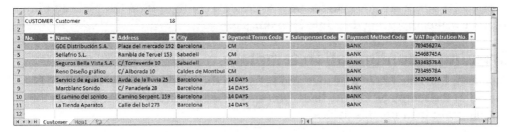

Do not change the columns in the worksheets. If they are moved, changed, or deleted, the worksheet cannot be imported into Microsoft Dynamics NAV.

11. In the configuration worksheet, click on the **Import from Template** option and import your customers' file. Use the **Package Data** option to check the data and then click on the **Apply Data** option.

12. Click on the **Database Data** option to see the records that have been created in the `Customer` table.

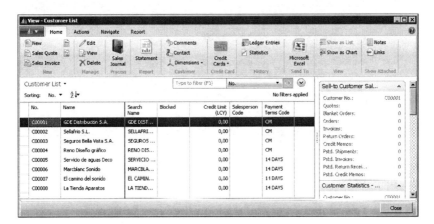

Configuration templates

Templates are used to fill in preconfigured data. When you import data such as items into Dynamics NAV, you only enter general information, such as item number, description, and price, and then collect the rest of the mandatory field data from a template.

You usually create templates for the master data, such as customers, vendors, and items master data.

 You can also use data templates for daily operations to create records that are based on templates.

In this section, we are going to see how to create a configuration template and how to use it while importing data into Dynamics NAV.

Creating a configuration template

Each template consists of a header and lines. On the header, you specify the table related to the template. On the lines, you specify which fields are included in the template and their default values.

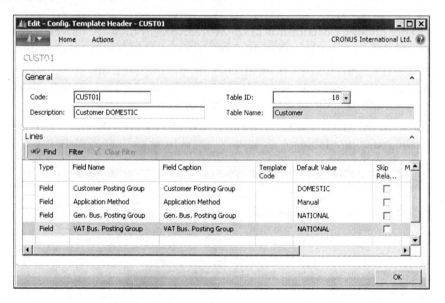

Follow the ensuing steps to create the configuration template shown in the preceding screenshot:

1. Open the **Templates** page and click on the **New** button.

2. In the `Code` field, enter a unique ID for the template. On the `Description` field, enter a description.

3. In the `Table ID` field, enter the table to which this template has been applied.

4. Create a new line, select the **Field Name** field. The **Field List** window displays the list of fields in the table. Select a field and then click on the **OK** button.

5. In the **Default Value** field, enter an appropriate value.

Using configuration templates

Using configuration templates with RapidStart Services is as simple as selecting the template we want to use on a line of a configuration package. The following steps will demonstrate this:

1. Open the **Packages** page.

2. From the list of packages, open the **CUSTOMER** package we created earlier in this chapter.

3. Find the **Customer** table included in the package. In the **Data Template** field, select the template that we created in the previous section.

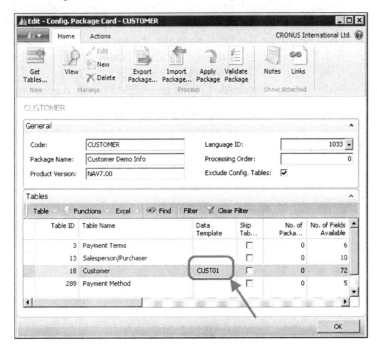

And we are done! When importing new customers using the package, the template will be applied:

Configuration questionnaire

Configuration questionnaire is used to collect data from users to help configure a new company. You can create a list of questions and provide it to the users as an Excel or an XML file. When the user completes the questionnaire, you import the file into the new Microsoft Dynamics NAV company and then apply it to the database. Follow the steps described in the following section to create and complete configuration questionnaires.

Creating a configuration questionnaire

Follow the steps listed in this section to create a configuration questionnaire:

1. Open the **Questionnaire** page and click on the **New** option.

2. Provide a code and a description.

3. Click on the **Questions Areas** option found on the ribbon bar.

4. In the **Code** field, enter a code for the question area.

5. In the **Table ID** field, choose the ID of the table for which you want to collect information.

6. Click on the **Update Questions** option found on the ribbon bar. Each field in the table is added to the questionnaire with a question mark following its label. You can rephrase the label to make it clear how the question should be answered. For example, if a field is called **Name**, you could edit it to state `What is the name of <data being collected>`. As needed, you can also delete questions that you do not want to include in the questionnaire.

7. Repeat these steps to add additional question areas.

In the following screenshot, you can see an example of a questionnaire for the inventory setup area.

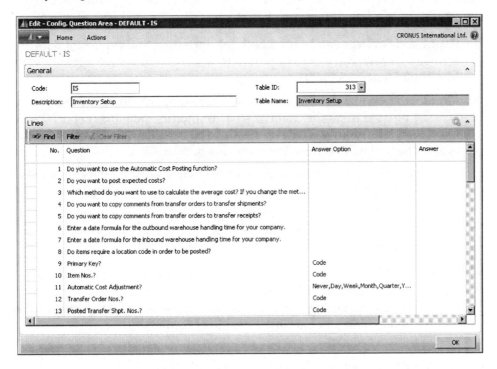

Completing the configuration questionnaire

1. Open the **Questionnaire** page, click on the **Export to Excel** option found on the ribbon bar, and save the file.

2. Complete the configuration questionnaire by entering the answers in the Excel workbook. There are worksheets for each of the question areas that have been created for the questionnaire. Save the file.

3. Back in the questionnaire, click on the **Import from Excel** option. Select the XLSX file that you have saved.

4. Click on the **Question Areas** option, and select one question area to begin the process of validating and applying the answers to the setup questionnaire.

5. To apply the process of validating and applying the answers to the whole questionnaire, click on the **Apply Answers** option of the **Questionnaire** page.

6. To apply answers for a specific question area, click on the **Apply Answers** option from the **Question Areas** page.

Summary of RapidStart Services

We have already covered the RapidStart Services. Before moving to another tool to migrate, there are a few things you should know about RapidStart Services:

- RapidStart Services can be used both for importing and exporting data. It is not a tool reserved just to import data when you first start working with Microsoft Dynamics NAV.

- RapidStart Services does not only insert new data into the database, it can actually be used to modify data as well. To modify data, first export it to an Excel template, modify whatever needs to be modified, and import the data again. The tool will perform the following actions:
    - Create a new record in the corresponding table if no record exists with the same values on primary key fields as the imported record.
    - Update a record in the corresponding table if the record imported already exists in the table. The record will be updated with all the information coming from the imported record.

- RapidStart Services consume a lot of time while importing and exporting data. It took us 1 minute to import 5,000 customers and almost 5 minutes to apply them. Importing that exact same data using an **XMLport** (the next tool we will explain) took us just a couple of seconds.

Using XMLports to migrate data

An XMLport is a Microsoft Dynamics NAV object type used to import and export data encapsulated in XML format. Fixed text and variable text formats are also available on an XMLport to import and export data from a plain text file, just as we used to do with **dataports** (a Dynamics NAV object type that has been discontinued in the previous release of the application). XMLports have their own designer, **XMLport Designer**, which can be found in **Object Designer**.

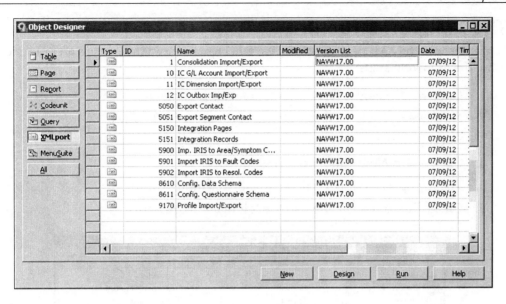

Using XMLport Designer, we will specify all the XML tag names and their type (element or attribute). We will also map those tag names to data structures (tables, records, or fields) in the Dynamics NAV database.

We will create an **XMLport** to import customers, just as we did on the Configuration Worksheet section. By performing the same example with both the tools, we will be able to compare them and have some elements to decide which one we will use in our migrations.

We will be importing the following data into the Customers table:

- Name
- Address
- City
- Salesperson code
- Payment method code
- Payment terms code
- VAT registration number

The XMLport structure

To understand the XMLport structure, we will create a new XMLport as an example, using the following steps:

1. Open the Dynamics NAV Development Environment.

2. Navigate to **Tools | Object Designer** (or press *Shift + F12*).

3. Select XMLport.

4. Click on the **New** button (or press *Alt + N*).

5. The XMLport Designer will open with an empty XMLport.

6. Create the structure shown in the following screenshot:

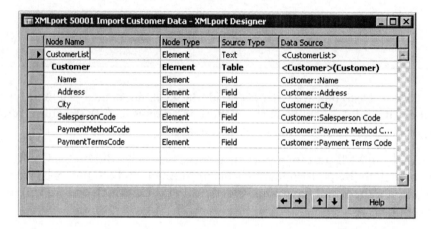

7. Save the XMLport by clicking on **File | Save** (or press *Ctrl + S*).

8. Give your XMLport an ID, **50001** and a name, **Import Customer Data**.

9. Click on the **OK** button.

The following are the elements of our XMLport:

- The **Node Name** column indicates the tag names that will be used in the XML document.

- The **Node Type** column, where we will indicate which type of tag it will be, whether element or attribute.

- The **Source Type** column, from which we can select whether the mapping of the element or attribute is with a text source, a table source, or a field source.

- The **Data Source** column, where we will indicate the text for text sources, the Dynamics NAV table for table source types, and the Dynamics NAV field for field source types.

For both table and field source types, we can click on the up arrow that appears in the column to select the appropriate Dynamics NAV data structure. When a table source type has been selected, a list of Dynamics NAV tables will be shown. When a field source type is selected, a lookup field will appear for us to select a field in any of the tables selected as table source type on the XMLport. When using a text source type, the information imported from the XML document will be put in a text variable with the name specified in the **Data Source** column. This variable can be used as a global C/AL variable.

Child nodes have to be indented under their parent elements using one indentation per level. To indent elements, use the left and right arrows that can be found in the lower right corner of the **XMLport Designer** window. Nodes have to be entered in the exact same order that they appear in the XML document.

If you check the XMLport properties by placing the cursor on the first empty line of the XMLport and clicking on **View** | **Properties** (or pressing the *Shift + F4* key combination), you will see a property called format, which is set to xml. Other options for this property are variable text and fixed text. By selecting either variable text or fixed text, you will be able to import/export data in a plain text format rather than in an XML format.

Running the XMLport

We will be importing a file called Customer.xml that has the following structure and data:

```xml
<?xml version="1.0" encoding="UTF-16" standalone="no"?>
<CustomerList>
  <Customer>
    <Name>GDE Distribución S.A.</Name>
    <Address>Plaza del mercado 192</Address>
    <City>Barcelona</City>
    <SalespersonCode />
    <PaymentMethodCode />
    <PaymentTermsCode>CM</PaymentTermsCode>
  </Customer>
  <Customer>
    <Name>Sellafrio S.L.</Name>
    <Address>Rambla de Teruel 153</Address>
    <City>Sabadell</City>
    <SalespersonCode />
    <PaymentMethodCode>BANK</PaymentMethodCode>
```

```
      <PaymentTermsCode>CM</PaymentTermsCode>
    </Customer>
  </CustomerList>
```

To import the file, follow these steps:

1. Open the Dynamics NAV Development Environment.
2. Click on **Tools | Object Designer** (or press *Shift + F12*).
3. Select the **XMLport** option.
4. Click on the **Run** tab (or press *Alt + R*).
5. The Windows client will open, and the **Edit – Import Customer Data** page will also open.
6. Select the **Import** tag in the **Direction** field.
7. Click on the **OK** button.
8. Navigate to the XML file you want to import and click on the **Open** tab.
9. The file will be imported.

Check the customer list to see the records that have been created by the XMLport. You will notice that the OnInsert and OnValidate triggers for each of the fields, have been run (each customer has a number, so the **OnInsert** trigger has been run, and the field **Search Name** has been filled in, which means that at least the **OnValidate** trigger for the **Name** field has been run as well).

Writing code inside the XMLport

With an XMLport, you can write your own code to handle multiple situations. You can either write data on multiple Dynamics NAV tables or create secondary records while importing master data.

In our example, you can write code to create new payment methods if the payment method code filled for one customer does not exist on the database.

XMLports do also offer the capability of importing data into different Dynamics NAV tables that have a link relation between them, such as in a **Sales Order** table. In a **Sales Order** table, data has to be imported into the **Sales Header** and **Sales Line** table, which have a header/line relation through the **Document Type** and **Document No.** fields.

The document structure

Imagine we have an XML document, like the one shown in the following screenshot, which we want to import into Dynamics NAV.

```xml
<?xml version="1.0" encoding="UTF-16" standalone="no" ?>
<SalesOrder>
 <Header>
  <SalesHeader Date="18/01/12">
     <CustomerName>Deerfield Graphics Company</CustomerName>
   <Lines>
    <SalesLine>
        <ItemNo>LS-10PC</ItemNo>
        <Quantity>12</Quantity>
        <UnitOfMeasureCode>BOX</UnitOfMeasureCode>
        <UnitPrice>57</UnitPrice>
        <LocationCode>WHITE</LocationCode>
     </SalesLine>
    <SalesLine>
        <ItemNo>LS-150</ItemNo>
        <Quantity>8</Quantity>
        <UnitOfMeasureCode>PCS</UnitOfMeasureCode>
        <UnitPrice>120</UnitPrice>
        <LocationCode>WHITE</LocationCode>
     </SalesLine>
    </Lines>
   </SalesHeader>
  </Header>
 </SalesOrder>
```

We analyze the XML document tag structure and decide that we will have to import the data into the **Sales Header** and **Sales Line** tables, and we design an XMLport with the following structure:

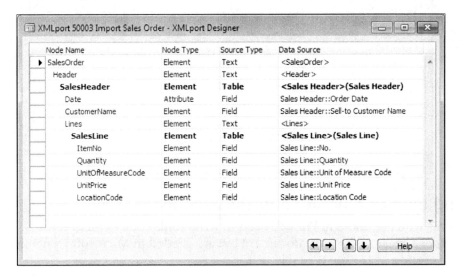

Node Name	Node Type	Source Type	Data Source
SalesOrder	Element	Text	\<SalesOrder\>
Header	Element	Text	\<Header\>
SalesHeader	**Element**	**Table**	**\<Sales Header\>(Sales Header)**
Date	Attribute	Field	Sales Header::Order Date
CustomerName	Element	Field	Sales Header::Sell-to Customer Name
Lines	Element	Text	\<Lines\>
SalesLine	**Element**	**Table**	**\<Sales Line\>(Sales Line)**
ItemNo	Element	Field	Sales Line::No.
Quantity	Element	Field	Sales Line::Quantity
UnitOfMeasureCode	Element	Field	Sales Line::Unit of Measure Code
UnitPrice	Element	Field	Sales Line::Unit Price
LocationCode	Element	Field	Sales Line::Location Code

In this XMLport structure, we have used all XML tags detected on the XML document and we have mapped them to Dynamics NAV tables (the **SalesHeader** element is mapped to the **Sales Header** table and the **SalesLine** element is mapped to the **Sales Line** table) and Dynamics NAV fields in the corresponding tables.

Note that the **Date** tag, which has been mapped to the **Order Date** field of table **Sales Header** has a node type of attribute. We have designed it that way because, while analyzing the XML document, we have seen the **Date** tag as an attribute of the preceding tag, **SalesHeader**.

```
<SalesHeader Date="18/01/12">
```

In the properties of the **SalesLine** tag, which is mapped to the `Sales Line` table, we have indicated that this tag has a link relation with table **Sales Header**, we have specified which fields offer the link in the **LinkFields** property, and we have set the **LinkTableForceInsert** property to `Yes`. This means that we force the record on the link table (`Sales Header`) to be inserted before we start writing anything into the linked table (`Sales Line`).

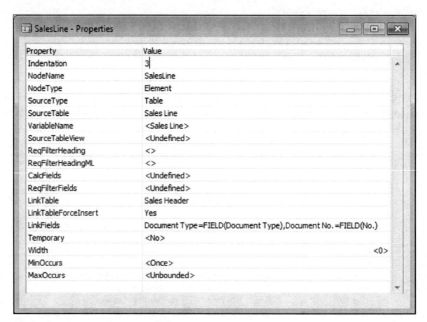

Filling data not included in the XML file

All of this won't be enough. We will need to write some code to fill in some fields that do not appear in the XML document but are needed in Microsoft Dynamics NAV to create a `Sales Order` table.

For example, we will have to fill-in the **Document Type** field in both the **Sales Header** and **Sales Line** tables. We will have to fill-in the **Type** field in the **Sales Line** table. We will also need to find the customer number as only the name of the customer appears in the XML document, but in Dynamics NAV we will have to inform the **Sell-to Customer No.** field as well. Now, declare the global variables as shown in the following screenshot:

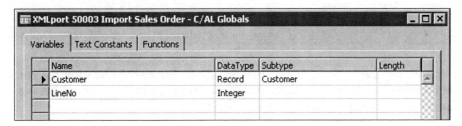

Write the code as stated in the following screenshot:

```
XMLport 50003 Import Sales Order - C/AL Editor
SalesHeader - Import::OnAfterInitRecord()
"Sales Header"."Document Type" := "Sales Header"."Document Type"::Order;
LineNo := 10000;
```

When initializing the Sales Header record, assign Order as the **Document Type** field and assign an initial value of 10000 to the global variable LineNo.

```
XMLport 50003 Import Sales Order - C/AL Editor
Date - Import::OnAfterAssignField()
"Sales Header".VALIDATE("Document Date","Sales Header"."Order Date");
```

Assign the **Document Date** field the same value as the **Order Date** field.

```
XMLport 50003 Import Sales Order - C/AL Editor
CustomerName - Import::OnAfterAssignField()
Customer.SETRANGE(Name,"Sales Header"."Sell-to Customer Name");
IF Customer.FINDFIRST THEN
  "Sales Header".VALIDATE("Sell-to Customer No.",Customer."No.");
```

Find the customer number by setting a filter on its **Name** field and assign it to the **Sell-to Customer No.** field, as shown in the following screenshot:

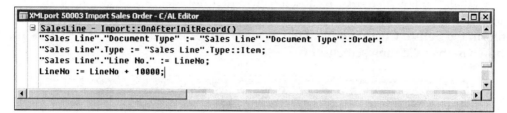

When initializing the `Sales Line` record, assign `Order` as the **Document Type** field, `Item` as the **Type** field, and the value of global variable **LineNo** as the **Line No** field. Then increment variable `LineNo` to be used in the next line.

Save and compile the XMLport with the number `50003` and the name `Import Sales Order`.

Run the XMLport and take a look at the `Sales Order` that has been created:

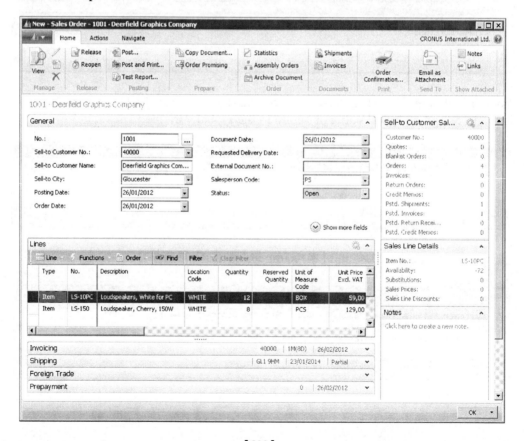

Validation order may change our data

Everything seems to be fine, except the order and document dates, which were set to 18/01/12 in the XML document but have the value 26/01/2012 in the **Sales Order** table.

To find out what happened, you can run the import codeunit for **XMLport 50003 Import Sales Order** again, with the debugger option turned on. If you follow the code in the debug mode, you will see that the order and document dates are first set to 18/01/2012, but, when the OnInsert trigger for the **Sales Header** table is run, they are set to the date, Workdate, which in the example is **26/01/2012**.

We will have to change something in our XMLport to prevent this behavior. What we will do is save the **Order Date** field in a global variable and validate it against the table field after the OnInsert trigger is run.

Create a global variable named **OrderDate** as the **Date** field. Modify the code in the XMLport to insert the highlighted code lines in the Date - Import::OnAfterAssignField() trigger.

```
XMLport 50003 Import Sales Order - C/AL Editor                    _ □ ×
 ⊟ Date - Import::OnAfterAssignField()
    "Sales Header".VALIDATE("Document Date","Sales Header"."Order Date");
    OrderDate := "Sales Header"."Order Date";
```

Also add the highlighted code line in the SalesLine - Import::OnAfterInitRecord() trigger.

```
XMLport 50003 Import Sales Order - C/AL Editor                    _ □ ×
 ⊟ SalesLine - Import::OnAfterInitRecord()
    "Sales Header".VALIDATE("Order Date",OrderDate);
    "Sales Header".VALIDATE("Document Date",OrderDate);
    "Sales Header".VALIDATE("Posting Date",OrderDate);
    "Sales Header".MODIFY(TRUE);

    "Sales Line"."Document Type" := "Sales Line"."Document Type"::Order;
    "Sales Line".Type := "Sales Line".Type::Item;
    "Sales Line"."Line No." := LineNo;
    LineNo := LineNo + 10000;
```

When the **Date** tag is assigned to the **Order Date** field, we can also assign it to a variable called OrderDate.

When the sales line record is being initialized (it means the **OnInsert** trigger for table **Sales Header** has already been run), we once again assign the saved date to the **Order Date**, **Document Date**, and **Posting Date** fields and we modify the **Sales Header** record.

Back in Microsoft Dynamics NAV, if we take a look at the **Sales Order** table that has been created, we will see that, finally, all data is correct.

Writing your own tools

The tools provided by Microsoft Dynamics NAV to import data only allow you to import data in a very specific Microsoft Office Excel format, in an XML format, or in plain text.

What if we have the data in a completely different format? In that case, you probably have two options:

- Manually manipulate the document you may have, to give it the format expected. This may be a good option for a one-time import process. Manual manipulation of data and formats may lead to errors, but if you just have to do it once, do it carefully, take your time, and check everything afterwards. The time consumed in doing all this work will probably not be as much as developing a tool to import the data, so yes, it is probably a good option.

- Write your own tool to import data. Make your tool meet the exact format as it appears in the original document, so no manual manipulation of data is needed.

 You can use a **codeunit**, a report, or even a page to write your own code. You will find several examples in the Dynamics NAV code on how to read from files or how to use the Excel Buffer table to read from an Excel file. Use variables of type record for as many tables as you have to import data to.

We will not be giving any examples on how to develop a tool to import data as it is not within the scope of this book. We just wanted to point out that this is always an option, although if possible, it is better to use the tools provided by Dynamics NAV. That will probably save you a lot of time.

Converting data from the old system to suit Dynamics NAV's needs

The company's old system will probably have a very different data structure. A conversion process must be done in the meantime. In this chapter we'll explain a few tips to convert data to meet Dynamics NAV's needs.

In most of the Dynamics NAV tables, the primary key uses a code field type. For example, all master and document tables do. You can write either numbers or characters in a code field. If a code contains only numbers, people expect the data to be ordered by number. But Dynamics NAV does not act this way. A code is always sorted by character, even if it only contains numbers. This may confuse the user, so using fixed-length number codes is recommended. Let's see this with an example:

Number Sort	Dynamics NAV Sort	Fixed length sort
1	1	01
2	10	02
3	2	03
10	3	10

As you can see, if you use fixed length codes, the way these codes are sorted in Dynamics NAV is the same as the number sort. Therefore, we recommend that you identify those codes in the old system data and convert them before importing the data into Dynamics NAV.

In Dynamics NAV, posting groups are used in master tables (customers, vendors, items, banks, fixed assets, and other such master tables) to identify which accounts must be used while posting entries related to them. This information may not be available in the old system or may need to be transformed. For instance, the company could use a system that used one single account for each customer. In Dynamics NAV, just a few accounts are necessary, so you may have to figure out which posting group fits all master data the best.

You also need to know what fields are mandatory for each master table in order to use its registers. For instance, a customer needs to have the **Customer Posting Group** field filled in order to create a new order; items need the **Base Unit of Measure** field. You may not find this information in the old system, but you need to define how to fill those fields during the migration process.

In general, find all Dynamics NAV required fields and also the fields required by the company's business logic. Determine how they are going to be filled, and fill them during the migration process.

Master data

Master data can be defined as information key to the operation of a business that is often nontransactional but, supports transactional processes and operations.

Customers are a good example of master data. Data about customers (their names, addresses, phone numbers, and so on) is not transactional data but will support a transactional operation, for example, a sales order for a customer.

Microsoft Dynamics NAV has several master data tables, namely, **Customer**, **Vendor**, **Item**, **Contact**, **Resource**, **Fixed Asset**, and so on. Each master data table is the primary table in an application area. The Customer table is the main table in the sales application area, while the **Vendor** table is the main table in the **Purchases** application area.

Secondary tables, such as Sales Prices, also support transactions just as master tables do. You will also need to take secondary tables into account while migrating master data.

Master and secondary tables that will be used in Microsoft Dynamics NAV have to be identified and a migration plan has to be defined in order to get all this information into the system.

The migration plan for master data tables will include:

- Table name and number
- List of fields that will be migrated and their possible values (if applicable)
- The format in which data will be presented
- The possible requirement of data manipulation before importing it to Dynamics NAV
- The tool that will be used to import the data
- Date on which a migration test will be done
- The go-live migration date
- Person responsible for providing the data
- Person responsible for importing the data into Microsoft Dynamics NAV
- Person responsible for testing and validating the migrated data

To import master data into Microsoft Dynamics NAV, all concepts introduced in the *Converting Data from the old system to suit Dynamics NAV's needs* section will have to be taken into account. Use the tool that best meets your requirements for importing master data into the Dynamics NAV database.

Open entries

Open entries are transactions that haven't reached their final status yet, and are not included in the *Open documents* section. You can only post open entries when the corresponding master data is already imported. In a common scenario, the open entries include:

- **Customer entries**: It means all the money each customer owes on the day of the migration
- **Vendor entries**: It means all the money the company owes to each of their vendors on the day of the migration
- **Bank entries**: It means the money the company has in each bank account
- **Item entries**: It means the stock the company has in each location on the day of the migration
- **Accounting Balances**: It means the balance that each account has on the day of the migration

In a more advanced scenario, this may also include:

- **Fixed asset entries**: It means all the company's assets with their initial cost and the amount depreciated, as on the day of the migration.

All these entries must be posted through their corresponding journal and must use a specific posting date. The posting date must be at least one day prior to the migration date. For instance, if you choose to go live on April 1, you should use March 31 as the posting date for all open entries. The easiest way to migrate open entries is to use the Configuration Worksheet described earlier in this chapter.

Customer entries

Customer entries are all the money that each customer owes on the day of the migration. We need to create at least one customer entry to summarize all of the money that the customer owes. If the company wants to control due dates from Dynamics NAV for the open entries, we need to create at least one summarized entry for each due date, or we can create one entry for each pending invoice.

The minimum information needed is as follows:

- **Posting date**: Use one day before migration day for all the entries.
- **Account type**: Use the **Customer** option for all the entries.
- **Account number**: Use the customer code given to the customer.
- **Document number**: You can use the invoice number extracted from the old system, or you can give it a document number such as OPENING.
- **Description**: Give the entry a description. You can use the invoice description extracted from the old system, or you can give a description such as Opening Entries to all the entries.
- **Currency**: Leave it blank if the amounts are in local currency. Write the currency code otherwise. Keep in mind that if a currency code is filled, amounts must be in that currency.
- **Amount**: It's the money the customer owes. Write a negative amount if it's the company which owes money to the customer, either because of credit memos or advance payments.

Other information that can be provided are as follows:

- **Document date**: In case you are creating one entry for each pending invoice, the document date corresponds to the date of the original invoice
- **Due date**: In case you are creating one entry for each pending invoice, the due date corresponds to the date when the customer has to pay their debt
- **Payment method**: In case you are creating one entry for each pending invoice, the payment method corresponds to how the debt will be paid

Actually, you can provide information for any field included in the **Gen. Journal Line** table. But for migration purposes, the previously listed fields are enough.

Let's see, with an example, how to migrate customer entries. We'll just take the minimum information needed. The following steps are involved while migrating a customer entry:

1. Provide an Excel template; we'll use the RapidStart Services. The data has to be imported into the General Journal, to create customer entries when posted.
2. Create an Excel template for the table **81** and include the fields **Account Type, Account No. , Posting Date, Document No., Description, Currency Code**, and **Amount**. Refer to the *Create the migration structure* section in this chapter for more information on this step.

3. Ask someone in the company to fill in the template, extracting data from the old system using the extraction tools available. You are a Dynamics NAV expert, and you may not know how data is stored in the old system, so don't try to do it yourself.

> Remember that your job is to import data into Dynamics NAV the way Dynamics NAV expects it. It is the company's responsibility to assure that data is consistent and of good quality.
>
> As a Dynamics NAV expert, you will be responsible for filling in the fields corresponding to the primary key of the table. In this case, these would be the **Journal Template Name**, **Journal Batch Name**, and **Line No.** fields.

The final document will look similar to the following screenshot:

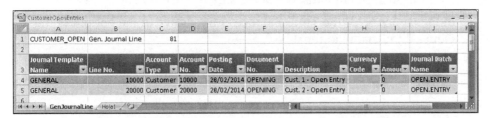

4. Once the template is completely filled, it's time to import it to Dynamics NAV and apply it. Refer to the *Migrate your data* section in this chapter for more information on this step.

5. Open the General Journal. The data is almost ready to be posted. Once posted, Dynamics NAV won't allow you to delete or modify the created entries, so take your time before posting. Check, check, and check your work. Once you are done, check it again. Also ask the user who provided you the information to check it. Use this checklist:

Question	Answer
Does the Total Balance shown in the Journal correspond with all the money customers owe?	
Is the Posting Date set to one day before go-live?	
Does each Customer owe the Amount shown in its Journal line?	

Do not check it with the template you just imported; you will easily get a positive answer. Instead, ask someone in the company to check it with their old system. If you added extra fields to the template, add at least one question for each new field.

Once the lines are posted, new customer ledger entries will be created. G/L entries will also be created. When a new **Gen. Journal Line** table is created, Dynamics NAV copies the posting group from the customer card to the **Gen. Journal Line** table. The receivables account found in each posting group is used to determine which account must be used to post the amount each customer owes. Now, add another question to your checklist.

Question	Answer
Group all the lines by posting group. Get the receivables account for each posting group. Will each account receive the expected amount?	

Since G/L entries will be created, the accounting rules must be followed. One rule says that any transaction must be balanced. The sum of the debit amounts in each line must equal the sum of the credit amounts.

In Dynamics NAV the **Total Balance** entry shown at the bottom of the **General Journal** field must be 0.

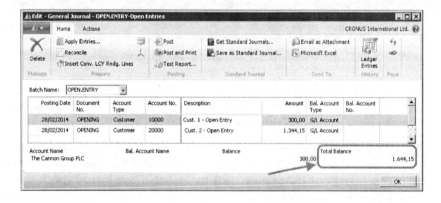

6. In our example, the total available balance is **1.644,15**. We need to perform an extra step to make it 0 and balance the whole transaction. There are a few options we can use to accomplish this. Let us explain two of those options which we are aware of:

   ° Fill in the **Bal. Account Type** field with **G/L Account**. Also fill in the **Bal. Account No.** field with the receivables account on the customer posting group assigned to each customer. In the example, both customers have the domestic customer posting group. The receivables account for them is 2310. If you try to use the 2310 account in the **Bal. Account No.** field you will get the following error:

Direct Posting must be equal to 'Yes' in G/L Account: No.=2310. Current value is 'No'.

This is because Dynamics NAV has a mechanism to prevent accounts included in any posting group from receiving entries directly. You will have to skip this control in order to post the customer open entries. Go to the account card and uncheck the **Direct Posting** field. Don't forget to check it again when the migration process is over!

Your journal lines will now look like those in the following screenshot, and the transaction will be balanced and ready to post.

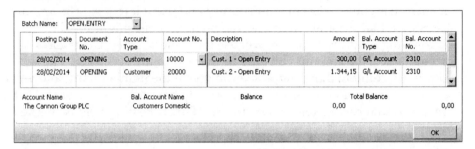

Of course, these two new fields could be added to the migration template to fill them at the outset.

Let's see the general ledger entries that have been created after the posting process:

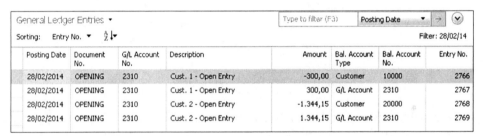

As you can see, the same account has been used. The balance of the account is **0,00** , even if it has four entries. If you run a balance report, you will see that no amount is shown in the **Accounts Receivable** line. It feels weird, doesn't it? Don't worry, this will be solved once the balance open entries are imported.

 In the company CRONUS International Ltd., open entries are posted balancing the transactions this way.

- ° Some countries include a temporary account in their chart of accounts to post transactions when the balance account is unknown at the moment of posting. The balance posted in that account can only be there for a short period of time and when known, must be transferred to the right balance account.

In the Spanish chart of accounts, for instance, we can find the `555` group, named `Movements pending application`. Ask the company accountant if such an account exists in your country and use it if it does. The amount posted on that account will be cleared later on while migrating the accounting balances. Since we will use the same posting date regarding accountancy, the amount will only be there for one day. Create a new posting account in that group. You can give it the number `5551`, and you can name it `Customer - Opening entries`. Then write `Balance Sheet` in the **Income/Balance** field and ensure that the **Direct Posting** field is checked.

Now, go back to the **General Journal** page and manually insert a new line with the following information:

Field	Value
Posting date	March 31
Document number	OPENING
Account type	G/L account
Account number.	5551
Amount	-Total balance

Note that, after introducing this new line, the transaction becomes balanced, as shown in the following screenshot. Now it can be posted.

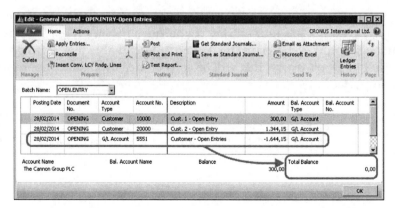

We like this way of balancing opening transactions because it follows accountancy rules. The accountant in the company will easily understand what we are doing. Plus, after the transaction is posted, if you run a balance report, the posted amount will be shown in the accounts receivable line. This looks much better.

7. We are done! You can repeat this process as many times as you want.

Vendor entries

Vendor entries are pretty much the same as customer entries. Just follow the steps described in the previous section. There are a few differences explained as follows:

- When you fill in the data migration template, account type must have the vendor value.
- You have to reverse the sign of the amounts.
- The balancing account will be found in the **Payables Account** field in the **Vendor Posting Group** table.
- If you choose to use a temporary account to balance the transaction, create a new posting account. In the Spanish chart of accounts, you would create the 5552 account. Give it a description such as Vendor - Opening entries.

Bank entries

Bank entries are pretty much the same as customer entries. Just follow the steps described in the previous section. The few differences are explained as follows:

- When you fill in the data migration template, account type must have the bank account value.
- The balancing account will be found in the **G/L Bank Account No.** field in the **Bank Account Posting Group** table.
- If you choose to use a temporary account to balance the transaction, create a new posting account. In the Spanish chart of accounts, you would create the 5553 account. Give it a description such as Bank - Opening entries.

Item entries

Item entries are a bit different from the entries described so far. First of all, another journal must be used, the item journal. Also, you can choose whether the posting of items entries creates general ledger entries or not.

The data migration tool has limitations here, so follow the recommendations to work around them.

The minimum information needed is:

- **Posting date**: Use 1 day before migration day for all the entries
- **Entry type**: Use **Positive Adjmt.** for all the entries
- **Document number**: You can use a generic document number, such as OPENING
- **Item number**: Use the item code given to the item
- **Location code**: Leave it blank if the company is not using locations; otherwise, write the location code
- **Quantity**: Fill in the quantity in terms of the base unit of measurement of the item
- **Unit cost**: Fill in the unit cost in the base unit of measurement of the item

Note that the **Item Journal Line** table contains a field called **Unit of Measure Code**. So, you could use a different unit of measurement and therefore quantity and unit cost will refer to the new unit. When you import data using RapidStart Services, the OnValidate trigger of each field is run. By default, the fields are validated in the same order that they are declared in the table.

The **Unit Cost** field has the field number 17, whereas the **Unit of Measure Code** field has the field number, **5407**. The **Unit Cost** field will be validated before the **Unit of Measure Code** field. If you fill in the **Unit of Measure Code** field in the template, code will be run. In this particular case, unit cost will be recalculated and you will not get the unit cost you filled in the template.

To avoid this situation, you will have to change the default validation order, as explained in the *RapidStart Services* section.

Usually, the automatic cost posting is disabled, since in most scenarios it is not recommended that this functionality should be used.

To check whether the automatic cost posting is disabled, go to **Departments/Financial Management/Inventory/Setup** and open the **Inventory Setup** page. There is a field called **Automatic Cost Posting**. If this field is not checked, the functionality is disabled.

Even if, in your case, the automatic cost posting must be used, disable the functionality while posting the initial item open entries. The cost will be posted in the corresponding account later on, when accounting balances are imported.

Run the data migration tool to import the data into the item journal and post it. The item entries will be created.

Fixed-asset entries

Migrating fixed assets is a bit tricky. Here, we are not talking just about assets that have pending depreciation but all active assets in the company. Two types of entries have to be posted, cost entries and depreciation entries. Plus, there is more than one account involved with a singular asset. You could post fixed asset entries from two different journals:

- The general journal will post fixed asset entries as well as general ledger entries
- The fixed asset journal will only post fixed asset entries, general ledger entries will not be posted

We will now explain how to post fixed asset entries using the fixed asset journal. Accounting entries related to them will be posted while importing the accounting balances later on.

To use the fixed asset journal, you must uncheck the G/L integration for the acquisition cost and the depreciation. Go to **Departments/Financial Management/ Fixed Assets/Setup/Depreciation Book**. Open the **Depreciation Book Card** page and uncheck the fields, as shown in the following screenshot:

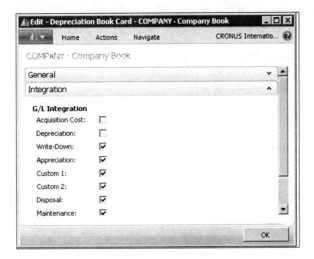

From the fixed asset journal, the minimum information needed for the acquisition cost entries is:

- **FA posting date**: Use 1 day before migration day for all the entries
- **Document number**: You can use a generic document number, such as OPENING
- **FA number**: Use the fixed asset code given to the asset
- **FA posting type**: Use the **Acquisition Cost** value
- **Amount**: Fill in this field with the amount of the original invoice

Import this information using the data migration tool and post it.

From the fixed asset journal, the minimum information needed for the depreciation entries:

- **FA posting date**: Use 1 day before migration day for all the entries
- **Document number**: You can use a generic document number, such as OPENING
- **FA number**: Use the fixed asset code given to the asset
- **FA posting type**: Use the depreciation value
- **Amount**: Fill in this field with the total amount already depreciated for each asset
- **Number of depreciation days**: Count 30 days for each month depreciated

Import this information using the data migration tool, and post it. Do not forget to check the G/L integration again in the depreciation book card. If you have been using a temporary account in the past sections, we recommend that you post general ledger entries for the fixed assets entries that you just posted.

In the Spanish chart of accounts, you would create the 5554 and 5555 accounts. Give them descriptions such as FA - Opening Cost entries and FA - Opening Depreciation entries, respectively.

Summarize all asset acquisition cost entries, grouped by posting group. In the general journal, create one line for each posting group. Use the acquisition cost account found in the FA posting group. Use the FA - Opening Cost entries account to balance the whole transaction.

Do the same with the depreciation entries and use the FA - Opening Depreciation entries account to balance the transaction.

Accounting balances

Accounting balances are the backbone of all open entries. When accounting balances are posted, everything else must match. It is like putting in the last piece of a puzzle. The sad part is that sometimes you find that your last piece does not fit. Don't worry about this right now; at the end of this section, we will explain how to check whether everything is ok and how to solve problems.

While other open entries could be imported and posted in many iterations, accounting balances must be posted all at once because the whole transaction must be self-balanced. Follow the steps described in the *Customer Entries* section of this chapter, but keep in mind these few differences:

- When you fill in the data migration template, **Account Type** must have the G/L account value
- If an account has a debit amount, the amount for that account must be positive
- If an account has a credit amount, the amount for that account must be negative

If you have been using a temporary account in the past sections, all 555 accounts must be 0 after posting the balance. To achieve this, you have to replace some accounts with the temporary accounts. The accounts needed to be replaced are as follows:

- Customer accounts must be replaced by the 5551 account
- Vendor accounts must be replaced by the 5552 account
- Bank accounts must be replaced by the 5553 account
- Fixed asset accounts must be replaced by the 5554 account
- Accumulated depreciation accounts must be replaced by the 5555 account

If no temporary accounts were used, you have to be sure that the amount you are about to post is the same as the sum of all the corresponding entries. You can run the following reconciliation reports:

- **Reconcile Cust**: This report and the **Vend. Accs.** report can be found at **Departments/Financial Management/General Ledger/Reports/ Miscellaneous**
- **Inventory – G/L Reconciliation**: This report can be found at **Departments/ Financial Management/Inventory/Analysis & Reporting**

No standard reconciliation report for bank accounts or fixed assets exists exist, so you will have to check it yourself.

Since accounting must always be balanced, if 555 accounts are not 0 or the reconcile reports show any difference, it will mean that some other account does not have the correct balance. Find this other account and you will find the solution to your problem.

Historical data

When moving from an ERP system to another ERP system such as Microsoft Dynamics NAV, a lot of companies want to import their historical data into the new ERP. For example, companies may want to import all inventory entries made for the previous year for statistical purposes; or, if they start working with Microsoft Dynamics NAV in the middle of a fiscal year, they may want to import all G/L entries made in the old system for the current fiscal year.

In Microsoft Dynamics NAV, this kind of data is stored in ledger entry tables. If you have to conduct a migration of such data, never import it directly into ledger entry tables. Use journals instead, and post the data. That way, Microsoft Dynamics NAV will create the ledger entries for you in a consistent way.

For item ledger entries, for instance, not only is the item ledger entry created, but the value, item register, item application entries and other entries are created as well. If a journal is used, all those entries will consistently be created for us and we won't have to worry about anything.

Several journals exist in Microsoft Dynamics NAV. Choose the right journal for the ledger entries that have to be imported. If item ledger entries have to be imported, use the item journal. If G/L entries have to be imported, use the general journal. Some journals use the same underlying table but have specific values in some fields or use specific fields. General Journals and Recurring Journals use the same **Gen. Journal Line** table, and item journals and revaluation journals use the same **Item Journal Line** table.

If you have to import data into those tables, make sure the right fields are being filled and that the right options are used.

A good idea would be to create some journal lines manually, through the interface provided by Microsoft Dynamics NAV, and compare those lines with the ones created through an import process. That way, we will know whether we are missing something in our import process code and will be able to correct it. Let's see all of this in a step-by-step example.

Item number `70061` has previously been created in the master data migration process. The item will start to be used in Microsoft Dynamics NAV on **01/01/2013**. We want to import all inventory movements done for this item in 2012, which are:

Date	Type	Quantity	Unit of Measure	Unit Cost	Location
05/01/2012	Sale	20	PCS		BLUE
01/02/2012	Purchase	1	BOX	40	BLUE
23/04/2012	Sale	10	PCS		BLUE
13/06/2012	Sale	5	PCS		BLUE
07/09/2012	Sale	15	PCS		BLUE

We will use the item journal:

1. Using RapidStart Services, create a package including table **83**, **Item Journal Line**, and all the fields shown in the following screenshot. Change the **Processing Order** column for the **Unit Cost** field so that it is the last one to be processed.

    We need to change the **Processing Order** column because, after the **Location Code** field is entered, the **Unit Cost** field resets to 0. Why is that happening? Well, Dynamics NAV acts like this in many places. As item unit costs are maintained at location level, when the location is entered, the unit amount is updated. In this case, it resets to 0 because this is a new item that (still) has no associated costs.

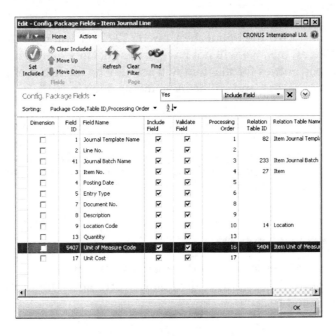

2. Use the **Export to Excel** option to create the Excel template.

3. Fill in the template as shown in the following screenshot:

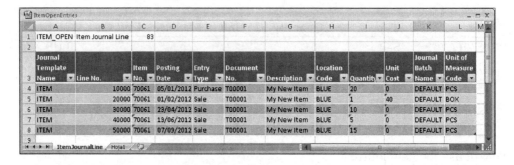

4. Import the Excel template and apply it.

5. Open the item journal and post it.

Now let's check the Item card for item **70061** and create the **Item Ledger Entries**.

It looks relatively good so far, but we are still missing something. The entries have been correctly posted, but the Item Card shows an inventory of -10.

What we have actually missed is creating a first entry for the initial inventory. Do you remember which scenario that was? We wanted to start working with Dynamics NAV on 01/01/2013 and also wanted to import all movements done for the item in 2012.

We should have imported the initial stock on 31/12/2011 and then the movements for year 2012. With all this, we will not have to conduct any extra import to get item open entries as open entries for the item will actually be the result of posting the initial stock on 31/12/2011 and all the movements done in 2012.

> All of this does also apply to any other kind of historical data you may want to import. Import the initial value one day before the beginning of the period for which you are importing historical data. You don't have to import data about open entries now as open entries will already be in the system as the result of the previous actions.

Open documents

The day a company moves to Microsoft Dynamics NAV, they can start creating all kinds of documents in the system for their daily work: sales orders, purchase orders, production orders, and so on.

Some chances exist, that some documents on the old system have not yet been completed, for example, sales orders that have not yet been shipped, purchase orders that have not yet been received, or production orders that have yet not been finished.

What should be done with all these documents?

The first recommendation would be to have the least possible open documents on the old system on the day you start working with Dynamics NAV.

For those documents that could not be finished before migrating to Dynamics NAV, there are a couple of strategies you could follow:

- Finish them in the old system and recreate the movements in Dynamics NAV. This will mean doing double the manual work and some manual checks and asking users to function somewhat differently from how they have been taught to in Dynamics NAV. All of this added to the fact that users may still not be 100 percent comfortable with the new system may lead to some errors. But it may be an option to be taken into account.

  How should users act if this is the chosen option?

  When an open sales order is shipped in the old system, you will have to do a negative adjustment in Dynamics NAV to reflect the inventory decrease. No sales shipment will exist in NAV, though, the person responsible for posting sales invoices will not have the information in NAV for what to invoice. He will have to check the old system as well and do a manual invoice in Dynamics NAV. This will be done using a G/L account and not the item number since we do not want the inventory decrease to be posted again while posting the invoice.

  You could think of similar strategies for all other kinds of documents that still exist on the old system and that will be finished at some point.

- Create them in Dynamics NAV and finish them in the new system. This strategy may also involve some manual work, extra checks, and acting differently for these documents. You could create all open documents in Dynamics NAV using any of the migration tools explained in this chapter, keeping in mind that:
  - If a sales order line, for instance, has already been partially shipped in the old system, only the pending quantity should be transferred to Dynamics NAV.

    ○   In some cases, most of the lines of a document may have been finished, but the document is open because a single line is still pending. In this case, only this line should be transferred to Dynamics NAV.

    ○   For tracing purposes, whenever it is possible, try to create the documents in Dynamics NAV using the same document number they were given on the old system.

- If the documents are created in Dynamics NAV, you will be able to finish them without having to do any extra work or extra checks. You will be able to act normal in Dynamics NAV.

- You will probably have to do an extra check and extra work with all the partially finished documents. Let's imagine you had a partially shipped sales order on the old system. Only the pending lines and quantities have been transferred (and finished) in Dynamics NAV. Imagine the company does not post the invoice for the sales order until the sales order has been completely shipped. The sales order (and sales shipment) in Dynamics NAV will not have complete information about the original sales order. To be able to post the sales invoice in Dynamics NAV, you will have to use the sales shipment existing in NAV, but you will also have to complete the sales invoice with information that is in the old system.

Open documents can be handled, but they imply extra work. That is actually why our recommendation was to try to finish as many documents as possible in the old system before migrating.

You could think of some other strategies, for example, you could have created the open documents in Dynamics NAV in a way in which no extra work is needed in any of the processes to actually finish the document.

In the sales order case, you could have created the pending lines for the pending quantities and also the lines already shipped but not yet invoiced.

For those last lines, you could have used G/L accounts instead of items. After creating them in Dynamics NAV, they should be posted. That way, we have a scenario in which:

- The complete information of the sales order exists in Dynamics NAV

- Posting the already shipped but not yet invoiced lines as G/L entries will not lead to wrong inventory information for the items

- Posting the already shipped but not invoiced lines will create a sales shipment that you will be able to use while doing the sales invoice (although in Dynamics NAV the sales shipment may be given a different document number, from what was given in the old system, which may lead to mistakes or misunderstandings).

Even more elaborate strategies can be used. Think of all possible strategies, analyze them, and determine how much work is needed in the migration process (define the data to be imported, the migration tool to be used, and so on), how much work is needed by the users to finish those documents, and so on. After analyzing all of them, choose the one that best meets your requirements.

Choosing a go-live date

If you ask, what date we should choose to start working with Dynamics NAV, most companies will answer, "January 1", without considering any other option. The reason behind this answer is that, for most companies, January 1 is the beginning of their fiscal year. It has advantages, no doubt, but it also has drawbacks. The year has 364 additional days to work, but limiting yourself this much is not worth the hassle and stress.

In this section, we will see the pros and cons of going live at the beginning of a fiscal year versus going live on any other date. With all this information, you should be able to choose the best date in your case and know the consequences of your choice.

Going live at the beginning of the fiscal year

All companies analyze information at least annually. Among other reasons, because the tax authorities require certain documentation submitted annually as balance sheets. Starting to use Dynamics NAV at beginning of the year has another major advantage; there is no need to do anything special to get annual information. There is no need to seek information in two different systems and add it somewhere, and then to repeat this process every time you need to analyze information.

We are not just talking about accounting. Accounting information is the easiest to be add. That's because accounting is an area where everything is regulated, and so there will not be many differences between the old system and Dynamics NAV. No major problem here. But there are other areas where it may be impossible to obtain information from the old system. We will never have complete information in the first year.

Okay, maybe we messed it up a bit. What do we mean by other areas? Let's see an example. Imagine a company that sells items. In their old system, the company had no way to classify items by category, but in Dynamics NAV, they do. Now they want to analyze sales by item category. As you can imagine, there will be no way to have complete information on an annual basis as the old system did not have this information. Therefore, the only way to get complete information from any area is migrating at the beginning of a fiscal year.

As you can see, the major (and the only) advantage here is having complete information on an annual basis for analytics and statistics purposes.

What cons do we have? Quite a few!

A project is, by definition, a temporary endeavor with a defined beginning and end, undertaken to meet unique goals and objectives. Implementing Dynamics NAV is a project. At the beginning of the project you have some requirements which give you the details of the amount of work needed to accomplish it. Along with the resources available, you can perfectly plan when each task must be done in order to get the entire job done before January 1. However, when it comes to software projects, changes in requirements are on the agenda all the time.

Each project has three main constraints that must be balanced; time, cost, and scope. This is known as the iron triangle.

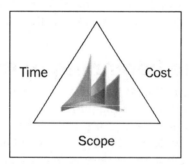

In order to keep the triangle balanced, any change on one of the sides modifies at least one of the other sides. Therefore, any change in the requirements (scope) produces a change in the cost, the time, or in both of them.

If you choose January 1 as the migration day, the time side will be pretty difficult to change. You will have to wait a whole year for it to be January 1 again. Your other option is to increase the cost side. You can put in more resources to help finish the project on time. But this is not an easy solution. Resources are not always available, plus you will have to teach them what the project is all about. Wouldn't it be easier if you could just go-live two weeks later?

More cons are that the month prior to the go-live date is quite busy, both at the implementer's and at the customer's ends. All the training has to be done, all the development has to be tested, and the new requirements usually come at the end! Plus, usually the customer is asked to leave as few things pending as possible, and complete most of the tasks. This again means an extra effort. Besides, December is not the best time of year to ask people for extra effort. It's Christmas, kids are off school, and moms and dads want to be with their children playing with the new toys Santa brought them.

Okay, there are not that many cons on the list. Just two, but they are important enough to consider another date.

Going live in the middle of a fiscal year

Here the pros and cons are just the opposite of those in the case we discussed earlier.

The main advantage is that the starting date can be moved. Don't get us wrong; it does not mean that you can play with the date with no consequences. Your customer will always ask you to be committed with a date. But in case of some change within the iron triangle, you will always have the chance to negotiate a change on the time side to balance the triangle.

It is better to go-live a few days late with guarantees than do it on time if some new feature hasn't been implemented or tested yet.

Choose a date, bearing in mind what is your customer's busiest time of year and try to avoid it. As we mentioned before, the month before the go-live date is a pretty busy month. Actually, the month after it is also a very busy one.

Therefore, the main con is that, in some cases, the company won't have complete information, on an annual basis, during the year they start to work with Dynamics NAV. But don't worry, you also have the option of doing an extra job to mitigate it. You can post historical data, such as accountant entries or item entries, into Dynamics NAV. Read the *Historical data* section in this chapter for more information. If you choose to migrate historical data, the main con of going live in the middle of a fiscal year is gone and only the pros stay.

So, there is no reason not to choose a date different from January 1.

Summary

Several kinds of data may be imported into Microsoft Dynamics NAV. There are different ways to import that data into Microsoft Dynamics NAV and a variety of ways to present that data.

Do you remember anything about statistical classes? Let's remember some basics:

Several x Different x Many x A bunch = Too many options.

That means that migration processes should be carefully designed and planned. Everyone, both at the partner and at the customer ends, should know what will be migrated, how it will be migrated, when it will be migrated, who is responsible for retrieving or filling in the data, how the data has to be presented, and what the result in Microsoft Dynamics NAV will be.

The tools that can be used, the way you can use them, and the kind of data that is commonly migrated has been covered in this chapter. We hope all of this helps you to plan all your migration processes.

In the next chapter we will learn how to upgrade Dynamics NAV from previous versions to Dynamics NAV 2013.

7

Upgrading to Microsoft Dynamics NAV 2013

In previous chapters we have covered the implementation process of Microsoft Dynamics NAV 2013 for new customers—companies that had not used Microsoft Dynamics NAV before.

What about companies already using Microsoft Dynamics NAV that want to upgrade to the latest version?

Upgrading to a different version of Dynamics NAV is not a **Next-Next-Finish** process. It is a whole project that has to be planned and executed carefully. In this chapter we will explain the migration process coming from almost all previous versions of the application. For all of them, we will explain the steps that have to be done and the tools that are out there to help us execute the whole process.

The topics covered in this chapter are as follows:

- An explanation of the upgrading philosophy in Dynamics NAV
- A brief checklist of all steps required to upgrade for all previous versions since Navision Attain 3.60
- An in-detail explanation of all the steps pointed in the checklist
- The tools that must be used in the upgrade process
- The tools that can be used on the upgrade process to make the whole process easier

Upgrading philosophy

We have a customer who is currently working with a previous version of Microsoft Dynamics NAV. They know that a new version of the product is about to come out and they always want to be up to date, so they asked about migrating to the latest version.

We said: "Well, that is something that cannot be done in 5 minutes. Upgrading is a project! Let's take a look at it and we will come back to you with a project proposal and quotation."

We prepared the skeleton of the project, evaluated its implementation of Dynamics NAV to determine the effort required to upgrade to the current version, and presented to him the quotation.

The first thing the customer said after they had the quotation in their hands was: "Have you gone nuts? Do you really need all this time to upgrade my implementation of Microsoft Dynamics NAV? How is that possible? Every once in a while automatic updates are installed in Windows through Windows Update, and many other applications check online for the existence of available updates and install them themselves. Why does Microsoft Dynamics NAV not work that way? Why do we have to pay for this project?"

That is definitely a good point. But Microsoft Dynamics NAV doesn't have automatic updates, and there is a reason for that.

Customization is actually the reason.

Microsoft Dynamics NAV is an application that can be customized. Some companies do customize their implementation of Microsoft Dynamics NAV a lot. Some others, just a little bit.

Microsoft Dynamics NAV could be used with no customization at all—sure, but the truth is that we don't know of any implementation of the application that has zero customizations. At least, the printing of documents such as **Sales Invoices** or **Sales Shipments** have some customizations, but we have not seen any implementation with only those customizations. Customizing Microsoft Dynamics NAV is so easy that usually many customizations are done; there is no need of other applications to edit the application code since Dynamics NAV has its own code editor; no need of full compilations of code projects; no need of deployment of the new solution since modifications can be done on the fly and they get to end users right away, and so on.

They can be minor customizations such as adding an existing field to a page or creating a new field in an existing table. They can be mid-size customizations such as modifying some minor standard behavior. Or they can be major customizations such as developing a whole new functionality or changing the way major standard functionalities behave.

Some applications do have different code layers. The standard application code is in a base code layer and customizations are done in other code layers that are built on top of the base code layer. That way, the base code layer could be updated, for example, and customizations will still apply.

Unfortunately, that is not the case in Dynamics NAV. The layer concept in Dynamics NAV does not exist, although you could think of it as a single code layer on which both the standard application code and the customized code are written. It is not just the customized code that is written in the same layer as the standard application code. The standard application code can actually be modified or even deleted.

When you get a new version of Microsoft Dynamics NAV and a new standard application code file, a merge process has to be done to ensure that customizations done in a specific version of Microsoft Dynamics NAV are carried out into the new version of the application. That process cannot be done automatically (although we will explain in this chapter some tools that will make the process easier). Some steps in the merge process will have to be done manually by a Microsoft Dynamics NAV developer. Some others will have to be done manually by a Microsoft Dynamics NAV implementer.

An upgrade project in Microsoft Dynamics NAV can be an easy task or a large project. It really depends on how customized the Dynamics NAV application is and which previous version of Dynamics NAV you are coming from:

- If you have a Microsoft Dynamics NAV 2009 R2 implementation that has not been modified at all, upgrading to the latest version of the product will probably be an easy task

- If you have a Microsoft Dynamics NAV 2009 R2 implementation that has customizations on, let's say, 30 percent of the application objects and hundreds of new objects, upgrading to the latest version of the product doesn't necessarily have to be an extremely complex project, but what is for sure is that it will require more time and effort

- And if you have a Microsoft Business Solutions–Navision 4.0 SP3 implementation with 30 percent of the application objects modified and hundreds of new objects, upgrading to the latest version of the product will require much more time and effort

Summarizing the processes that have to be completed for an upgrade project are:

1. Compare and merge objects to carry out customizations to the latest version of Dynamics NAV.

2. Create a new database in the latest version of Dynamics NAV.

3. Restore a backup of your old database into the new database.

4. Run processes to upgrade your data.

5. Import the merged objects (new version objects with customizations).

Keep in mind that the processes to upgrade data into Microsoft Dynamics NAV 2013 are intended to upgrade data only from the previous version of Dynamics NAV – Microsoft Dynamics NAV 2009 (including SP1 and R2). If your old implementation of Dynamics NAV is in any earlier version, some extra steps will have to be taken.

Imagine you have a Microsoft Business Solutions–Navision 4.0 SP3 implementation. To upgrade to Microsoft Dynamics NAV 2013, data will have to be upgraded firstly from Version 4.0 SP3 to Version 5.0 SP1, then from Version 5.0 SP1 to Version 2009 R2, and finally from Version 2009 R2 to our final version, 2013.

That means that steps 2, 3, and 4 will have to be done as many times as versions that exist between your old implementation version and the latest version of Microsoft Dynamics NAV.

In the following section, we will do a checklist of detailed steps that have to be taken to upgrade to Microsoft Dynamics NAV 2013 from every version since Navision Attain 3.60. We will do that in the reverse order, though. That is, we will first expose the checklist of actions to upgrade from Microsoft Dynamics NAV 2009 (also SP1 and R2), which is the immediate previous version that will have the least number of steps to upgrade; and then from Microsoft Dynamics 5.0 (also SP1), which will have all steps to upgrade from 2009 plus some extra steps; and so on.

After that, we will explain every single step with all kinds of details.

Upgrading process checklist

Upgrading is supported only from Dynamics NAV 2009, including the original version, the SP1 version, or the R2 version. If your current version is not Dynamics NAV 2009, you have to upgrade to Dynamics NAV 2009 R2 before you can upgrade to Dynamics NAV 2013.

If you are on older versions, the official documentation tells you to follow the Microsoft Dynamics NAV 2009 upgrade guide for details. If you check that guide, it will tell you that if you are coming from versions previous to X, you will have to follow guide Y, and so on. If you follow all the steps detailed on all the guides, it will take forever.

But there is good news. If you are planning to upgrade from previous versions, you can skip some steps, or only do them once. You really don't need a complete upgrade to Microsoft Dynamics NAV 2009. In this section we will see the steps you need to follow to upgrade from Version 3.60 to Version 2013. You can use this section as a checklist for your upgrade process.

The steps that you will have to follow to upgrade from any version to Dynamics NAV 2013 can be spread out into three groups:

- Preparing to upgrade
- Upgrading the application code
- Upgrading the data

The first group will be the same for all versions. The second and third group will be different depending on which version you intend to upgrade to Microsoft Dynamics NAV 2013.

We will first enumerate the steps for the preparing to upgrade group, and then enumerate the steps in the other two groups depending on the version.

Preparing to upgrade

There are two things that have to be done before upgrading to Dynamics NAV 2013, no matter the previous version from which you are upgrading:

1. Migrate to SQL Server database if you are using the Microsoft Dynamics NAV native database.

2. Test the database. If the test fails, follow the workflow for repairing damaged databases.

Upgrading from 2009, 2009 SP1 or 2009 R2

Upgrading to Dynamics NAV 2013 is officially supported only from those versions. In this section we will enumerate the steps that have to be performed to upgrade from those versions.

Upgrading the 2009 application code

The steps that have to be performed to upgrade the application code from Dynamics NAV 2009 to Dynamics NAV 2013 are listed as follows:

1. Get the objects' versions.

2. Convert old objects' version files to Microsoft Dynamics NAV 2013 format.

3. Compare your database objects to the standard objects of your current version to determine the objects that have been customized.

4. Carry out your customizations to the new standard code for the new version of Microsoft Dynamics NAV.

 You can use any generic text-comparing application to do this job. It will be easier, though, if you use an application specifically designed for Microsoft Dynamics NAV, such as **MergeTool**, which will be explained later in this chapter.

5. If you have a Microsoft Dynamics NAV 2009 classic client installation, transform your own forms to pages.

6. If you have a Microsoft Dynamics NAV 2009 classic client installation, carry out your customizations on existing forms and into its corresponding page object.

7. Transform your reports to the new report definition of Microsoft Dynamics NAV 2013.

8. Revise and modify your customized code for better performance in Microsoft Dynamics NAV 2013.

Upgrading the 2009 data

Data and field structure has changed between Microsoft Dynamics NAV 2009 and Microsoft Dynamics NAV 2013. That's why a data upgrade process has to be run. The data upgrade is done in two steps: one still in the old version and the other in the new version.

The data conversion process can be seen in the following figure:

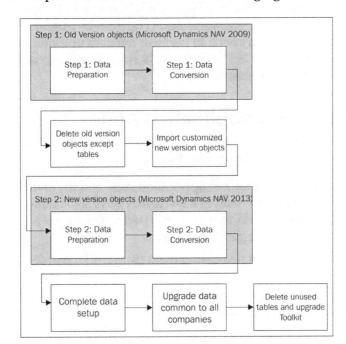

Follow these steps to perform the data conversion process:

1. On your old customized database, import a file called Upgrade Step 1 Objects.

2. Run the data conversion process for the objects of the old version.

3. Create a new Microsoft Dynamics NAV 2013 database.

4. Restore the database that was being upgraded.

5. Import all customized Microsoft Dynamics NAV 2013 objects.

6. Import a file called Upgrade Step 2 objects.

7. Run the data conversion process for the objects of the new version.

8. Delete the Upgrade Toolkit objects.

Upgrading from 5.0 or 5.0 SP1

To upgrade to Microsoft Dynamics NAV 2013 from any Microsoft Dynamics NAV 5.0 version, you will have to upgrade first to Microsoft Dynamics NAV 2009, and then follow the upgrade steps to upgrade from Microsoft Dynamics NAV 2009 to Microsoft Dynamics NAV 2013.

Even if having to upgrade first to NAV 2009, a full upgrade to the intermediate version will not be necessary. For example, you will not need to upgrade your application code to NAV 2009. The application code can be upgraded directly to Dynamics NAV 2013. You don't need to perform the data upgrade process while upgrading from Dynamics 5.0 to Dynamics 2009 since there is no table structure changes between those two versions.

Upgrading the 5.0 application code

The steps that have to be performed to upgrade the application code from Dynamics NAV 5.0 to Dynamics NAV 2013 are listed as follows:

1. Import both your customized application code and the standard application code of your current version in a Dynamics NAV 2009 database. Compile all objects. Use those objects that are converted to Dynamics NAV 2009 format for comparing and merging purposes.

2. Get the objects' version (exporting them from the Dynamics NAV 2009 database).

3. Compare your database objects to the standard objects of your current version to determine the objects that have been customized.

4. Carry out your customizations to the new standard code for the new version of Microsoft Dynamics NAV.

 You can use any generic text-comparing application to do this job. It will be easier, though, if you use an application specifically designed for Microsoft Dynamics NAV, such as MergeTool, which will be explained later in this chapter.

5. Transform your own forms to pages.

6. Carry out your customizations on existing forms to its corresponding page object.

7. Transform your reports to the new report definition of Microsoft Dynamics NAV 2013.

8. Revise and modify your customized code for better performance in Microsoft Dynamics NAV 2013.

Upgrading the 5.0 data

Data and field structure has changed between Dynamics NAV 5.0 and Dynamics NAV 2013. That's why a data upgrade process has to be run. However, data and field structure did not change at all between Dynamics NAV 5.0 and NAV 2009. So the data upgrade tools available for NAV 2009 do also apply to NAV 5.0. The only extra thing you will have to do is to convert your database to Dynamics NAV 2009.

The data conversion process can be seen in the following figure:

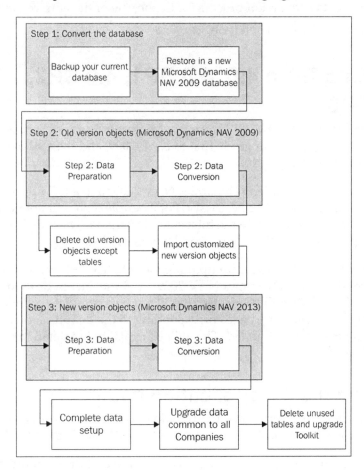

The steps required to upgrade the data are listed as follows:

1. Create a new Microsoft Dynamics NAV 2009 database.

2. Restore your Microsoft Dynamics NAV 5.0 database in the new 2009 database.

3. Import a file called `Upgrade Step 1 Objects`.

4. Run the data conversion process for the objects of the old version.

5. Create a new Microsoft Dynamics NAV 2013 database.

6. Restore the database that was being upgraded.

7. Import all customized Microsoft Dynamics NAV 2013 objects.

8. Import a file called `Upgrade Step 2 objects`.

9. Run the data conversion process for the objects of the new version.

10. Delete the Upgrade Toolkit objects.

Upgrading from 4.0, 4.0 SP1, 4.0 SP2, or 4.0 SP3

To upgrade to Dynamics NAV 2013 from any Microsoft Business Solutions–Navision 4.0 version, you will have to upgrade first to NAV 2009, and then follow the steps to upgrade to Dynamics NAV 2013.

Even when having to upgrade to Dynamics NAV 2009 first, a full upgrade to the intermediate version will not be necessary. For example, you will not need to upgrade your application code to the intermediate version. The application code can be upgraded directly to Microsoft Dynamics NAV 2013.

You will, however, need to do a data upgrade though, from Microsoft Business Solutions–Navision 4.0 to Dynamics NAV 2009. To do so, an application code upgrade from 4.0 to 2009 will be needed. It will not be a complete code upgrade, however. Only the application code corresponding to the definition of all tables' structures will have to be upgraded. This will be explained in detail in the *Upgrade steps in detail* section.

Upgrading the 4.0 application code

The steps that have to be performed to upgrade the application code from Microsoft Business Solutions–Navision 4.0 to Dynamics NAV 2013 are listed as follows:

1. Import both your customized application code and the standard application code of your current version in a Microsoft Dynamics NAV 2009 database. Compile all objects. Use those objects that are converted to Microsoft Dynamics NAV 2009 format for comparing and merging purposes.

2. Get the objects' version (exporting them from the Microsoft Dynamics NAV 2009 database).

3. Compare your database objects to the standard objects of your current version to determine the objects that have been customized.

4. Carry out your customizations to the new standard code for the new version of Microsoft Dynamics NAV.

 You can use any generic text-comparing application to do this job. It will be easier, though, if you use an application specifically designed for Microsoft Dynamics NAV, such as MergeTool, which will be explained later in this chapter.

5. Transform your own forms to pages.

6. Carry out your customizations on existing forms to its corresponding page object.

7. Transform your reports to the new report definition of Microsoft Dynamics NAV 2013.

8. Revise and modify your customized code for better performance in Microsoft Dynamics NAV 2013.

9. Compare your database table objects to the standard table objects of your current version to determine the changes in data structure.

10. Carry out your customizations to the table object's data structure. This will be similar to the standard table object's data structure of Microsoft Dynamics NAV 2009.

Upgrading the 4.0 data

Data and field structure has changed between Microsoft Business Solutions–Navision 4.0 and Microsoft Dynamics NAV 2013. That's why a data upgrade process has to be run. However, the data upgrade tool available is only to upgrade from NAV 2009 to NAV 2013. Data and field structure did also change between Microsoft Business Solutions–Navision 4.0 and Microsoft Dynamics NAV 2009. We will first have to upgrade our data to a Dynamics NAV 2009 data and field structure, and then we will be able to finish the upgrade process to Microsoft Dynamics NAV 2013.

The data upgrade from NAV 4.0 to NAV 2009 is very similar to the one described for NAV 2009 to NAV 2013. The steps are exactly the same, but the *upgrade* objects will be different.

The data conversion process can be seen in the following figure:

The steps required to upgrade the data are listed as follows:

1. On your old customized database, import a file called Upgrade Step 1 objects from Upgrade Toolkit found in the Microsoft Dynamics NAV 2009 installation media.

2. Run the data conversion process for the objects of the old version (Microsoft Business Solutions–Navision 4.0).

3. Create a new Microsoft Dynamics NAV 2009 database.

4. Restore the database that was being upgraded.

5. Import customized Microsoft Dynamics NAV 2009 table objects.

6. Import a file called Upgrade Step 2 objects from Upgrade Toolkit found in the Microsoft Dynamics NAV 2009 installation media.

7. Run the data conversion process for the objects of the new version (Microsoft Dynamics NAV 2009).

8. Delete the Upgrade Toolkit objects.

At this point, a data upgrade from Microsoft Business Solutions–Navision 4.0 to Microsoft Dynamics NAV 2009 has been completed. From now on, a data upgrade to Microsoft Dynamics NAV 2013 will have to be done.

1. In the Microsoft Dynamics NAV 2009 database, import a file called Upgrade Step 1 objects.

2. Run the data conversion process for the objects of the old version (Microsoft Dynamics NAV 2009).

3. Create a new Microsoft Dynamics NAV 2013 database.

4. Restore the database that was being upgraded.

5. Import all customized Microsoft Dynamics NAV 2013 objects.

6. Import a file called `Upgrade Step 2 objects`.

7. Run the data conversion process for the objects of the new version (Microsoft Dynamics NAV 2013).

8. Delete the Upgrade Toolkit objects.

Upgrading from 3.60 or 3.70

To upgrade to Microsoft Dynamics NAV 2013 from any Navision Attain 3.*xx* version, you will have to upgrade first to Microsoft Dynamics NAV 2009 and then follow the upgrade steps to upgrade to Microsoft Dynamics NAV 2013.

Even when having to upgrade to Dynamics NAV 2009 first, a full upgrade to the intermediate versions will not be necessary. For example, you will not need to upgrade your application code to the intermediate versions. The application code can be upgraded directly to Microsoft Dynamics NAV 2013.

You will, however, need to do a data upgrade though, from Navision Attain 3.*xx* to Microsoft Dynamics NAV 2009. To do so, an application code upgrade from 3.*xx* to 2009 will be needed. It will not be a complete code upgrade, however. Only the application code corresponding to the definition of all tables' structures will have to be upgraded. This will be explained in detail in the *Upgrade steps in detail* section.

Upgrading the 3.60 or 3.70 application code

The steps that have to be performed to upgrade the application code from Navision Attain 3.60 or 3.70 to Dynamics NAV 2013 are listed as follows:

1. Import both your customized application code and the standard application code of your current version in a Microsoft Dynamics NAV 2009 database. Compile all objects. Use those objects that are converted to Microsoft Dynamics NAV 2009 format for comparing and merging purposes.

2. Get the object's version (exporting them from the Microsoft Dynamics NAV 2009 database).

3. Compare your database objects to the standard objects of your current version to determine the objects that have been customized.

4. Carry out your customizations to the new standard code for the new version of Microsoft Dynamics NAV.

 You can use any generic text-comparing application to do this job. It will be easier, though, if you use an application specifically designed for Microsoft Dynamics NAV, such as MergeTool, which will be explained later in this chapter.

5. Transform your own forms to pages.

6. Carry out your customizations on existing forms to its corresponding page objects.

7. Revise and modify your customized code for better performance in Microsoft Dynamics NAV 2013.

8. Compare your database table objects to the standard table objects of your current version to determine the changes in data structure.

9. Carry out your customizations in table objects data structure to the standard table object data structure of Microsoft Dynamics NAV 2009.

Upgrading the 3.60 or 3.70 data

Data and field structure has changed between Navision Attain 3.*xx* and Microsoft Dynamics NAV 2013. That's why a data upgrade process has to be run. However, the data upgrade tool available is only to upgrade from NAV 2009 to NAV 2013. Data and field structure did also change between Navision Attain 3.*xx* and Microsoft Dynamics NAV 2009. We will first have to upgrade our data to a Microsoft Dynamics NAV 2009 data and field structure, and then we will be able to finish the upgrade process to Microsoft Dynamics NAV 2013.

The data upgrade from NAV 3.*xx* to NAV 2009 is very similar to the one described for NAV 2009 to NAV 2013. The steps are exactly the same, but the upgrade objects will be different.

The data conversion process can be seen in the following figure:

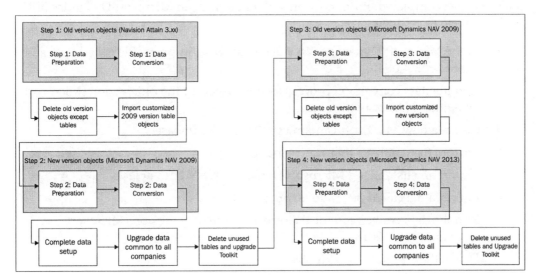

The steps required to upgrade the data are listed as follows:

1. On your old customized database, import a file called `Upgrade Step 1 objects` from Upgrade Toolkit found in the Microsoft Dynamics NAV 2009 installation media.

2. Run the data conversion process for the objects of the old version (Navision Attain 3.*xx*).

3. Create a new Microsoft Dynamics NAV 2009 database.

4. Restore the database that was being upgraded.

5. Import customized Microsoft Dynamics NAV 2009 table objects.

6. Import a file called `Upgrade Step 2 objects` from Upgrade Toolkit found in the Microsoft Dynamics NAV 2009 installation media.

7. Run the data conversion process for the objects of the new version (Microsoft Dynamics NAV 2009).

8. Delete the Upgrade Toolkit objects.

At this point, a data upgrade from Navision Attain 3.xx to Microsoft Dynamics NAV 2009 has been completed. From now on, a data upgrade to Microsoft Dynamics NAV 2013 will have to be done.

1. In the Microsoft Dynamics NAV 2009 database, import a file called Upgrade Step 1 Objects.

2. Run the data conversion process for the objects of the old version (Microsoft Dynamics NAV 2009).

3. Create a new Microsoft Dynamics NAV 2013 database.

4. Restore the database that was being upgraded.

5. Import all customized Microsoft Dynamics NAV 2013 objects.

6. Import a file called Upgrade Step 2 objects.

7. Run the data conversion for the objects of the new version (Microsoft Dynamics NAV 2013).

8. Delete the Upgrade Toolkit objects.

Upgrading steps in detail

In the preceding sections we have seen all the steps that you have to do in order to upgrade from older versions of Dynamics NAV to Dynamics NAV 2013. In this section we will explain all those steps in detail.

Preparing to upgrade

No matter what your current version of Microsoft Dynamics NAV is, before you can upgrade to Microsoft Dynamics NAV 2013, a migration to SQL Server is needed if you are using a native database, because it is no longer available.

A test of the database is also needed before starting the upgrade process. In this section we will explain how to perform those two processes.

Migrating to SQL Server

Microsoft SQL Server (on its 64-bit version) is the only database supported in Microsoft Dynamics NAV 2013. The native database is gone. If you are using a native database in previous versions of Microsoft Dynamics NAV, you should upgrade to SQL before you start the upgrade process to Microsoft Dynamics NAV 2013.

The steps to upgrade to SQL Server will not be explained in this book. You can use the official Microsoft Dynamics NAV documentation to do that.

Testing the database

This is a required step to upgrade to Microsoft Dynamics NAV 2013. The steps to test the database are as follows:

1. Open your current database in the classic client (testing the database can be done in any version of Microsoft Dynamics NAV; if you are upgrading to Microsoft Dynamics NAV 2013 from any version previous to Microsoft Dynamics NAV 2009, you can do the test of the database in your current version).
2. Go to **File | Database | Test**.
3. The **Test Database** form will open.
4. Click on the **Options** tab.
5. Select the file's output and enter or browse to a path and filename.
6. Click on the **General** tab.
7. Choose **Normal** to test everything except field relationships between tables.
8. If the test fails, follow the workflow for repairing damaged databases.
9. Open the **Test Database** form again (**File | Database | Test**).
10. Choose **Custom** and then check **Test field relationships between tables** to test field relationships between tables.

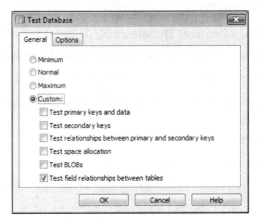

This will determine if there is any data inconsistency on your database. You should determine whether errors detected on this test will affect the upgrade process.

11. Compile all the objects in the database. Repair any objects that are not compiling correctly.

Upgrading the application code

Customers will typically want all customizations that have been implemented in their old Microsoft Dynamics NAV databases to be implemented in their new Microsoft Dynamics NAV 2013 database.

To achieve this goal, a sequence of development actions intended to fully transfer the functionality of a customer's solution to the latest version of Microsoft Dynamics NAV have to be performed.

Getting object versions

When working with code upgrade, it is important to analyze and process the changes by comparing and evaluating three separate versions of the Microsoft Dynamics NAV database:

- **The old base version**: This is a standard version of the current version of the Dynamics NAV database

- **The old custom version**: This is the old base's database plus the customer's changes and add-on solutions

- **The new base version**: This is a standard version of the Microsoft Dynamics NAV 2013 database

Follow these steps to obtain the three .txt files:

1. Open a standard Microsoft Dynamics NAV database of your current version.
2. Navigate to **Tools | Object Designer** (or press *Ctrl + F12*).
3. Click on **All** to see the list of all the application objects.
4. Select all objects (clicking on the upper-left corner of the grid will select all objects).
5. Go to **File | Export**.
6. Select the destination folder and give the file the name OldBase.txt.
7. Open your current customized Microsoft Dynamics NAV database.
8. Navigate to **Tools | Object Designer** (or press *Ctrl + F12*).
9. Click on **All** to see the list of all the application objects
10. Select all objects (clicking on the upper-left corner of the grid will select all objects).
11. Click on **File | Export**.
12. Select the destination folder and give the file the name OldCustom.txt.

13. Open a standard Microsoft Dynamics NAV 2013 database.

14. Navigate to **Tools | Object Designer** (or press *Ctrl + F12*).

15. Click on **All** to see the list of all the application objects.

16. Select all objects (clicking on the upper-left corner of the grid will select all objects).

17. Go to **File | Export**.

18. Select the destination folder and give the file the name `NewBase.txt`.

At this point, you should have three `.txt` files named `OldBase.txt`, `OldCustom.txt`, and `NewBase.txt`.

Converting objects to the Dynamics NAV 2013 format

There is a tool called **TextFormatUpgrade2013** that is explained later in this chapter, in the *Upgrading tools* section. Right after the `OldBase.txt` and `OldCustom.txt` files are obtained, they have to be converted to the format used in Microsoft Dynamics NAV 2013.

This will make comparisons to the new standard application code (the `NewBase.txt` file) much easier.

New custom objects that do not exist in the standard application but only on the customized application (custom objects in the range of 50000 to 99999 or in add-on ranges), cannot be directly imported in Microsoft Dynamics NAV 2013 in a `.fob` file (`.fob` is the extension of Dynamics NAV object files). Doing so will cause the application to crash as soon as the objects are accessed. For those objects, you have to use the TextFormatUpgrade2013 tool to do the appropriate formatting change, import them in Microsoft Dynamics NAV 2013 in text format, and compile the objects in Microsoft Dynamics NAV 2013.

Refer to the *Upgrading tools* section to know what exactly the tool does and how to use it.

Carrying out customizations to the new version

As explained in the *Upgrading philosophy* section, carrying out customizations to the new version is actually the main point of the whole upgrade process.

There are a couple of ways to achieve this:

- Rewriting your customizations from scratch in Microsoft Dynamics NAV 2013
- Using any merge tool to follow a compare-and-merge process to finally get the customized code into Microsoft Dynamics NAV 2013

As the implementer, feel free to use the approach that best suits your needs. You would probably go for the rewriting method when just a few customizations exist, and use the compare-and-merge one when the old database has been customized a lot.

Where to put the line between a few and a lot? We really don't know.

To rewrite your customizations, you will probably want to use a text compare tool to compare your old base application code to your new base application code. That way, you will understand what the differences are and you will be able to write them again on a Microsoft Dynamics NAV 2013 database.

To do a compare-and-merge process, you will need a tool that allows you to compare three text files at the same time (`OldBase.txt`, `OldCustom.txt`, and `NewBase.txt`) and automatically creates the new application code (`NewCustom.txt`).

In the *Upgrading tools* section, we will talk about comparing the text tools and about MergeTool, which can be used for the purpose of the current section. Refer to them to get a detailed view of how to use them to carry out customizations to a new database.

Transforming forms to pages

The object type "form" is no longer available in Microsoft Dynamics NAV 2013. The process of transforming forms to pages had to be done when upgrading to Microsoft Dynamics NAV 2009 with an RTC installation.

If you intend to upgrade to Microsoft Dynamics NAV 2013 from Microsoft Dynamics NAV 2009 with an RTC installation, just skip this section. It's not for you.

For those using a classic installation in any previous version of Microsoft Dynamics NAV, this is a required step. Your own forms have to be transformed to pages. Also, standard customized forms should be transformed to pages to carry out the customization done in the form to the standard page.

There isn't a form-transformation tool specific for Microsoft Dynamics NAV 2013. The form-transformation tool that was released with Microsoft Dynamics NAV 2009 can be used.

Refer to the *Upgrading tools* section to learn more about the form-transformation tool.

Transforming reports

The report definition had already changed in Microsoft Dynamics NAV 2009 compared to previous versions of Microsoft Dynamics NAV. In Microsoft Dynamics NAV 2013, the report definition changes again. So, no matter which version you are upgrading to Microsoft Dynamics NAV 2013 from, you will have to go through a report-transformation process.

The report-definition changes in Microsoft Dynamics NAV 2013 include:

- Report sections and section triggers are no longer available
- The request form is no longer available
- The RDLC definition of reports has changed

With the release of Microsoft Dynamics NAV 2013, a tool for report transformation included in Microsoft Dynamics NAV 2013 Development Environment has been shipped. This is the tool to use. It can be used for reports in Microsoft Dynamics NAV 2009 that have both a classic definition and an RDLC definition and for reports in Microsoft Dynamics NAV 2009, or any previous version, that only have a classic definition.

Refer to the *Upgrading tools* section to get detailed information on how to use this tool.

Revising and modifying customized code

The data stack has been completely redesigned in Microsoft Dynamics NAV 2013 for better performance.

In previous versions, some coding structures were used to get better performance. With this redesign, those coding structures are not needed anymore. In fact, if you keep using those structures, you might even get a significant lower performance in Microsoft Dynamics NAV 2013!

If you care about performance and you have always coded for performance, you should revise all your customizations if you intend to carry them over to Microsoft Dynamics NAV 2013.

In *Chapter 2, What's New in NAV 2013*, we discussed new development considerations in Microsoft Dynamics NAV 2013. Refer to that chapter to revise your customized code.

Upgrading the data

The steps explained to upgrade your data have been summarized to reflect the most important steps involved in that process. There are many other minor steps that are required to successfully upgrade your data to Microsoft Dynamics NAV 2013. A complete list of all the steps can be found in the official documentation provided by Microsoft, which can be downloaded from PartnerSource from the following link:

```
https://mbs.microsoft.com/customersource/downloads/servicepacks/
msdyn_nav2013rtmdownload_cs.htm
```

In this link, navigate to the **Microsoft Dynamics NAV 2013 Documentation** section and download the *Upgrade Quick* guide.

If you are upgrading from Microsoft Business Solutions–Navision 4.0 or from Navision Attain 3.*xx*, download that same guide, but from the Microsoft Dynamics NAV 2009 download page, which follows:

```
https://mbs.microsoft.com/customersource/downloads/servicepacks/
microsoftdynamicsnav2009r2.htm
```

Follow the steps described on those documents to perform a data upgrade.

If you are upgrading from Microsoft Business Solutions–Navision 4.0 or from Navision Attain 3.*xx*, to do the first data upgrade to Microsoft Dynamics NAV 2009 you will not need a full application code upgrade to Microsoft Dynamics NAV 2009. You really only need to do an application code upgrade to Microsoft Dynamics NAV 2009 for your table objects; and even for those, you don't have to upgrade all your code, you only have to upgrade your own customized fields.

That is, just compare your old database version object tables to Microsoft Dynamics NAV 2009 standard object tables to determine which fields were created by the customization and create those same fields in a Microsoft Dynamics NAV 2009 database. There is no need to upgrade any other application code.

Upgrading tools

There are several tools that will help us in the upgrading process. Some of them must be used at some point of the upgrade process (like the text format upgrade tool). Some others can be used to help us in the upgrade process, but are not mandatory (like MergeTool). In this section we will explain them all.

Upgrade Toolkit

Upgrade Toolkit is included in the Microsoft Dynamics NAV 2013 installation media.

For the W1 version of Microsoft Dynamics NAV 2013, Upgrade Toolkit only includes two folders: Data Conversion Tools and Object Change Tools. For country versions, it also includes an extra folder: Local Objects.

In both the Data Conversion Tools and Local Objects folders, there are two .fob files that have to be used in the data upgrade process. If you are upgrading an old W1 version database, the objects found on Data Conversion Tools should be used. If you are upgrading any old localized version database, use the objects under the Local Objects folder instead.

In upgrading the data section from the different versions of Microsoft Dynamics NAV, we have explained at what point those objects have to be imported and used.

In the Object Change Tools folder, there is a .exe file that will help us transform our new customized objects that have a Dynamics NAV 2009 object definition, into objects with a Dynamics NAV 2013 object definition.

Text format upgrade

As part of Upgrade Toolkit, there is a folder called `Object Change Tools`, which contains a tool called **TextFormatUpgrade2013**.

This tool has to be used during the application code upgrade process.

There are several object properties, parts, triggers, text in code, and so on, that are no longer available in Microsoft Dynamics NAV 2013. Some of them have been replaced by other properties, parts, or triggers. Some of them have just been removed.

As part of a code upgrade to Dynamics NAV 2013 we have to get rid of all the old stuff and get a *clean* object for the new application version.

The text format upgrade tool does the following:

- Replaces the `LookupFormID` table and page property with `LookupPageID`
- Replaces the `DrillDownFormID` table property with `DrillDownPageID`
- Replaces the text form with the text page on the value of former table properties `LookupFormID` and `DrillDownFormID`
- Replaces code `FORM.RUN(FORM::` and `FORM.RUNMODAL(FORM::` with `PAGE.RUN(PAGE::` and `PAGE.RUNMODAL(PAGE::`
- Replaces all form variables declared in the application code with a page variable, taking the same variable ID and name
- Deletes the whole definition of the request form in reports
- Replaces the `UseRequestForm` XMLport property with `UseRequestPage`
- Replaces the value form with the value page in the `MenuSuite` property, `RunObjectType`
- Replaces the `RunFormLink` page property with `RunPageLink`
- Replaces the `CardFormID` page property with `CardPageID`
- Replaces the `RunFormView` page property with `RunPageView`

- Replaces the SubFormLink page property with SubPageLink
- Replaces the RunFormMode page property with RunPageMode

We may have skipped some individual replacements, but we are pretty sure you got the idea. Actually, summarizing, what the tool does is the following:

- Replaces all references to the former form object with the page object in the following:
    ○ Object properties
    ○ Application code
- Deletes the definition of request form in reports

So now, how do we use that tool? Well, it is a command-line tool that can just take one parameter, so it's pretty easy to use! Just follow these steps:

1. Open a Microsoft Dynamics NAV 2009 database.
2. Select all objects except forms and dataports.
3. Export them in the .txt format.
4. Open the command-line interface.
5. Execute the following command:

   TextFormatUpgrade2013.exe <PathToTheTxtFileOrFolder>

   Which can, for instance, be:

   **TextFormatUpgrade2013.exe
   C:\ImplementingDynamicsNAV2013\OldCustom.txt**

   Or just:

   TextFormatUpgrade2013.exe C:\ImplementingDynamicsNAV2013

   In this second case, we have just specified the folder containing different .txt Dynamics NAV files (OldBase.txt and OldCustom.txt), and the tool will convert all the text files inside the folder during the same execution.

6. The tool will start its execution. Wait for the process to finish.

7. The result of the execution of the tool will be a text file with the same name as the original text file, but it will be stored in a directory called `Converted` inside the directory where the original file was.

You can now use those new text files for merging purposes by following the instructions explained in previous sections. If you use the old text files instead, any comparison to the new standard application code of Microsoft Dynamics NAV 2013 will result in hundreds or thousands of modifications purely because of object property changes, even if the object has not changed between two versions. Using those new files instead, will let us just compare *real* object modifications.

Form transformation

For those who upgrade to Microsoft Dynamics NAV 2013 from Microsoft Dynamics NAV 5.0 or previous versions, or from Microsoft Dynamics NAV 2009 in a classic environment, you have to know that your form objects have to be transformed to pages. Customizations done in standard form objects have to be carried out to the corresponding standard page object and new custom form objects have to be fully transformed to new custom page objects.

This process is not new for Microsoft Dynamics NAV 2013. It was already a requisite if you wanted to upgrade to Microsoft Dynamics NAV 2009 in an RTC environment.

There was a form-transformation tool available with Microsoft Dynamics NAV 2009. You will find the tool in the Microsoft Dynamics NAV 2009 installation media, on a folder called `TransformationTool`.

There is no form-transformation tool shipped with Microsoft Dynamics NAV 2013. So, if you have to transform forms into pages, you will have to use the tool shipped with the 2009 version.

We will not explain how to use this tool in this book. If you have never used the tool and want to learn how to use it, you can consult the online help available at `http://msdn.microsoft.com/en-us/library/dd338789.aspx`.

Report transformation

With Microsoft Dynamics NAV 2009, a new way of reporting was introduced: **Reporting Definition Language Client-side (RDLC)**. The old way of reporting, the classic way, was kept for compatibility reasons to use it with the classic client. That is, in Microsoft Dynamics NAV 5.0 and previous versions, only classic reporting was available; in Microsoft Dynamics NAV 2009, hybrid reporting was available (reporting in classic and RDLC at the same time); and now, in Microsoft Dynamics NAV 2013, only RDLC reporting is available.

For RDLC in Microsoft Dynamics NAV 2009, classic sections were the base to construct the layout of the report, and Report Viewer 2008 was used. In Microsoft Dynamics NAV 2013, the base of the RDLC layout is not the Classic report structure anymore (because it has disappeared). The new report structure is the report dataset. Along with that, RDLC 2005 (the RDLC version used in Microsoft Dynamics NAV 2009) has been upgraded to RDLC 2008, and the report viewer used is the 2010 version.

All of this means that old reports done in previous versions of Microsoft Dynamics NAV 2013 will not run anymore in the new version. They have to be converted to the new report format and structure.

The method of upgrading reports to Microsoft Dynamics NAV 2013 differs for Hybrid reports (those that have both a native Dynamics NAV and a RDLC definition) and Classic reports (those that only have a native Dynamics NAV definition).

Upgrading Hybrid reports

The steps required to upgrade a Hybrid report to Microsoft Dynamics NAV 2013 are the following:

1. Export the Hybrid report in `.txt` format from a Microsoft Dynamics NAV 2009 database.

2. Use the text format upgrade tool described earlier in this section to transform its definition to a Microsoft Dynamics NAV 2013 format.

3. Import them in a Microsoft Dynamics NAV 2013 database.

4. Compile the imported reports. The reports must be compiled in order to finish the report transformation. If there is any report that does not compile because it refers to tables, fields, or any structure that does not exist in Dynamics NAV 2013 anymore, make the report compile by redefining it.

5. In Microsoft Dynamics NAV 2013 Development Environment, go to **Tools | Upgrade Report**.

   When the **Upgrade Report** tool is run, the report data is upgraded to a valid Microsoft Dynamics NAV 2013 dataset definition and the layout is upgraded to RLDC 2008.

6. Save and compile the report.

Upgrading Classic reports

The steps required to upgrade a Classic report to Microsoft Dynamics NAV 2013 are the following:

1. Export the Classic report in `.txt` format from a Microsoft Dynamics NAV 2009 database.

2. Use the text format upgrade tool described earlier in this section to transform its definition to a Microsoft Dynamics NAV 2013 format.

3. Import them in a Microsoft Dynamics NAV 2013 database.

4. Compile the imported reports. The reports must be compiled in order to finish the report transformation. If there is any report that does not compile because it refers to tables, fields, or any structure that does not exist anymore in Dynamics NAV 2013, make the report compile by redefining it.

5. In Microsoft Dynamics NAV 2013 Development Environment, go to **Tools | Upgrade Report**.

6. When the Upgrade Report tool is run, the report data is upgraded to a valid Microsoft Dynamics NAV 2013 dataset definition, the request form is deleted, and the RDLC 2008 layout is generated by using the layout suggestion tool.

7. Manually adjust the RDLC layout in Visual Studio.

8. Manually create a request page if needed, or use the form-transformation tool to transform the former request form into a request page.

9. Save and compile the report.

Comparing text tools

To upgrade your application code to a new version of Microsoft Dynamics NAV, you have to compare your customized application code with the old original standard application code to determine which customizations have been made and where they have been made.

A second comparison has to be done, between the old original standard application code and the new original standard application code to determine what differences exist between those two versions, so that we can decide whether the old customized objects can still be used (if the original object hasn't changed) or if the customization has to be manually carried out to the new version of Dynamics NAV.

There are several generic compare text tools that you could use for this purpose. A web search will present you with several tools that you can use. We will not explain any of these tools here. We just want to point out that you can use any of them for application code upgrade purposes.

MergeTool

MergeTool is a third-party application that can be used for free by Microsoft Partners. This application is developed inside Microsoft Dynamics NAV. Using this application to help you out in your application code upgrade will probably save you a lot of time in analyzing text, as it will let you concentrate only on real customizations.

When using any generic text compare tool, you have to deal not only with customizations but also with object structure changes that may exist between a Microsoft Dynamics NAV version and its preceding versions. Dealing with object structure changes is useless.

Downloading MergeTool

MergeTool can be downloaded from www.mergetool.com. In the download section of the web page, you will find a ZIP or RAR file containing all the objects of the application. Download it onto your hard disk and unzip the file.

The version of MergeTool at the time of writing was MGT1.30.37. This version contains four .fob files that can be imported into Microsoft Dynamics NAV 2013, two help files, one Microsoft Visio file, and one readme file.

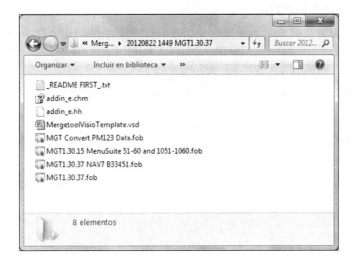

Installing MergeTool

The steps to install MergeTool are as follows:

1. Create a new Dynamics NAV 2013 database.
2. Open the development environment for the new database.

3. Open the **Object Designer** page by navigating to **Tools | Object Designer** or by pressing *Shift + F12*.

4. Navigate to **File | Import**.

5. Select the `MGT1.30.37 NAV7 B33451.fob` file.

6. A message will be prompted saying that all objects have been examined and no conflicts were found. Choose **Yes** to import all objects.

The steps to install the help files for MergeTool are as follows:

1. Copy the file `addin_e.hh` to the folder `C:\Program Files\Microsoft Dynamics NAV\70\Service\ENU` in the server where Microsoft Dynamics NAV 2013 services are installed.

2. Copy the file `addin_e.chm` to the folder `C:\Program Files\Microsoft Dynamics NAV\70\RoleTailored Client\en-US` in all PCs where the Microsoft Dynamics NAV 2013 client is installed.

3. Restart the Microsoft Dynamics NAV 2013 service.

4. Restart the Microsoft Dynamics NAV 2013 client.

Using MergeTool

MergeTool will allow us to compare our customized application code with the old standard application code and merge the customizations to the new standard application code, creating a new customized application code.

Follow the steps explained in the *Upgrade steps in detail* section.

1. Get the object's version to get the files `OldBase.txt`, `OldCustom.txt`, and `NewBase.txt`.

2. Open your Microsoft Dynamics NAV MergeTool database.

3. Open the MergeTool menu by navigating to **Departments | MergeTool**.

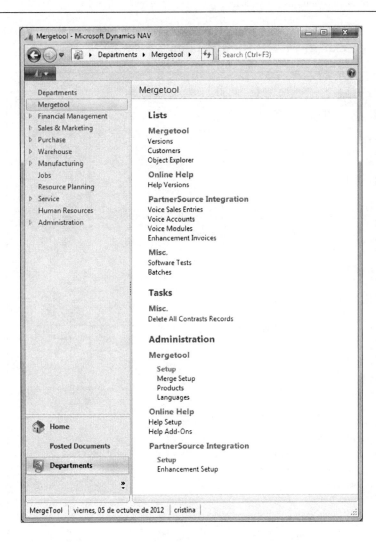

In this menu you will find everything that can be done with MergeTool.

We will start by importing the old base version of our current Microsoft Dynamics NAV database. That is, the `OldBase.txt` file.

Importing the old base version

To import the old base version, follow these steps:

1. Click on **Versions**.

2. Click on the **Import Object Text File** process option that appears on the ribbon bar.

3. Select the `OldBase.txt` file, give this version a name in field **Version**, and put a checkmark on **Navision Version**.

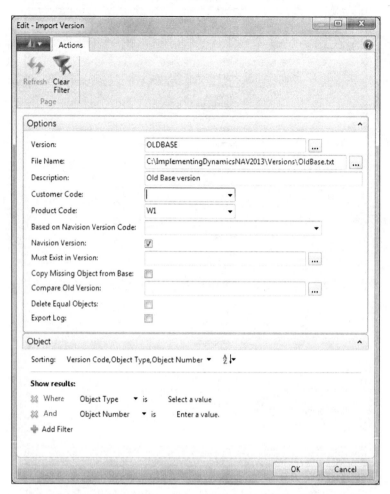

4. Click on **OK**.
5. The text file will be imported.

In the example we are using, the old version is a Microsoft Dynamics NAV 2009 R2 database. This version has **4232** different objects (excluding forms and dataports), which gets reflected in the version list of MergeTool once the file has been completely imported.

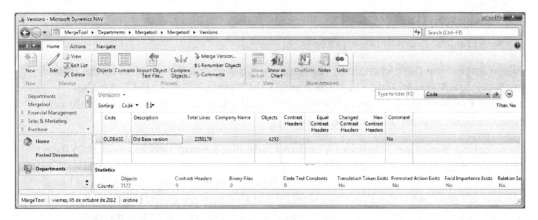

Importing the old custom version

We will now import our old customized database, that is, the `OldCustom.txt` file:

1. Click on the **Import Object Text File** process option that appears on the ribbon bar.

2. Select the `OldCustom.txt` file, give this version a name in the **Version** field, select **OLDBASE** in the **Based on Navision Version Code** field and also in the **Compare Old Version** field, and select **Delete Equal Objects**.

3. Click on **OK**.

4. The text file will be imported.

When importing the old custom version, we have selected a version in the **Based on Navision Version Code** and **Compare Old Version** fields and have also selected **Delete Equal Objects** because this will allow us to concentrate only on customizations done on the base code.

By selecting **Based on Navision Version Code**, the import process will skip those objects in our custom version that do not exist in the base version. Objects that exist in a custom version but do not exist in its base version are objects that have been created for the customization. You don't need to compare them to anything, you will just import those on the new custom database. That's why we skip them.

By selecting **Compare Old Version** and **Delete Equal Objects**, the import process will first compare the custom objects against those on the base version and, if they have not changed at all, will skip them. As we have seen on the first import process, a Microsoft Dynamics NAV database has thousands of objects. In a customization, probably not all of them have been customized. Probably only a few dozens or even some hundreds of objects have been modified, but all 7,000 objects are not customized. We want to skip objects that have not been modified because we want to concentrate only on those that have actually been modified.

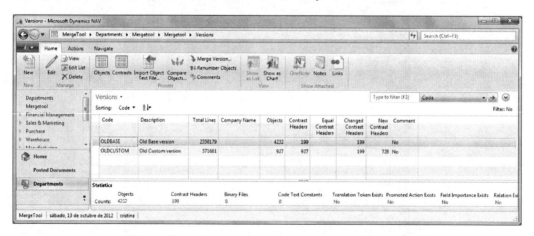

Once the old custom version has been imported, compared against the old base version, and equal objects have been deleted, our old custom version has only 927 objects. Only 927! We don't need to go through all 4,232 objects for the application code upgrade. We really only need to concentrate on those 927 that have actually been modified. That's great! That will save us a lot of time!

But we can further reduce those 927 objects by a little. How is that? Well, sometimes it happens that you open an object in the design mode through the **Object Designer** page because you want to check something. You finally leave the object without modifying anything at all, but the editor asks you whether you want to save the changes made to the object or not. If you say yes, object properties such as `Date` and `Time` will be modified. Since there is something that has changed, even if it's just those object properties, MergeTool has determined that you will have to compare and merge those objects. Wouldn't it be great to be able to delete those objects from comparison so that only real modifications have to be compared and merged?

That is possible with MergeTool. That's cool, right?

Let's see how to delete objects that has only object property changes (date, time, and version list):

1. Navigate to **Departments | MergeTool | Versions**.
2. Click on the **Navigate** tab that can be found on the ribbon bar.
3. Click on **Find Object Properties Changes**.
4. The **Find Object Properties Changes** process will open.
5. Select the version **OLDCUSTOM** in the **Version** field.
6. Select **Delete Objects**.

If we go back to the **Versions** list, only **914** objects are on the **OLDCUSTOM** version now. That means that 13 objects had only object properties changes and have been removed. Great! As we go on, we will be saving more and more time. Now we will only have to concentrate on 914 objects!

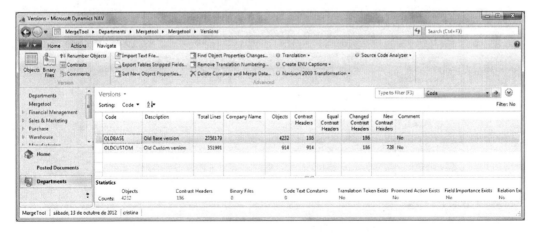

Importing the new base version

Now it is time to import the new base version, that is, the NewBase.txt file.

1. Click on the **Import Object Text File** process option that appears on the ribbon bar.

2. Select the NewBase.txt file, give this version a name in the **Version** field, place a checkmark on **Navision Version**, and select **OLDCUSTOM** in the **Must Exist in Version** field.

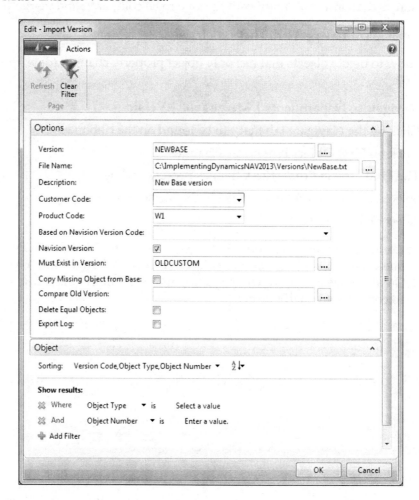

3. Click on **OK**.

4. The text file will be imported.

When importing the new base version, we have selected a version in the **Must Exist in Version** field because this will allow us to concentrate only on customizations done on the base code. In previous steps we have seen that only 914 objects were really modified or new in the custom application code used in that example. For the new version, we only want to import those 914 objects. Microsoft Dynamics NAV 2013 has 4,053 objects. But we only want to focus on the 914 that were modified or new in our custom version. For the rest of the objects, we will use the standard objects of Microsoft Dynamics NAV 2013. By selecting the **OLDCUSTOM** version in the **Must Exist in Version** field, we are telling MergeTool that we only want to import the new object of the new version if it was an object modified in our custom version.

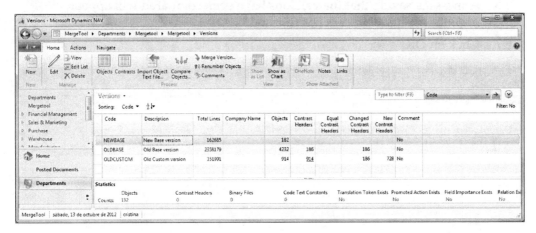

The result is shown in the previous screenshot. Only 182 objects are shown in the new base version. That means 732 objects that were modified on the old custom version do not exist anymore in Microsoft Dynamics NAV 2013 or they were new customized objects.

The main thing is that now we have just a few objects to concentrate on. Our customizations on those objects will have to be carried out to the new application code version.

To do so, the first thing we need to know is if the standard code for those 182 objects has been modified at all. If there are no modifications in the standard code, carrying our customizations will be easy. If there are modifications in the standard code, we will have to take a closer look to see how to carry out our customizations to the new objects.

Comparing the old base and new base versions

Let's first compare the old base and new base versions:

1. On the ribbon bar, click on **Compare Objects**.

2. Select **OLDBASE** in the **Old Version** field.

3. Select **NEWBASE** in the **New Version** field.

4. Click on **OK**.

5. The compare process will start.

6. A message saying that the versions have been compared will appear once the compare process has finished.

7. Click on **OK**.

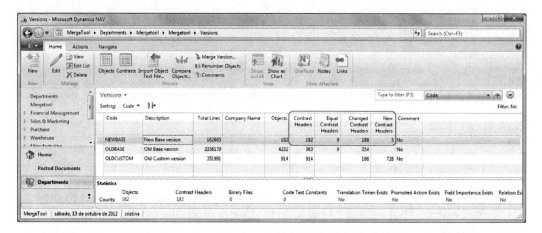

Take a new look at the **Versions** list. Contrast fields have been updated. A contrast is a group of code lines that have some differences (change in code, added code, or deleted code) respective to the two versions. MergeTool does not treat modifications on a line-by-line basis. It actually treats modifications as groups of line codes.

Imagine the modification in an object consists of creating a new function with hundreds of code lines and a call to that function from within the same object. There aren't hundreds of modifications for the hundreds of code lines added. There are only two modifications: added code for the definition of a function and added code for the call to that function. It's easier to deal with two modifications than with hundreds of modifications. And that's what MergeTool does.

MergeTool groups contrasts in **Contrast Headers**. There is one contrast header per object in the new base version. Each contrast header may have several contrasts inside.

The screenshot taken after **NEWBASE** was compared against **OLDBASE** and it tells us that there are **182** contrasts:

- **Equal Contrast Headers – 9**: These contrasts correspond to **9** whole objects out of the 182 new base version's contrasts that have not changed at all.

- **Changed Contrast Headers – 168**: Those contrasts correspond to 168 objects that have changed.

- **New or Added Contrast Headers – 5**: Those contrasts correspond to **5** objects that are new in **NEWBASE** (they did not exist in **OLDBASE**). Even if they did not exist in **OLDBASE**, they did actually exist in **OLDCUSTOM**. Otherwise they would not be on **NEWBASE**, because of the import options we have selected. Standard objects that were not in **OLDBASE** but were in **OLDCUSTOM**, now remain the same in **NEWBASE**. This may seem weird, but it's not. They probably correspond to hot fixes or new functionalities released by Microsoft that we have applied to our customized version of Microsoft Dynamics NAV and that were not part of the original standard code for our old version of the application.

We can navigate to the contrast to analyze the differences. To do so, click on the type of contrast you want to analyze (for all: by clicking on the **Contrast Headers** field; for equal contrasts: by clicking on the **Equal Contrast Headers** fields; for changed contrasts: by clicking on the **Changed Contrast Headers** field; for new contrasts: by clicking on the field **New Contrast Headers**) and the list of contrasts will be shown. Select then the specific contrast you want to analyze and click on **Lines** (log), which can be found on the ribbon bar.

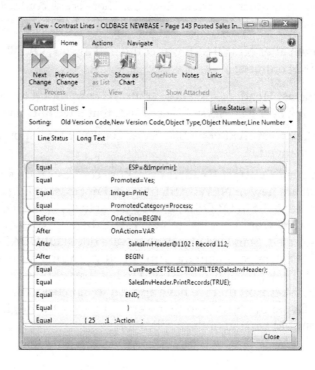

In the previous screenshot we can see what a contrast looks like. The code lines in green remain the same in both versions (**Line Status** is **Equal**). The code lines in red tell us what the code was on the old version (**Line Status** is **Before**). The code lines in orange tell us what the code is in the new version (**Line Status** is **After**).

In the example, a line of code has been replaced by three lines of code. Three lines of code are involved in the change but there is only one change—a local variable has been defined for an action in **Page 143 Posted Sales Invoices**.

In the **Contrast Headers** list, we can see how many groups of changes exist between the two versions. In the example, we have 182 contrast headers (objects) with a total of 4,018 groups of changes: 330 changes in properties groups, 2,368 changed groups, 893 inserted groups, and 427 deleted groups.

We definitely do not want to deal with all 4018 groups of changes by manually looking at all the differences in code. We want MergeTool to deal with them automatically and just let us decide on those that cannot be merged automatically by the application. That's what we are going to do on the last part of this section.

Merging all versions

We will go back to the version list page of MergeTool and we will follow these steps:

1. Click on the **Merge Version** action that can be found on the ribbon bar.
2. Select **OLDBASE** in the **Old Base** field.
3. Select **NEWBASE** in the **New Base** field.
4. Select **OLDCUSTOM** in the **Custom Version** field.
5. Write **NEWCUSTOM** in the **New Custom Version** field.
6. Give this new version a description in the **New Custom Version Description** field.
7. Put a checkmark in the **Skip if Manual Merge** field. We are selecting that option because on the first merge we want MergeTool to automatically merge everything that can be merged without our intervention. On the second run we will uncheck this option to deal with those changes that MergeTool cannot automatically deal with.
8. Leave the rest of the options to their default value.

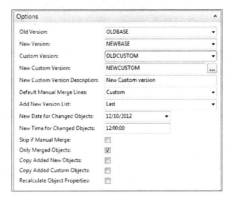

9. Click on **OK**.
10. The merge process will start.
11. When the merge process is completed, a message will appear saying that the NEWCUSTOM version has been created and the number of objects that require manual merging.

12. Click on **OK**.

If we go back to the MergeTool version list, we will see that a new version, **NEWCUSTOM**, has been created, with a few objects—the ones that were completely merged automatically.

We will now do a second run of the merge process, unselecting the **Skip if Manual Merge** field. Once the merge process starts again, when a manual merge is required, the process will prompt a page with all the versions (the old base code, the old custom code, the new base code, and the new merged custom code). MergeTool has merged the changes to the new merged custom code, but we have to decide if we accept the merge or if we want to do any extra modification. Let's see an example of that.

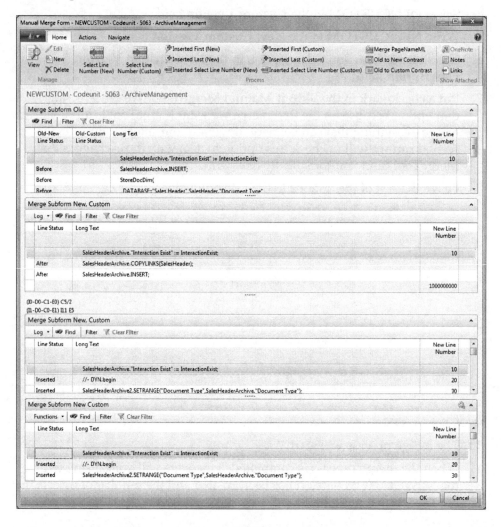

The first subpage corresponds to the old base code. Before, we had the assignation of a value to a field, then a record was inserted into the database, and finally the call to a function to store document dimensions.

The second subpage corresponds to the new base code. On the new application code, there is an extra code line between the assignation of a value to a field and the insertion into the database, and the call to a function to store document dimensions has disappeared.

The third subpage corresponds to the old custom base code. To see the whole customization, we will have to scroll through the subpage. The customization consists of a group of 11 code lines added between the assignation of a value to a field and the insertion of the record into the database.

The fourth subpage corresponds to the new custom code. There is a conflict. The custom code inserts code lines in a specific place and the new code inserts different code lines in the same place. MergeTool cannot automatically merge this because the tool cannot decide if only the custom-added code lines have to be inserted, if only the new code lines have to be inserted, or if both the added code lines have to be inserted in the new custom version; and, in this case, in which order.

Let's take a better look at the fourth subpage, at the proposal made by MergeTool in the following screenshot:

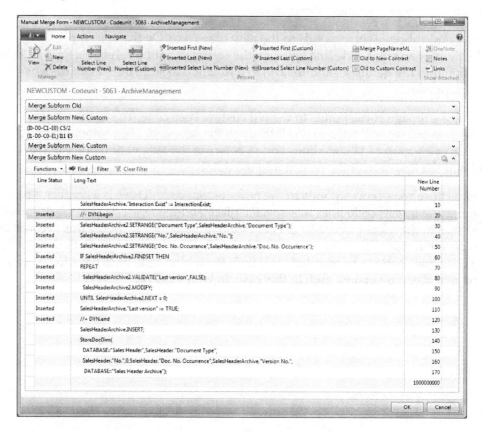

As we can see, the merge proposal consists of using only the customized code. Even the old call to the `StoreDocDim()` function has been used in the custom-merged code. MergeTool has made this proposal because of the option **Default Manual Merge Lines** used on the merge options, which we have left to its default value, **Custom**. That is, we have actually told MergeTool to use the custom version for the first proposal when merging lines manually.

In this particular example, we actually want both groups of added lines (the ones coming from the old customization version and the ones coming from the new base version) to be added to the new customized version, and we want the call to the function to be deleted from the new customized version, as this function is no longer available in Microsoft Dynamics NAV 2013 because of the dimension functionality redesign.

The way to move code lines from any version to the new customized version in MergeTool is through the **New Line Number** field that can be found in any of the subpages. If there is a number in the **New Line Number** field in any line code of the three first subpages, which correspond to the three code versions used for the merge process, that line will show up on the fourth subpage, on the new customized code. The number used in this field will determine the order in which the code lines will be shown in the fourth subpage.

In this particular example, we want to do the following:

1. Delete the **New Line Number** field values on the third subpage (custom version) for lines 140 to 170. That is, we do not want the call to the `StoreDocDim()` function to be on our new customized version.

2. Leave the proposed **New Line Number** field values as is, on the third subpage for lines 20 to 120. That is, we want our 11 customized code lines to be on our new customized version.

3. Give a value of `15` to the **New Line Number** field on the second subpage (new version), to the second line:

   ```
   SalesHeaderArchive.COPYLINKS(SalesHeader);
   ```

To do so, we will use the functions found on the **Actions** tab of the ribbon bar.

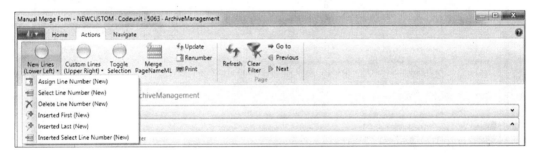

In the **New Lines** action, there are several functions to assign a value to the **New Line Number** field to code lines in the second subpage, the one corresponding to the new base version.

In the **Custom Lines** action, we will find the same functions but they apply to code lines in the third subpage, the one corresponding to the old custom version.

The final result is the one that can be seen in the following screenshot:

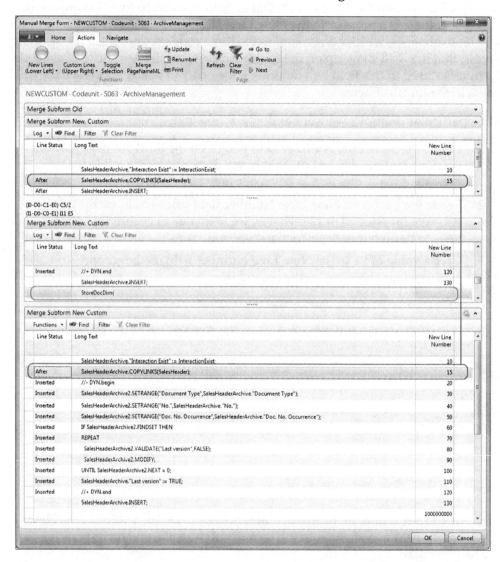

In the new custom version, we have our customized code and we have the code line added in the new version, and the call to the StoreDocDim() function is not there anymore.

Once we are done, we will click **OK** and MergeTool will move on to the next merge conflict.

Exporting the new custom version

Once we are done with the whole merge process and we have a good new custom version, we can go back to the MergeTool versions list and export this version as a `.txt` file. To do so, there is an action in the **Actions** tab of the ribbon bar, called **Export Object Text File**. Select **NEWCUSTOM** as the version to export and select a destination folder and file name.

Importing the new custom version to a Dynamics NAV 2013 database

The last part of the merge process is to get a new database, with all the new objects, and import into that database the `.txt` file we have just exported with the customizations merged into the new code version. After importing the `.txt` file, we will have to compile all objects and solve any additional issues that may exist.

And that's it. We have a brand new full application code with standard objects for all those objects that we have not modified in the old version and with the customizations carried out to this new version.

We would still have to import into that new database the new objects created in our customization. To do so, we will first have to do the following:

- Transform form objects to pages
- Transform reports to the new RDLC definition

Summary

Companies that already use Microsoft Dynamics NAV can also be benefitted by the release of the latest version of the ERP—Microsoft Dynamics NAV 2013. To do so, they have to go through an upgrade process to get their current implementation to the latest version. In this chapter we have covered this whole process. Even if upgrading to Microsoft Dynamics NAV 2013 is only supported from Microsoft Dynamics NAV 2009, we have also explained how to upgrade from previous versions of the application.

In the next chapter we will be talking about developing in Microsoft Dynamics NAV 2013.

8
Development Considerations

Almost every Dynamics NAV implementation implies development. The customized code must fit inside the application standard code and it should look like it was a part of the standard. This makes it easier for users to understand how customized modules work and for partners to support it. A good initial development also makes any future change easier and cheaper, for both the customer and the partner.

In this chapter we will go through the main development considerations you should take into account while developing for Dynamics NAV. The topics covered in the chapter are:

- Setup versus customization
- The data model principles
- How the posting processes are developed
- Where to write customized code
- How to write customized code

Setup versus customization

Dynamics NAV offers many configuration options on all its sectors. Those options make Dynamics NAV work differently in each company depending on the option selected; for example, you could define that your locations will use warehouse documents for shipping and receiving.

When you set up a new company, you will find more than 200 tables that can be considered setup tables. You will find the setup table of each module, plus journals and its sections, the accounting periods, and the payment terms or the dimensions.

Whenever possible, use the setup options instead of writing customized code. This will save time and money to the company acquiring Dynamics NAV, now and in the future, since any customized code will add cost for migrating to a newer Dynamics NAV version.

Even if Dynamics NAV is not the most configurable ERP in the market, you will find hundreds of setup options. The combination of all of them leads to thousands of possibilities. It is really difficult for a single person to be aware of all these options and the impact that a single option will have on other areas of the application. However, for a developer it is very easy to think about adding a new field on a table. A good consultant/developer will not fall into the temptation of starting to develop right away. Before this, it is important to invest time to investigate all the setup options. On many occasions you will find small features that you never heard of, that are very useful.

Let's see an example of what we are talking about. The Spanish version of Dynamics NAV has a module called Cartera that is used to manage the receivables and payables. Once, while giving support to a customer, I saw that someone created a new field on a table. It was a Boolean field that was used to identify whether the customer had given a promissory note or not. On that table a field called `Category Code` already existed. Instead of creating a new field, the user could just create a new entry on the `Category Code` table, called `PromissoryNoteDelivered` (or something like that), and then just assign this classification code to any receivable needed.

For the user, the result is the same. Plus, the `Category Code` table offers many more possibilities than the Boolean field that the developer created.

It is normal that the consultant or the developer does not know about the existence of all those small features found all over the application. But doing a research and discovering those features every time we face a new situation is a great way to expand our knowledge in Dynamics NAV and provide more value to our work.

This is not only good for us as professionals, but is good for the Dynamics NAV channel. On more than one occasion we've heard complaints from customers asking how it is possible that this requirement is not covered in the standard application? Probably, in many of these occasions there is a little feature that can help our customer, but we cannot offer it due to ignorance. However, if we invest a little of our time to discover them, we could offer them to our customers and increase the overall Dynamics NAV satisfaction.

How can we discover and know how all those small features work? Basically, there are three options: read, research, and ask others.

- **Read**: Microsoft provides two portals: the **PartnerSource** and the **CustomerSource**, where you will find manuals on the Dynamics NAV modules and fact sheets on certain features. If you work for a Dynamics NAV partner, ask for the credentials to access the PartnerSource portal. If you work for a Dynamics NAV customer, ask for the credentials to access the CustomerSource portal. The manuals of Dynamics NAV also gives you some information (not much) about the features that are behind each window.

  Reading manuals helps you to better understand the application. Although we agree with you that the functional documentation on Dynamics NAV is rather sparse. Besides, the existing documentation only covers the big features and their common usage, without giving much details. I have found myself discovering something new every time I review the current documentation. And even when you don't learn anything new, they are a good source of ideas to investigate on our own.

  Besides the official manuals, you will find many other books related to Dynamics NAV, like this one and other books that you will find on the Packt Publishing library (`http://packtlib.packtpub.com/`). Unfortunately, most of them cover only technical aspects.

  You will also find information on the Internet. You can find multiple blogs with very interesting posts about Dynamics NAV. We recommend you to subscribe to them. It is a good way to learn something new every day. Again, most of them cover only technical aspects.

- **Research**: This is one of the best ways to discover all the features that Dynamics NAV can offer, in a step-by-step manner. Every time a customer raises a need, do investigate. Do not start to develop a new feature; before this, you must try to fulfill the need using the standard options. For example, if the need of your customer is related to items, start by looking at each single field in the item table. If you don't know what a certain field is used for, use tools to help you see where the field is used and why.

- **Ask others**: Your coworkers are your best allies; use them. They have had different experiences than you have. They may have had to solve similar problems on others projects. Apart from your coworkers, Dynamics NAV has a large online community that can help you with a specific problem. Our recommendation is to ask the community just after you have tried to solve it yourself. You can state the problem by explaining what have you tried so far. Generally, the community will be more receptive if you tried first, rather than you throwing the question without investigating beforehand. You must understand that the community is there to help you, not to work for you.

As we have seen, it is important to invest time in finding ways to use the standard features before starting to develop. This implementation project will be easier and you will also increase your knowledge of the product, which will be very useful on your future projects.

For your customer, the benefit is also clear. Apart from saving the cost of unnecessary developments, they are also saving the cost of upgrading the customized developments to new versions of Dynamics NAV.

Data model principles

After analyzing the standard functionality, if we finally find out that we will have to develop our own customized code to cover the project needs, it is important that we develop following the same structure that Dynamics NAV uses in its modules.

The users that are going to use our development are users that are also going to use standard parts of the application. To avoid confusing them, it is essential to use the same philosophy and the same structure everywhere. This way, once a user knows one part of the application, he/she can intuitively use other modules.

This is something that will also help us; we do not have to reinvent the wheel every time. There is no need for us to consider how to structure our data on each development. Take the existing structure as your basis, and just grow its functionality to meet your needs. With this, we are not only making the developer's life easier, but also the life of others who will participate in the project, such as the consultant, the implanter, the trainer, or the person who will support the customer once they start to run with Dynamics NAV. And to develop our own application, using the principles and structure of what already exists, it is important to know what already exists. This is what we will cover in the next section.

Basic objects

In Microsoft Dynamics NAV 2013, you can find seven basic object types; they are as follows:

Object	Description
Table	This object is used to store data in the database. Most of the time it is within this object that data is validated or calculated so that it follows the business rules described on each application area. Understanding tables is the key to using all the other objects.

Object	Description
Page	This object is used to display data to the users. Pages allow users to add records to a table, and to view and modify records. Pages can also be exposed as Web Services so that other applications can also read, insert, modify, or delete data, just like users do.
Report	These objects are mostly used to summarize and print detailed information by using filters and sorting, selected by the users. On some other occasions, reports are also used to batch process data.
XMLport	This object is used to export and import table data in XML format.
Codeunit	This object is used to group code of a particular functional area.
MenuSuite	This object is used to contain menus that are displayed in the department page. It is the user's door to access the functionalities of a certain area.
Query	This object is used to specify a set of data from the Dynamics NAV database.

Even if we are talking about objects, it is important to note that Dynamics NAV is not object-oriented, but object-based. You have seven object types that you can use, but you cannot create new object types. This may seem limiting, and it actually is, but it also makes development work much easier.

Each object is created using a specific designer. For example, tables are created using the **Table Designer**, pages are created with the **Page Designer**, and so on.

To open the development environment, you will have to install **Dynamics NAV Development Environment**. Open it and navigate to **Tools | Object Designer** (or press *Shift + F12*); the following window will open:

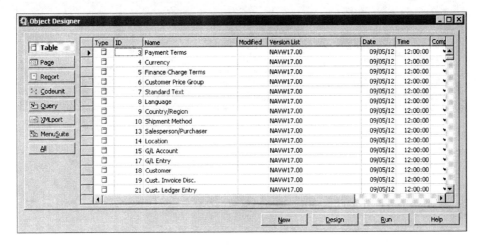

On the left-hand side you will find a number of icons representing the different objects available. On the right-hand side, you will see a list of all existing objects of the object type selected. In the previous screenshot, we can see a list of objects of the `Table` type.

All application objects are identified by an ID number. There are, however, restrictions about which numbers can be used while creating application objects. As a general rule, when you are developing for a customer you will use ID numbers between 50000 and 99999 when creating new objects, although you will have to check the exact IDs that can be used for a specific customer license. You will be allowed to modify the standard objects, but you cannot create them.

To modify an existing object, you must select it and then click on the **Design** button. This will open the object in its corresponding designer. In the following screenshot, we can see the **Table 18 Customer - Table Designer** window:

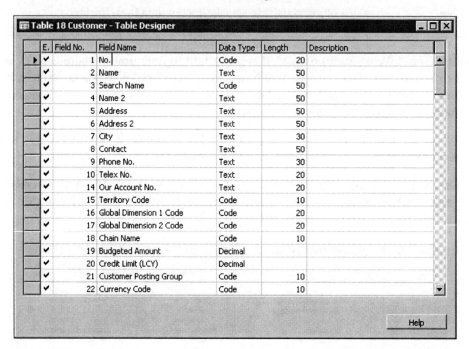

Object elements

Each object has its own fundamentals. A table contains properties, triggers, fields, and keys, which are related to each other, as we can see in the following image:

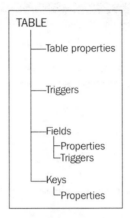

To access the table properties, from the table designer scroll down and put the cursor on an empty line at the bottom of the Table Designer. Then navigate to **View | Properties**, or click on the properties icon on the toolbar, or press *Shift + F4*. The **Table - Properties** window opens and shows the properties of the table. Here, developers can view and modify the properties for the **Customer** table.

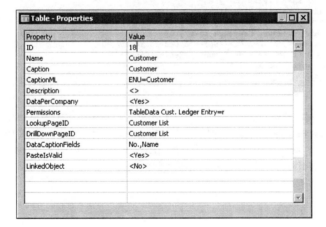

To access the triggers from the Table Designer, go to **See | C/AL Code** (or press *F9*). The following window will open, showing all the triggers of the table, including the field triggers:

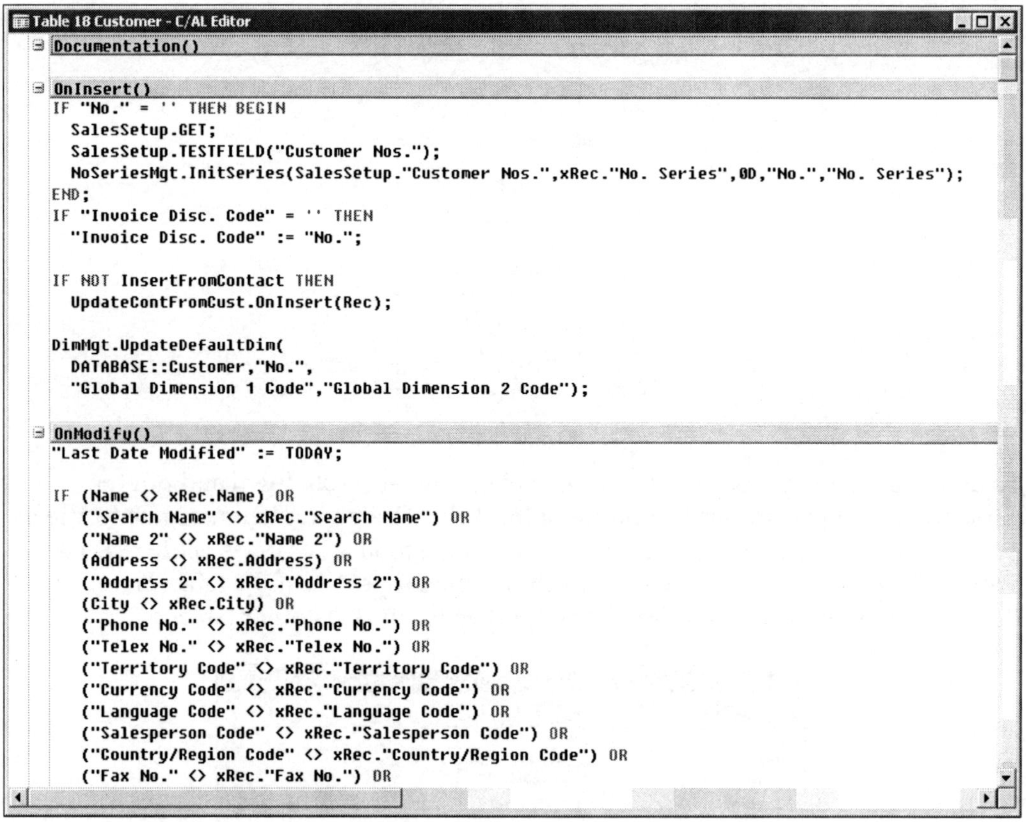

```
Table 18 Customer - C/AL Editor                                      _ □ X
  Documentation()

  OnInsert()
  IF "No." = '' THEN BEGIN
    SalesSetup.GET;
    SalesSetup.TESTFIELD("Customer Nos.");
    NoSeriesMgt.InitSeries(SalesSetup."Customer Nos.",xRec."No. Series",0D,"No.","No. Series");
  END;
  IF "Invoice Disc. Code" = '' THEN
    "Invoice Disc. Code" := "No.";

  IF NOT InsertFromContact THEN
    UpdateContFromCust.OnInsert(Rec);

  DimMgt.UpdateDefaultDim(
    DATABASE::Customer,"No.",
    "Global Dimension 1 Code","Global Dimension 2 Code");

  OnModify()
  "Last Date Modified" := TODAY;

  IF (Name <> xRec.Name) OR
    ("Search Name" <> xRec."Search Name") OR
    ("Name 2" <> xRec."Name 2") OR
    (Address <> xRec.Address) OR
    ("Address 2" <> xRec."Address 2") OR
    (City <> xRec.City) OR
    ("Phone No." <> xRec."Phone No.") OR
    ("Telex No." <> xRec."Telex No.") OR
    ("Territory Code" <> xRec."Territory Code") OR
    ("Currency Code" <> xRec."Currency Code") OR
    ("Language Code" <> xRec."Language Code") OR
    ("Salesperson Code" <> xRec."Salesperson Code") OR
    ("Country/Region Code" <> xRec."Country/Region Code") OR
    ("Fax No." <> xRec."Fax No.") OR
```

Field properties can be accessed from the Table Designer. Put the cursor on the field you want to check and then navigate to **View | Properties**, or click on the properties icon on the toolbar, or press *Shift + F4*. The properties window from the selected field opens as shown in the following screenshot:

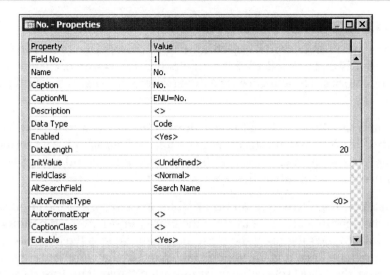

Keys can be accessed from the Table Designer, by navigating to **View | Keys** as shown in the following structure:

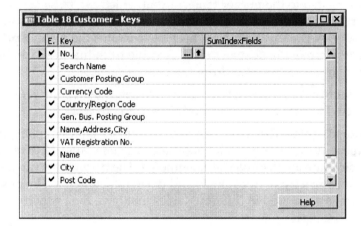

The properties of the keys can be accessed the same way you accessed the table properties or the field properties. Select the key you want to check, and navigate to **View | Properties**. Not all objects have the same elements as the ones shown for the tables, but they have similar elements that can be accessed in a similar way.

How tables are structured

Tables are the most fundamental objects among Microsoft Dynamics NAV objects. They store records that are collected through pages, for example, customers, sales, and inventories. These records are then presented to users through pages and reports.

The table's structure is the base of the structure of the whole application. We have already covered the table structure in *Chapter 3, Dynamics NAV General Considerations*, but we go a bit deeper in this section. In the standard application, we find different kinds of tables that are used for different purposes.

- **Master tables**: We will find master tables in each area of the application; they are the ones that are used to store the more important information of each module. In the sales area, the most important table is the Customer table; in the purchase area, it is the Vendor table; and in the warehouse management module, the Item table is the most important table; therefore they are called master tables.

- **Secondary or subsidiary tables**: These are tables that store secondary data, usually related to the master table, or that which can be selected from a master table. An example of a secondary or subsidiary table would be the Customer Price Group table. This table contains the distinct price groups that are set up in the Company table. A value from this table can be selected and assigned to a customer from the Customer table.

- **Setup tables**: All modules have their own setup table; different options can be selected to specify how the module is going to work.

- **Document tables**: We always find the document tables in pairs, because a document always has a Header table and a Lines table. Orders, shipments, or invoices are all examples of documents. The documents can also be divided between live documents and posted documents. The posted documents are stored in different tables that have the property of being protected tables.

- **Entry tables**: Entry tables are used to keep track of all transactions related to a master table. On the Customer ledger Entry table, for instance, we can find an entry for each invoice, credit memo, or payments for a single customer.

- **Register tables**: Register tables are used to keep track of entries created on the same posting process. For instance, the posting of a single sales invoice creates different G/L entries (an entry in the customer account, another in the sales account, another in the VAT account, and so on). All those entries are grouped on the `G/L Register` table as they all belong to the same posting process, the posting of a specific sales invoice.

- **Journal tables**: These are the tables that the posting process uses to create entries. It is the system that introduces data as a previous step on the journal tables while posting a document. The user can also manually introduce data on journal table if he wants to post a transaction without a document. We can find many processes that create data on journal tables but don't post them. The user is responsible for checking that data and finally posting it. That's what the calculate depreciation process does. For each fixed asset, it calculates the corresponding depreciation, and creates a line that reflects those calculations. The user has to go to the journal, review the lines, and post them.

Understanding table structures

The best way to understand a concept is to see it in practice. This is why we are going to analyze the structure of the tables on a particular area, the warehouse management area.

Master tables

The master table of the warehouse management area is the `Item` table. It holds the main data in this area and everything else relates to it. Usually, the primary key of a master table is a field named `No.`. Typically, a series number is used to assign a new `No.` value each time a new item is created. Field `No.` gets replicated on different tables to refer to a specific item.

Secondary tables

In the item card, you will find fields that can be filled by selecting data from a secondary table, such as the `Base Unit of Measure` field that can be filled by selecting data from the `Item Unit of Measure` table. For each item, you can indicate its sales price on the `Sales Price` table, which is also a secondary table.

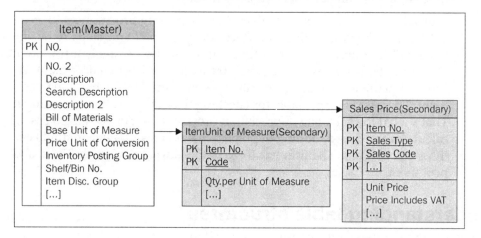

Any table (it doesn't matter if it's a master table, a secondary table, a setup table, or any other kind of table) can be used in other application areas. The `Sales Price` table, which we've seen, is also a secondary table of the sales area.

In the example we've only seen a couple of secondary tables related to the `Item` master table. We'll find many other secondary tables, such as the `Item Category` table, the `Product Group` table, the `Tariff Number` table, the `Item Tracking Code` table, and the `Item Variant` table, just to give a few examples.

Setup tables

The setup table of the warehouse management area is called the `Inventory Setup` table. The series number used to code the items can be set up on this table; also, other information, such as whether we want the item cost to get automatically posted to the general ledger or not, is available. Other setup tables also affect how the warehouse management area works. For instance, in the `General Ledger Setup` table you can indicate the rounding precision of the unit prices of the items in the `Unit-Amount Rounding Precision` field.

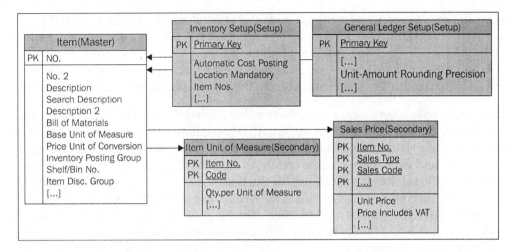

The master table, the setup tables, or the secondary tables are meant to create and define an item.

Document tables

Now it's time to start using the item on documents, to purchase or sell them. The item can now be used on the lines of a document. In the following example, we've used a sales document, the sales order. There are other sales documents where an item can be used, like the sales quote, the sales invoice, the sales return order, or the sales credit memo. In fact, all these sales documents are stored on a single document structure composed of the Sales Header table and Sales Line table. Each one is identified by the Document Type field that is part of the primary key of the tables.

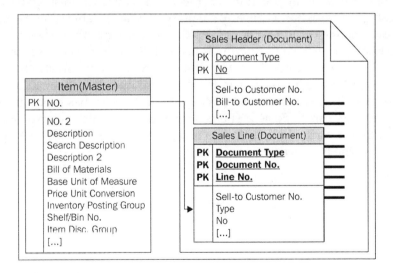

When an item is used in a document, not only is the item number stored on the `Sales Line` table, but many other fields from the `Item` table are also copied. Fields like the `Inventory Posting Group` field, the `Description` and `Description 2` fields, the `Gen. Prod. Posting Group` field, or the `VAT Prod. Posting Group` field—just to name a few—are copied from the `Item` table to the `Sales Line` table.

It may seem redundant; why are all those fields copied if the information is already stored in the item card? Well, this information is copied for two reasons. Firstly, this information is considered default data; and secondly, it gets copied to allow users to change a field value on a specific order. As an example, you can change the item description, the sales unit of measure, or the item VAT group on a specific order. Other fields, such as `Inventory Posting Group`, are also replicated on the `Sales Line` table, but users cannot modify their value. It may take some time between creating the order and finally posting it. In the meantime, the item configuration may have changed. However, it is not acceptable for a specific order to post something different to when it was created, which is probably when the user checked it.

The same is true for the item price. When we create a sales order for the item, the system calculates and proposes a price for the item. This is the price we have configured, either on the item card or in the `Sales Price` table. We have told our customer the selling price so that he can approve the order before we ship the item. Imagine that in the meantime, the item price changes. We all agree that the new price is for new orders. It would be unacceptable for the system to change the existing price without warning.

Copying data from the master table to a document table is part of Dynamics NAV philosophy. It is something that we can find in all application areas and in all documents. It has a clear pro: it makes the system flexible. It also gives us a lot of traceability. It also has a con: any change on a master table is not reflected immediately. Existing document lines keep the old configuration. The user has to refresh the line if the new configuration is needed. From our experience, some users have difficulty understanding this. They don't know when to refresh a line. During training, we will have to invest time to tell them and make sure they understand when to refresh a line. When the order is ready and the item has been shipped to the customer, the order can be posted. The posting routines, which are explained later on, are in charge of verifying that all data is correct and to create all the required entries to reflect the transaction.

Concerning documents, a shipment is created by inserting records on the `Sales Shipment Header` and `Sales Shipment Lines` tables. In the next step, the invoice will be created by inserting records on the `Sales Invoice Header` and `Sales Invoice Lines` tables. We can see this in the following diagram:

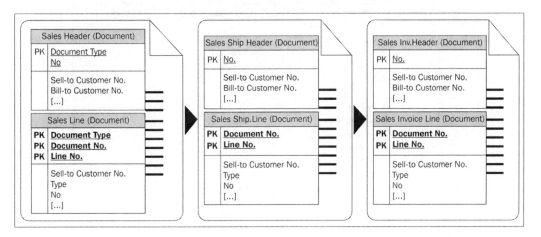

Records representing the shipment and the invoice are almost exact copies of the original order. Take a look at the fields found on the `Sales Line` table, which has been shown in the following screenshot:

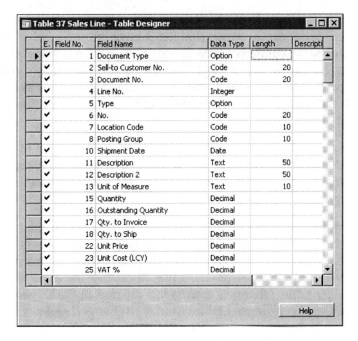

And now take a look at the fields found on the `Sales Shipment Line` table, which has been shown in the following screenshot:

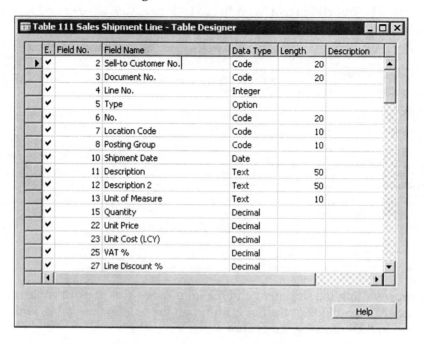

As you can see, we can find almost the same fields, with the same name and the same type. The most important part is that fields have the same value on the `Field No.` property. This is important because to copy values from one table to another, the `TRANSFERFIELDS` instruction is used. This instruction copies fields based on the `Field No.` property. For each field in the `Record` (the destination) table, the contents of the field with the same `Field No.` property in the `FromRecord` (the source) table will be copied, if such a field exists.

So, if you create a new field on the `Sales Line` table and you need to propagate the value of the field along the different documents, you just have to create the same field with the same `Field No.` property on the tables where the documents are stored. There is no need for extra coding.

We have not seen them in this example, but there are other document tables related to the warehouse management area. For instance, the `Transfer Header` and `Transfer Line` tables, with its corresponding historical documents `Transfer Shipment Header`, `Transfer Shipment Line`, `Transfer Receipt Header`, and `Transfer Receipt Line`. Historical documents are part of the Dynamics NAV protected tables. Data on protected tables cannot be changed and nor can you directly insert new records on those tables; the posting routines are the ones in charge of inserting data in those tables.

To refresh our memory, so far we have covered the types of tables that are shown in the following diagram:

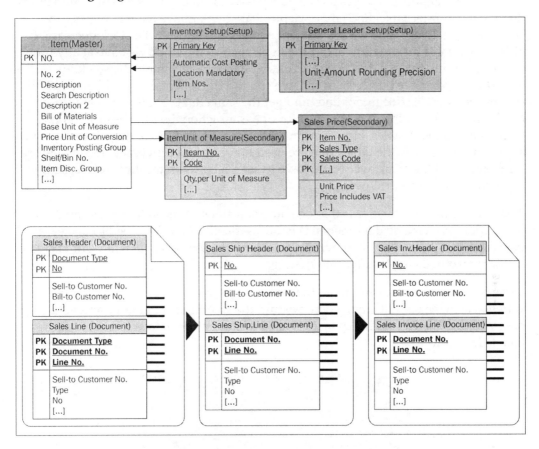

Only `Entry` and `Journal` tables are left and we will cover them in the following section.

Entry tables

As we have mentioned, the purpose of entry tables is to keep track of all transactions done with a master table. Each time we purchase an item, we have to register the stock increase. Every time we sell an item, we have to register the stock decrease. It gives us valuable information about the item, such as the stock we have at any time. One might think that we don't need an entry table to determinate the stock. As we've seen before, when we purchase or sell, we create a document. We could just add all purchases and sales document lines and get the same data. Again, we seem to be duplicating information. It is true that for one transaction the same information is to be copied to a lot of tables. However, in each case we want to see the information in a different way. Also, the tables that are used for sales and purchases documents are different; to get the stock, we would have to search between multiple tables. This will make the whole system slower.

Another element to consider is that on some occasions we need to register an item transaction but have no documents. What if we break a box? We need to decrease the item stock but there is no document to reflect this. In this case, we will want to create a new record in the table entry and that's it.

Some master tables will need more than one entry table. This is the case of the warehouse management area, where we find the `Item Ledger Entry` and `Value Entry` tables. The `Value Entry` table is used to store more details related to each item ledger entry.

Item Ledger Entry (Entry)		Value Entry (Entry)	
PK	**Entry No.**	**PK**	**Entry No.**
	Item No.		Item No.
	Posting Date		Posting Date
	Entry Type		Item Leader Entry Type
	[...]		[...]

The primary key for all entry tables is a field called `Entry No.`, which is an auto-incremental integer. All entry tables also have a field named `Posting Date`.

Additionally, when new records are inserted on entry tables, the system also creates new records on tables called `Register`. In the warehouse management area, we find the `Item Register` table. The `Item Register` table is used to keep track of when entries are created (regardless of the posting date), which user created them, and also how many entries have been created for each transaction. The `Item Register` table can be considered a secondary table.

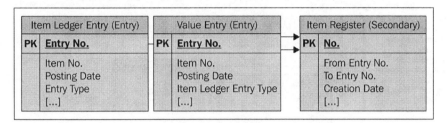

Journal tables

Last but not the least, we find the journal tables. Journal tables are very important since they contain most of the business logic of the application. All the posting processes found on the application are based on journal tables. In the warehouse management area, we find the `Item Journal Line` table.

If the posting is made from a document, the posting process converts the document lines to journal lines by creating temporary registers on the `Item Journal Line` table. The user can also manually create lines on the `Item Journal Line` table and then post them, without using a document at all.

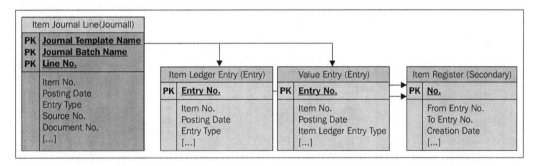

The final picture

And at last we can see the final picture of how tables are structured in Dynamics NAV, as shown in the following diagram:

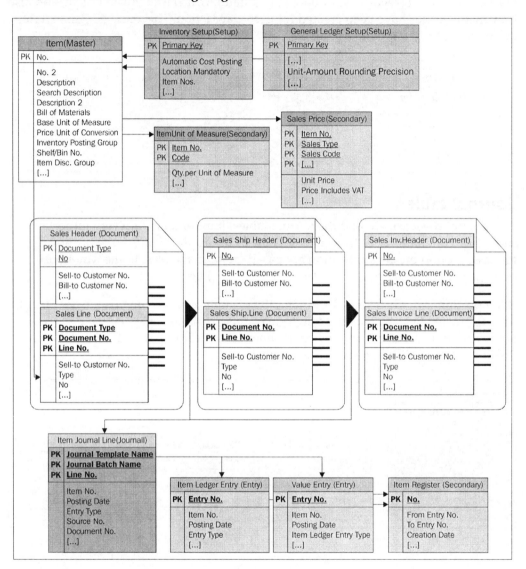

In reality, you will find many other secondary tables, setup tables, document tables, and entry tables that are not shown in the diagram, but the structure remains the same.

Remember that all existing areas in the applications follow this structure; therefore users are used to it. Keep this structure in mind while building your own applications.

The structure of pages

In the previous section we've seen the table's structure and how important it is to keep the same structure in all the areas to help users understand how the area works. Pages are also important; they are the objects through which users interact with Dynamics NAV. Users do not see tables, but pages. Thus, maintaining consistency in the page structure is vital for the user to perceive the consistent application structure. In the standard application, we find different kinds of pages that are used for different purposes, such as:

- **Role center pages**: This is the first page that users see when accessing Dynamics NAV. Depending on each user's role, the page shows a quick view of the work that the user is responsible for.

- **Card pages**: Card pages show data from a single table and also from a single record. All master tables have a card page associated with them, which is also the only way to insert, edit, or delete records. Some secondary tables with sufficient entity (many fields) also use card pages.

- **List pages**: List pages show multiple records from a single table. For each card page, you will find a list page that shows data from the same table. In fact, the users access the card page from the list page. These pages are not editable and are only used to show data, not to modify or delete it. Most secondary tables don't have a card page, but all of them have a list page. When no card page can be found for a table, the list page is editable. We are allowed to insert, modify, or delete records from the list page.

- **Document pages**: These pages are used to show the two tables related to a document: the header and the lines. Document pages are used to show data related to the header, and they include a link to a **ListPart** page where lines are shown.

- **ListPart pages**: ListPart pages are pages with the same characteristics as those of a list page, but the difference is that they are always used inside other pages.

- **Worksheet pages**: These pages are based on a template, batch, or name structure and have a control for selecting a template, batch, or name. Journals are a good example of worksheet pages.

- **ConfirmationDialog pages**: These are pages that pose a question to the user, have no input fields, and require that the user select **Yes** or **No**.

- **NavigatePage pages**: These pages are used for wizards, which consist of a number of user input screens or steps linked together, enabling users to carry out infrequently performed tasks.

Understanding page structures

As in the previous section, we will analyze the structure of pages on a particular area, the warehouse management area.

Role center pages

The following screenshot shows the default role center page for a user that has the shipping and receiving profiles assigned:

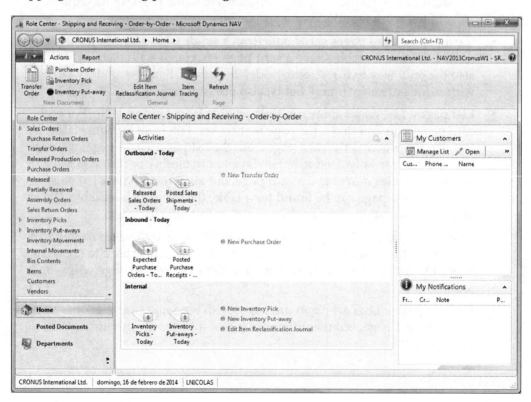

The Role Center page has a central area called **Activities**. This area contains a few cues that provide a visual indicator of the work that a user has to do each day. Cues are different for each role. The **Activities** area also contains actions so that the user can start new transactions right from the Role Center.

Card pages

Card pages show data from a single table and also from a single record. In the following screenshot, you can see the **Item Card** page. It contains all fields that can be stored in the Item table, except for a few fields that are used for internal purposes.

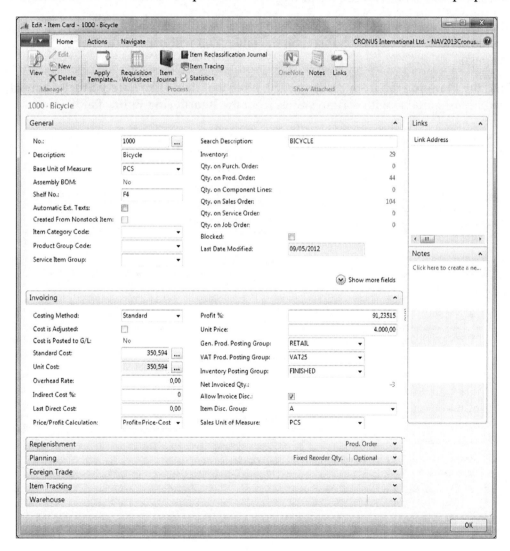

Data is shown in different tabs, grouping fields that are used for similar purposes. In the **Item Card** page, we can find all those tabs: **General**, **Invoicing**, **Replenishment**, **Planning**, **Foreign Trade**, **Item Tracking**, and **Warehouse**.

If you need to create your own card page, keep a similar structure. Keep in mind that all cards start with a tab called **General**. Card pages are always editable, which means that the user can insert, modify, or delete data on this page. Only a few fields are not editable, such as the `Last Date Modified` field. But you don't have to define this as an editable page because it is a property of the field in the table where you define whether a field is editable or not.

There is one exception to that. If one field has to be editable only in certain circumstances, you cannot define it on the table. You will need to do that on the page.

Find the **Planning** tab from the item card. Note that fields like **Safety Stock Quantity** can only be editable with certain values from the **Reordering Policy** field.

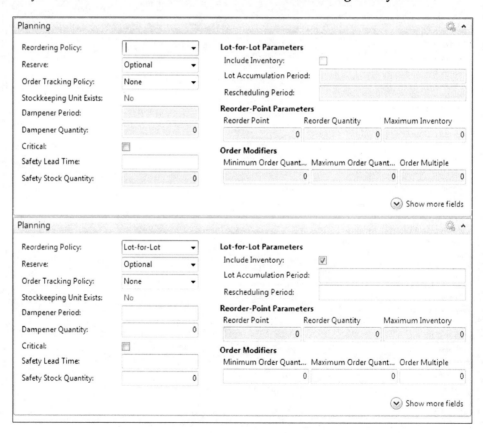

When the **Reordering Policy** field has no value entered into it, the **Safety Stock Quantity** field is not editable. This is recognizable because the field has a grey background. When you change the value to Lot-for-Lot, the **Safety Stock Quantity** field becomes editable. You can identify it because the fields have a white background.

As we mentioned before, this behavior has to be coded from the card page. Follow these steps to see how it is achieved in the item card page:

1. Open Dynamics NAV Development Environment
2. Navigate to **Tools | Object Designer**

Find **Page 30 Item Card** and click on the **Design** button.

Navigate to **View | C/AL Code**. The following screenshot shows what you will see:

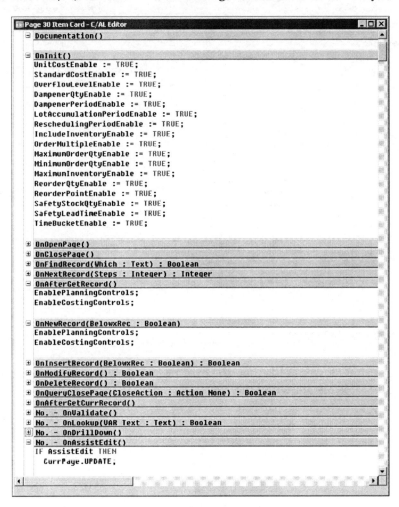

Only a few lines of code are present for the non-editable fields, but no code for inserting or deleting a record or when validating a field.

List pages

List pages show multiple records from a single table. For each card page, you will find a list page that shows data from the same table. In fact, the users access the card page from the list page. These pages are not editable and are only used to show data, not to modify or delete it.

The following screenshot shows the item list page:

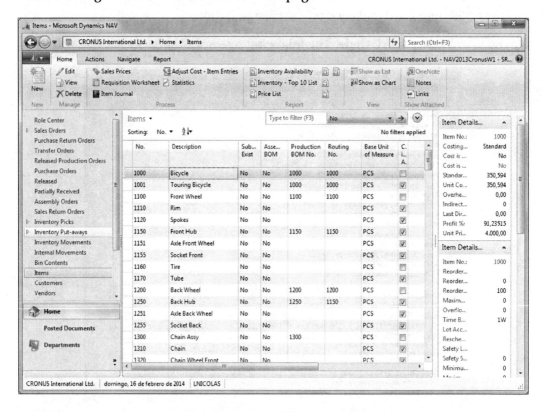

The list pages show fewer fields than the card pages. Only the most important fields of each master table are shown in the list.

By clicking on the related information icon, you will find a link to all kinds of tables that contain information related to the item. The options that are used most often have a shortcut key so that users can access it without using the mouse.

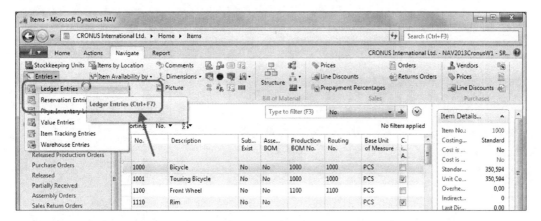

In the previous screenshot we can see that the **Ledger Entries** option can be accessed with *Ctrl + F7*. Remember to enable shortcut keys while creating your own list pages, and always use the same shortcut keys for the same actions in all the pages in the application, no matter what kind of page it is! This applies to all kind of pages, not only the list pages.

All options that can be found on the **Actions** pane can also be found on the item card page. Therefore, while creating a new option, remember to make it accessible from the list page and also from its corresponding card page.

Most secondary tables don't have a card page, but all of them have a list page. When no card page can be found for a table, the list page is editable. We are allowed to insert, modify, or delete records from the list page.

This is the case of the **Item Units of Measure** page, which can be accessed from the **Actions** pane, the **Navigate** tab, the **Item** entry, and the **Units of Measure** icon. You will find the option both from the item card and the items list.

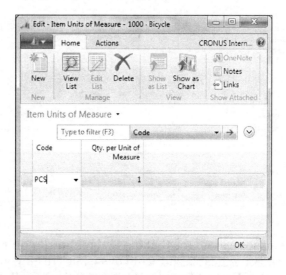

Those list pages need to show all fields (except internal use fields) to the user, so that he/she can fill them with the required data. By default, the **Item Units of Measure** page shows only two fields, but many others are also available to the user.

Put the cursor anywhere on the header of the table, where it says the name of the fields. Right-click on the mouse and select the **Choose columns** option as shown in the following screenshot:

A new window opens and allows the user to customize the page. On the **Available columns** grid, you will find all the fields that are available for the page but are not shown at the moment, as shown in the following screenshot:

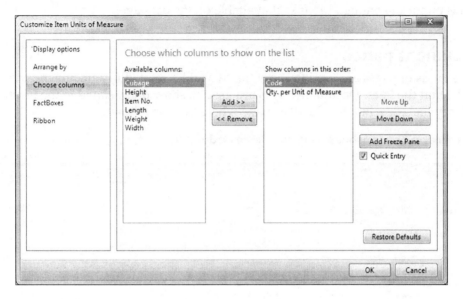

Select one of them and click on the **Add >>** button. Do the same with all the remaining fields, and then click on the **OK** button. You will end up with the **Item Units of Measure** page as shown in the following screenshot:

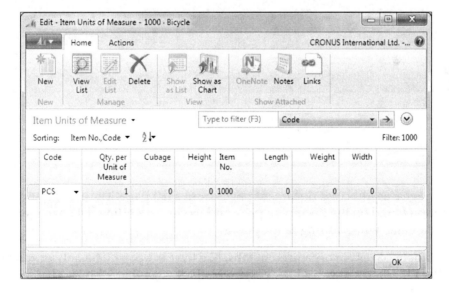

So remember that if you want a field from a secondary table to be filled by the users, you will have to make the field available from the list page. With master tables, you will have to make the field available from the card page and then decide if the new field is important enough to make it available on the list page.

Document pages

These kinds of pages are used to show the two tables related to a document: the header and the lines. Document pages are used to show data related to the header, and they include a link to a ListPart page where lines are shown.

The following screenshot shows the **Sales Order** page:

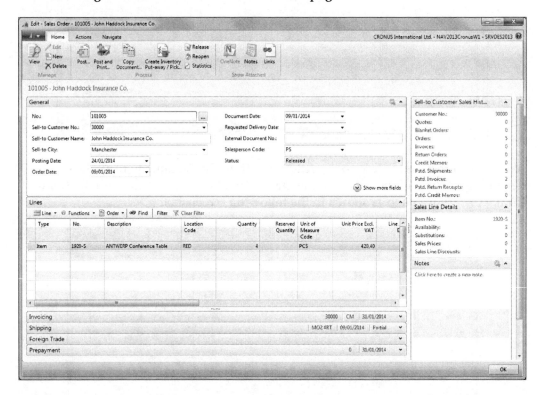

As card pages, users access document pages from a list page. The actions and related information found on the document page and its corresponding list page must remain the same while adding new options.

The document pages are organized in tabs, like the card page. The only difference is that the **Lines** tab shows another page, a ListPart page that is embedded into the document part.

On the right-hand side of the previous screenshot, you can find a few tabs showing data related to the document, the customer, or the item on the order. Those tabs are a particular type of page, called **CardParts**. These pages are associated to the FactBox pane of the document page.

ListPart pages

ListPart pages are pages with the same characteristics of a list page, but the difference is that ListPart pages are always used inside other pages. Actions can also be defined for ListPart pages.

The following screenshot shows the sales order **Subform** page, which shows the lines associated to the order:

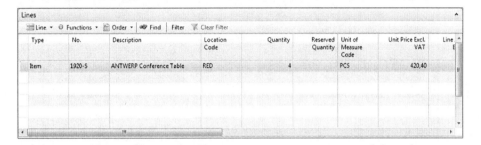

Worksheet pages

Worksheet pages are based on a template, batch, or name structure and have a control for selecting a template, batch, or name. Journals are a good example of worksheet pages, but there are other worksheet examples such as the account schedule or the requisition worksheet functionality. The following screenshot shows the **Item Journal** page:

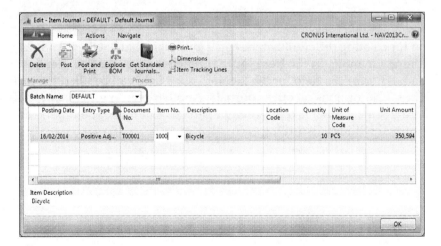

The **Item Journal** page is based on a batch and has a control for selecting the batch, as you can see in the previous screenshot.

Only the lines associated with the selected batch are shown in the page. It's similar to the header-lines structure. In this case, the header is the batch and has only one field, its name.

Users can create as many batches as needed on each journal. If you click on the **Batch Name:** field, the window shown in the following screenshot opens, showing all the available batches:

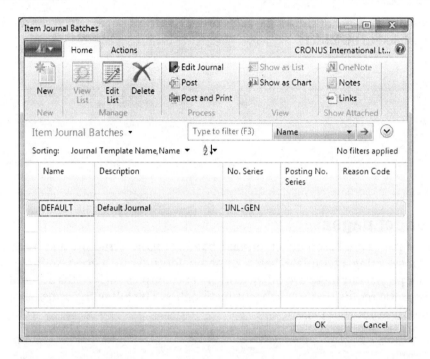

The reason for creating different batches on a journal is that batches can be set up to act in a different manner. In the **Item Journal Batches** page, the No. Series field, the Posting No. Series field, or the Reason Code field can be filled for each batch. You will find other options on other journals. Another reason for creating different batches on the same journal is that different persons can work at the same time on the same journal without disturbing each other's work.

ConfirmationDialog pages

ConfirmationDialog pages are pages that pose a question to the user, have no input fields, and require that the user select the **Yes** or the **No** button.

The **Check Availability** page shown in the following screenshot is a good example of a ConfirmationDialog page:

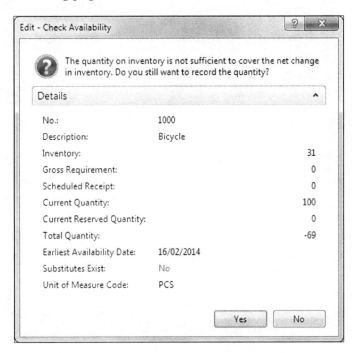

This page will pop up when the quantity filled in a line, either a document line or a journal line, is bigger than the current availability of the item.

NavigatePage pages

These pages are used for wizards, which consist of a number of user input screens or steps linked together, enabling users to carry out infrequently performed tasks.

Dynamics NAV also has a functionality called Navigate, and the page that shows this functionality is a NavigatePage type of page.

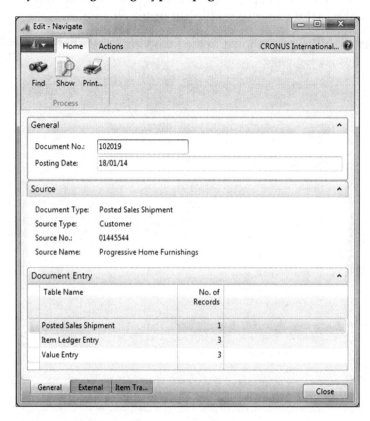

The navigate functionality shows all documents and entries posted using the same document number on the same posting date. This is a very useful way to see all the entries a particular transaction has created. If you create your own entry or posted document tables, don't forget to add them to the Navigate functionality.

The final picture

Well, there is no final picture for this section. Since we were talking about structure and the importance of maintaining the same structure on customized area, we wanted to maintain the same structure of the last section! Just kidding. We hope that after those two sections, you have a clear idea of the basic structure of an area of Dynamics NAV. We encourage you to follow the same structure on any new area you develop.

The posting process

The posting process is the most important process of the system. Actually, there are a few different posting processes, but they all follow the same structure. The posting process is complicated. If you try to debug a posting process, you will see that a lot of code from a lot of functions is executed to achieve the purpose of the posting process. In fact, many functions are executed many times. This section does not cover the posting process in depth; refer to *Chapter 3, Dynamics NAV General Considerations* for detailed information. Instead, this section shows the existing post codeunits and how they are structured.

There are several posting routines, one for each journal table and one for each group of documents. All posting routines use more than one codeunit. In Dynamics NAV, you can find more than 80 codeunits with the word *post* on their description. That's quiet a few!

Let's see a couple of examples of the posting's codeunits structure. The first example is posting codeunits for sales documents. In the second example, we will see posting's codeunits for general journal lines.

The codeunit structure for sales posting

The sales posting routine consists of 4 codeunits. The following diagram shows the schema that shows how each codeunit relates to one another:

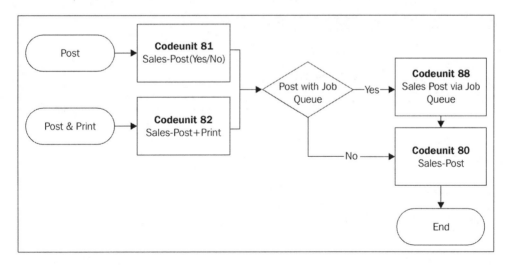

A user can start the posting process by selecting the Post or the Post & Print action, which will run Codeunit 81 Sales-Post (Yes/No) and Codeunit 82 Sales-Post + Print respectively. Both codeunits perform the same action; the only difference is that the Codeunit 82 Sales-Post + Print prints the posted sales document at the end. Both codeunits ask a confirmation from the user and check whether the post with the job queue is activated. If the post with job queue is activated, they call the Codeunit 88 Sales Post via Job Queue, which creates new records on a queue table to post the document later in a batch job. When the record in the queue is processed, Codeunit 80 Sales-Post is called in order to end the posting routine. If the post with the job queue is not activated, Codeunit 80 Sales-Post is called from Codeunit 81 or Codeunit 82.

Codeunit 80 Sales-Post is the most important one. It checks data, inserts records into the historical document tables, and creates all the required journal lines. It also calls the posting routines for the journal lines. You will find similar structures in other document-posting routines.

The codeunit structure for general journal posting

The general journal routine consists of 7 codeunits. The following screenshot shows us the schema of how each codeunit relates to each other:

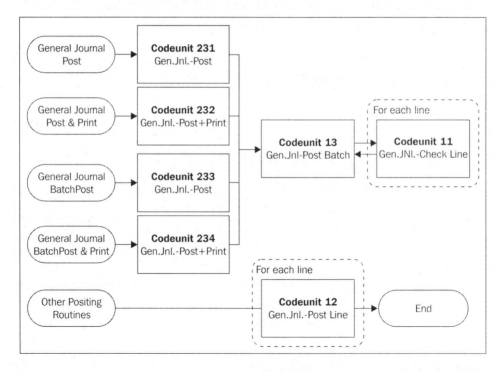

The general journal posting routine can start from several places. Either from a general journal page or a general journal batch page, or the user can start the routine by selecting the Post or the Post & Print action. This will run one of the following codeunits: Codeunit 231 Gen. Jnl.-Post, codeunit 232 Gen. Jnl.-Post + Print, codeunit 233 Gen. Jnl.-B.Post, or codeunit 234 Gen. Jnl.-B.Post + Print.

All these codeunits ask for confirmation from the user, and codeunits 232 and 234 also print the posted entries at the end. After that, they all call codeunit 13 Gen. Jnl.-Post Batch. This codeunit checks the consistency of all the lines individually, by calling Codeunit 11 Gen. Jnl.-Check Line. Codeunit 13 also checks that all lines in the transactions are balanced, and if so it inserts some secondary data into the records.

Finally, codeunit 13 calls codeunit 12 Gen. Jnl.-Post Line for each line. Codeunit 12 is the one in charge of creating the corresponding ledger entries. If some other posting routines need to post General Journal Lines, they do so by calling codeunit 12 directly.

Where to write customized code

While writing your own customized code for Dynamics NAV, it is important to choose where to write that code. If you try, you will see that the same code can be written in different places and the application will still work as you had intended. Unfortunately, not all places are equally good. Depending on where we write our code, it will be easier or more difficult to expand or change functionality. That's why we have to choose the best site. In this section we will give you some guidelines for choosing where to write your code.

Validating fields

When a field is filled, a special trigger runs the `OnValidate` trigger of the field. For a given field, you will find an `OnValidate` trigger on the page where the user enters the data and also on the table itself. Whenever possible, write your code on the `OnValidate` trigger of the table.

A field can be shown on multiple pages. If you choose to validate the field on the page, you will have to replicate your code in all the pages where the field is shown. This will make your code difficult to maintain.

Checking data

Dynamics NAV checks if certain fields are filled or filled with certain data only when the system needs it. As an example, you can create a new customer just by giving it a number, which is the way to identify the customer. Then you can leave the customer card without filling any other field. You are not using the new customer yet, so the system allows you to do it. However, if you try to select the newly created customer on a sales order, you will get the following error:

> ⊗ Gen. Bus. Posting Group must have a value in Customer: No.=C00010. It cannot be zero or empty. (Select Refresh to discard errors)

The system does not need you to fill the `Gen. Bus. Posting Group` field of a customer until you want to use the customer on a transaction, either a document or a journal line. Some other fields from the customer card are also mandatory in order to select the customer on a new transaction. Dynamics NAV checks the needed data one by one and also gives message errors one by one. If you enter the customer card and fill in the required field, you will get the following error:

> ⊗ Customer Posting Group must have a value in Customer: No.=C00010. It cannot be zero or empty. (Select Refresh to discard errors)

You will get an error one after another until all required fields are filled. When you have finally inserted the sales order and tried to post the shipment, many other validations are done. In fact, the posting routines are the ones that do the big job, data checking.

Posting dates, dimensions, item availability, posting groups' setup, and many other questions are checked while posting. This means that it is when posting that most of the data is required.

Batch jobs

Batch jobs are written using a `Report` object. Typically, batch jobs are not to be done for all records on a table, but for a set of them. In most cases, it is the user who selects what set of data has to be processed. `Report` objects are the ones that best suit those requirements, since they have an interface that allows users to select options or filter data.

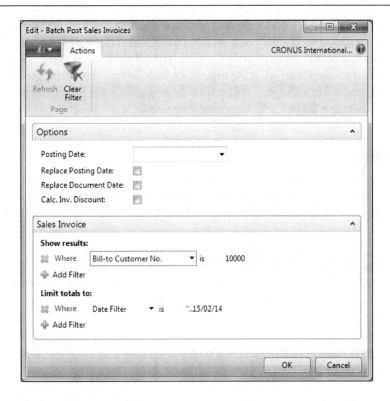

The previous screenshot is an example of a **Batch Post Sales Invoices** report. It is used to post multiple invoices. As we can see in the screenshot, there is an **Options** tab, and a **Sales Invoice** tab that allows users to filter data. In the example, we have chosen to only post invoices from customer number **10000** onwards.

In this section we have seen where to write customized code. Besides following the guidelines given in this book, there are other options that will help you choose where to write your code. When you need to write a new functionality, you can search for a similar functionality on the standard application and try to mimic the structure.

How to write customized code

Writing customized code is easy; customized code should look like standard code. How to write customized code? Like standard code! You have to keep in mind that any code you write today will probably be maintained by others in the future. If you follow your own programming conventions, we are pretty sure you'll find them easier to write and read. Unfortunately, others may not be used to your conventions, so you'll be making their work harder.

Like it or not, all Dynamics NAV developers are used to reading code from the standard application. If everyone writes customized code like the standard application does, everybody will only be able to read their own code. To make it easy to maintain an application, it is important to follow a few strict guidelines while writing C/AL code. This chapter will cover these guidelines. The information found in this section is taken from *C/AL Programming Guide*.

Language

In the standard application, all C/AL code is entered in English (United States). If all code is in the same language, it is easier to maintain the applications, including add-ons for several countries.

Spacing and alignment

There must be exactly one space character on each side of binary operators such as assignment or plus, as shown in the following example:

```
y := (a + b) / 100;
```

There must not be any space between a unary operator and its argument, as shown in the following example:

```
y := -x;
```

In general, use an indentation of two character spaces, as shown in following the example:

```
IF a <> '' THEN
  Record.TESTFIELD(b);
```

When you split a C/AL statement into two or more lines, indent the continuation line by two characters, as shown in the following example:

```
MyVariable :=
  Variable1 + Variable2 * 2 + Variable3 * 3;

MyFunction(
  Expression1,Expression2,
  Expression3,Expression4);
```

Comments

Always start comments with // followed by one character space. Never use curly brackets ({ and }). To emphasize a comment, put it on a separate line and insert one empty line before it, as shown in the following example:

```
// Comment
x := x * 2;
```

If the comment is on the same line as the C/AL code, add one character space before the comment sign, as shown in the following example:

```
x := '....'; // Comment
```

Text constants

Error messages and other message strings must be entered as text constants. That way, the message can be easily translated and the users can see the same message in their own language.

Text constants will automatically be assigned unique IDs by **C/SIDE**. You can see the ID by opening the **C/AL Globals** window, selecting the text constant, and navigating to its **Properties** window.

When you are working in the **C/AL Editor** window, place the cursor on a text constant and the content of the text constant will be shown in the message line.

C/AL statements

The IF and THEN statements should normally be on the same line. The ELSE statement should be on a separate line as shown in the following example:

```
IF x = y THEN
  x := x + 1
ELSE
  x := -x - 1;
```

If the last statement in the THEN part of an IF-THEN-ELSE statement string is an EXIT command or an ERROR command, do not continue with an ELSE statement, as shown in the following code snippet:

```
IF x <> y THEN
  EXIT(TRUE);
x := x * 2;
```

When the BEGIN statement follows the THEN, ELSE, or DO statement, it should be on the same line, preceded by one character space as shown in the following snippet:

```
IF (x = y) AND (a = b) THEN BEGIN
  x := a;
  y := b;
END;
```

REPEAT should always be alone on a line. Indentation of REPEAT statements is shown in the following example snippet:

```
REPEAT
  <Statement>;
UNTIL <expr>;

REPEAT
  <Statement>;
UNTIL <expr> AND
        <expr>;
```

When you use a CASE statement, indent the possibilities by two character spaces. Two or more possibilities on the same line are separated by commas (with no spaces), and the last possibility on a line is immediately followed by a colon (with no preceding space).

The action starts on the line after the possibility, further indented by two character spaces. If there is a BEGIN statement, it should be placed on a separate line unless it follows the ELSE statement. In this case, it should be on the same line as the ELSE statement.

```
CASE Field OF
  Field::A:
    BEGIN
      x := x + 1;
      y := -y - 1;
    END;
  Field::B:
    x := y;
  Field::C,Field::D:
    y := x;
  ELSE BEGIN
    y := x;
    a := b;
  END;
END;
```

If there are more than two alternatives, use a CASE statement; otherwise, use an IF statement.

Naming conventions

Precise and consistent terminology helps the end user work with the application. Rules for naming and abbreviating everything will also help programmers gain an understanding of the base application and develop new features faster.

Remember that the user will see the value of the caption property but not the name property. But you, as a developer, must follow the naming convention in this section both for the name in English (United States) and for the caption in your local language.

Naming objects

Two objects of the same type must not have the same name. In general, each object must be named in a way that leaves no doubt as to what it is concerned with (for example, an object can be specifically related to customers, items, or resources). Do not give a table the name Status, for example, because the word is too general and could refer to something in almost every table.

Table objects

The names of table objects are always singular. That is, the table name corresponds to what one record in the table is called.

Page objects

The name of a page depends on the page type. A card page has the singular form of the table name and a list page has the plural form of the table name. This gives the users an idea of the type of page they have selected or that which will be presented. If a table can be accessed by both a card page and a list page, the page names should explicitly describe the page types (for example, item card and item list). This tells the user that there is more than one way to access the table. Other page types (for example, statistics) are given names that are as descriptive as possible.

Report objects

The naming of reports is as important as that of pages and tables. For example, users see the caption of a report object when they need to identify a sales invoice, or when they modify or create reports. The caption is also shown in the request page. This is why the caption (and the name in English) should be as descriptive as possible and not include abbreviations. Whenever possible, the caption should be the same as the heading in the actual report.

Table fields

The name and caption of a field should be as descriptive as possible and should be able to stand alone, that is, the user should not need to see the caption in the context of other fields in order to understand what it is.

The field contents and the field type should be described in the caption. For example, include `Date` while you name a date field (for instance, `Posting Date`). If the field contains a percentage, include it. This is displayed with the percentage sign, for example, `Profit %`. Include `Quantity` (or `Qty.`) when you name a quantity field, for example, `Quantity Shipped`. Replace `Quantity` with `No.` while referring to the number of entries, for example, `No. Printed` and `No. of New Records`. Include `Amount` (or `Amt.`) while you name an amount field, for example, `Debit Amount`.

Codeunit objects

A codeunit is named almost like a report, except that the name begins with the object that the codeunit processes, followed by a dash. The object is normally a record abbreviated as a variable (see rules for this in the next section). The description of the codeunit is written in the imperative (without abbreviations, if possible), for example, `Purch-Explode BOM`.

Variables

Use the existing terminology whenever possible; for instance, the standard application usually names variables that refer to the `General Journal Line` table as `GenJnlLine`. Blanks, periods, and other characters (such as parentheses) that would make quotation marks around a variable necessary, must be omitted. For example, the periods and blanks are omitted in the `GenJnlBatch` variable. In addition, currency unit signs, such as `$`, should be replaced by the corresponding currency unit code, for example, `AmountUSD`.

User-defined functions

While naming user-defined functions, if possible start with a verb in the imperative, for example, `ApplyCustLedgEntry`. Usage of function name prefixes are shown in the following examples:

- If the code posts something, use `Post` as a prefix
- If the code makes something, use `Make` as a prefix
- If the code inserts something, use `Insert` as a prefix
- If something is checked, use `Check` as a prefix

Using small functions

Every Dynamics NAV object allows you to create functions inside itself. Instead of writing all your code in an existing trigger, break up your code into small steps. Write each small step's code in a separate function, give the function a name so that it explains what it does, and call your function from where you need it. This will ensure that you do not not write the same thing twice.

If the functions you are creating are to be called from one single object, create them on the object. If the functions are to be called from many objects, create them in a codeunit to group them all, or create them on a table if the function refers to a record of a table.

Summary

In this chapter we have seen that Dynamics NAV offers many configuration options and workarounds that we should use before starting to write our own code. If you need to write customized code, it is important to do it following the same structure as the standard application, to avoid confusing the users. The structures of the tables and the pages are the most important ones, and we've seen them in depth.

The posting process, or posting routines, are the ones in charge of creating historical documents and entries. If you need to modify them, you have to be careful and know what you are doing. That's why we have explained the main idea of posting routines. Last but not least, we have seen where and how to write customized code on Dynamics NAV objects.

In the following chapters we will see how to implement functional changes on existing and running Dynamics NAV implementations.

9

Functional Changes on Existing Implementations

The world changes constantly. So do the way companies work and the way they interact with other companies.

A changing company may require functional changes on their Microsoft Dynamics NAV implementation. A whole new project should start. It may not be an implementation project, but some of the steps that have to be taken on an implementation project also apply. There are some other things to take into account though, and this chapter will explain how to handle a project like this one by analyzing the actions to be performed by using four examples of a functional change in Dynamics NAV:

- Requisition Worksheet
- Fixed Assets
- Item Tracking
- Extending a customized functionality

General guidelines

All functional changes are different. Some will just require a few actions to complete the change; some others may require many actions, not just on the functionality being changed, but also somewhere else. There are a few things you have to take into account when implementing a functional change. In this section we will provide some general guidelines. Later on, we will follow the guidelines for all the examples of the chapter.

The following figure shows the general steps that will have to be performed to implement a functional change:

1. The first step is to clearly define the functional change.

2. After that, we have to think about how this change will affect other Dynamics NAV functionalities and whether those other functionalities will have to change somehow.

3. Once all the changes are clear, we will have to define a clear list of all the actions that will have to be completed to be able to implement the functional change.

4. Having the whole picture of the effort required to implement the functional change, we will be able to choose the right time to actually implement the change.

5. And finally, plan everything so that all actions are completed on time and the functional change can be implemented on the chosen day.

What is a functional change

A functional change in a Dynamics NAV implementation is to start using an application functionality not used before, or to change the way certain application functionalities were used in the past.

The Requisition Worksheet

Imagine a distribution company that purchases items from its vendors and sells those same items to its customers. This company does not have any kind of automation on its purchase order creation process. It manually determines when purchase orders have to be created, for which items, and in what quantities. In the aim of automating this process to reduce the time invested in purchase order creation, the company wants to start using the Requisition Worksheet, which according to the replenishment parameters established in every item, will calculate the replenishment needs of the company and, upon user acceptance, automatically create the corresponding purchase orders.

Fixed Assets

You could also think of a company that has never used the Fixed Assets functional area of Dynamics NAV and has only kept accounting information of its fixed assets by posting manual accounting transactions using the General Journal and now wants to start using the Fixed Asset functionality to better manage its fixed assets.

Item Tracking

A company may have been working with items for a long time and now it wants to have information of lot and serial numbers for its inventory.

If you try to enable the Item Tracking functionality on your existing items, you will get an error message over and over saying that the Item Tracking Code cannot be changed because one or more ledger entries exist for the item. Some actions will have to be performed to allow this functional change to be possible.

Extending a customized functionality

We have a recent example of implementing a functional change in an existing Dynamics NAV implementation.

In this customization, Volume Discounts were calculated for each sales invoice line, according to a set of predefined rules, and they were stored as Volume Discount Ledger Entries.

When thousands of Volume Discount Ledger Entries existed in the system, the company wanted to be able to apply those ledger entries to other ledger entries, so that they could know which ledger entries were still open, partially open, or closed. This is similar to how an application of Customer Ledger Entries or Vendor Ledger Entries works in standard Dynamics NAV.

Interactions with other functionalities

If you have to make a functional change in a Dynamics NAV implementation that has been working for a while, the questions that should be answered are does the functionality being changed (or that will begin to be used) have interactions with other Dynamics NAV functionalities? Which are those interactions? How will those other functionalities have to change?

The easiest scenario is when no interactions exist or when the interactions don't require any change on any other Dynamics NAV functionality than the one that is actually being changed.

The Requisition Worksheet

The Requisition Worksheet has interactions with the Purchase functionality of Dynamics NAV, since purchase orders are created as the result of running the Requisition Worksheet. However, it also has interactions with items (as they hold the replenishment parameters that the Requisition Worksheet will use), with the Sales functionality, (since the Requisition Worksheet will check this functionality to get the demand of items) and other functionalities that represent the demand of items (item transfers between locations, production components, service orders, and so on), and again with the Purchase functionality (since the Requisition Worksheet will check this functionality to get the supply of items) and other functionalities that represent the supply of items (item transfers between locations, inventory, production, and so on).

The answer to the question of how those functionalities will have to change, in the case of using the Requisition Worksheet, is that they do not have to change at all. Not in standard Dynamics NAV at least. You will have to check if some customizations in those areas in your Dynamics NAV implementation will interfere with the Requisition Worksheet and require further customization.

What will definitely have to change is the way users create purchase orders. The old procedure will not be used anymore, as it will be replaced by a new procedure.

Fixed Assets

The Fixed Assets functionality interacts with the Financial Management functionality.

The acquisition costs and depreciations of the company's fixed assets have probably already been posted to the General Ledger by posting manual transactions using the General Journal. But this will have to change in the future. Those transactions will not be posted anymore by creating manual transactions, but using standard functionality offered by the Microsoft Dynamics NAV Fixed Assets module. The accounting procedure will have to be changed.

Fixed assets also interact with Microsoft Dynamics Sales and Purchases functionalities, as fixed assets can either be sold or purchased using those functionalities. The user's procedures to post those transactions will change when the new functionality starts being used.

Item Tracking

The Item Tracking functionality interacts with all the Dynamics NAV areas that use items to post item transactions, such as:

- Sales and marketing
- Purchase
- Warehouse
- Manufacturing
- Jobs

Every single item posting transaction will have to change since Item Tracking will have to be informed prior to posting. Examine all places where you use items. Very often items have some kind of customization in Microsoft Dynamics NAV. When determining interactions with other Microsoft Dynamics NAV functionalities, take into account those customizations. They may not have been developed to support Item Tracking.

Item Tracking also interacts with Item Ledger Entries. Even if the actual inventory of an item is 0, Dynamics NAV will not allow you to start using Item Tracking that involves either **SN Specific Tracking** or **Lot Specific Tracking** if the item has had any kind of movement in the past.

That is a big problem for most companies, as the only way (without customizing Dynamics NAV) to start using Item Tracking for already used items is to use the official workaround, which involves the following steps:

1. For the item in question, reduce the quantity in hand to 0 by making a negative adjustment.
2. Rename the item in question.
3. Create a new item and give it the name of the original item.
4. Set up an Item Tracking Code for the new item.
5. For the new item, increase the quantity in hand to the original amount by making a positive adjustment.

Companies don't like this workaround. It involves a lot of work and a lot of problems.

- This workaround involves doubling your list of items (if Item Tracking has to be used in all items).
- It involves "losing" your item's history (entries, orders, and so on), as this will be under the renamed item and not under the new item.

- When renaming, not only the history of the item will be renamed, but also all kinds of related data (units of measure, sales and purchase prices, sales and purchase discounts, item variants, extended texts, cross references, stockkeeping units, bill of materials, and so on) and documents. However, not only historical documents (posted documents) will point to the renamed item, but pending documents as well. So you will have to go to all pending documents, one by one, and change the **Item No.** field so that the new item is shipped, received, or manufactured instead of the old one. You will also have to check bills of materials where that item was used, because you probably also want to point it to the new item.

- Creating a new item involves not only creating the item itself, but also its related data (units of measure, sales and purchase prices, sales and purchase discounts, item variants, extended texts, cross references, stockkeeping units, bill of materials, and so on).

If you have to do this for thousands of items and you have a lot of related data to your items and a bunch of pending documents, then completing all those steps can take a lot of hours (even days).

You could also think about customization. Do not check if Item Ledger Entries exist for the item and allow the Item Tracking functionality to be turned on. If you do so, we recommend a lot of testing work. If Microsoft Dynamics NAV doesn't allow this change to be done, it is probably because the application has not been designed to do it under those circumstances. If you plan on turning on Item Tracking on your existing items without using the official workaround and allowing it through customization, test the application so that no data inconsistency is introduced due to the change.

By testing, you may find odd behaviors that you will have to take into account in the future.

For instance, an undo action on a Sales Shipment posted prior to the change (so posted without any Item Tracking information) may not work as expected. There is no tracking information for the undo action to use, but the item now requires this information. The standard functionality of Microsoft Dynamics NAV hasn't been designed to allow the user to introduce Item Tracking information when undoing a Sales Shipment. The posting action will require Item Tracking but there will be no way to introduce that information, so there will be no way to undo a Sales Shipment posted prior to the change.

Let's actually take a look at that situation in a step-by-step example. We will create a new item (with no Item Tracking) and post a purchase order for it. We will also post a sales order for that same item. Having Item Ledger Entries for the item, we will enable the Item Tracking functionality for it and will try to undo the Sales Shipment to see what happens.

Creating a new item

Follow the given steps to create a new item:

1. Navigate to the item list.

2. On the **Home** tab, click on **New** to create a new item.

3. Place the cursor on the **No.** field on the **General** tab.

4. Press *Enter*. Microsoft Dynamics NAV will give you a new item number. The item number in this example is **70061**.

5. Enter the following information for the item:

Tab Name	Field Name	Field value
General	Description:	**Item Tracking Test**
General	Base Unit of Measure:	**PCS**
Invoicing	Gen. Prod. Posting Group	**MISC**
Invoicing	VAT Prod. Posting Group	**VAT25**
Invoicing	Inventory Posting Group	**RESALE**

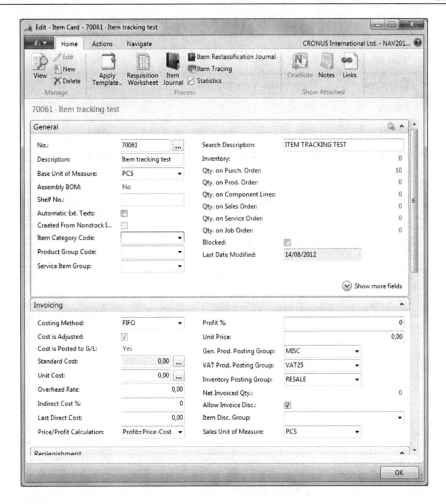

Creating and posting a purchase order for the new item

Follow the given steps to create and post a purchase order for the new item:

1. Navigate to the **Purchase Order** list.

2. On the **Home** tab, click on **New** to create a new purchase order.

3. Place the cursor on the **No.** field on the **General** tab.

4. Press *Enter*. Microsoft Dynamics NAV will give you a new purchase order number.

5. Enter the following information for the purchase order:

Tab Name	Field Name	Field value
General	Buy-from Vendor No.:	10000
Lines	Type	Item
Lines	No.	70061
Lines	Location Code	BLUE
Lines	Quantity	10
Lines	Direct Unit Cost Excl. VAT	1

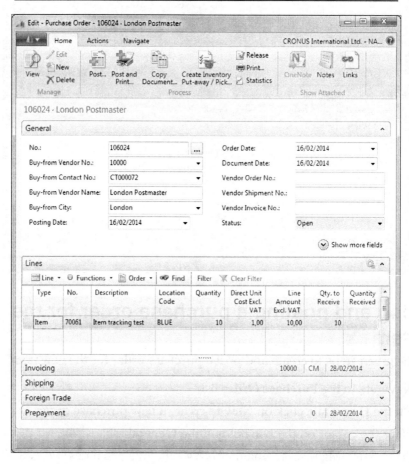

6. Make sure the **Qty. to Receive** field in the line has a value of **10**.

7. On the **Home** tab, click on **Post** to post the purchase order.

8. A dialog will open with options **Receive, Invoice,** and **Receive and Invoice**. Select **Receive** and click on **OK**.

9. The purchase order has been posted (received).

Creating and posting a Sales Order for the new item

Follow these steps to create and post a Sales Order for the new item:

1. Navigate to the **Sales Order** list.

2. On the **Home** tab, click on **New** to create a new Sales Order.

3. Place the cursor on the **No.** field on the **General** tab.

4. Press *Enter*. Microsoft Dynamics NAV will give you a new Sales Order number.

5. Enter the following information for the Sales Order:

Tab Name	Field Name	Field value
General	Sell-to Customer No.:	20000
Lines	Type	Item
Lines	No.	70061
Lines	Location Code	BLUE
Lines	Quantity	2
Lines	Unit Price Excl. VAT	1.5

6. Make sure the **Qty. to Ship** field in the line has a value of **2**.

7. On the **Home** tab, click on **Post** to post the Sales Order.

8. A dialog will open with options **Ship**, **Invoice**, and **Ship and Invoice**. Select **Ship** and click on **OK**.

9. The Sales Order has been posted (shipped).

Turning on Item Tracking for the new item

Follow these steps to turn on Item Tracking for the new item:

1. Navigate to the items list.

2. Select item 70061.

3. On the **Home** tab, click on **Edit**.

4. The **Edit – Item Card** for item 70061 opens.

5. On the **Item Tracking** tab, enter the LOTALL value in the **Item Tracking Code** field.

6. The **You cannot change Item Tracking Code because there are one or more ledger entries for this item** error message will be displayed.

Customization will have to be done in Dynamics NAV to allow the Item Tracking Code to be informed in items that have had any kind of ledger entry.

1. Close the **Edit – Item Card** window.

2. Open the Microsoft Dynamics NAV Development environment.

3. Open the **Object Designer** by navigating to **Tools | Object Designer**.

4. Select **Table 27** named **Item**.

5. Click on the **Design** button.

6. Select field **6500 Item Tracking Code**.

7. Click on **View – C/AL Code**.

8. The C/AL Code for Item Tracking Code triggers will be shown.

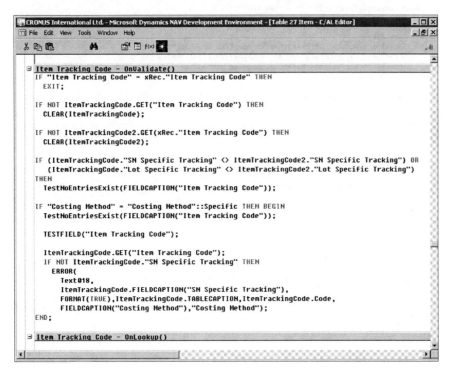

The call to function TestNoEntriesExist() in the fourth IF sentence is what tests whether Item Ledger Entries exist and throws the error we have seen when turning on Item Tracking.

9. Comment all lines involved in the fourth IF sentence by placing two backslashes (//) in front of those lines.

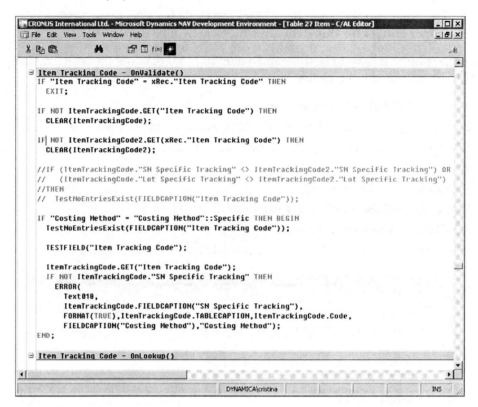

 This is just for demonstration purposes. Do not leave these lines of code uncommented in any live environment. It may lead to data inconsistency and to unpredictable behavior.

10. Navigate to **File | Save** to save the changes.

11. Close the Microsoft Dynamics NAV Development Environment.

12. Once again open the **Edit – Item Card** for item 70061.

13. On the **Item Tracking** tab, enter the LOTALL value in the **Item Tracking Code** field.

Undoing the Sales Shipment posted for the new item

Follow these steps to undo the Sales Shipment posted for the new item:

1. Navigate to the Posted Sales Shipments list.
2. Find Sales Shipment No. 102036.
3. On the **Home** tab, click on **View** to view the Sales Shipment.

    The **View – Posted Sales Shipment** window for Sales Shipment 102036 opens.
4. On the **Lines** tab, navigate to **Functions | Undo Shipment**.
5. A dialog will be prompted with the following question: **Do you really want to undo the selected Shipment lines?**.
6. Click on **Yes**. The following error message will appear:

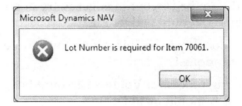

7. Click on **OK**.
8. Close the **View – Posted Sales Shipment** window.

This step-by-step example was meant to show you a problem you may encounter if you turn on Item Tracking on an item that had one or more Item Ledger Entries.

If you test around, you will probably find many other problems. If you do such a customization, you need to know all the problems you may encounter in the future.

Don't use the development done in this example in real environments. To allow the change in the **Item Tracking Code** field on an item, at least check that no Open Ledger Entries exist, rather than not checking anything at all.

Extending a customized functionality

In this example we are talking about a customized functionality in which Volume Discounts were calculated for each sales invoice line, according to a set of predefined rules, and stored as Volume Discount Ledger Entries.

The functionality had to be extended to allow users to apply those ledger entries to other Volume Discount Ledger Entries, so that they could know if Volume Discount Ledger Entries were completely open, partially open, or closed.

In this case there are no interactions with other Dynamics NAV functionalities. The interaction is actually with the customized Volume Discount functionality itself.

Since the functionality was developed to follow the same philosophy behind Customer Ledger Entries or Vendor Ledger Entries, the extension of the functionality had to follow the same philosophy as well.

That means creating a Detailed Volume Discount Ledger Entry table (similar to tables Detailed Cust. Ledg. Entry or Detailed Vendor Ledg. Entry) and then creating extra fields, the most important ones being **Remaining Amount**, **Open**, and **Amount To Apply**, in the already existing Volume Discount Ledger Entry table.

For all of this to work, the development of the functionalities' extension had to:

- Insert a Detailed Volume Discount Ledger Entry of type **Initial Entry** when inserting a Volume Discount Ledger Entry
- Develop the functionality to be able to select which Volume Discount Ledger Entries have to be applied
- Develop the posting process of Volume Discount Ledger Entries' Applications, which should include:
  - Inserting Detailed Volume Discount Ledger Entries of type **Application**
  - Updating field **Open** for the corresponding Volume Discount Ledger Entries

That is great and the extended functionality will work for new Volume Discount Ledger Entries. But, what happens with existing Volume Discount Ledger Entries? They do not have a Detailed Ledger Entry of type **Initial Entry**. And their **Open** field will indicate **No** (the default value for fields of type **Boolean**), but some of the existing Volume Discount Ledger Entries, especially the newest ones at the moment of implementing the new functionality, are probably open, so their **Open** field should actually indicate **Yes**.

When implementing the new functionality, some actions will have to be done to create Detailed Volume Discount Ledger Entries for all existing Volume Discount Ledger Entries. And a big initial application will have to be created so that only existing Volume Discount Ledger Entries that are really open indicate so on their Open field.

Writing a to-do list to implement a change

Several actions will have to be performed to implement a functional change. All of them will have to be written down so that everyone is aware of what has to be done for the new functionality to work properly.

The Requisition Worksheet

Let's examine the Requisition Worksheet implementation. The actions that have to be performed are as follows:

1. Study the different reordering policies Microsoft Dynamics NAV offers.

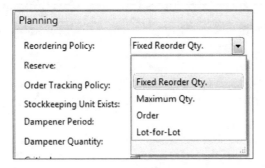

2. Determine which replenishment parameters apply to each reordering policy. Notice that some replenishment parameters are non-editable when you select a specific reordering policy. This means that those parameters do not apply to the selected reordering policy.

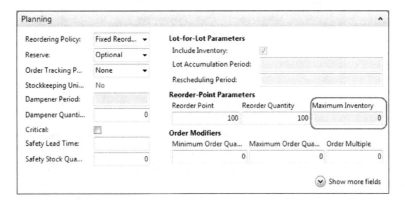

In the previous screenshot, you can see that the **Maximum Inventory** field is non-editable when the **Fixed Reorder Qty.** reordering policy is selected.

3. Establish which reordering policies will be used in every group of items. Different kinds of items will probably best fit in different reordering policies.

4. Calculate the appropriate replenishment parameters for every item using statistical information of sales or any other information.

5. Set the **Vendor No.** for every item.

6. Set the **Lead Time Calculation** for every item.

7. If the company manages different locations and replenishment parameters are different for every location, create **stockkeeping units** and inform the replenishment parameters in the stockkeeping unit card rather than on the item card.

8. If the company uses item variants and replenishment parameters are different for every variant, create stockkeeping units and inform the replenishment parameters in the stockkeeping unit card rather than on the item card.

9. If the company uses both different locations and item variants, create stockkeeping units per variant and per location.

That makes nine actions, and some of them may require a lot of time and effort to complete. As you go on, you may find several other actions that have to be done. Write them all down so that nothing is forgotten. Consider using flow charts for a clearer picture of what has to be done and in which order, if the order matters.

If you have a reasonable amount of items, this project will not be difficult or time consuming.

If you have thousands of items, you may want a Dynamics NAV developer to help you out with some of the steps, especially in the calculation of the replenishment parameters. You could think of an algorithm to calculate and inform replenishment parameters in your items or stockkeeping units and ask a Dynamics NAV developer to develop it for you.

Fixed Assets

Imagine a company that has been using Microsoft Dynamics for a while. This company has never used the Fixed Assets functionality. Now they want to start managing their fixed assets with Dynamics NAV.

How many actions do you think will be needed to complete the project? Let's go through them:

1. Get a list of the fixed assets. This may require that you perform a Fixed Asset Physical Inventory in your company.

2. Check the existing FA posting groups. Modify the existing FA posting groups if they do not meet your accounting requirements, or create new ones if you need to. To do so, navigate to **Departments/Financial Management/ Administration** and click on **FA Posting Groups**.

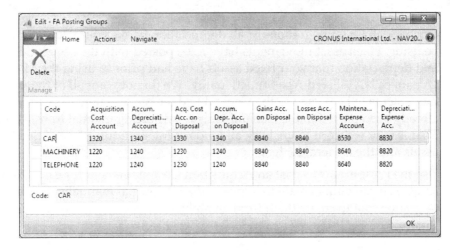

3. Study the different depreciation methods Microsoft Dynamics NAV offers. The **Depreciation Method** field can be found on a fixed asset card; the options for this field are shown in the following screenshot:

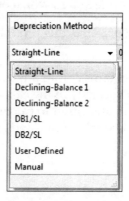

4. Choose the appropriate **FA Posting Group** for each fixed asset in your list.

5. Choose the appropriate **Depreciation Method** for each fixed asset in your list.

6. Determine the **Depreciation Starting Date** and **Depreciation Ending Date** for each fixed asset in your list.

7. Determine the **Acquisition Cost** for each fixed asset in your list.

8. Manually create all the fixed assets in Microsoft Dynamics NAV or choose a data migration tool and format to create fixed assets from an archive.

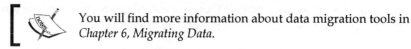

You will find more information about data migration tools in *Chapter 6, Migrating Data*.

9. Uncheck all G/L integrations of all depreciation books your company will be using. Fixed asset movements have to be posted with the acquisition cost and depreciation that your fixed assets have had prior to using the Microsoft Dynamics NAV Fixed Asset functionality. We do not want all of those movements to be posted to the General Ledger because they have probably already been posted to the General Ledger by posting manual transactions. That is why we want to uncheck all kinds of integrations between fixed assets and the General Ledger.

10. Use the FA Journals to post an Acquisition Cost movement for each fixed asset. You can either create the lines in the FA Journal manually or use a data migration tool to create them from an archive.

11. Use the FA Journal to post depreciation movements for each fixed asset. You can either create the lines in the FA Journal manually or use a data migration tool to create them from an archive.

12. Make sure both acquisition costs and depreciation movements match with transactions previously posted to the General Ledger.

13. Check G/L integrations again of all depreciation books your company will be using.

In this example, 13 actions had to be completed to implement this functional change. All the steps can be done by an end user using standard Dynamics NAV functionality.

If you have a reasonable amount of fixed assets, this project will not be difficult or time consuming.

If you have thousands of fixed assets, you may want a Dynamics NAV developer to help you out with some of the steps, especially in the creation of thousands of FA Journal lines to post acquisition costs and depreciations.

Item Tracking

In this example, we are talking about turning on Item Tracking for existing items that have at least one Item Ledger Entry. This is a casuistry in which Dynamics NAV will not allow us to turn Item Tracking on.

In the previous section we have already talked about some of the steps that will have to be performed for this to be possible. We will follow the official workaround to implement this functional change, as we have seen that some other solutions can lead to data inconsistency, unpredictable behavior, or some other functionalities to not work as expected.

Let's write down the list of actions we need to perform in order to turn on Item Tracking for existing items that have at least one Item Ledger Entry:

1. Reduce the quantity in hand to zero by making negative adjustments of all items for which Item Tracking will be turned on.

2. Rename all those items.

3. Create new items and give them the name of the original items.

4. Create and configure related data for the new items that include:
    ° Units of measure
    ° Sales prices
    ° Sales discounts

- ° Purchase prices
- ° Purchase discounts
- ° Vendors
- ° Item variants
- ° Extended texts
- ° Translations
- ° Cross references
- ° Stockkeeping units
- ° Bill of materials
- ° Substitutions
- ° Dimensions
- ° Customized related data

5. Set up the Item Tracking Code for the new items.

6. Do a physical inventory of those items, specifying quantities and their tracking (serial number, lot number, and expiration date).

7. Increase the quantity in hand of the new items by making positive adjustments in which quantities and tracking will have to be specified.

8. Review open documents and change the item number to point to the new item instead of the renamed one, so that the item that will be shipped, received, or manufactured is actually the new one and not the renamed one.

- ° Sales documents
- ° Purchase documents
- ° Service documents
- ° Transfer orders
- ° Manufacturing documents
- ° Job planning lines
- ° Item journals
- ° Warehouse journals
- ° Requisition Worksheets

Extending a customized functionality

In this example we are talking about a customized functionality in which Volume Discounts were calculated for each sales invoice line, according to a set of predefined rules, and stored as Volume Discount Ledger Entries.

The functionality had to be extended to allow users to apply those ledger entries to other Volume Discount Ledger Entries, so that they could know if Volume Discount Ledger Entries were completely open, partially open, or closed.

In the *Interactions with other functionalities* section, we said that this extension actually had only interactions with the functionality itself, and we have already pointed out some of the actions that will have to be performed, such as creating Detailed Volume Discount Ledger Entries of type **Initial Entry** for all existing Volume Discount Ledger Entries and doing a big initial application of Volume Discount Ledger Entries so that only real open Volume Discount Ledger Entries indicate so on their **Open** field.

The actions to be performed in this example are as follows:

1. Develop the extended functionality as per requirements.

2. Develop a process that will create Detailed Volume Discount Ledger Entries of type **Initial Entry** for all existing Volume Discount Ledger Entries.

3. Develop a process that will set the recently created **Open** field to **Yes** in the table Volume Discount Ledger Entry.

4. Determine which existing Volume Discount Ledger Entries are actually open and what **Remaining Amount** they should have.

5. Implement the development change.

6. Execute the process that will create Detailed Volume Discount Ledger Entries of type **Initial Entry** for all existing Volume Discount Ledger Entries.

7. Execute the process that will set the recently created **Open** field to **Yes** in the table Volume Discount Ledger Entry.

8. Use the new Volume Discount Application functionality to do a big initial application posting so that at the end of this process, only real open Volume Discount Ledger Entries are marked as open and they have the correct Remaining Amount.

Choosing the right time

It is important to choose the right time to make a functional change on an existing Dynamics NAV implementation. Some functional changes can be implemented at any time. Some of them may require a lot of time and no users to be working and changing data; you may want to choose a weekend for that. Some others could be implemented at any time, but to keep a better track of the time at which it began to work differently, you might want to choose the start of a fiscal year or the start of a month.

The important thing is to think about it, analyze it, and choose the right time for every functional change implementation.

The Requisition Worksheet

Using the Requisition Worksheet to automatically calculate and plan the replenishment of items is something that could be done at any time. It could even be done progressively, starting with a few items to get familiar with the requisition functionality and adding new items to this process by progressively configuring their replenishment parameters.

In this case, the right time is anytime, whenever you are ready for it.

Fixed Assets

Using the Fixed Assets functionality when previously only accounting tracking has been kept of the fixed assets is something you may want to do at the beginning of a fiscal year because of the accounting implications.

That way you will always know that fixed assets costing and depreciation accounting transactions were done in a certain way until the end of a certain fiscal year, and another way for the following fiscal years.

This doesn't actually mean that you have to do it on January 1, if that is the date when your fiscal year starts. It can be done any other day of the year, but with that date in mind.

In the previous section, when talking about the actions required to start using Microsoft Dynamics NAV Fixed Assets functionalities, we said that fixed asset movements will have to be posted with the acquisition cost and depreciation the fixed assets may have prior to start using the new functionality.

Even if you implement the change any day of the year, you could post acquisition cost and depreciation entries up to December 31 of the previous year and make sure they match with acquisition costs and depreciations posted directly to the General Ledger also up to that date.

After that, you will be able to calculate the depreciation of all fixed assets for the whole fiscal year. It will be calculated the same way (through Dynamics NAV functionality) for the whole year.

If you choose any other date to implement this functionality, there will be a fiscal year in which depreciations will be calculated partially by Dynamics NAV and partially by any other method. This could be difficult to keep track of, but not impossible.

But there are other things to take into account. We said in the previous section that to perform the first action, getting the list of fixed assets of the company, could require performing a Fixed Asset Physical Inventory in your company. Depending on how large the company is, this could be done in a few hours or could require a lot of time.

Taking all variables into account and knowing the implications of everything, choose the right time for you.

Item Tracking

If you turn Item Tracking on for your items, it is because you want or need to be able to have traceability of your products.

Choose an appropriate time to do so because you will have to know when your traceability begins and that before that date there is no traceability at all.

You may have a legal requirement that says that after a specific date, traceability will be mandatory for the kind of items you sell or manufacture. If this is the case, that date will probably be the right time.

If this is not the case, or you have a period of time to implement it, you will have to choose a specific date. The beginning of a fiscal year or the beginning of a specific month are dates that are easy to remember for anyone. They could be good candidates.

But you also have to take into account that turning Item Tracking on, especially if it has to be done for a large number of items, or if you have a lot of data related to your items, or a lot of pending documents, is something that will be time consuming. You will have to rename old items, create new items, create their related data, and go through all pending documents. You will also have to reduce the quantity in hand of the old items and do a physical inventory of the new items to write down their tracking, and be able to increase the inventory of the new items and assign them the right tracking.

Even if you develop a process to rename items, create new items and all their related data and go through all pending documents. You have to know that this will be a time-consuming process if that has to be done for a lot of items, because the renaming instruction in Dynamics NAV takes a lot of time to execute. I did it once for a company with around 15 thousands items and the process took three complete days to finish. And besides that process, there is a physical inventory, which could also be a time-consuming action.

There is something else to take into account. When doing all of this, you do not want any users to be posting any item entries.

Keeping all of this in mind, you will probably have to choose a time to implement the change on items outside regular working times: a long weekend or a holiday period.

You could also choose to implement Item Tracking progressively, a few items at a time. That will take a shorter time per partial implementation, so it will be easier to find the time to do it, but the global process will take longer and there will not be a single date on which Item Tracking functionality was turned on.

Extending a customized functionality

In this example in which a functionality of Volume Discounts—which has Volume Discount Ledger Entries—wants to be extended by adding application functionality similar to how applications work both in Customer Ledger Entries and Vendor Ledger Entries, any time is good to implement the change. Whenever it is developed and ready to go live will be considered a good time to implement this change.

The only thing to take into account is that the list of Open Ledger Entries has to be prepared for the initial application to be done. Some manual work will have to be done to post this initial application, but there is no need to stop working, to not allow other people to post other kinds of transactions, and so on.

Planning the change

Good planning (and actually sticking to it) is something you always need. As we have seen, some implementations may require a lot of actions to be done, some of them before the new functionality is implemented, some during the implementation process, and some others right after the implementation process is completed. Some implementations can even be done progressively, so they could last weeks or even some months.

Everything has to be planned and scheduled so that all needed work for the implementation of the functionality is ready on the chosen date to go live.

Take the to do list written in the previous section and determine the following for each action:

- Determine when the action has to be done:
    ◦ Before the implementation date
    ◦ During the implementation process
    ◦ After the implementation process is completed

- Estimate the time that will be needed to complete the action
- Establish relations between actions (some actions have to be completed so that another action can start; some other actions have no relations with other actions so that two or more actions can be performed simultaneously)
- Determine the date on which the actions should be completed
- Determine the person or persons responsible to perform the action

The Requisition Worksheet

Let's take the actions required for this implementation and determine relations between them, estimation of time, and when they should be performed. In the example, we will not be determining the due date and the people responsible for the action.

The estimation of time will depend upon the number of items the company implementing this functionality may have.

1. Study the different reordering policies Microsoft Dynamics NAV offers:
    ◦ **When**: Before the implementation
    ◦ **Estimation of time**: 1 day
    ◦ **Previous action**: None

2. Determine which replenishment parameters apply to each reordering policy:
    ◦ **When**: Before the implementation
    ◦ **Estimation of time**: Half a day
    ◦ **Previous action**: Action 1

3. Establish which reordering policies will be used in every group of items:
    - ◦ **When**: Before the implementation
    - ◦ **Estimation of time**: 1 day
    - ◦ **Previous action**: Action 2

4. Calculate the appropriate replenishment parameters for every item using statistical information of sales or any other information:
    - ◦ **When**: Before the implementation
    - ◦ **Estimation of time**: 3 days
    - ◦ **Previous action**: Action 3

5. Set the **Vendor No.** for every item:
    - ◦ **When**: Before the implementation
    - ◦ **Estimation of time**: 1 day
    - ◦ **Previous action**: None

6. Set the **Lead Time Calculation** for every item:
    - ◦ **When**: Before the implementation
    - ◦ **Estimation of time**: 1 day
    - ◦ **Previous action**: None

7. If the company manages different locations and replenishment parameters are different for every location, create stockkeeping units and inform the replenishment parameters in the stockkeeping unit card rather than on the item card:
    - ◦ **When**: Before the implementation
    - ◦ **Estimation of time**: Half a day
    - ◦ **Previous action**: None

8. If the company uses item variants and replenishment parameters are different for every variant, create stockkeeping units and inform the replenishment parameters in the stockkeeping unit card rather than on the item card:
    - ◦ **When**: Before the implementation
    - ◦ **Estimation of time**: Half a day
    - ◦ **Previous action**: None

9. If the company uses both different locations and item variants, create stockkeeping units per variant and per location:

    ◦ **When**: Before the implementation

    ◦ **Estimation of time**: Half a day

    ◦ **Previous action**: None

Fixed Assets

Let's take the actions required for this implementation and determine relations between them, estimation of time, and when they should be performed. In the example, we will not be determining the due date and the people responsible for the action.

The estimation of time will depend upon the number of fixed assets the company implementing this functionality may have.

1. Get a list of fixed assets:

    ◦ **When**: Before the implementation

    ◦ **Estimation of time**: 2 days

    ◦ **Previous action**: None

2. Check the existing **FA Posting Groups**.

    Modify the existing **FA Posting Groups** if they do not meet your accounting requirements or create new ones if you need to:

    ◦ **When**: Before the implementation

    ◦ **Estimation of time**: Half a day

    ◦ **Previous action**: None

3. Study the different depreciation methods Microsoft Dynamics NAV offers:

    ◦ **When**: Before the implementation

    ◦ **Estimation of time**: Half a day

    ◦ **Previous action**: None

4. Choose the appropriate **FA Posting Group** for each fixed asset in your list:

    ◦ **When**: Before the implementation

    ◦ **Estimation of time**: Half a day

    ◦ **Previous action**: Actions 1 and 2

5. Choose the appropriate **Depreciation Method** for each fixed asset in your list:
    - ° **When**: Before the implementation
    - ° **Estimation of time**: Half a day
    - ° **Previous action**: Actions 1 and 3

6. Determine the **Depreciation Starting Date** and **Depreciation Ending Date** for each fixed asset in your list:
    - ° **When**: Before the implementation
    - ° **Estimation of time**: 1 day
    - ° **Previous action**: Action 1

7. Determine the acquisition cost for each fixed asset in your list:
    - ° **When**: Before the implementation
    - ° **Estimation of time**: 1 day
    - ° **Previous action**: Action 1

8. Create all the fixed assets in Microsoft Dynamics NAV:
    - ° **When**: Before or during the implementation
    - ° **Estimation of time**: Half a day
    - ° **Previous action**: Actions 1 to 7

9. Uncheck all G/L integrations of all depreciation books your company will be using:
    - ° **When**: During the implementation
    - ° **Estimation of time**: Half an hour
    - ° **Previous action**: None

10. Use the FA Journals to post an acquisition cost movement for each fixed asset:
    - ° **When**: During the implementation
    - ° **Estimation of time**: Half a day
    - ° **Previous action**: Actions 8 and 9

11. Use the FA Journal to post depreciation movements for each fixed asset:
    - ° **When**: During the implementation
    - ° **Estimation of time**: Half a day
    - ° **Previous action**: Action 11

12. Make sure both acquisition costs and depreciation movements match with transactions previously posted to the General Ledger:
    - ° **When**: During the implementation
    - ° **Estimation of time**: Half a day
    - ° **Previous action**: Action 11

13. Check G/L integrations again of all the depreciation books your company will be using:
    - ° **When**: After the implementation
    - ° **Estimation of time**: Half an hour
    - ° **Previous action**: Action 12

Item Tracking

Let's take the actions required for this implementation and determine relations between them, estimation of time, and when they should be performed. In the example, we will not be determining the due date and the people responsible for the action.

The estimation of time will depend upon the number of items the company implementing this functionality may have.

1. Reduce the quantity in hand to zero by making negative adjustments of all items for which Item Tracking will be turned on:
    - ° **When**: During the implementation
    - ° **Estimation of time**: Half a day
    - ° **Previous action**: None

2. Rename all those items:
    - ° **When**: During the implementation
    - ° **Estimation of time**: 1-2 days
    - ° **Previous action**: Action 1

3. Create new items and give them the names of the original items:
    - ° **When**: During the implementation
    - ° **Estimation of time**: Half a day
    - ° **Previous action**: Action 2

4. Create and configure related data for the new items:
   - ° **When**: During the implementation
   - ° **Estimation of time**: Half a day
   - ° **Previous action**: Action 3

5. Set up the Item Tracking Code for the new items:
   - ° **When**: During the implementation
   - ° **Estimation of time**: Half a day
   - ° **Previous action**: Action 3

6. Do a physical inventory of those items, specifying quantities and their tracking (serial number, lot number, and expiration date):
   - ° **When**: During the implementation
   - ° **Estimation of time**: 1 day
   - ° **Previous action**: None

7. Increase the quantity in hand of the new items by making positive adjustments in which quantities and tracking will have to be specified:
   - ° **When**: During the implementation
   - ° **Estimation of time**: Half a day
   - ° **Previous action**: Action 6

8. Review Open documents and change the **Item No.:** field to point to the new item instead of to the renamed one, so that the item that will be shipped, received, or manufactured is actually the new one and not the renamed one:
   - ° **When**: After the implementation
   - ° **Estimation of time**: Half a day
   - ° **Previous action**: Action 2

Extending a customized functionality

Let's take the actions required for this implementation and determine relations between them, estimation of time, and when they should be performed. In the example, we will not be determining the due date and the people responsible for the action.

The estimation of time will depend upon the number of Volume Discount Ledger Entries the company implementing this functionality has.

1. Do the required development of the extended functionality:
   - ° **When**: Before the implementation
   - ° **Estimation of time**: 4 days
   - ° **Previous action**: None

2. Develop a process that will create Detailed Volume Discount Ledger Entries of type **Initial Entry** for all existing Volume Discount Ledger Entries:
   - ° **When**: Before the implementation
   - ° **Estimation of time**: Half a day
   - ° **Previous action**: Action 1

3. Develop a process that will set the recently created Open field to **Yes** in the table Volume Discount Ledger Entry:
   - ° **When**: Before the implementation
   - ° **Estimation of time**: Half a day
   - ° **Previous action**: Action 1

4. Determine which existing Volume Discount Ledger Entries are actually open and which **Remaining Amount** they should have:
   - ° **When**: Before the implementation
   - ° **Estimation of time**: 1 day
   - ° **Previous action**: None

5. Implement the development change:
   - ° **When**: During the implementation
   - ° **Estimation of time**: Half an hour
   - ° **Previous action**: Action 1

6. Execute the process that will create Detailed Volume Discount Ledger Entries of type **Initial Entry** for all existing Volume Discount Ledger Entries:
   - ° **When**: During the implementation
   - ° **Estimation of time**: Half an hour
   - ° **Previous action**: Action 5

7. Execute the process that will set the recently created **Open** field to **Yes** in the table Volume Discount Ledger Entry:

    ○ **When**: During the implementation

    ○ **Estimation of time**: Half an hour

    ○ **Previous action**: Action 5

8. Use the new Volume Discount Application functionality to do a big initial application posting so that at the end of this process, only real open Volume Discount Ledger Entries are marked as open and they have the correct Remaining Amount:

    ○ **When**: After the implementation

    ○ **Estimation of time**: Half a day

    ○ **Previous action**: Action 4

Summary

In this chapter we have seen that Microsoft Dynamics NAV implementations are not only for companies that have never used this ERP before and that will start doing it. An implementation can also be done for companies already using Dynamics NAV. They will not be complete implementations, of course, probably just the implementation of a new module or functionality. There are some things to take into account in these kinds of implementations. We have talked about them using different examples.

In the next chapter we will be talking about reporting in Microsoft Dynamics NAV and how to analyze the data stored in the database.

10
Data Analysis and Reporting

Data analysis and reporting is an important part of the management of a company. Having a system where you can do accounting, invoicing, warehouse management, and all kinds of things a company does is great. Dynamics NAV is a good data entry system and offers ways to provide a flow to the information and make it available when it is needed to complete the company's processes. Sales processors enter sales orders, which are then available to warehouse employees so that they know what has to be shipped. Once warehouse employees are done with the shipping, invoicing people have the needed information to make the invoice.

But companies do also need to analyze all this information. Do we ship our orders on time? Which item category is the most profitable? Are our departments generating value for the company? We have to be able to answer these kinds of questions. That is what analysis and reporting can do.

In this chapter we will see the tools available to analyze Dynamics NAV data, both inside and outside the application.

This chapter covers the following topics:

- Analyze data using filters and FlowFilters
- Statistics
- Charts
- Reports
- Analysis views
- Account schedules
- Extract Dynamics NAV data
- Report development

Using filters and FlowFilters

A good and powerful way to view and analyze data is to use **filters** and **FlowFilters** inside the application.

We have explained the use of filters in the *Navigating through your data* section in *Chapter 3, Dynamics NAV General Considerations*. Refer to that chapter to get some examples on how to use filters to analyze your data.

In that same chapter we explained what the SIFT technology is and how to define fields on tables to use that technology. What we have not explained in that chapter is that FlowFilters can be applied over fields defined to use SIFT to narrow-down the calculated results. That is actually what we will be explaining now.

We will be looking at the **Chart of Accounts** page to explain how to apply FlowFilters and the results they produce.

1. Enter Chart of Accounts in the search box of the Dynamics NAV Windows client.

2. Select **Chart of Accounts**.

3. The **Chart of Accounts** page will be shown.

   The following screenshot shows part of the **Chart of Accounts** page. We have removed all fields on that screen and we are just showing the fields **No.**, **Name**, **Net Change**, and **Balance** because those are the relevant fields for this example.

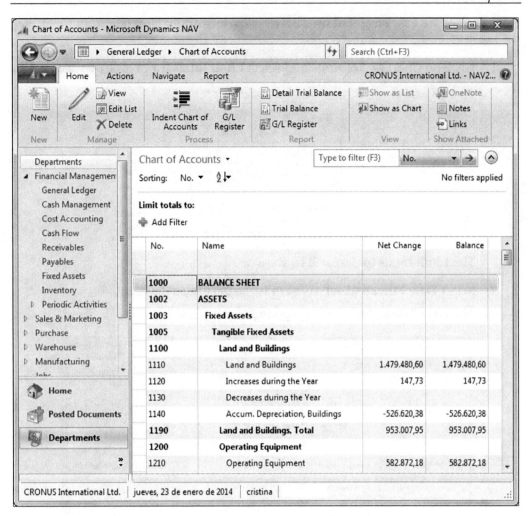

Fields **Net Change** and **Balance** are FlowFields that use the SIFT technology. They both show the sum of G/L entries amounts for the different accounts.

Now that we are on a page that uses FlowFields, let's apply FlowFilters and look at the results.

1. Click on **Chart of Accounts** and select **Limit totals** (or press *Ctrl* + *Shift* + *F3*).

The **Limit totals to** part will be shown.

2. Select **Date Filter** and set 01/01/13..31/12/13 as the filter.

3. The **Net Change** field will be updated.

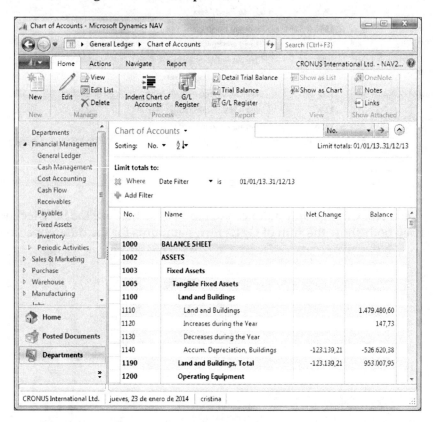

Not all FlowFilters apply to all FlowFields. In the example, we have seen that after applying a date FlowFilter, the **Net Change** field gets updated and now shows only the sum of G/L entries amounts in the specified period, while the **Balance** field has remained the same. This is because of the definition of the fields. The definition of the **Net Change** field states that the calculation of this field will take into account a date filter, while the **Balance** field does not.

Limit total is the place where a user can apply FlowFilters. It can be found in all the application pages where a FlowFilter is available, and also in the **Filter** section of reports, which will be seen later in this chapter.

Creating Views

We have seen how to apply filters and FlowFilters to the application. But once we leave the page and come back to the same page, the filter is gone. We have to apply the same filter or FlowFilter over and over again if we want to see the same results. Wouldn't it be great if we could save the filters applied so that we could apply them as many times as we wish without having to select the fields we want to filter and writing the filter expression again? That is possible with Dynamics NAV Views.

To create a View follow the given steps:

1. Follow the steps from the previous section to apply a FlowFilter to the **Chart of Accounts** page.

2. Click on **Chart of Accounts** and select **Save View As...**.

The **Save View As** dialog will open.

3. Enter `Chart of Accounts - Year 2013` in the **Name** field and select **Home** in the **Activity Group** field.

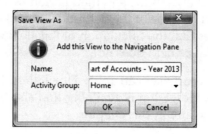

4. Click on **OK**.
5. The View will be saved.

Every time you want to see your saved View, follow the given steps:

1. Click on **Home**.
2. Click on your saved View.

Statistics

All the master data has one or more statistical page associated where the most important statistical information about the record is shown.

Statistics can be found under the **Navigate** tab of the ribbon.

Follow the given steps to view Customer Statistics:

1. Type `Customer` in the search box of the Dynamics NAV Windows client.
2. Select **Customers**. The Customers list will be shown.
3. Click on the **Navigate** tab of the ribbon.
4. Select **Statistics**. The **Customer Statistics** page for the current selected customer will be shown. This page shows the most important economic information about the customer.

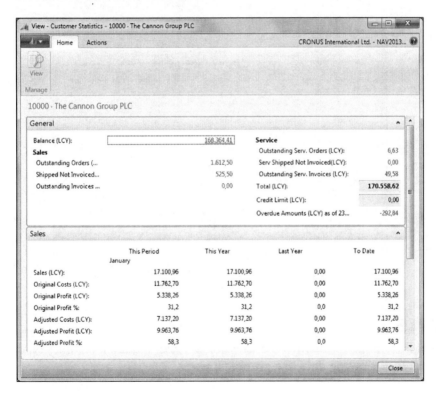

Other statistics pages offer dynamical information, like the Customer Sales statistics. To open the **Customer Sales** statistics page, follow the given steps:

1. Type Customer in the search box of the Dynamics NAV Windows client.

2. Select **Customers**. The Customers list will be shown.

3. Click on the **Navigate** tab of the ribbon.

4. Select **Sales**. The **Customer Sales** page for the current selected customer will be shown. This page shows customer sales on time basis.

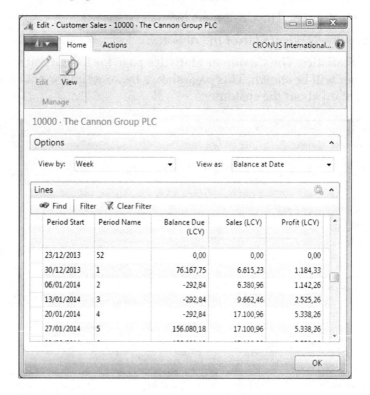

Charts

Graphical information is always useful when analyzing data. Dynamics NAV offers various ways of viewing data in a graphical way.

The Show as Chart option

Whenever the information shown on the screen can be viewed as a chart, the **Home** tab of the ribbon will contain a section called **View** where users can switch the view of the information from **List** to **Chart** and vice versa.

Let's see an example of how to build a chart based on the customer list.

1. Type `Customer` in the search box of the Dynamics NAV Windows client.
2. Select **Customers**. The Customers list will be shown.
3. Click on **Show as Chart**. An empty chart will be shown. We will have to select a measure and the dimensions we want to use to build our chart.

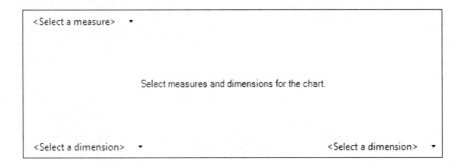

4. Select **Sales (LCY)** as the measure.
5. Select **Country/Region Code** as the dimension on the right of the chart.
6. The chart will be drawn.

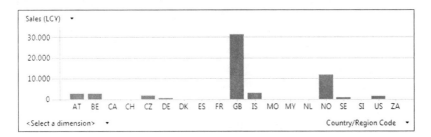

We can quickly see that GB is the country where our sales are concentrated.

Adding charts to the Role Center page

Dynamics NAV has a set of predefined, generic charts that can be added to the **Role Center** page.

To add a chart to the home page, follow the given steps:

1. Click on **Home**.
2. Click on the Application [ ] icon, choose **Customize**, and then **Customize This Page**. The **Customize the Role Center** window will open.

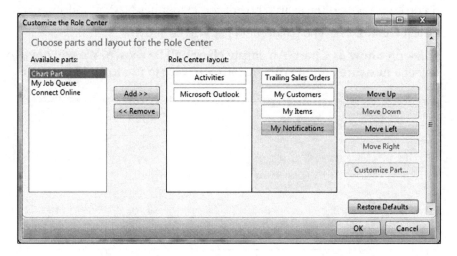

3. Select **Chart Part** from the **Available parts** field and click on the **Add** button.
4. A **Blank Chart** will appear in the **Role Center layout** field.

5. Select the **Blank Chart** and click on the **Customize Part** button. A list of available charts will appear.

6. Select the **Customer Sales and Profit** chart.

7. Click on **OK**.

8. Click on **OK** to close the **Customize the Role Center** window.

9. The selected chart will be displayed on the **Role Center** page.

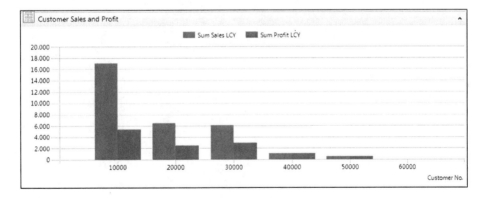

 The data in this chart is displayed after the customers on the **My Customer** list. If you have no customers on the **My Customer** list, this chart will show no data.

Creating and configuring charts

If the predefined generic charts are not enough for you, you can define other generic charts and make them available to all users, so that they can add your chart to their **Role Center** page.

To create and define a generic chart, follow the given steps:

1. Type `Generic Charts` in the search box of the Dynamics NAV Windows client.

2. Select **Generic Charts**. The **Generic Charts** list will be shown.

3. Click on **New** to create a new generic chart.

4. Give the new generic chart an ID (MYCHART) and a name (My Chart).

5. Select **Table** as **Source Type**.

6. Select **18** as the **Source ID**.

7. In the **Required Measure** row, select **Sales (LCY)** in the **Data Column** field, **Sum** as **Aggregation**, and **Column** as **Graph Type**.

8. In the **Optional Measure** row, select **Profit (LCY)** in the **Data Column** field, **Sum** as **Aggregation**, and **StepLine** as **Graph Type**.

9. Select **Country/Region Code** in **X-Axis Field**. The entire configuration of the generic chart is shown in the following screenshot:

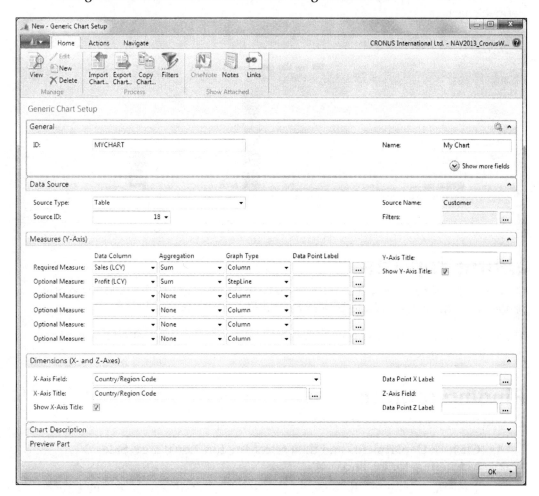

10. Click on **OK**.

A new chart is now created and configured. Follow the steps in the previous section to add this new chart to your **Role Center** page. The following screenshot shows the defined chart:

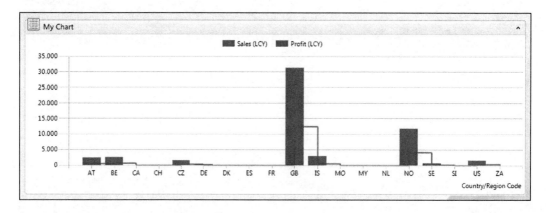

Using reports

Dynamics NAV has a bunch of reports that can be used out of the box. Some other reports may have been added by a partner and can also be used.

The first thing you need to know to be able to execute the application reports is where to find them.

Finding reports

To find the application reports, follow the given steps:

1. Click on **Departments** and then select any functional area, **Sales & Marketing**, for instance.

2. The main menu for the selected functional area will appear on the screen. Every item you can find inside a menu for an application area has a category associated with it. In the menu, there is a way to view items according to their category. The following screenshot illustrates the existing categories in Dynamics NAV:

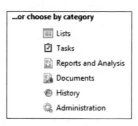

3. Select **Reports and Analysis**.

4. All items under the **Reports and Analysis** category for the functional area selected will be shown. The previous screenshot shows all the items under the **Reports and Analysis** category for the **Sales & Marketing** functional area.

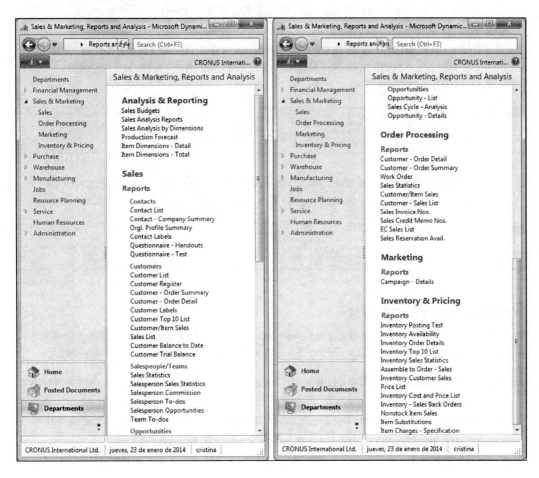

But reports are not only found on the main menu. They can also be found in many application pages where only the reports that are valuable for the data shown on the page will be found.

Follow the given steps to see an example:

1. Click on **Departments**, then choose **Sales & Marketing**, and then choose **Sales**.

2. Click on **Customers** to open the Customers list. In the **Home** tab of the ribbon, a section called **Report** contains the most relevant reports regarding customers.

On the **Report** tab of the ribbon, the reports regarding Customers will be shown and grouped according to the application area to which they belong.

Running reports

Now that we have found all the available reports, it is time to execute them and see what kind of information they show. To execute a report, follow the given steps:

1. Click on the report that you want to execute. For instance, click on **Customer Top 10 List**.

2. The Request page for the report will be shown. The following screenshot shows the Request page for the **Customer Top 10 List** report:

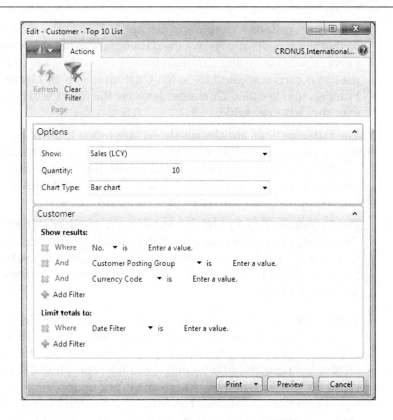

Request pages for reports have three different sections:

 ° The **Options** section – Here users can choose among different options
   to define the behavior of the report. This section is always called
   Options and is shown as the first section of a report request page.
   The **Options** section may not be shown in some reports if the report
   actually has no options for the user to select.

   In the **Customer Top 10 List** report, the **Options** section is shown
   and the users have three different fields (**Show, Quantity**, and **Chart
   Type**) to define what they want to see (using the **Show** field), how
   many customers they want to list (using the **Quantity** field), and
   which kind of chart they want to see on the report (using the **Chart
   Type** field).

○ The **Filter** sections – Here users can apply filters over their data so that the report only shows the data the users are interested in. **Filter** sections may take different names depending on which data the filters can be applied to. In the **Customer Top 10 List** report, the **Filter** section is called **Customer** because the filters will be applied over the customer table.

The **Filter** sections are always shown after the **Options** section. A report may have no **Filter** sections if there are no filters that users can apply to the data shown on the report, or may have several **Filter** sections if the report combines data from multiple tables and filters can be applied over the data of the different tables.

The **Customer Top 10 List** report has a single **Filter** section, **Customer**, but the **Customer – Order** detail report, which can be found under the **Reports and Analysis** category of the **Sales & Marketing** functional area, has two **Filter** sections, **Customer** and **Sales Order Line**.

○ The **Buttons** section – Here users can choose to either **Print** the report in different formats (print it using one of the available printers in the system by using the **Print** option, print the report into a PDF archive by using the **PDF** option, print the report into a Microsoft Word archive by using the **Microsoft Word** option, or print the report into a Microsoft Excel archive by using the **Microsoft Excel** option), **Preview** the report on the screen, or **Cancel** the execution of the report.

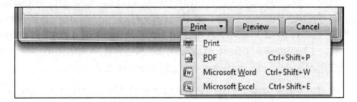

 All four existing options on the **Print** button can also be found afterward on the **Preview** screen.

3. Click on **Preview** to see the results of the report on the screen.

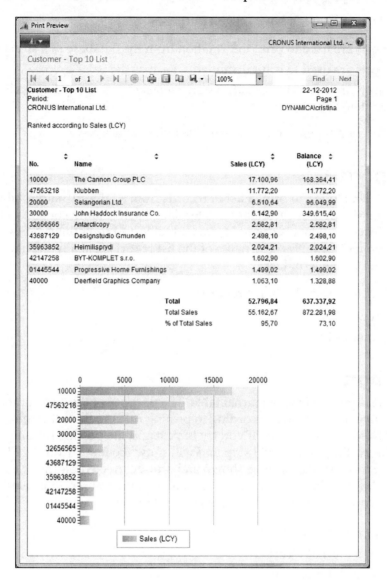

Types of reports

Reports in Dynamics NAV have several purposes:

- Reports are used to print information from the database in a structured way
- Reports are used to print documents, such as the Sales Invoice
- Reports are used to automate recurring tasks, such as updating all the prices in an item list

There are different types of reports available in Dynamics NAV.

List reports

A list report is intended to print a list of records from a table, usually a table containing master data or secondary master data. Each column contains a field from the table. Most of the data is printed from that table and sometimes brought in or calculated from other tables. The name of the list report is usually the name of the table followed by the term List.

The following are examples of list reports:

- Customer List
- Inventory - List

Test reports

A test report is printed from a journal table. The purpose of this kind of report is to test each line of the journal according to posting rules so that all errors can be found and fixed before posting. If you try to post and the posting routine encounters an error, the posting routine will stop and will show the first encountered error. If several errors exist, they will be shown and, thus, corrected one at a time. A test report will show all the existing errors. The name of the test report is usually the name of the corresponding Journal, followed by the term Test.

The following are examples of test reports:

- General Journal – Test
- Resource Journal – Test

Posting reports

A posting report prints from a register table. It lists all the transactions (ledger entries) that are posted into the register. This kind of report can be very useful for auditing. The name of the posting report is usually the name of either the register table or the master table of the corresponding ledger entries.

The following are examples of posting reports:

- G/L Register
- Job Register

Transaction reports

A transaction report has the following characteristics:

- It lists all the ledger entries for each record in the ledger table.
- It contains a subtotal for each master table record, and a grand total for all tables printed.
- It is used to view all transactions for a particular master record.
- It has no standard naming convention. A transaction report usually has one or more data items, including the master and the corresponding ledger table.

The following are examples of transaction reports:

- Detail Trial Balance
- Customer – Detail Trial Bal.

Document reports

A document report prints a document, such as a Sales Invoice or a Purchase Order. Document reports have a different layout than all other reports. The header information of the document is printed as if filling out the document at the top of the page and is repeated on every page. The information on the lines of the document resembles other kinds of reports because it is printed in rows and columns.

The following are examples of document reports:

- Sales – Invoice
- Order

Report Selection

A user can select which document report will be printed with each document type. To view and select the document reports that will be printed with each document type, follow the given steps:

1. Type `Report Selection` in the search box of the Dynamics NAV Windows client.

2. Select **Report Selection Sales**. The **Edit - Report Selection - Sales** window will open.

The following screenshot shows that report number **204**, which is called **Sales - Quote**, will be used to print sales quotes:

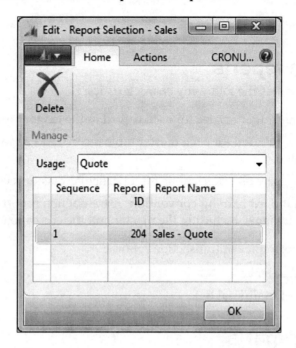

By selecting other usages (**Order, Invoice, Credit Memo, Shipment, Order Archive**, and so on) you will be able to see and to choose which report(s) to print for each type of sales document.

By default, there is usually only one report selected for each type of document, but you can add more reports to the list so that more than one record is printed for each document type.

Other reports

Most reports consist of a tabular listing with records listed horizontally and each field displaying in its own column. Many times, there is a group heading or total to split the lines among various categories and to subtotal the lines by categories.

The following are examples of other reports:

- Customer/Item Sales
- Vendor/Item Purchases

Account schedules

The account schedules functionality is part of the **Analysis & Reporting** section of the **Financial Management** area. It is meant to create customized financial reports based on the General Ledger information, the Budget information, or on the analysis views information. Account schedules can group data from various accounts and perform calculations that are not possible directly on **Chart of Accounts**.

When defining account schedules, both the information that will be displayed on rows and columns can be defined.

Just to see how it works, we will create a simple account schedule that will compare budgeted amounts versus real amounts. To do so, we will follow the given steps:

1. Navigate to **Departments/Financial Management/Reports and Analysis** and choose **Account Schedules**.

2. Click on **New** to create a new account schedule.

3. For the new account schedule, select **EXAMPLE** as **Name**, **Comparing budget versus reality** as **Description**, and **ACT/BUD** as **Default Column Layout**.

4. Click on **Edit Account Schedule**. An empty page will open. We will define our account schedule on this page.

5. Define the account schedule as shown in the following screenshot:

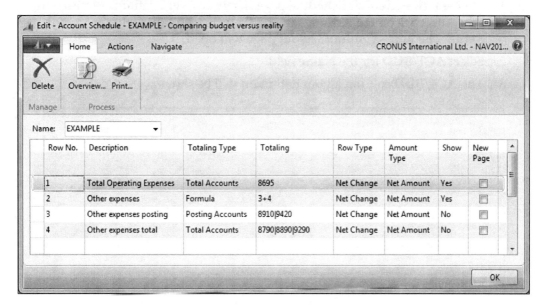

Row No.	Description	Totaling Type	Totaling	Row Type	Amount Type	Show	New Page
1	Total Operating Expenses	Total Accounts	8695	Net Change	Net Amount	Yes	☐
2	Other expenses	Formula	3+4	Net Change	Net Amount	Yes	☐
3	Other expenses posting	Posting Accounts	8910|9420	Net Change	Net Amount	No	☐
4	Other expenses total	Total Accounts	8790|8890|9290	Net Change	Net Amount	No	☐

- ° The first row gets the net amount of account **8695**, a totaling account that summarizes all operating expenses.

- ° The second row uses a formula to sum up the results of rows **3** and **4**. That is because other expenses couldn't be summarized together in a single account schedule row, as some of the other expenses are summarized in **Chart of Accounts** on totaling accounts, but there are a couple of other expenses that have to be taken directly from the posting accounts.

- ° The third row gets the net amount of other expenses from the posting accounts. The posting accounts used are **8910** and **9420**. As this row is only used for calculation purposes and is not intended to be shown on the report, the **Show** field has been set to **No**.

- ° The fourth row gets the net amount of other expenses from totaling accounts. The totaling accounts used are **8790**, **8890**, and **9290**. As this row is only used for calculation purposes and it is not intended to be shown on the report, the **Show** field has been set to **No**.

The account schedule is fully defined now. The account schedule defines the rows that will be shown on the report.

Columns are defined at the Column Layout. In the example, we have used an existent column layout called **ACT/BUD**. Let's see what this column layout will show.

1. On the **Edit – Account Schedule** page where we were defining our account schedule, click on the **Actions** tab and then click on **Edit Column Layout Setup**. The **Edit – Column Layout** page will open.

2. Select **ACT/BUD** for the **Name** field.

3. The **ACT/BUD** column layout definition will be shown.

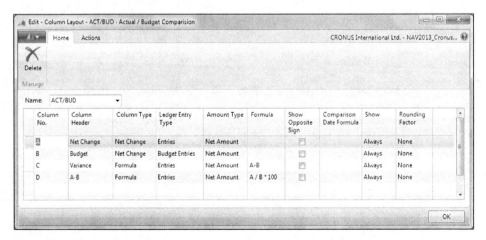

Column No.	Column Header	Column Type	Ledger Entry Type	Amount Type	Formula	Show Opposite Sign	Comparison Date Formula	Show	Rounding Factor
A	Net Change	Net Change	Entries	Net Amount				Always	None
B	Budget	Net Change	Budget Entries	Net Amount				Always	None
C	Variance	Formula	Entries	Net Amount	A-B			Always	None
D	A-B	Formula	Entries	Net Amount	A / B * 100			Always	None

- ° The column layout defines that the report will have four columns called **Net Change**, **Budget**, **Variance**, and **A-B**.
- ° The **Net Change** column will show the net amount for G/L entries.
- ° The **Budget** column will show the net amount for budget entries.
- ° The **Variance** column will show the difference between the first and the second column.
- ° The **A-B** column calculates the percentage that the first column represents versus the second column.

Now that we have both the account schedule and the column layout defined, it is time to see the results of our account schedule.

1. Navigate to **Departments/Financial Management/Reports and Analysis** and select **Account Schedules**.
2. Select the account schedule that we have created in this section.
3. Click on **Overview**.
4. The report will be shown on the screen.

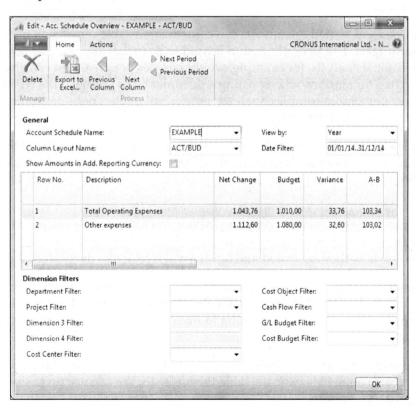

The results can be seen in different time periods and filters can be applied over the calculation to get more accurate results. The results can be exported to Excel and can also be printed.

Analysis views

Analysis views are used to analyze the information about dimensions from general ledger entries, budgets, and cash flow forecast entries.

Let's first have a look at what dimensions are, and then we will be able to see how to analyze the information that dimensions provide using analysis views.

Understanding dimensions

A dimension can be seen as information linked to an entry, something like a tag or a characteristic. The purpose of dimensions is to group entries with similar characteristics so that you can report on the data in a way that is meaningful to the company. Each company can define its own dimensions according to how they need to analyze their data.

Posted entries and posted documents can contain analyzable dimension information as well as budgets. The term dimension is used to describe how analysis occurs. A two-dimensional analysis, for example, would be sales per area. You can also apply more than two dimensions when posting a document or a journal. This will allow you to carry out a more complex analysis, for example, sales, per sales campaign, per customer, or group per area.

Each dimension can have unlimited dimension values that are subunits of the dimension. For example, a dimension called Department can have subunits called Sales, Administration, and so on. These departments are dimension values.

Dynamics NAV 2013 supports unlimited dimensions. This means that you can create as many dimensions as needed according to how you are currently categorizing areas of the business. However, even if you can create unlimited dimensions, there are some restrictions on how they are stored and how easy it is to access their information.

In Dynamics NAV, all dimensions are stored in special dimension tables. Some dimensions are also stored in fields inside the table they refer to. We can group dimensions in three categories according to their access level (how easy it is to access them).

- **Global dimensions** – Their value is stored on special dimension tables and also on fields inside the table they refer to. We can use up to two global dimensions.

- **Shortcut dimensions** – Their value is stored on special dimension tables. Although the value is not stored inside the table they refer to, in some occasions they are shown on pages as if they were stored on the table. We can use up to eight shortcut dimensions. Two of them correspond to global dimensions.

- **The rest of the dimensions** – Their value is only stored on special dimension tables.

Setting up new dimensions

Imagine in our company we have two different divisions: one responsible for selling items, and another responsible for renting items. We decide to use dimensions to analyze the results of each division. So, we are going to create a dimension called DIVISION.

To create new dimensions, access **Departments/Financial Management/Setup/Dimensions** and follow the steps described in this section.

1. Click on the **New** icon found on the ribbon bar.

2. Create a new dimension by assigning some values as shown in the following screenshot.

3. Click on the **Dimension Values** icon found on the ribbon bar. A new page will open.

4. Create two different dimension values by giving them the values shown in the following screenshot:

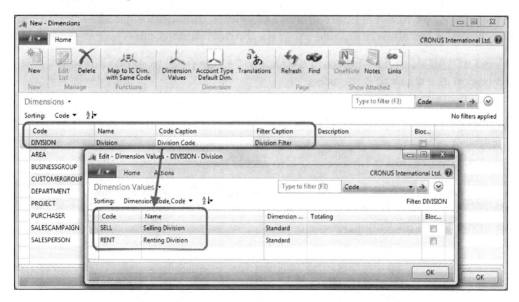

Categorizing dimensions

We have already created a new dimension along with its dimension values. Now we must determine if it is going to be a global dimension, a shortcut dimension, or one of the rest of the dimensions.

To do so, open the **General Ledger Setup** by navigating to **Departments/Financial Management/Setup/General Ledger Setup**. Select the **Dimensions** tab.

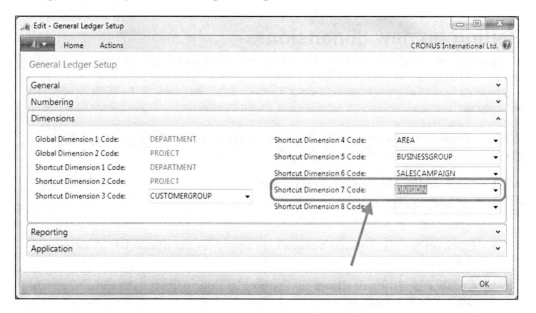

In the company CRONUS International Ltd., global dimensions are already defined. The company has already defined up to six shortcut dimensions.

Select **DIVISION** in the **Shortcut Dimension 7 Code** field, to define our new dimension as a shortcut dimension.

Accessing dimensions

As we said earlier in this chapter, the difference between global, shortcut, and the rest of the dimensions is how easy it is to access them.

We are going to see how to access the **DEPARTMENT** global dimension, the **DIVISON** shortcut dimension, and the **SALESPERSON** dimension, which is one of the rest of the dimensions.

To see how dimensions can be accessed to fill them when creating documents, follow the given steps:

1. Open the **Sales Invoices** page that you will find by navigating to **Departments/Sales & Marketing/Order Processing/Sales Invoices**.

2. Click on the New [🗐New] icon found on the ribbon bar to create a new sales invoice.

3. In the **Sell-to Customer No.** field, select customer **62000**.

4. Create a line for item 1000 to sell 1 PCS.

5. On the **Lines** tab, click on the setup icon and select **Choose Columns....**

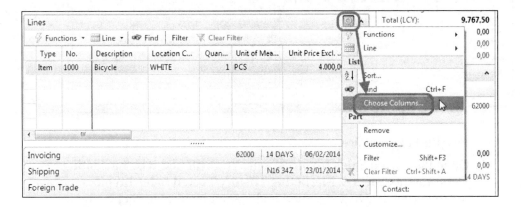

6. Add **Department Code** and **Division Code** in the column titled **Show columns in this order**. Then click on **OK**.

    Salesperson Code cannot be selected because it is not a global dimension or a shortcut dimension.

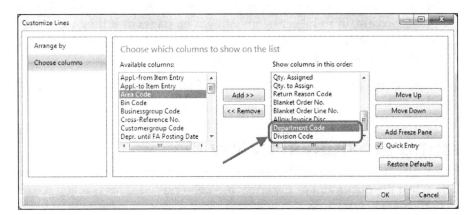

7. Back to the sales line, fill in the value **Sales** for the **Department Code** field. Also fill in the value **Sell** for the **Division Code** field.

8. To fill in a value in the **Salesperson Code** field, click on **Line** and then **Dimensions** to open the **Edit Dimension Set Entries** page.

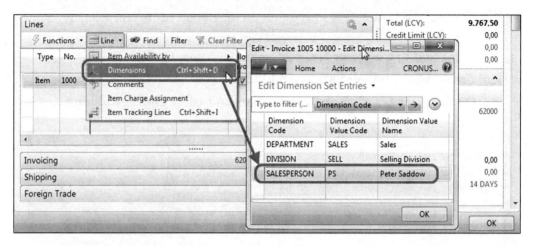

9. Post the Sales Invoice.

10. Open the **Posted Sales Invoices** page. You will find it by navigating to **Departments/Sales & Marketing/History/Posted Sales Invoices**. Locate the invoice we have just posted and open it by double-clicking on it.

11. Open the **Customize Lines** page, as we did in step 6.

12. Add **Department Code** in the column titled **Show columns in this order**. Notice that you will not find **Division Code** available in the column titled **Available columns**.

    This is because division is a shortcut dimension. As we said earlier, shortcut dimensions are, in some occasions, shown on pages as if they were stored on the table. Usually they are shown in pages meant to enter information, but not on pages meant to show posted information.

13. Access all the dimensions by clicking on **Line** and then **Dimensions**, as we did in step 8.

Creating an analysis view

As we have seen, there are several dimensions that are not easily accessed by users, especially when the document or the entry has been posted. This is when we need to analyze the data.

Analysis views are specially meant to access all the dimensions in the same easy way, in groups of a maximum of four dimensions at the same time. The four dimension group may seem a limitation, but it is not, since we can create as many analysis views as needed combining all the dimensions we want.

With analysis view, we can view data from the general ledger. Entries are grouped by criteria, such as:

- G/L accounts
- Period
- Business units
- Up to four dimensions

In other words, if a G/L entry has been posted to a particular account with one of the four dimensions selected, the G/L entry information will be included in the analysis view as an analysis view entry. You can also include G/L budget entries in an analysis view to compare reality and budget.

Follow the given steps to set up an analysis view:

1. Open the **Analysis Views** page by navigating to **Departments/ Administration/Application Setup/Financial Management/Dimensions/ Analysis Views**.

2. The **Analysis Views** page will open showing the existing analysis views.

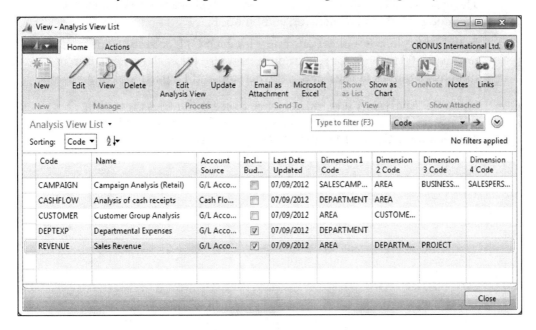

3. Click on the **New** icon found on the ribbon bar. The analysis view card will open.

4. Fill up the analysis view card with the data shown in the following screenshot:

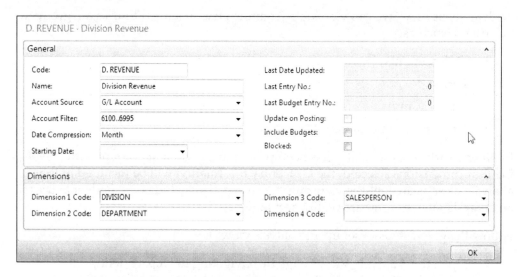

5. Click on the **Update** option found on the ribbon bar to create analysis view entries based on the criteria that you set up on the card.

   The system will create one summarized analysis view entry for each G/L account, period, and dimension combination.

   In the example, we will get one entry for each G/L account from account number 6100 to 6995, for each month, and also for each combination of dimension values of the **Area**, **Salesperson**, and **Department** dimensions.

6. Open the **Analysis View Entries** page to see the entries created by the system. You can find it by navigating to **Departments/Financial Management/General Ledger/History/Analysis View Entries**.

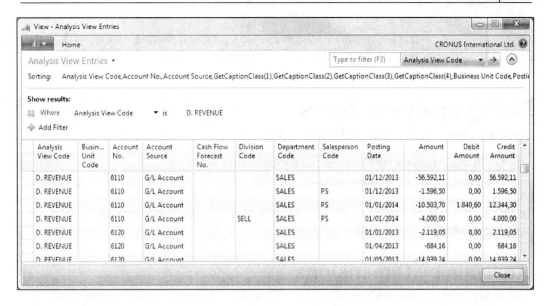

Updating analysis views

An analysis view is a fixed photo of the posted G/L entries grouped with specific criteria.

If you change any of the fields found on the analysis view card, for instance, if you change the **Starting Date** field, you will get the following message:

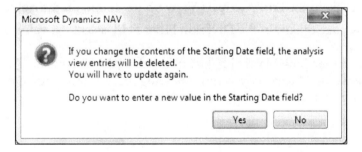

If you select **Yes**, all entries will be deleted and you will have to click on the **Update** option again to create analysis view entries according to the new criteria.

You will also have to use the **Update** action to include new general ledger entries posted after you last updated the analysis view. Although you can also let the system update it automatically when new G/L entries are posted by checking the **Update on Posting** field found on the analysis view card.

It is not recommended to use the **Update on Posting** option because it penalizes performance when posting.

Using analysis views

Analysis views can be used in different scenarios:

- In the Analysis by Dimensions functionality
- As source for account schedules

In this section we are going to see an example of using analysis views on each of the scenarios detailed.

Analysis by Dimensions

The analysis by dimensions functionality is used to display and analyze the amount derived from the existing analysis views.

Follow the steps to see an example of how Analysis by Dimensions work:

1. Open the **Analysis View List** page by navigating to **Departments/Financial Management/General Ledger/Analysis & Reporting/Analysis by Dimensions**.

2. Locate the D. REVENUE analysis view that we created earlier in this chapter. Then click on the **Edit Analysis View** option found on the ribbon bar.

3. A new page opens. In the **Division Filter** field, select the value **SELL**.

4. Click on the Show Matrix [] icon found on the ribbon bar. The **Analysis by Dimensions Matrix** page is now showing the amounts posted on the general ledger under the **SELL** value of the **Division** dimension.

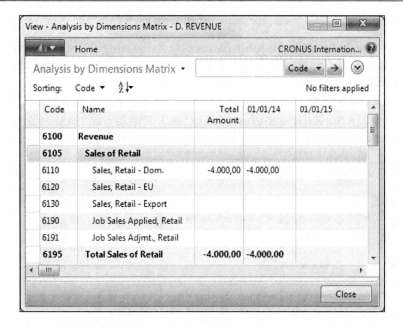

5. Close the current page and go back to the **Analysis by Dimensions** page.

6. Select different values for the following fields, and click on **Show Matrix** to see the results. The main fields you can change to analyze data are **Show as Lines, Show as Columns, Dimension Filters, Show, Show Amount Field, View by,** and **View as**.

Analysis views as a source for account schedules

If analysis views are selected as a source for account schedules, the amounts in the account schedules are calculated based on analysis views entries. Since analysis views entries are based on general ledger entries, the result should be the same.

The difference is that, when analyzing account schedules, you can only filter the amounts based on global dimensions. If you use analysis views as a source for account schedules, then you can filter on any of the four dimensions selected on the analysis view card. Those dimensions can be global dimensions, shortcut dimensions, or any other dimensions.

To use analysis views as source for account schedules follow the given steps:

1. Open the **Account Schedules Names** by navigating to **Departments | Financial Management |General Ledger | Analysis & Reporting |Account Schedules**.

2. Locate the **REVENUE** account schedule. Notice that an analysis view is selected in the **Analysis View Name** field. This is what makes it possible to use the analysis view as a source for the account schedule.

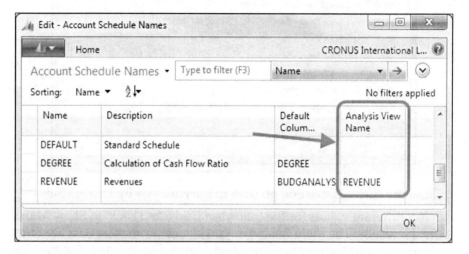

3. Click on the **Overview** option found on the ribbon bar.

4. The **Acc. Schedule Overview** page opens. Notice that you can now filter on any of the three dimensions that were set up on the analysis view. Select different values on those fields to see the results.

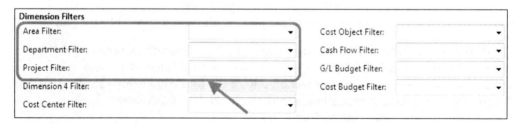

Extracting data

Dynamics NAV offers several ways of analyzing and reporting data inside the application. If that is not enough, you can also extract data from the application and use an external tool to report and analyze your data.

In this section we will see the different ways you can extract your data from Dynamics NAV. Once it is outside the application, you can use the most convenient tool for you.

Data in Dynamics NAV can be extracted in different ways:

- Sending data to Microsoft Office applications
- Using web services

Sending data to Microsoft Office applications

Dynamics NAV data can be sent to either Microsoft Word or Microsoft Excel by users.

Whenever that is possible, which is in all pages in Dynamics NAV except on the **Role Center** page and on menu pages under the **Department** area, the export option will be available on the application menu.

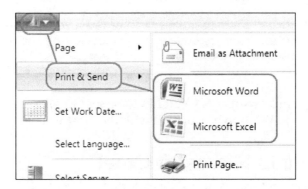

The data exported will be the one that the user is seeing at the moment, including filters and columns shown/hidden on a list. Imagine you are looking at the customer list. In that list you have only chosen columns **No.**, **Name**, and **Contact**, and you have applied a filter to only see blocked customers. When you export that to either Word or Excel, you will export only those three fields and only the customers within the filter.

Sending data to Microsoft Word

The following screenshot shows how data exported to Microsoft Word looks:

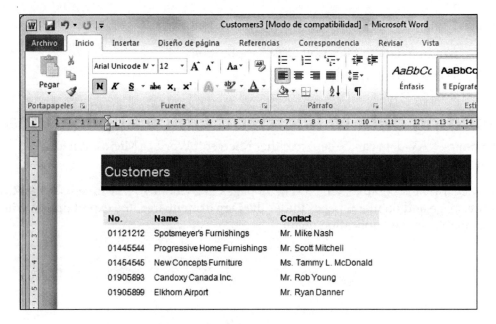

When data changes in Dynamics NAV, it has to be sent to Microsoft Word again if you want your data in Word to be updated with the most recent changes.

Sending data to Microsoft Excel

The following screenshot shows how data exported to Microsoft Excel looks:

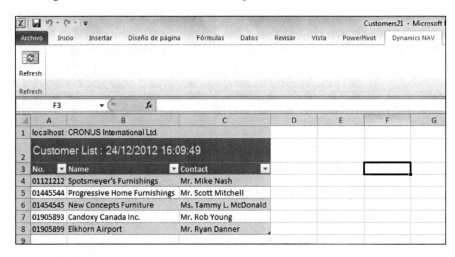

Notice the **Dynamics NAV** tab on the Microsoft Excel ribbon and the **Refresh** button in that tab. When data changes in Dynamics NAV, there is no need to send it again to Excel. You can click on the **Refresh** button and the data in Excel will be updated with the most recent data from Dynamics NAV.

The Dynamics NAV add-in for Excel gets installed when you install the Dynamics NAV Windows client.

Extracting data through web services

Any Dynamics NAV codeunit, page, or query can be published as a web service. Codeunits will be published as SOAP web services. Pages will be published as both SOAP web services and OData web services. Queries will be published as OData web services.

 Refer to the *OData web services* section in *Chapter 2, What's New in NAV 2013*, to get a detailed step-by-step explanation on how to publish a web service.

Any application that can consume SOAP web services or OData web services will be able to extract Dynamics NAV data.

In *Chapter 12, The Query Object*, we have included an example of consuming a query OData web service using Excel.

Other ways to extract Dynamics NAV data

Dynamics NAV data is actually stored in a Microsoft SQL database, and thus, all available tools for SQL to extract data could be used for the Dynamics NAV database.

Understanding report development

Report development is completely different from what it used to be. The report development experience changed in Dynamics NAV 2009 with the introduction of **Report Definition Language Client-side (RDLC)** report, but it changes again with the actual release of the application.

With Dynamics NAV 2009, RDLC-based reports were introduced, but reports were still compatible with the classic definition of reports in Dynamics NAV. RDLC reports were actually based on the classic definition of the report.

With Dynamics NAV 2013, the reports classic definition has disappeared and only RLDC-based reports are available. This is why the report development experience has changed again. It now resembles the development experience of pages, queries, or XMLPorts.

Reports anatomy

Creating reports includes designing both the business logic that covers the kind of information the report will contain, and the layout that deals with how the report will look when it is printed.

In Microsoft Dynamics NAV 2013, to design a client report definition (RDLC), you design the data model with Report Dataset Designer and the layout with Visual Studio Report Designer. To do this, Visual Studio 2010 Professional or above is required.

Visual Studio Report Designer offers several new options and features. Furthermore, due to its thorough integration with Microsoft SQL Server, it is possible to take advantage of the reporting capabilities of Microsoft Report Viewer, including the following:

- Richer formatting
- Interactive sorting
- Graphics and charts
- Export possibilities (PDF, Microsoft Office Excel, and Microsoft Office Word)

A report object is composed of a report dataset and a visual layout. You design a report by first defining the dataset and then designing the visual layout. Report objects also contain properties, triggers, code, and an optional request page.

The following diagram shows components of a report and how they are related in Microsoft Dynamics NAV 2013.

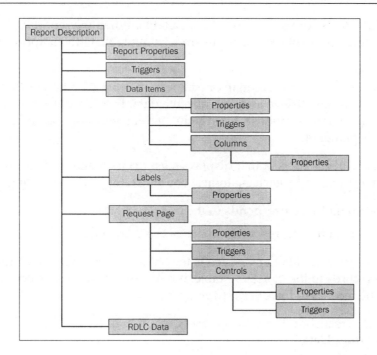

Reports in Dynamics NAV 2013 are executed in two steps, which reflect the two steps in the report design. The first data set design in C/SIDE followed by report layout design in Visual Studio.

1. The C/AL runtime retrieves the data from the involved source tables, performs necessary calculations, and combines the data in a single flattened dataset. This is performed by the NAV server.

2. The produced dataset is transferred to the report viewer's runtime hosted on the NAV client, which, in turn, renders the dataset data according to the report layout definition.

Defining the dataset

The dataset is defined on the Report Dataset Designer in the Microsoft Dynamics NAV development environment. The report dataset is built from data items and columns. A data item is a table. A column can be one of the following:

- Field in a table
- Variable
- Expression
- Text constant

Typically, data items correspond to fields in a table. When the report is run, each data item is iterated for all records in the underlying table with an appropriate filter defined.

When a report is based on more than one table, you must set relations between the data items so you can retrieve and organize the data. In Report Dataset Designer, you indent data items to establish a hierarchy of data items and control how the information is gathered.

For example, to create a report that displays a list of customers and lists the sales orders that were placed by each customer, you must define the following data items:

- A data item that corresponds to the Customer table
- A data item that corresponds to the Sales Line table

You indent the second data item, which is the Sales Line table. As the report works through the records in the Customer table, it finds each customer's sales orders by examining the records in the Sales Line table.

The following screenshot shows the dataset definition of **Report 108 Customer – Order Detail**:

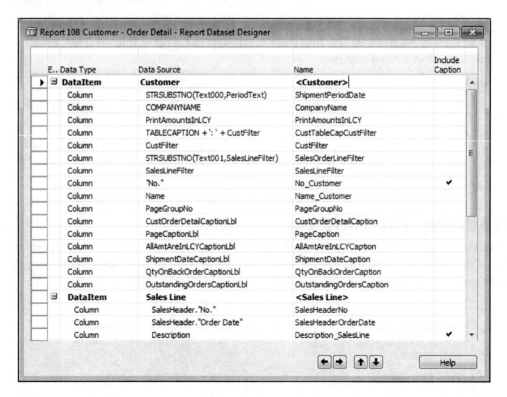

And this is how the dataset looks on Visual Studio:

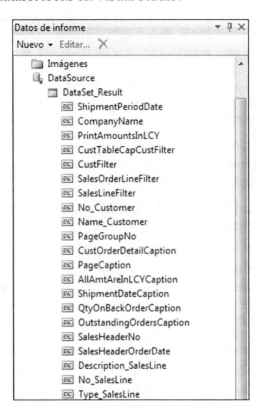

Designing the visual layout

You build the visual layout of a report by arranging data items. A report that is displayed or printed must have a client report definition (RDLC) layout. You use Visual Studio Report Designer to design the RDLC layout. Microsoft Dynamics NAV 2013 supports RDLC 2008. You generally display most data in the body of a report, and you use the header to display information before any data item record is displayed. For example, you can display a report title, company, and user information in the header of a report.

With Visual Studio Report Designer, you can add useful features to your report layouts, such as:

- Links from a field on a report to either a page or another report
- Images and graphs

- The ability to toggle columns so you can hide or display data
- The ability for users to interactively change the column on which data in the report is sorted
- The ability to display RTF text

A report in Visual Studio always has exactly one body, and it is not possible to add more than one. Optionally, it can have one page header and one page footer. Extra headers or footers cannot be added.

When the report runs, it first runs the page header, then the page body, and then the page footer. It will not run the page body for each record. Looping through records is done by using a data region in the body section.

However, now it is possible in RDLC2008, in the page header sections, to work with data fields. This is different from RDLC2005 that was used to define RTC reports in Dynamics NAV 2009.

Reports use a variety of report items to organize data on a report page. The design surface is not *what you see is what you get*. The report items have an initial layout position that can change when the report is processed. The following list describes typical uses for different report items:

- **Textbox** – It is used on titles, date stamps, and report names.
- **Table, Matrix** – It is used to display tabular data from a report dataset. Table and matrix are templates of a Tablix data region and provide a starting grid layout for data from a report dataset.
- **Chart** – It is used to graphically display data from a report dataset.
- **Gauge** – It is used to present a visual image for a single value within a range of values.
- **List** – It is used to create free-form layout, such as the forms on a webpage.
- **Image** – It is used to add existing images to a report.
- **Line** – It uses lines as graphical elements.
- **Rectangle** – It can be used as a container for other report items. Rectangles are often used to help control how report items appear on a report page when the report is rendered.

The following screenshot shows the layout definition of the **108, Customer – Order Detail** report:

«Expr»										[&ExecutionTime]
«Expr»										«Expr»
«Expr»										[&UserID]
«Expr»										
«Expr»										
«Expr»										
[First(Shi	[@Tyl	[@No SalesLir	[@Description SalesLineCapti	eCaption]	«Expr»	OrderCaption]	esLineCaption]	sLineCaption]	LineCaption]	«Expr»
[No Cust	[Name Customer]									
	«Expr»	«Expr»								
[Shipmen	[Type	[No SalesLine]	[Description SalesLine]	SalesLine]	[Qty SalesLine]	BackOrderQtv]	Price SalesLine]	Amt SalesLine]	mt SalesLine]	OrderAmount]	[Sales]
	[Name Customer]								derAmount]	[Sales]
								[TotalCaption] Amt CurrTotalBuff2] [Buff2]		

Rules for flattening data

The RoleTailored client report works with a flattened dataset. This means that data from multiple tables is joined before it is sent to the client.

In the Report Dataset Designer, there can be multiple data items that might or might not be indented. Depending on the indentation and relations between data items, a resultset is generated at runtime. This resultset is the result of the flattening of the indented data items into a two-dimensional resultset.

The rules for flattening data can be described as follows:

- **Reports with one data item** – This corresponds to a single SELECT Column FROM Table statement. The result can be displayed in the body section.

- **Reports with indented data items** – This is similar to the following SQL statement:

```
SELECT Column FROM Table A INNER/OUTER JOIN Table B ON
    Table A.Column = Table B.Column.
```

  If PrintOnlyIfDetail is set to True on the parent, an INNER JOIN is used. If PrintOnlyIfDetail is set to False on the parent data item, an OUTER JOIN is used. The resulting set can then be displayed using grouping and filtering.

- **Reports with multiple data items on the same level** – This is similar to a UNION statement. Again, grouping and filtering can be needed to display the correct records. The difference with a UNION statement is that both data items will have different fields and a different number of columns. Actually, it is more like a concatenation of multiple resultsets.

When working with flattened datasets, the result of queries will be one single dataset containing information from multiple tables. Once the dataset is available, the dataset can be processed using filtering and sorting and the report can be rendered.

The following is the result of the flattened dataset when report **108, Customer – Order Detail** is run:

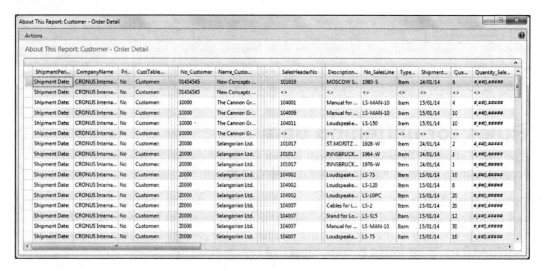

Report design guidelines

Designing reports with Visual Studio brings you many possibilities and options to define the report look and feel. You could be creative and use a new look and feel each time you create a new report, but it will be time consuming and you might confuse the end users. It is much easier, both for developers and users, to have reports with similar look and feel.

These are the general guidelines and recommendations regarding the user interface of Dynamics NAV 2013 reports. All standard reports follow these guidelines.

Report title	
Attribute	**Value**
Font	Segoe UI 14 pt Bold
Cell height	20 pt
Cell padding	left: 5 pt, right: 5 pt, top: 0 pt, bottom: 0 pt
Text alignment	Document reports: Right and All other reports: Left

Other text in the header

Attribute	Value
Font	Segoe UI 14 pt Regular
Cell height	10 pt
Cell padding	left: 5 pt, right: 5 pt, top: 0 pt, bottom: 0 pt

Space to body

Attribute	Value
Height	20 pt

Headers in the body

Attribute	Value
Font	Segoe UI 8 pt Bold
Cell height	10 pt
Cell padding	left: 5 pt, right: 5 pt, top: 0 pt, bottom: 0 pt

All other text

Attribute	Value
Font	Segoe UI 8 pt Regular
Cell height	10 pt
Cell padding	left: 5 pt, right: 5 pt, top: 0 pt, bottom: 0 pt

Line spacing

Attribute	Value
Height	10 pt. Multiplication of 10s. (As a designer/ developer, you can use your discretion to space the content).

Table Header

Number of row	Attribute	Value
Row 1 (Title)	Font	Bold
	Vertical align	Bottom
	Height	Up to 30 pt in height if required (allowed to be up to 3 lines)
Row 2	Height	2.5 pt
	Border	Bottom; black; solid
	Width	1 pt
Row 3	Height	2.5 pt
Row 4 (Text)	Vertical align	Bottom

The output of the previous table is as follows:

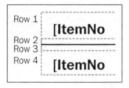

Table content

Attribute	Value
Height	10pt
Cell padding	left: 5 pt, right: 5pt, top: 0 pt, bottom: 0 pt (if row needs to be indented, add +10 pt to left padding)
Vertical align	Top (default)

Cell colors

Type of report	Value
List reports	Alternate BackgroundColor= mod 2, "WhiteSmoke", "White"

Logo

Attribute	Value
Height	40 pt
Space below logo	10 pt

Text Alignment	
Attribute	**Value**
Numeric fields	Right aligned (included header)
Text fields	Left aligned
Numeric text	Left aligned (for example, Customer No.)
Date/time	Left aligned

Colors	
Where	**Value**
Link	Blue (no underline)
Chart	Palette: Bright Pastel

Report 108, Customer – Order Detail has been designed following these guidelines. You can see the result in the following screenshot:

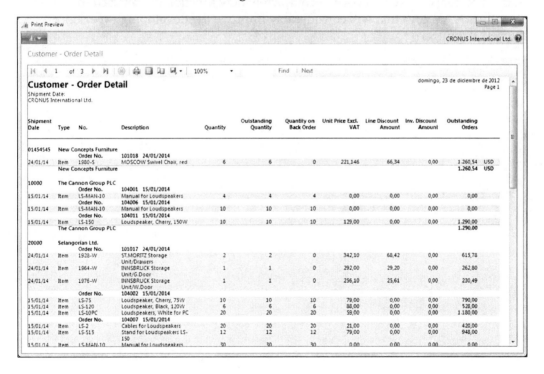

Summary

In this chapter we have learned that there are several ways of analyzing and reporting data inside Dynamics NAV. We can use filter and FlowFilters, create views, take a look at the statistics pages of Dynamics NAV, define charts and use them in multiple pages, use all the available reports, use analysis views to analyze our data based on dimensions, and use account schedules to analyze our accounting information.

If that is not enough, we have learned that there are several ways to extract data from Dynamics NAV and do the analysis and reporting outside the application using external tools.

And finally, we can create our own Dynamics NAV reports if none of the earlier ways are useful to us. We have learned the basics about report development in this chapter.

In the next chapter, we will cover a completely new functionality offered in Dynamics NAV 2013 that will considerably improve the developing experience: the new debugger.

11
Debugging

Debugging is twice as hard as writing the code in the first place. Therefore, if you write the code as cleverly as possible, you are, by definition, not smart enough to debug it. – Brian Kernighan

Microsoft Dynamics NAV 2013 introduces a brand new debugger. Debugging will no longer be a painful task in Microsoft Dynamics NAV. Conditional breakpoints, debugging other user sessions, and debugging C/AL code in the RTC client instead of incomprehensible C# code. All these new features will convert the debugging experience to a happy experience.

The following topics are covered in this chapter:

- The art of debugging
- Starting the debugger
- Placing breakpoints
- Line-by-line execution
- Code coverage

The art of debugging

By definition, debugging is a methodical process of finding and reducing the number of bugs in an application. Normally, the first step in debugging is to attempt to reproduce the problem. On some occasions, the input of the program may need to be simplified to make it easier to debug. Then you use the debugger tool to examine the program stats (values of variables, call stacks, and so on) and track down the origin of the problem(s), to finally be able to fix it.

Debugging however, can do so much more than just solving issues. It is a fantastic way to understand how an application works. You could just open the involved object, read the written code, and follow it up. But it will be hard.

First of all, because Dynamics NAV code is run after an event occurs. If you take a look at an object, you will see code in the events, but it will be hard to know when an event occurs, or which event is the one that first causes the code to be executed.

It will also be hard to just read the code because you don't know which values a variable is taking. If you turn the debugger on, you read the code with a specific example that makes variables take specific values. And this is really helpful!

Of course, this means that depending on specific variable values, some lines of the code won't be executed and you won't be able to follow them. Therefore, you will have to create significant and varied examples in order to cover all (or almost all) code in a given object.

Debugging in Dynamics NAV 2013

Debugging in Dynamics NAV 2013 has never been this easy. With the release of Dynamics NAV 2013, we can find a brand new debugger that offers the developers tools that they did not have before. Conditional breakpoints or debugging other users sessions are very nice features that will make debugging an easy job.

Starting the debugger

The debugger starts from the Dynamics NAV development environment. The user with which you are logged in must be assigned the SUPER permission set. Go to **Tools | Debugger | Debug Session**.

If you did not have a company open, the system will prompt you to select a company as shown in the following screenshot:

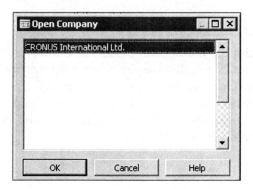

If you already had a company open in the development environment, the system will skip this step. However, you can manually change the company by clicking on **File** and then going to **Company | Open**.

The **Session List** page will open as shown in the following screenshot:

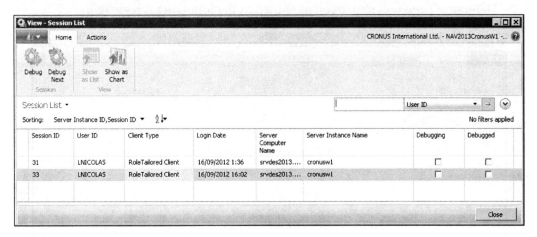

Note that the page shows all sessions on the current database from all companies. This means that it doesn't really matter what company you select from the Dynamics NAV development environment.

The session you select can be any of the following:

- A **RoleTailored Client** session
- A **Microsoft Dynamics NAV Portal Framework for Microsoft SharePoint 2010** session
- An **OData Web Services** session
- An **SOAP Web Services** session
- An **NAS Services** session
- A background session started by using the STARTSESSION function.

Place the cursor on the line corresponding to the session you want to debug and then click on the **Debug** button from the ribbon bar. You can select your own session or any other session from any other user. You can also click on the **Debug Next** option, to debug a session that is not on the session list. The next session can be a session of any client mentioned before.

The user won't be able to work with his/her session while you are debugging; so, whenever possible, open your own session and debug your session. If you cannot reproduce the bug because of user setup conditions, debug the session of the user that is encountering the problem but remember to warn him/her.

The **Debugger** page will now open as shown in the following screenshot:

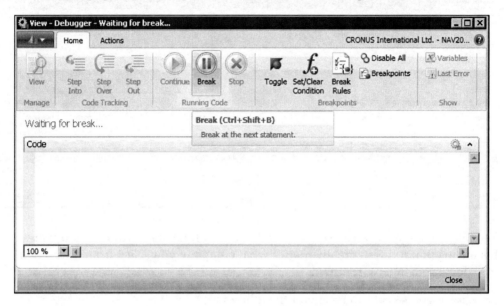

Note that the **Code** area is blank. You can still work with the session you have selected, but no code appears on the debugger. There are two options to actually start to debug code:

- Place a breakpoint on an object and wait until the session reaches the breakpoint. The *Placing breakpoints* section of this chapter explains how to do this.

- Click on the **Break** icon on the ribbon bar. The debugger will stop on the next line of code that the session executes.

You will notice that in the **Debugger** page you can only see the **Code** area, but you are missing two important parts that you will need to debug. The **Call Stack FactBox** is a list that shows the functions and triggers that are currently active. The **Watches FactBox** will allow you to select variables to see their current value.

Follow these steps to enable those options:

1. Click on the Dynamics NAV icon at the upper-left side of the page, and then go to **Customize | Customize This Page...** as shown in the following screenshot:

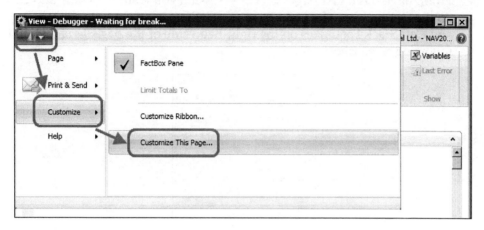

2. On the left side, select the **FactBoxes** option. From the **Available FactBoxes** lists, select **Watches** and click on the **Add >>** button. Do the same with the **Call Stack** option. Click on **OK**.

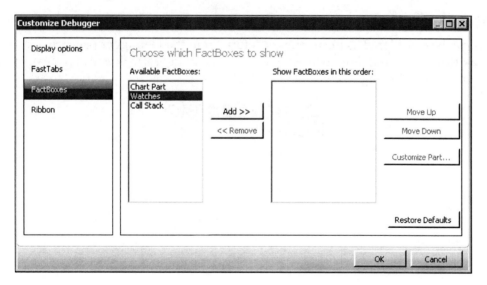

3. The system warns you that you will have to reopen the **Debugger** page for customizations to take effect. Click on **OK**, and then click on **Close** to close the **Debugger** page.

4. From the **Session List** page, select the session you want to debug, and click on the **Debug** icon. The **Debugger** page will open again, with the **Watches** and **Call Stack** FactBoxes on the right-hand side of the page, as shown in the following screenshot:

Break Rules

This can be considered as the debugger setup. From the **Debugger** page, click on the **Break Rules** icon found on the ribbon bar. The **Debugger Break Rules** page opens as shown in the following screenshot:

In Dynamics NAV 2013, you can find three basic options on the debugger feature:

- **Break On Error**: If the debugger is set to break on errors, it breaks execution both on errors that are handled in code and on unhandled errors. By default, the debugger is set to break on errors.

- **Break On Record Changes**: If the debugger is set to break on record changes, it breaks before creating, modifying, or deleting a record. Therefore, the debugger stops on any of the following statements: INSERT, MODIFY, MODIFYALL, DELETE, DELETEALL.

  By default, the debugger is not set to break on record changes.

- **Skip Codeunit 1**: Many of the triggers in codeunit 1 Application Management are not important for debugging a business scenario. This is due to the fact that they are seldom important for debugging and because the codeunit 1 triggers are called frequently in the application. So you can specify that the debugger skips all code in codeunit 1. If you skip codeunit 1, when you break on the next statement the debugger does not break on code in codeunit 1. It continues until the first line of code after codeunit 1. In addition, when you step through the lines of code, the debugger does not step into code in codeunit 1. If you skip codeunit 1, you also implicitly skip all code that is called from codeunit 1.

  If you explicitly set a breakpoint in codeunit 1 or in code that is called from codeunit 1, the debugger breaks execution when it hits the specific breakpoint, regardless of whether you have selected the setting to **Skip Codeunit 1**.

  By default, the debugger is set to **Skip Codeunit 1**.

If the debugger is set up to break on error, the best way to determine the cause of a runtime error is to disable all breakpoints and click on **Continue**. The debugger will automatically stop the execution of the code when it encounters an error.

Placing breakpoints

A breakpoint is an intentional stop or pause placed in an object. It is a mark that you can set on a statement. When the program flow reaches the statement, the debugger intervenes and suspends execution until you instruct it to continue. During the interruption, you can inspect the environment or start a line-by-line code execution.

There are several ways of placing and removing breakpoints. This section will show you all the different ways so that you can choose the one that best suits your debugging needs.

From the Object Designer

From the Microsoft Dynamics NAV development environment, select **Table 270 Bank Account** and click on the **Design** button to open the **Table Designer** window. Then press *F9* or click on **View, C/AL Code** to open the C/AL Editor.

Place the cursor on one statement, a line of code, and press *F9*. A red bullet will appear on the left-hand side of the statement. Press *F9* again; the bullet is now a white bullet. Press *F9* again and the bullet disappears; you have removed the breakpoint.

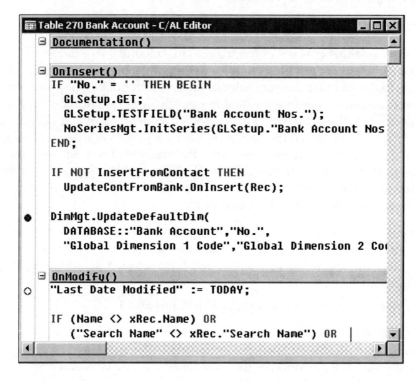

The red bullet indicates that a breakpoint is enabled for that statement. The debugger will stop when the program flow reaches the statement.

The white bullet indicates that a breakpoint was placed before, but it is now disabled. This means that the debugger will not stop on that statement.

In the current statement of the debugger

With the debugger on, place the cursor on one statement, a line of code, and press
F9. A red bullet will appear on the left-hand side of the statement. Press *F9* again; the
bullet is now a white bullet. Press *F9* again and the bullet disappears. You have now
removed the breakpoint.

Instead of pressing *F9*, you can also use the **Toggle** icon found on the ribbon bar, as
shown in the following screenshot:

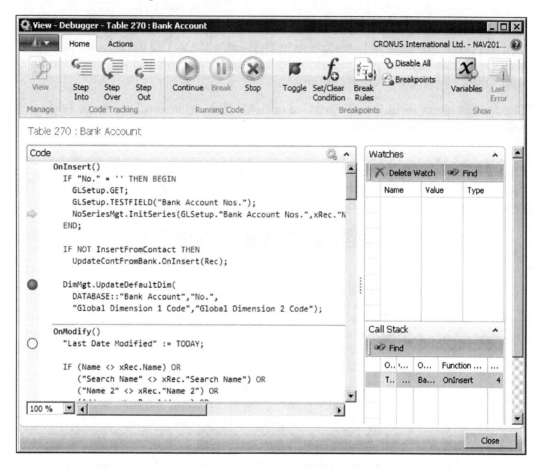

Red and white bullets indicate the same breakpoints as explained in the last section.
This means that you can place breakpoints from the **Object Designer** window or
from the debugger with the same effect.

The only difference is that breakpoints placed from the **Object Designer** window are seen from the debugger, but breakpoints placed from the debugger cannot be seen from the **Object Designer** window.

The end of each function contains a blank statement where you can also place a breakpoint. If you do so, the execution flow will stop right after all the code on the function has been executed and right before returning to the calling function. This is something we could not do in the previous versions of Dynamics NAV.

Conditional breakpoint

You can place a conditional breakpoint in Dynamics NAV. The debugger will only stop the execution if the program flow reaches the breakpoint and the condition is true. Otherwise, the execution continues.

The condition can include any variables or fields that are currently in scope of the following types: BigInteger, Boolean, Code, Decimal, Integer, Option, Text, WideText.

Place the cursor on the statement where you want to place the conditional breakpoint, and the click on the **Set/Clear Condition** icon found on the ribbon bar. The following page will now open:

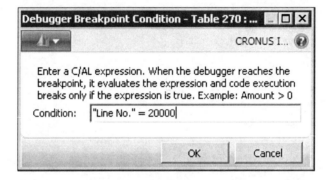

Write your condition using any of the supported operators: =, < >, <, >, <=, >=. Then click on **OK** to go back to the debugger.

On the left-hand side of the statement, a red bullet with a white cross inside will appear. This indicates that the statement has a conditional breakpoint.

The debugger breakpoint list

From the debugger breakpoint you can view, set, enable, disable, or delete breakpoints. You can also set, modify, or delete conditions for the breakpoints.

From the **Debugger** page, click on the **Breakpoints** icon found on the ribbon bar to open the **Debugger Breakpoint List** window, as shown in the following screenshot:

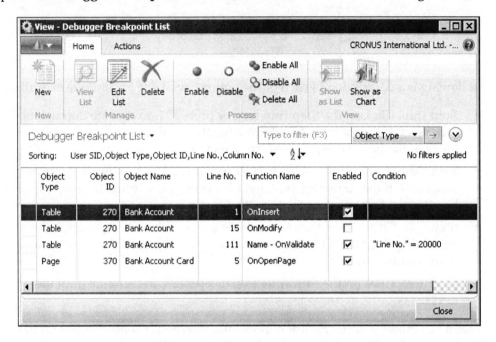

On the ribbon pane of the page, you will find options to create new breakpoints and to enable or disable the existing ones. You can also modify the **Condition** column of any existing breakpoint.

Line-by-line execution

When the debugger stops the execution of the program flow, you have four options to continue the execution. You can find those options on the ribbon pane of the **Debugger** page, as shown in the following screenshot:

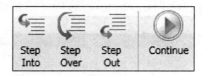

The following is a description of each of the options available to continue execution:

- **Step Into**: Click on the **Step Into** icon or press *F11*, to execute the current statement. If the statement contains a function call, execute the function and break at the first statement *inside* the function.
- **Step Over**: Click on the **Step Over** icon or press *F10*, to execute the current statement. If the statement contains a function call, execute the function and break at the first statement *outside* the function.
- **Step Out**: Click on the **Step Out** icon or press *Shift + F11*, to execute the remaining statements in the current function and break at the next statement in the calling function.
- **Continue**: Click on the **Continue** icon or press *F5*, to continue until the next break.

Let's see an example of each execution mode: the insertion of a new record on the **Bank Account** table. We will use the same example for all the four options.

The Step Into option

Our "Step Into" execution starts with the first statement of the OnInsert trigger of the **Bank Account** table. The yellow arrow (in the following screenshot) shows the line that is currently going to be executed:

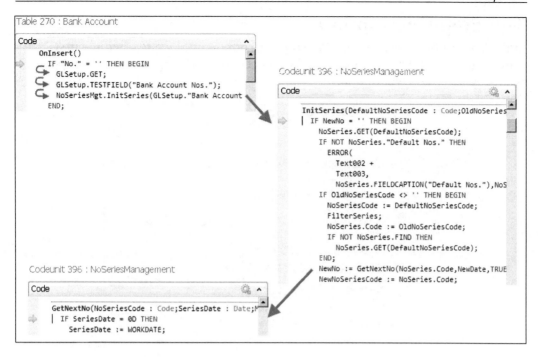

```
Table 270 : Bank Account
Code                                              ^
      OnInsert()
=>      IF "No." = '' THEN BEGIN
  ↳      GLSetup.GET;
  ↳      GLSetup.TESTFIELD("Bank Account Nos.");
  ↳      NoSeriesMgt.InitSeries(GLSetup."Bank Account
         END;
```

Codeunit 396 : NoSeriesManagement

```
Code                                              🔍  ^
      InitSeries(DefaultNoSeriesCode : Code;OldNoSeries
=>  |   IF NewNo = '' THEN BEGIN
          NoSeries.GET(DefaultNoSeriesCode);
          IF NOT NoSeries."Default Nos." THEN
            ERROR(
               Text002 +
               Text003,
               NoSeries.FIELDCAPTION("Default Nos."),NoS
        IF OldNoSeriesCode <> '' THEN BEGIN
          NoSeriesCode := DefaultNoSeriesCode;
          FilterSeries;
          NoSeries.Code := OldNoSeriesCode;
          IF NOT NoSeries.FIND THEN
            NoSeries.GET(DefaultNoSeriesCode);
        END;
        NewNo := GetNextNo(NoSeries.Code,NewDate,TRUE
        NewNoSeriesCode := NoSeries.Code;
```

Codeunit 396 : NoSeriesManagement

```
Code                                              🔍  ^
      GetNextNo(NoSeriesCode : Code;SeriesDate : Date;N
=>  |   IF SeriesDate = 0D THEN
          SeriesDate := WORKDATE;
```

If you press *F11* repeatedly, you will see how each statement is executed. Four statements later, we find a function call. The debugger then stops on the first statement of the `InitSeries` function. A few statements later we find a new function call, and the debugger goes to the first statement of the `GetNextNo` function.

Using these options, the debugger stops on each and every single statement. If you keep on debugging this example, you will see that after pressing *F11* 310 times and visiting 28 functions and triggers, the new bank account will get inserted.

Try to avoid this option unless you don't know what you are looking for and you have no other option than executing all the statements one by one, especially for long transactions.

The Step Over option

In the last section, we have used the **Step Into** option until we reached the first statement of the GetNextNo function. We will continue debugging from that point, but using the **Step Over** option.

If you press *F10* a few times, you will see that the debugger stops on each statement, just as the **Step Into** option does.

The seventh statement of the function is a call to the SetNoSeriesLineFilter function. If you use the **Step Over** option on that statement, the debugger will execute all the code inside the function without stopping and will stop on the first statement after the function call. That is, the next statement in the current function.

Use this option when you already know the code that executes inside the function and you know that the function that is going to be called does not contain the bug you are looking for.

The Step Out option

In the last section, we have used the **Step Over** option until we reached the first statement after the SetNoSeriesLineFilter function call, which is the GetNextNo function. We will continue debugging from that point, but using the **Step Out** option. Please refer to the following screenshot before proceeding:

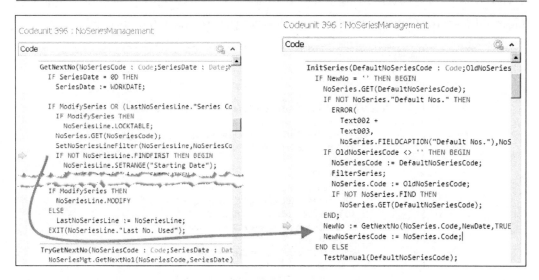

The **Step Out** option executes all the statements in the current function, and stops on the first statement of the calling function.

We are now on the `GetNextNo` function that was called from the `InitSeries` function, as we have seen in the *The Step Into option* section. If you click on the **Step Out** option, the debugger will execute all the remaining statements in the `GetNextNo` function, including the statements inside the new function call. After that, the debugger will stop on the next statement of the calling function, the `InitSeries` function.

Use this option if you have stepped inside a function to see its code and variables but, once inside the function, you have realized that the bug you are looking for is not there.

The Continue option

In the last section, we have used the **Step Out** option until we reached the next statement after the call of the `GetNextNo` function. We will continue debugging the code from that point, but using the **Continue** option.

With the **Continue** option, the execution of the code continues until:

- A breakpoint is reached
- We click on the **Break** option again
- An error occurs

Now, click on the **Continue** option on our example and see what happens.

In the **Code** part of the debugger, we keep seeing the code we had before the **Continue** option was clicked. But the yellow arrow that showed us the current line is not there anymore. At the top of the previous screenshot, we can read that the debugger is now waiting for a break.

The execution of the code has continued, a new bank account has been created, the user gets back the control of the execution, and the debugger is waiting for a new breakpoint.

You can use this option if you don't need to follow the code line by line and want to wait for a breakpoint instead. You also can use this option if an error occurs on a process and you want to know where the error occurs. In this case, you can turn on the debugger, reproduce the process that is causing the problem, and use the **Continue** option to let the debugger find the line causing the error. Of course, you will need the **Break on error** option enabled. You can read the *Break rules* section for more information about this option.

The Call Stack FactBox

The Call Stack FactBox shows the active functions of the current execution. The Call Stack FactBox gives us information about the function that is currently on execution, and also from where this function has been called.

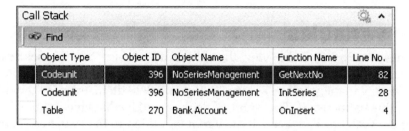

In the preceding screenshot, we can see the call stack corresponding to the code execution which we were analyzing in the **Step Into** option.

We started debugging on the OnInsert trigger of the **Bank Account** table. We used the **Step Into** option until we reached a call to the InitSeries function. With this, we kept using the **Step Into** option until we reached the GetNextNo function. The *The Step Into option* section stopped there.

And this is exactly what we see on the **Call Stack** FactBox.

The top line shows us the current function, while the bottom line shows the first function from where we started debugging. It also gives us valuable information, such as the object that contains the functions that are executed.

You can select any of the lines of the **Call Stack** FactBox. We have selected the bottom line. Now you can see that the **Code** area of the debugger changes, showing the code of the line selected on the **Call Stack** FactBox.

```
Table 270 : Bank Account

Code
    OnInsert()
     IF "No." = '' THEN BEGIN
        GLSetup.GET;
        GLSetup.TESTFIELD("Bank Account Nos.");
        NoSeriesMgt.InitSeries(GLSetup."Bank Account N
     END;

     IF NOT InsertFromContact THEN
        UpdateContFromBank.OnInsert(Rec);

     DimMgt.UpdateDefaultDim(
        DATABASE::"Bank Account","No.",
        "Global Dimension 1 Code","Global Dimension 2
```

Note that a green arrow shows us the last statement executed before the execution flow jumped to a new function.

We can now place a new breakpoint on the function, as can be seen a couple of statements after the green arrow.

Watch variables

The **Watches** FactBox is used to view the values of variables. You can select some variables from the **Debugger Variables List** window and add them to the **Watches** FactBox. Those variables will be shown until you delete them, even if they run out of scope. If this happens, the text **<Out of Scope>** will be displayed in the **Value** column of the **Watches** FactBox. All the variables added to the **Watches** FactBox persist between debugging sessions.

There are two ways to add a variable to the **Watches** FactBox:

- From the **Debugger Variable List** window
- From the code viewer.

Adding variables from the Debugger Variables List window

To add variables from the **Debugger Variables List** window, follow these steps:

1. On the **Debugger** page, click on the **Variables** option found on the **Actions** pane. The **Debugger Variable List** page will open as shown in the following screenshot:

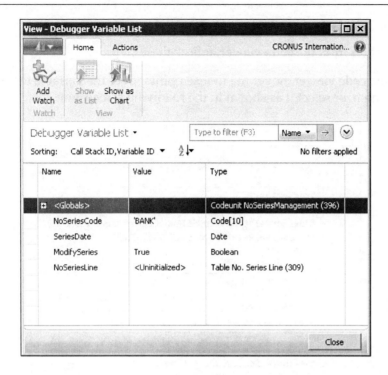

2. Select a variable from the list and click on the **Add Watch** icon. Then click on the **Close** button.

3. Back on the **Debugger** page, you will see the selected variable on the **Watches** FactBox. You can view the name of the variable, its value, and its type as shown in the following screenshot:

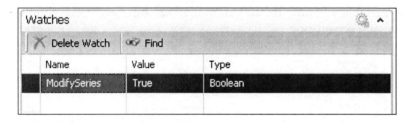

Adding variables from the code viewer

To add variables from the code viewer, follow these steps:

1. In the code viewer, hover the mouse pointer over the variable that you want to watch, or select it as shown in the following screenshot:

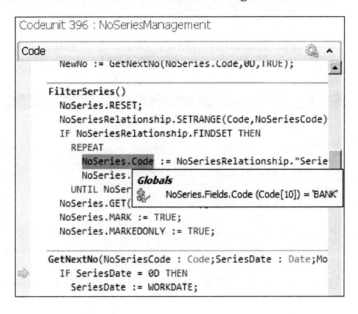

2. A data tip appears, as you can see on the preceding screenshot. Click on the watch icon found on the left-hand side of the data tip (the glasses with a green plus symbol).

3. The variable will now be shown on the **Watches** FactBox as shown in the following screenshot:

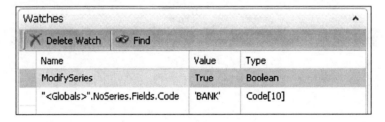

Code Coverage

The **Code Coverage** functionality keeps track of which objects and which lines of code have been executed by your own session since you started and stopped the coverage. We used this feature extensively in combination with the debugger to find and fix bugs and also to investigate how certain features work in Dynamics NAV.

Incomprehensibly, this functionality is no longer available as a standard feature in Dynamics NAV 2013. Doing some quick research on the Internet, we found a blog post written by Carsten Scholling on the *German NAV Developers Blog*. The blog post is titled *Pimp your NAV 2013: Code coverage upgrade in 30 minutes* (`http://blogs.msdn.com/b/german_nav_developer/archive/2012/08/26/pimp-your-nav-2013-code-coverage-in-30-minuten-nachr-252-sten.aspx`). Carsten has developed his own **Code Coverage** page. In this section, we will show you how to include this feature in your Dynamics NAV, and how it works.

Importing the Code Coverage objects

We have provided a file containing the Code Coverage objects that Carsten published on his blog. The file is called `CodeCoverage.txt`. Follow these steps in order to import the objects in to your Dynamics NAV environment.

1. Open the Microsoft Dynamics NAV development environment.
2. Click on **File** and then on **Import**. Select the `CodeCoverage.txt` file and click on **Open**.
3. Find **Page 50020** and **Page 50021**, and select them.
4. Objects imported from the `.txt` file are not compiled. Therefore, click on **Tools** and then on **Compile**.

How to use the Code Coverage feature

Follow these steps in order to use the Code Coverage feature in the small example we have been debugging: creating a new bank account.

1. From the Microsoft Dynamics NAV development environment, find page `50020`, go to **Code Coverage**, and click the **Run** button.

2. The **Code Coverage** page will open. Click on the **Start Code Coverage** option as shown in the following screenshot:

3. Open the **Bank Accounts** page, and click on the **New** option in order to create a new bank account. On the **Bank Account Card** page, click on **enter** to let the system give you a number from the number series configured for bank accounts.

4. Go back to the **Code Coverage** page and click on the **Stop Code Coverage** option. A list with all the objects used since you started the code coverage will appear as shown in the following screenshot:

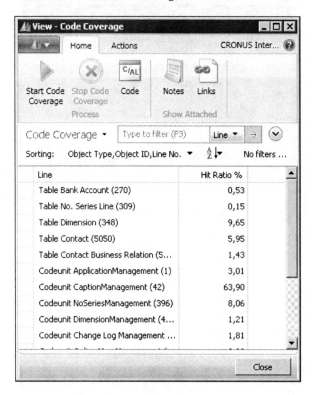

5. Select the **Table Bank Account (270)** line and click on the **Code** option found on the action pane.

6. The **Code Coverage Code** page will open, showing all the code of the selected object:

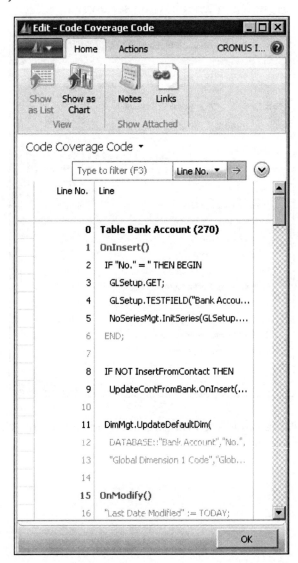

Note that different lines are shown in different styles. Each style has its own meaning. The following screenshot shows the meaning each style has in the Code Coverage feature, for Dynamics NAV 2013

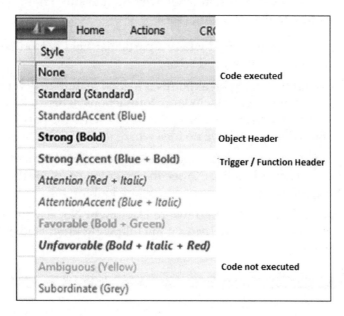

7. To see the code of all the objects, and not the selected object only, you can remove the current filter from the **Code Coverage Code** page.

8. To only see executed code, you can add the following filter to the **Code Coverage Code** page:

When to use the Code Coverage feature

You are free to use the Code Coverage feature whenever you find it useful. In this section, we will give you some tips on when we find it useful. We have used the Code Coverage feature in the following cases:

- On large transactions; to find where a particular field is modified, a record is inserted, a function called, and so on.

  We have found that using breakpoints is a good feature to debug only the code you need to follow. Especially in large transactions, where a lot of statements need to be executed before the program flow reaches the part you want to examine. But what if you have no idea where to place your breakpoint?

  On the **Code Coverage Code** page, you can remove all filters to see the code of all objects. Then add a filter to see the executed code. Next add a new filter on the **Line** column to find the code you are looking for.

  For example, if we want to find where **Document No.** is assigned during the sales posting routine, we can set the following filters and get the following result:

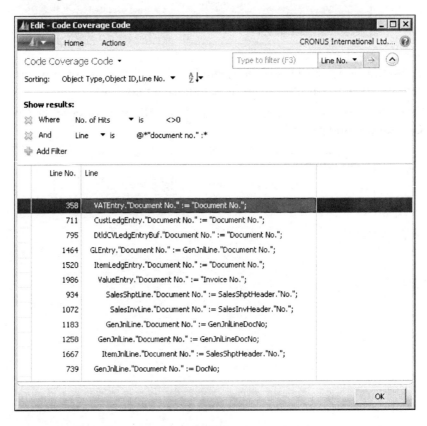

This gives us an idea about where to place breakpoints, where to start debugging and how a certain area works. This would be very helpful if we wanted to develop any feature regarding document numbers, or if we were finding a bug regarding the document numbers.

Let your imagination flow, because you can find any kind of information just by changing the filter of the **Line** column.

- With respect to permission setup, setting permissions on Dynamics NAV is a tedious task. To give permissions to a user to only perform certain tasks, you need to give the user permissions to all the objects that the task uses.

  Code Coverage is the perfect feature to help you determine all the objects used on a particular task. Just start **Code Coverage**, perform the task, and then go back to the **Code Coverage** page to get a complete list of all the objects that the user will need permission for.

We have seen two cases where the Code Coverage feature is useful. We are pretty sure that many people use Code Coverage for many other reasons. Just start using it while developing and we are pretty sure that you will find it very helpful.

We have never used it to track objects' usage, but it could work. If you could just start Code Coverage each time a session starts, track all the objects used, and save it in some kind of log, you would be able to see statistics of object usage that could be very helpful in making certain decisions.

Summary

In this chapter we have seen that debugging is kind of an art that is used to examine program stats, to find bugs, and to be able to fix them. In addition we have seen that debugging can also be used to understand how an application works.

We have also seen how to use the Dynamics NAV 2013 Debugger: how to start it, select a session to debug, place breakpoints, and do a line-by-line execution. We have also explained the **Call Stack** FactBox and the **Watches** FactBox.

We have also discussed the Code Coverage features and when such a feature is useful for developers.

In the next chapter we will talk about the Query object, the new object type included in Dynamics NAV 2013.

12
The Query Object

Microsoft Dynamics NAV 2013 introduces a new application object: **the query**. Although it is not yet, this new application object is meant to be "The Microsoft Dynamics NAV reading data object" in the future (notice the capital letter in the word "The"), so you better get familiar with it as soon as possible.

In this chapter, we will take an in-depth look at this new application object. We will go through the following topics:

- What is a query
- What can be done with a query
- Query Designer
- Defining a query
- Where queries can be used
- Query performance

What is a query

Query is the name of a new Dynamics NAV application object introduced in Microsoft Dynamics NAV 2013. This application object is only meant to retrieve data from the database. It is a read-only object. It cannot modify, delete, or insert new data into the database.

Queries are the ninth object type in Dynamics NAV, although only seven are available in Dynamics NAV 2013, now that forms and dataports are gone.

There are many things about queries in Dynamics NAV that will make you just love them:

- They allow us to retrieve data from multiple tables at the same time
- They allow us to retrieve only specific fields in a table
- They allow us to group the retrieved data according to certain fields without the need of any explicit key for them
- They allow us to total the retrieved data using different totaling methods (sum, count, average, min, and max)

If you are a Dynamics NAV programmer and you have worked with the previous versions of Dynamics NAV, you will see the advantages and the possibilities of this new object right away.

The query object makes programming easier and for the lovers of performance, it makes data retrieval a lot faster.

In this chapter, we will show you how to define a query using the query editor and where and how to use queries on your developments. Once we know how to write and execute queries, we will compare them both in time and effort of development and in speed, against the old ways of retrieving the exact same data out of the application.

Query Designer

Queries, just as any other object in Dynamics NAV, have their own designer or editor.

To open **Query Designer**, perform the following steps:

1. Open the Microsoft Dynamics NAV development environment.
2. The **Object Designer** window opens.

3. On the left pane of the **Object Designer** window, click on **Query** to see the list of existing queries, as shown in the following screenshot:

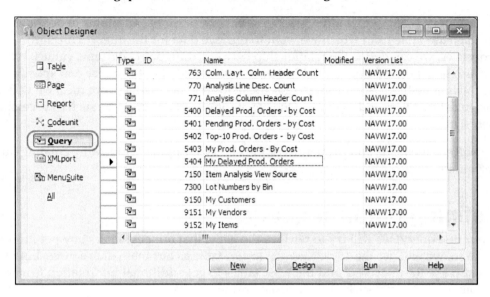

4. Select the query **9150 My Customers** (or any other existing query).

5. Click on **Design**.

6. The **Query Designer** window opens as shown in the following screenshot:

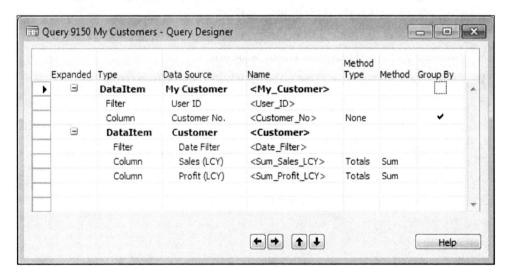

The **Query Designer** window looks a lot like the Page Designer or the new Report Dataset Designer. This will make it easier to get used to developing queries.

In the **Query Designer** window, we can select one or more **DataItems** to define the database table from which we want to retrieve data for the query. Through properties, we can define the relationship between different **DataItems** values. We can also select the columns or fields that will be included in the query and specify the totaling methods and grouping for the fields. Finally, using properties, we will be able to define filters and to modify the behavior of certain columns, such as reversing their sign.

We will see the fields and properties of the **Query Designer** window by creating our first query.

Defining our first query

In our first query, we will try to retrieve the items that our customers buy per month. To do so, we will use the Item Ledger Entry table as our main data source, but we will also use the Customer and the Item tables to get additional information from customers and items, such as their name or description.

Let's first define the main data source and the fields that will be retrieved:

1. Open the **Object Designer** window in the Microsoft Dynamics NAV development environment and select the **Query** object type on the left pane of the **Object Designer** window.

2. Click on **New** to create a new query.

3. An empty **Query Designer** window opens.

4. On the first line, in the **Type** column, choose **DataItem** from the drop-down list.

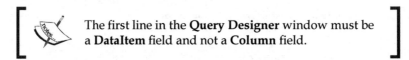

The first line in the **Query Designer** window must be a **DataItem** field and not a **Column** field.

5. Select **Item Ledger Entry** in the **Data Source** column.

You can choose the up arrow that will appear on the right-hand side of the **Data Source** column when you select it to see a table list and select the desired table. You can also type in the name or the number ID of the table (if you know the name or the number ID of the table) you want to use on your query.

6. The **Name** column will be automatically populated once a **Data Source** value has been selected. Default names are usually fine, but you can change them if you want to.

Names in queries must be **Common Language Specification** (**CLS**)-compliant. The first character must be a letter. Subsequent characters can be any combination of letters, integers, and underscores.

7. Display the **Properties** window for the data item. To do so, select the **DataItem** row and click on **View** | **Properties** (or press *Shift + F4*).

8. Select the property `DataItemTableFilter` and click on the **Assist Edit** button. The **Table Filter** window will open. Set **Field** to **Entry Type**, **Type** to **CONST**, and **Value** to **Sale**. Click on **OK**.

   Back at the **Properties** window, the value for the `DataItemTableFilter` property should be what is shown in the following screenshot:

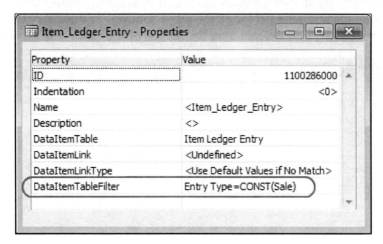

Using the `DataItemTableFilter` property, we have applied a filter so that only entries of type **Sale** are retrieved on this query. We are analyzing sales, we do not want other types of entries to be shown in our query.

9. Close the **Properties** window.

10. For the **Item Ledger Entry** data item, select fields **Item No.**, **Posting Date**, **Quantity**, and **Source No.** as **Column** in the rows below **DataItem**.

   Once you have selected all those fields, the **Query Designer** window should look like the following screenshot:

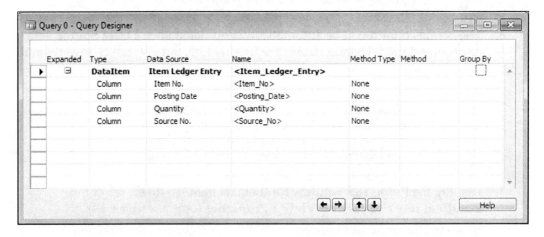

11. For the row **Posting Date**, select **Date** as **Method Type** and **Month** as **Method**.

12. For the row **Quantity**, select **Totals** as **Method Type** and **Sum** as **Method**.

   Notice that right after a **Totals** method type is selected, the **Group By** field is automatically selected for all the other columns in the query that are not of type **Totals**. This defines how the results of the query will be grouped.

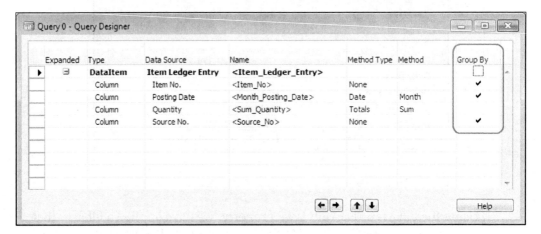

Group By is a read-only field that is automatically calculated. The value of this column cannot be modified.

13. In the **Properties** window of the **Quantity** field, select **Yes** for the property **ReverseSign**.

    We are analyzing sales. Sales represent a decrease in the item's inventory. Being a decrease, the **Quantity** field for entries of type **Sale** is a negative value. We want to reverse this sign because we want to see quantities sold as positive values.

14. Save and compile the query. To do so, click on **File | Save** (or press *Ctrl + S*).

15. We will be asked for an ID and a name for the query. We will set the **ID** attribute to 50000 and the **Name** attribute to My First Query.

16. The **Query Designer** window will be closed and we will be taken back to the **Object Designer** window. We will now run the query and take a look at the results. To do so, select **Query 50000 My First Query** and click on the **Run** button.

17. The Windows client will open and the result of the query will be shown as follows:

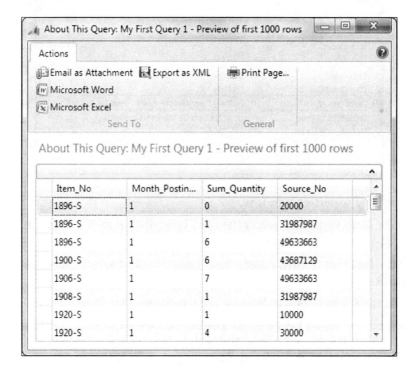

So far so good! We have defined a pretty simple query with a single data item, but we have already seen how to filter the results, the different method types, and how the results are grouped.

Adding complexity to the query

We will go further into the example by adding a couple of extra data items to the query.

1. In the **Object Designer** window, select **Query 50000 My First Query** and click on the **Design** button. The **Query Designer** window will open with the query we were creating.

2. On the first empty row, enter a **DataItem** value for the table **Item**.

3. Open the **Properties** window for the **Item** data item.

4. Click on the **Assist Edit** button for the property **DataItemLink**. Select **No.** as the **field**, the **Item_Ledger_Entry** data item as **reference DataItem**, and **Item No.** as the **reference field**. Click on **OK**.

    Back at the **Properties** window, the value for the **DataItemLink** property should be what is shown in the following screenshot:

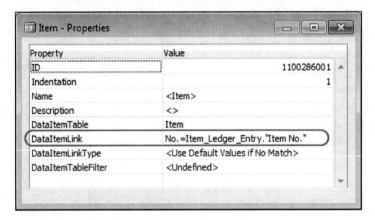

5. Close the **Properties** window.

6. For the **Item** DataItem, select the field **Description** as the **Column** type in the rows below the **DataItem** field.

7. On the first empty row, enter a new DataItem and select Customer as the Data Source.

8. Open the **Properties** window for the **Customer** DataItem.

9. Click on the **Assist Edit** button. For the property **DataItemLink**, select **No.** as the field, the **Item_Ledger_Entry** data item as the reference data item, and **Source No.** as the reference field. Click on **OK**.

10. Close the **Properties** window.

11. For the **Customer** DataItem, select the fields **Name** and **Customer Posting Group** as the **Column** type in the rows below the **DataItem** field.

    The final query should look like this:

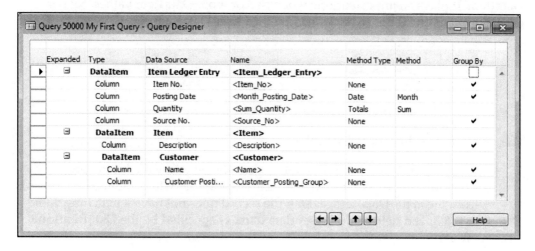

12. Save and compile the query.

13. Run the query to see the results:

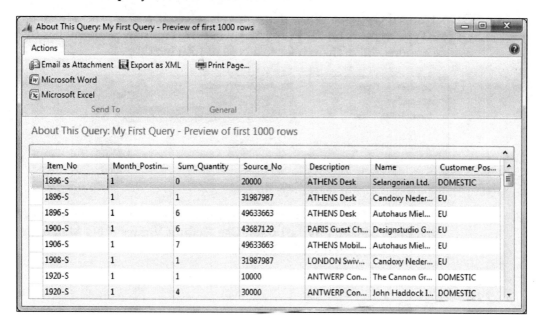

The DataItemLinkType property

Queries have other properties that did not come out in the query that we have created as an example. We will not go through all of them. We will however, explain an extra property. The **DataItemLinkType** property can be found only on the row of type **DataItem**. It plays an important role when two or more **DataItem** values exist on the same query and it has to be defined on the lower **DataItem** rows.

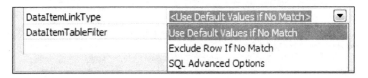

This property has three possible options:

- **Use Default Values if No Match**: This is the default value of the property. When this option is selected, the resulting data set will contain all the records from the *upper* DataItem, even if the record does not have a matching value in the linked field of the lower data item, as specified by the **DataItemLink** property.

- **Exclude Row If No Match**: When this option is selected, the resulting data set will only contain records from data item tables that have matching values for the fields that are linked by the **DataItemLink** property.

- **SQL Advanced Options**: When this option is selected, a new property called **SQLJoinType** appears on the **Properties** window. This new property has five possible options. All of them refer to a type of **Join** in SQL:

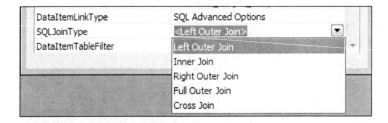

- ○ **Left Outer Join**: This is the default value of the property. It provides the same behavior as the option **Use Default Values if No Match** for the property **DataItemLinkType**.

The following illustration shows a **Left Outer Join** type between tables A and B. The shaded area indicates the records that are included in the resulting data set.

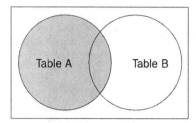

○ **Inner Join**: This option provides the same behavior as the option **Exclude Row If No Match** for the property **DataItemLinkType**.

The following illustration shows an **Inner Join** type between tables A and B. The shaded area indicates the records that are included in the resulting data set.

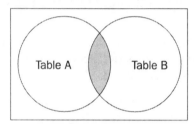

○ **Right Outer Join**: When this option is selected, the resulting data set will contain all the records from the *lower* data item, even if the record does not have a matching value in the linked field of the upper data item, as specified by the **DataItemLink** property.

The behavior is similar to the one provided by the **Left Outer Join** option. The **Left Outer Join** option sets all the upper data item records as the result while the **Right Outer Join** option sets all the lower data item records as the result.

The following illustration shows a **Right Outer Join** type between tables A and B. The shaded area indicates the records that are included in the resulting data set.

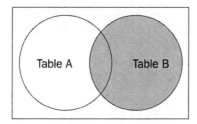

○ **Full Outer Join**: When this option is selected, the resulting data set will contain all the records from the upper data item and also all the records from the lower data item, including records that do not have a matching value for columns that are linked by the **DataItemLinkType** property.

It's like selecting **Left Outer Join** and **Right Outer Join** at the same time.

The following illustration shows a **Full Outer Join** type between tables A and B. The shaded area indicates the records that are included in the resulting data set.

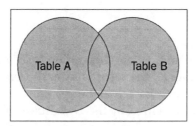

○ **Cross Join**. When this option is selected, the resulting data set will contain rows that combine each row from the upper data item table with each row from the lower data item table. Cross joins are also called **Cartesian products**.

In this type of join, there is no comparison between fields of the two involved data items, so the **DataItemLink** property must be left blank.

Where to use queries

Queries can be used in C/AL code or in Dynamics NAV charts. They can also be published as web services and thus consumed by external applications. In this section, we will see exactly where queries can be used.

C/AL code

Queries can be accessed from C/AL code. It is a good idea to use queries instead of writing C/AL code involving record variables when you want to read records from multiple tables at the same time.

Executing a query from C/AL code is as simple as defining a variable of type Query and typing the following sentences:

```
MyFirstQuery.OPEN;
WHILE MyFirstQuery.READ DO
  OutputData(MyFirstQuery.Item_No,
    MyFirstQuery.Month_Posting_Date,
    MyFirstQuery.Sum_Quantity,
    MyFirstQuery.Source_No,
    MyFirstQuery.Description,
    MyFirstQuery.Name,
    MyFirstQuery.Customer_Posting_Group);
```

In this example, we have defined a query variable called MyFirstQuery that points to the query created earlier on in this chapter.

We first have to open the query using OPEN and then read the results (READ) using a loop statement. On every READ, we will get a different result record.

We can access any of the columns defined in the query by typing the following:

```
<QueryVariableName>.<ColumnName>
```

In the example, we pass all the columns as parameters of a function called OutputData() that will handle the results.

Just a few sentences are needed to execute a query. Isn't that cool?

Designing the query has been easy. Executing the query has been even easier. How much effort do you think is needed to get the exact same result as in the query but using pure C/AL code? Examine the following code and evaluate it yourself:

```
ItemLedgEntry.SETRANGE("Entry Type",ItemLedgEntry."Entry Type"::Sale);
IF ItemLedgEntry.FINDSET THEN
REPEAT
  tmpItem.SETRANGE("No. 2",ItemLedgEntry."Item No.");
  tmpItem.SETRANGE(tmpItem."Vendor No.",ItemLedgEntry."Source No.");
  tmpItem.SETRANGE("Price Unit Conversion",DATE2DMY(ItemLedgEntry."Pos
ting Date",2));
  IF tmpItem.FINDSET THEN
  BEGIN
    tmpItem."Unit Price" := tmpItem."Unit Price" + ItemLedgEntry.
Quantity;
    tmpItem.MODIFY;
  END
  ELSE
  BEGIN
    IF Item.GET(ItemLedgEntry."Item No.") THEN;
    IF Customer.GET(ItemLedgEntry."Source No.") THEN;

    tmpItem.INIT;
    tmpItem."No." := FORMAT(tmpItemNo);
    tmpItemNo := tmpItemNo + 1;
    tmpItem."No. 2" := ItemLedgEntry."Item No.";
    tmpItem."Vendor No." := ItemLedgEntry."Source No.";
    tmpItem."Price Unit Conversion" := DATE2DMY(ItemLedgEntry."Posting
Date",2);
    tmpItem.Description := Item.Description;
    tmpItem."Description 2" := Customer.Name;
    tmpItem."Inventory Posting Group" := Customer."Customer Posting
Group";
    tmpItem."Unit Price" := ItemLedgEntry.Quantity;
    tmpItem.INSERT;
  END;
UNTIL ItemLedgEntry.NEXT = 0;

tmpItem.RESET;
IF tmpItem.FINDSET THEN
REPEAT
  OutputData(
    tmpItem."No. 2",
    tmpItem."Price Unit Conversion",
```

```
        tmpItem."Unit Price",
        tmpItem."Vendor No.",
        tmpItem.Description,
        tmpItem."Description 2",
        tmpItem."Inventory Posting Group");
    UNTIL tmpItem.NEXT = 0;
```

We first have to define all the variables used in the code, namely, `ItemLedgerEntry`, `Item`, `Customer` as record variables, `tmpItem` as a temporary record variable, and `tmpItemNo` as an integer.

We filter `ItemLedgerEntry` to only retrieve sales entry types. We loop through all the `ItemLedgerEntry` records and, in every loop, we check whether a temporary record exists or not for the grouping fields. If it does not exist, we create the temporary record with the appropriate values. If it exists, we just sum up quantities in the existing temporary record. Finally, we loop through all the temporary records, which have the same results as the query we defined earlier.

The code is confusing. There are no sentences in C/AL to group. We have to use some tricks to actually get that behavior. In this case, we use temporary records. There is no table in Dynamics NAV with the exact fields we need, so we just picked one-`Item`. We've used the fields in that table that had the type and length we needed, without really looking at the name of the fields.

Believe me, when I say; it was much easier to develop the query than this C/AL code.

Charts

The Windows client can display a set of predefined charts that use Dynamics NAV data. With Microsoft Dynamics NAV 2013, queries can be used as data sources for those charts.

We will use the query defined earlier on in this chapter as the data source of a chart and we will display it on the home page of the Dynamics NAV Windows client.

To define a query as the data source of a chart, perform the following steps:

1. Open the Windows client for Microsoft Dynamics NAV 2013.
2. Navigate to **Departments/Administration/Application Setup/RoleTailored Client**.
3. Select **Generic Charts**.
4. Click on **New** on the ribbon bar to add a new chart.
5. The **New-Generic Chart** setup page opens.

6. Give the new chart an **ID** value and a **Name** value. For example, set **ID** to `50000` and **Name** to `My Query Chart`.

7. On the **Data Source** tab, select **Query** as **Source Type** and **50000** as **Source ID**.

8. On the **Measures (Y-Axis)** tab, select **Sum_Quantity** as **Data Column** on the **Required Measure** row.

9. On the **Dimensions (X- and Z-Axes)** tab, select **Source_No** as **X-Axis Field**.

10. Click on **OK** to close the **New-Generic Chart** setup page.

To display the chart on the home page of the Windows client, perform the following steps:

1. Go back to the home page of the Windows client for Dynamics NAV 2013.

2. Click on the Dynamics NAV icon found on the upper-left corner of the page and select **Customize** and then **Customize This Page**.

3. Select **Chart Part** from **Available parts**.

4. Click on **Add**.

5. A blank chart will appear on the **Role Center layout** section. Select the blank chart and click on **Customize Part**.

6. Select chart **50000 My Query Chart** and click on **OK**.

7. Click on **OK** to close the **Customize the Role Center** page.

8. Back at the home page of the Windows client, the chart should be displayed as follows:

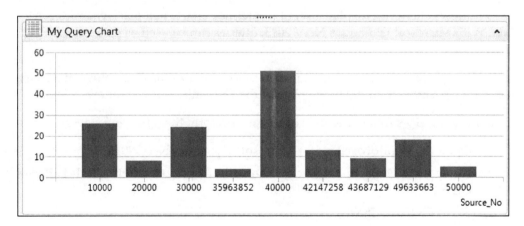

Web services

In Microsoft Dynamics NAV 2009, it was possible to publish page and codeunit objects as web services to allow external applications to access Dynamics NAV data and business logic. In Microsoft Dynamics NAV 2013, it is also possible to publish query objects as web services.

Page and codeunit objects can be accessed through SOAP web services. Queries can only be accessed through the new web services protocol introduced in Microsoft Dynamics NAV 2013: **OData web services**.

To publish a query as a web service, perform the following steps:

1. Open the Windows client for Microsoft Dynamics NAV 2013.
2. Navigate to **Departments/Administration/IT Administration/General**.
3. Select **Web Services**.
4. Select **New** on the ribbon bar to publish a new web service.
5. The **New-Web Services** page opens.
6. Select **Query** as **Object Type**.
7. Enter 50000 in the **Object ID** field.
8. Enter a name in the **Service Name** field. For example, let's use **MyQueryWS** as **Service Name**.
9. Check the **Published** field, as shown in the following screenshot:

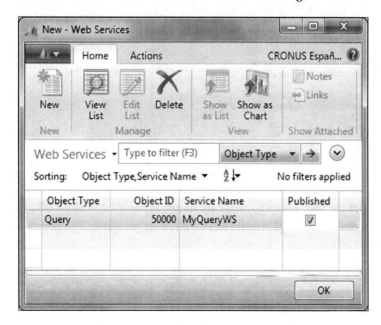

10. Close the Windows client for Microsoft Dynamics NAV 2013.

At this point, the query is already published as a web service. You can check to see if it is accessible using your browser. To do so, perform the following steps:

1. Open Internet Explorer (or any other browser).

2. Type the following on the address bar:

   `http://<ServerName>:<ODataPort>/<ServerInstance>/Odata`

   In a typical installation, `<ODataPort>` will be `7048`. `<ServerName>` will be the name of the server on which you have installed the server options of Microsoft Dynamics NAV 2013, and `<ServerInstance>` will be the name given to the Dynamics NAV service.

   If you are accessing the published web service on the server where Dynamics NAV is installed and you haven't changed the default port on which OData web services are published, you can use the following URL:

   `http://localhost:7048/DynamicsNAV70/Odata`

3. The published OData web services should be displayed in an XML format, as shown in the following screenshot:

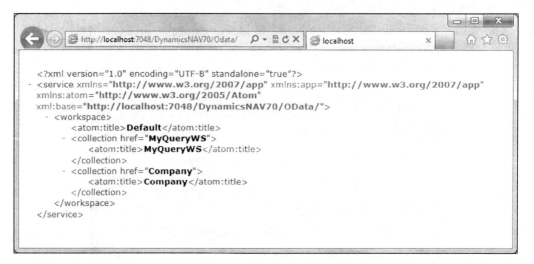

To access a concrete web service, enter its name at the end of the URL. In the case of the previous example, that would be `http://localhost:7048/DynamicsNAV70 /Odata/MyQueryWS`.

External applications

Because Dynamics NAV 2013 queries can be published as web services, they can be accessed by absolutely any application that can consume OData web services. There is no limit. It can be an external application developed by you for the only purpose of reading Dynamics NAV data or it can be a commonly-used application that supports OData web services.

In this section, we will see how to use Dynamics NAV 2013 queries in Microsoft Office Excel.

Excel and PowerPivot

Among all the applications that are out there, an extensively used one is probably Microsoft Office Excel. There is a free add-in for Excel called **PowerPivot** that can consume OData web services.

Great! How do we do that? Let's do it step by step:

1. You can download PowerPivot by performing a quick search on the Internet which will lead you to the download page.
2. Installing **PowerPivot** is an easy **Next**, **Next**, **Finish** install process.
3. The installation of PowerPivot will create a new tab in the ribbon bar of Microsoft Office Excel.
4. Publish a query as a web service. You can follow the instructions on the *Web services* section of this chapter to complete this action.
5. Open Microsoft Excel.
6. On the **PowerPivot** tab, select **PowerPivot Window**. A **PowerPivot for Excel** window will open.
7. Select **From Data Feeds**.

8. You will be asked to enter a friendly connection name and a data feed URL. Enter NAV2013MyQueryWS as **Friendly connection name** and http://localhost:7048/DynamicsNAV70/Odata/MyQueryWS as the value for **Data Feed URL**, as shown in the following screenshot:

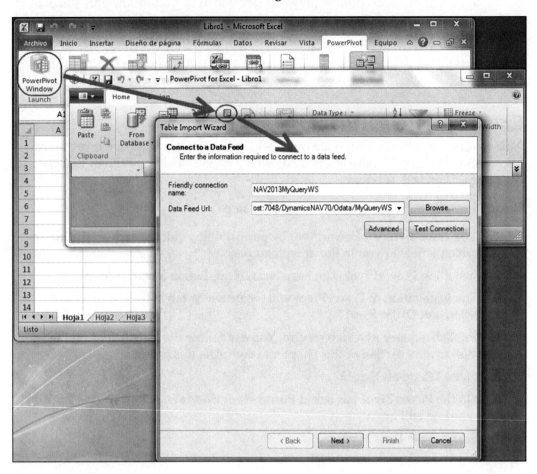

9. Click on **Test Connection** to check if PowerPivot can access the published web service.

10. Click on **Next** and then click on **Finish**.

11. An import process will start. Once it is finished, click on **Close**.

12. The imported data will be displayed on the **PowerPivot for Excel** window.

13. Close the **PowerPivot for Excel** window.

14. On the **PowerPivot** tab, select **PivotTable**.

15. A PivotTable that uses data from Microsoft Dynamics NAV 2013 will be created. Select the fields that you want to see on the PivotTable.

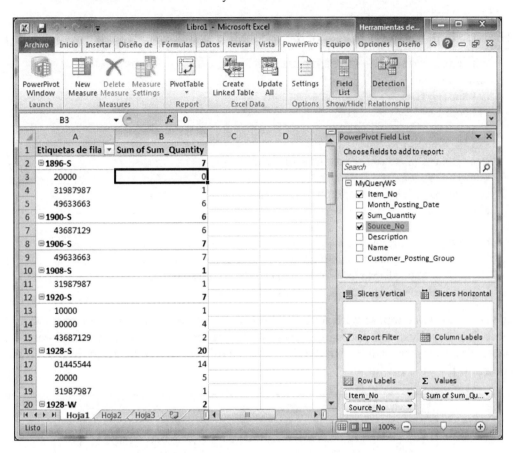

Query performance

In this chapter, we have defined a query and we have also written C/AL code to get the exact same results as the query; these are two different ways of performing the exact same action. But wouldn't it be great if we could compare their execution times to know how fast queries are?

We have put together in a single codeunit both the C/AL codes defined in the section *C/AL code* under *Where to use queries*. We have created a function called `QueryFunction()` in which we have copy/pasted the code corresponding to the execution of the query and a function called `CALFunction()` in which we have copy/pasted the code corresponding to the C/AL code that emulates the behavior of the query.

Before and after the call to each function, we retrieve the current system time. We will then compare ending time versus initial time to know the execution time of every function.

The code in the OnRun() trigger of the codeunit is as follows:

```
CALStartingTime := CURRENTDATETIME;
CALFunction;
CALEndingTime := CURRENTDATETIME;
CALCounter := Counter;

CLEAR(Counter);
QueryStartingTime := CURRENTDATETIME;
QueryFunction;
QueryEndingTime := CURRENTDATETIME;
QueryCounter := Counter;

MESSAGE('C/AL Code was executed in %1 returning %2 records\' +
        'Query was executed in %3 returning %4 records',
        CALEndingTime - CALStartingTime,CALCounter,
        QueryEndingTime - QueryStartingTime,QueryCounter);
```

We have used a database with only six thousand records on the Item Ledger Entry table. It is a really small database. This table has millions of records in many real databases. Even with such a small database, the difference in execution time of C/AL code and the query is huge.

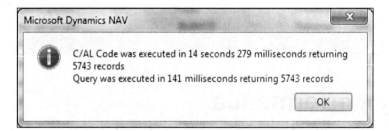

More than 14 seconds for the C/AL code and just one hundred and forty one milliseconds for the query.

That really points out that queries are good data readers. That's why they are meant to be "The Dynamics NAV reading object" of the future.

One of the things that can explain that time difference is that a regular loop in C/AL retrieves all the record fields in every looped record, even if only a few fields are needed in the loop, while queries only retrieve the fields that are really needed.

In the query, three tables were used, and only a few fields for each table:

Table name	Fields used	Fields retrieved
Item Ledger Entry	4	4
Item	2	2
Customer	3	3

Nine different fields were retrieved and used in the query.

In C/AL code, the same tables were used, but all their fields were retrieved:

Table name	Fields used	Fields retrieved
Item Ledger Entry	4	72
Item	2	189
Customer	3	142

Even if only nine fields were used, 403 were retrieved in every loop.

You can try out this example in your own databases. Both the query and the codeunit to run the query and the C/AL code are available to download. Import them in to your databases and check the results yourself.

Summary

In this chapter, we have taken a thorough look into the query object, a new Microsoft Dynamics NAV 2013 object, which is designed to read data from the database. We now know how to design new queries using the Query Designer. We also know that queries can be used in C/AL code or as data sources of Dynamics NAV Charts and that they can be published as web services and thus consumed by external applications. We also know that as a reading object, queries offer a good performance.

In the next chapter, we will see some third-party applications that are included in the Dynamics NAV license for free and that are fully integrated into Microsoft Dynamics NAV 2013.

13

Applications Included in Dynamics NAV

Jet Reports Express and Zetadocs Express are free versions of third-party applications recommended by Microsoft and compatible with standard versions of Microsoft Dynamics NAV. This chapter will explain what those applications are meant for, and how to install and configure them to work together with Microsoft Dynamics NAV 2013.

In this chapter we will cover the following topics:

- Downloading and installing Jet Reports Express
- How to configure and use Jet Reports Express
- Downloading and installing Zetadocs Express
- How to configure and use Zetadocs Express

Jet Reports Express

Jet Reports Express for Microsoft Dynamics NAV is a business-reporting tool meant to let users create high-impact reports in a familiar environment, such as Microsoft Excel. With Jet Reports Express, you can use all Excel capabilities, such as formatting, slicers, charting, and pivot tables.

This is a very good and profitable tool for many users. So don't wait for your customers to ask for it; instead, plan to install it on every new Dynamics NAV project and give users the necessary training to use it.

Visit the Jet Reports website for updated information of this application. In the website, you will also find a few demo videos that show you how to start using it. Don't worry, they are short videos that focus only on the information you need. It's worth seeing them.

In this section we will explain the following:

- Where to download Jet Reports Express from
- How to install Jet Reports Express
- How to configure Jet Reports Express
- How to create a Jet Reports Express report
- How to analyze data with Jet Reports Express
- The use of Jet Reports Express to retrieve data

Downloading Jet Reports Express

There are two components of Jet Reports Express to download, as follows:

- The installation files of Jet Reports Express
- A Microsoft Dynamics NAV 2013 FOB file

The installation files of Jet Reports Express can be downloaded from the following link:

`http://jetexpress.jetreports.com/en/index.php`

There is a 32-bit and a 64-bit installation file. You will be installing this application on the client computers that will be using Jet Reports Express. Choose the appropriate installation file for them; either one of the two files shown in the following screenshot:

The Microsoft Dynamics NAV 2013 FOB file can be downloaded from the following link:

`http://expresssupport.jetreports.com/viewtopic.php?f=9&t=134`

The name of this FOB file is `Jet Reports Objects.fob`.

Installing Jet Reports Express

Jet Reports Express has to be installed in Microsoft Dynamics NAV 2013 and also on every client computer that will be using Jet Reports.

Installing Jet Reports Express on client machines

Perform the following steps to install Jet Reports Express on client machines:

1. Run `Jet Express Setup (32-bit).exe` or `Jet Express Setup (64-bit).exe`.

2. Complete an easy **Next-Next-Next-Finish** installation process.

This will install a **Jet** tab in Microsoft Office Excel as shown in the following screenshot:

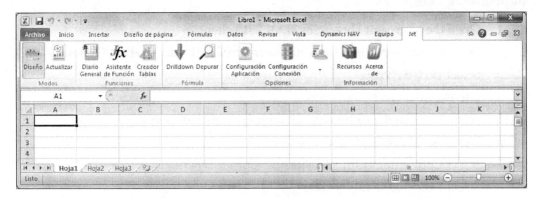

This installation has to be done on every single client machine using Jet Reports Express.

Installing Jet Reports Express on Dynamics NAV 2013

Perform the following steps to install Jet Reports Express on Dynamics NAV 2013:

1. Open the Microsoft Dynamics NAV Development Environment.

2. Go to **File | Import**.

3. Select the file `Jet Reports Objects.fob`.

4. A message will prompt, stating **All objects have been examined, and no conflicts were found**. Click on **Yes** to import all objects.

5. When the import is completed, click on **OK**.

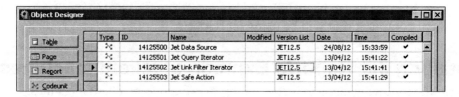

The Jet Reports objects for Microsoft Dynamics NAV 2013 are the Codeunits shown in the previous screenshot.

The codeunit **14125500 Jet Data Source** must be published as a web service to enable Jet Reports Express to operate. To publish this codeunit as a web service, complete the following steps:

1. Open the Microsoft Dynamics NAV 2013 client.
2. Navigate to **Departments/Administration/IT Administration/General**.
3. Select **Web Services**.
4. The **Web Services** page opens.
5. Select **New** on the ribbon bar to publish a new web service.
6. The **New – Web Services** page opens.
7. Select **Codeunit** as **Object Type**.
8. Select **14125500** as **Object ID**.
9. Set **Jet Data Source** as **Service Name**.
10. Select **Published** as shown in the following screenshot:

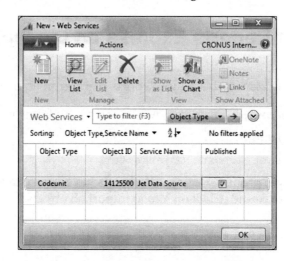

Configuring Jet Reports Express

Now it's time to configure Jet Reports Express on Microsoft Office Excel. This process will have to be done on every client machine where Jet Reports Express has been installed.

1. Open Microsoft Office Excel.
2. Select **Data Source Settings** from the **Jet** ribbon.
3. Use the **Data Source Version** drop-down button and select **Dynamics NAV 2013 and later**.
4. Select the **Web Service** tab.
5. Enter the **Server, SOAP Services Port**, and **Instance** values.

> Check your Dynamics NAV installation to know which server, SOAP services port, and instance you should use. On a typical installation, you will find the following installation setup:
> - **Server**: The name of the server machine where Dynamics NAV runs
> - **SOAP Services Port**: 7047
> - **Instance**: DynamicsNAV70

6. Select the company from which you want Jet Reports Express to retrieve your data.
7. Select **Jet_Data_Source** as the **Jet Codeunit** value.
8. Click on **OK**.

The configuration of Jet Reports Express is now complete.

The user can now access all the Microsoft Dynamics NAV 2013 data from the company selected while configuring Jet Report Express. All data? Not really! Jet Reports Express respects the roles and permissions assigned to users, so they will only see the data they are allowed to see.

Creating your first Jet Reports Express report

Let's see an example of how it works and all the capabilities it has. In the Jet Report's web page, you will find a few examples related to financial and sales information. We will not reproduce those examples; we will build a warehouse report instead.

We want to build a report to determinate the ABC items in the company so that we can rearrange our location based on this information. We will use the Item Ledger Entry table to analyze the data.

To do so, open Microsoft Excel, click on the **Jet** tab, and then click on the **Table Builder** icon as shown in the following screenshot:

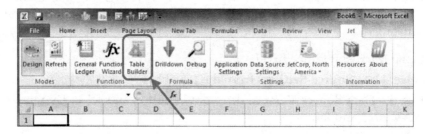

The **Table Builder** assistant opens. Click on the **Add Table** icon and a list of all available tables will appear. In the search area, type `Item Ledger Entry`. Once you find the table, select it by double-clicking on it.

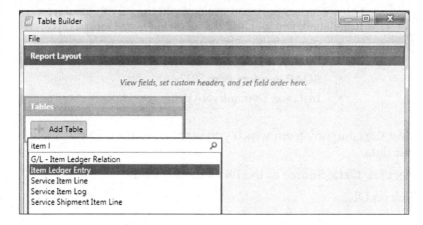

The next step is to select which fields we want to populate. All fields are available, including flowfields, which can retrieve delimited data by introducing fixed or user-defined filters on any flowfilter.

In our example, we need to select the following fields: **Item No.**, **Item Category Code**, **Location Code**, and **Quantity**. When selecting the table, you will see a list of all fields. You can scroll through the list or use the search area.

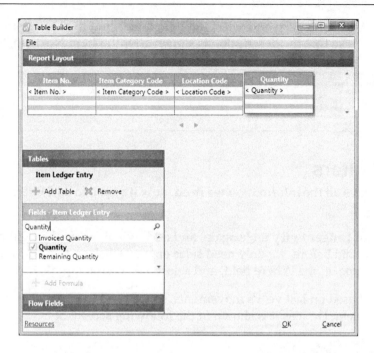

As you can see in the preceding screenshot, selected fields are shown at the top area of the screen. Fields are populated in the same order you have selected them, but you can also move any field position by selecting it and clicking on the left or right arrows that are placed just below the selected fields.

By default, the fields get the same name as defined in the Dynamics NAV table. You can select the field header and edit it if needed. In our example, we only need the sales item entries. We'll filter the information later on. We'll change the **Quantity** field header description to have a clear definition of what information we are getting. Edit the header and type Quantity Sold as shown in the following screenshot:

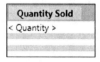

As you can imagine, the **Item No.** field does not have enough information to know what item we are talking about. The company may have hundreds or thousands of references, and it is impossible to know all their codes. A description of the item would be fantastic. In the **Item Ledger Entry** table you will find a field called **Description**, but it only gets filled if on a single entry the user has changed the description of the line. If the description hasn't changed, the **Description** field will be blank. So we need to use the **Description** field found on the Item Card instead.

Click on the **Add Table** icon and select the **Item** table. Find the **Description** field and mark it. Move it so that the description is shown after the **Item No.** field, like so:

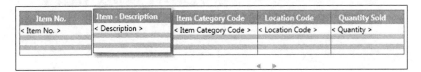

Item No.	Item - Description	Item Category Code	Location Code	Quantity Sold
< Item No. >	< Description >	< Item Category Code >	< Location Code >	< Quantity >

Adding filters

We already have all the information we need, now it's time to add filters to delimit the data we get.

Select the **Item Ledger Entry** table again, and add two filters on the right pane of the screen. As we said before, we only need sales entries. Click on the **Add Filter** icon, select **Entry Type** on the **Where** field, and select **Sale** on the **Equals** field.

Our report is based on last year's movements, so we need to add a filter on the **Posting Date** field. Do it as it is shown in the following screenshot:

 We have selected the **User Defined** option for the date filter. This way, every time you run the report you will be able to change the filter.

We've just finished the report definition. Click on the **OK** button to go back to the Excel sheet. A set of queries is generated inside Microsoft Excel that will return the report's information. If you are an end user, don't worry about what they mean; just let Jet Reports Express do the job for you. If you are a developer, you can edit this information to develop advanced reports, such as automatically sort the table by the value of a sum field. You can find all the information on the Jet Reports community web page at http://community.jetreports.com/.

 Even if you are not going to develop any report by editing its code, we recommend that you visit the community web page. You will find examples of good ready-to-run reports developed by members of the community.

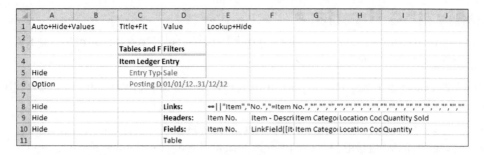

	A	B	C	D	E	F	G	H	I	J
1	Auto+Hide+Values		Title+Fit	Value	Lookup+Hide					
2										
3			Tables and F	Filters						
4			Item Ledger Entry							
5	Hide			Entry Typ	Sale					
6	Option			Posting D	01/01/12..31/12/12					
7										
8	Hide			Links:	==||"Item","No.","=Item No.","","","","","","","","","","","","","","","",""					
9	Hide			Headers:	Item No.	Item - Descri	Item Catego	Location Cod	Quantity Sold	
10	Hide			Fields:	Item No.	LinkField([It	Item Catego	Location Cod	Quantity	
11				Table						

Now click on **Refresh**. The **Report Options** window will open, so you can easily change the user-defined report options. At this moment, we would like to see the data for all of 2012, so we don't need to change the filter. Just click on the **Run** button as shown in the following screenshot:

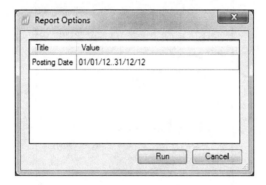

The report now looks like the following screenshot:

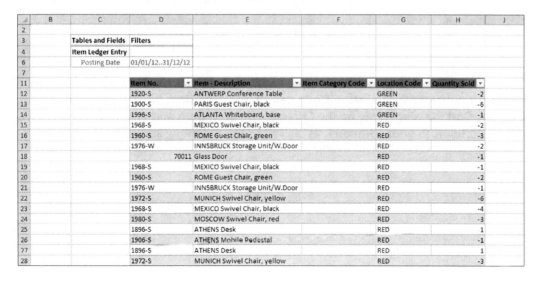

	B	C	D	E	F	G	H	J
2								
3		Tables and Fields	Filters					
4		Item Ledger Entry						
6		Posting Date	01/01/12..31/12/12					
7								
11			Item No.	Item - Description	Item Category Code	Location Code	Quantity Sold	
12			1920-S	ANTWERP Conference Table		GREEN	-2	
13			1900-S	PARIS Guest Chair, black		GREEN	-6	
14			1996-S	ATLANTA Whiteboard, base		GREEN	-1	
15			1968-S	MEXICO Swivel Chair, black		RED	-2	
16			1960-S	ROME Guest Chair, green		RED	-3	
17			1976-W	INNSBRUCK Storage Unit/W.Door		RED	-2	
18			70011	Glass Door		RED	-1	
19			1968-S	MEXICO Swivel Chair, black		RED	-1	
20			1960-S	ROME Guest Chair, green		RED	-2	
21			1976-W	INNSBRUCK Storage Unit/W.Door		RED	-1	
22			1972-S	MUNICH Swivel Chair, yellow		RED	-6	
23			1968-S	MEXICO Swivel Chair, black		RED	-4	
24			1980-S	MOSCOW Swivel Chair, red		RED	-3	
25			1896-S	ATHENS Desk		RED	1	
26			1906-S	ATHENS Mobile Pedestal		RED	-1	
27			1896-S	ATHENS Desk		RED	1	
28			1972-S	MUNICH Swivel Chair, yellow		RED	-3	

Analyzing the data

All the information you need is now in your Excel sheet. Now it's time to use the Excel capabilities to analyze this data.

In the **Item Ledger Entry** table, quantities for the sales movements are negative; they mean less stock in our warehouse.

Select any of the cells of the table and insert a pivot chart. A window will open with a few options. The table will already be selected, and we would want Excel to create a new sheet for our chart, so just click on the **OK** button. Drag the **Item No.** field into the **Row Labels** area, the **Quantity Sold** field to the **Values** area, and the **Location Code** field to the **Report Filter** area. This is depicted in the following screenshot:

The pivot table and the pivot chart are created on the fly in the Excel sheet. You can now filter either on the **Location Code** values or on the **Item No.** values to analyze the data. Sort the pivot table by the **Quantity Sold** column and you will easily see the most sold items in your company, as shown in the following screenshot:

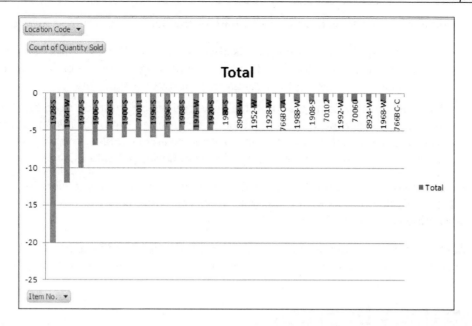

You will find more advanced examples on the **download** section of the Jet Reports Express web page. For instance, in the following screenshot, you can see the 3 NAV SALES - Sales Dashboard.xls report.

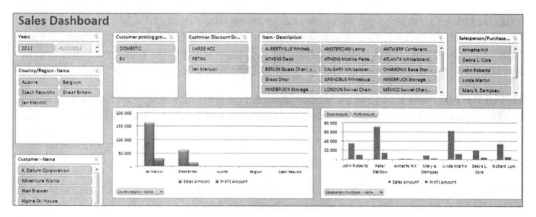

Using Jet Reports to retrieve data

Besides data analysis, Jet Reports Express can also be used to retrieve data. For example, you can retrieve all your customers' shipping addresses, or the item's cross references. This information can also be retrieved using the data migration tools explained in *Chapter 6, Migrating Data*.

But the data migration tools have a few limitations that Jet Reports Express overcomes.

- **Data filtering**: Data migration tools always retrieve all the records of a given table. There is no way to filter data when exporting it. For big tables, this may be an issue. However, Jet Reports Express allows multiple filters.

- **Table joining**: Data migration tools only retrieve information from one table at a time. There is no way to obtain joint or grouped data. For instance, if you want to retrieve information from the cross reference tables, you will be able to export the **Item No.** field but not the **Item Description** field.

To be fair with data migration tools, we also have to say that it allows users to import and update date, while Jet Reports Express can only be used to read. It has no writing capabilities.

Besides the Express edition, Jet Reports also has an Essentials edition and an Enterprise edition that give users more tools to analyze and share their data.

Zetadocs Express

Zetadocs Express is a tool for Microsoft Dynamics NAV meant to manage documents and apply workflows to them from within Dynamics NAV, using SharePoint 2010 or Office 365.

With Zetadocs Express, you can link one or more documents to a Microsoft Dynamics NAV record. The document will be uploaded to SharePoint, where it can follow a SharePoint Workflow. Workflows can be started from Dynamics NAV, and the status of the documents is also shown in Dynamics NAV.

Out of the box, you will find Zetadocs features on the sales and purchases processes in Dynamics NAV, but you can extend it to any other NAV functionality.

Check out the training video available online to see the tool in use (`http://download.equisys.com/pub/Express/Videos/ZetadocsExpressUserTraining.html`).

In this section we will explain how to install and configure Zetadocs Express, taking a special look at what has to be done in Dynamics NAV.

The first step is to download the tool. You can do it from the following website:

`http://www.equisys.com/zetadocsexpress`

A `.exe` file will be downloaded. When you execute it, you will get a folder with all the necessary files to use Zetadocs Express: documentation, language modules, FOB files, the Zetadocs Express client, and some configuration files, as shown in the following screenshot:

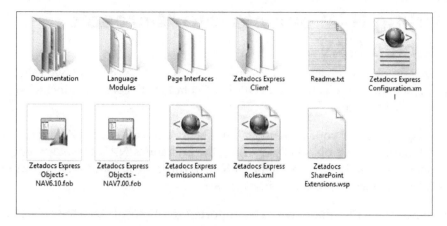

The installation and configuration process of Zetadocs Express includes:

- Installing the Zetadocs client
- Adding Zetadocs SharePoint Extensions
- Importing NAV objects into Microsoft Dynamics NAV
- Configuring Zetadocs in Dynamics NAV
- Installing the Zetadocs help files

Let's go step by step.

Installing the Zetadocs client

Run the `setup.exe` file that you will find inside the Zetadocs Express Client directory.

It's an easy **Next-Next-Next-Finish** installation process.

Adding Zetadocs SharePoint Extensions

You will have to add and enable Zetadocs SharePoint Extensions in your SharePoint site.

Follow the instructions provided with Zetadocs Express.

Importing NAV objects into Microsoft Dynamics NAV

If your Dynamics NAV license is dated prior to June 2011, you will have to refresh it, as this is the date in which granule 9041210 Zetadocs Express was included in all Dynamics NAV licenses.

You can check whether your Dynamics NAV license can access the Zetadocs Express Dynamics NAV objects by opening the Dynamics NAV Development Environment and navigating to **Tools | License Information** and making sure the 9041210 Zetadocs Express granule appears on your license.

There are two .fob files that have to be imported to Microsoft Dynamics NAV, as follows:

- **Zetadocs Express Objects (NAV7.00.fob)**: This file is located in the Zetadocs Express folder. It includes all Zetadocs Express objects in the Zetadocs Express granule numeration.

    To import these objects, open the Dynamics NAV Development Environment and navigate to **Tools | Object Designer** and click on **File | Import**. Select the appropriate .fob file and click on **Yes** to import all objects.

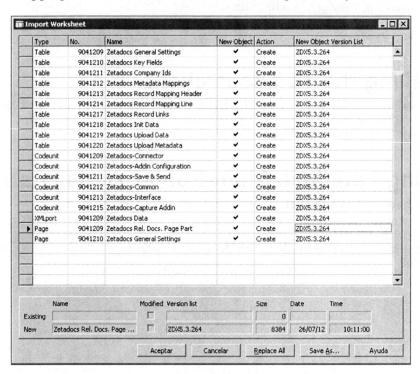

- **Zetadocs Express Interfaces (NAV7.00XX.fob):** The interface of Zetadocs Express consists of a FactBox added out of the box in all sales and purchases documents.

  There is a `.fob` file for each of the following country's versions of Microsoft Dynamics NAV: AU-NZ, NA, DK, FR, DE, IN, IE, IT, NL, ES, GB, W1, AT, BE, FI, NO, PT, SE, and CH. Select the appropriate one for your Dynamics NAV installation.

  If you have not modified any of the pages of the sales and purchases documents in your Dynamics NAV installation, you can import the Interface `.fob` file provided by Zetadocs Express. Otherwise, you can also manually add the Zetadocs FactBox to your pages.

  In the following screenshot, you can see the list of all pages modified by Zetadocs to include the Zetadocs FactBox:

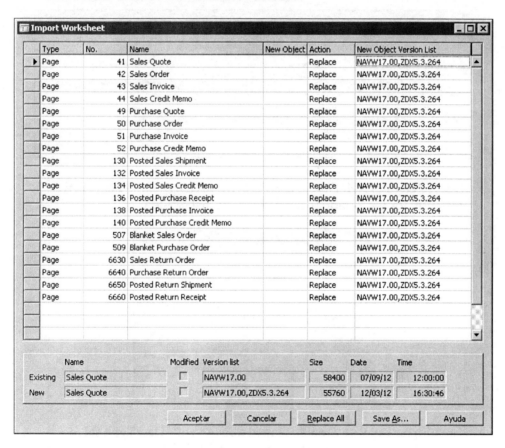

If you need to manually include the Zetadocs FactBox on those pages, or are planning on extending Zetadocs functionality to other Dynamics NAV functionalities, follow these steps:

1. Select the page in which you want to add the Zetadocs FactBox on the object designer and click on the **Design** button.

2. Add an entry for the Zetadocs FactBox as the first of the entries on the FactBox area, with the following values:

    ○   **Name: Zetadocs**

    ○   **Caption: Documents**

    ○   **Type: Part**

    ○   **Subtype: Page**

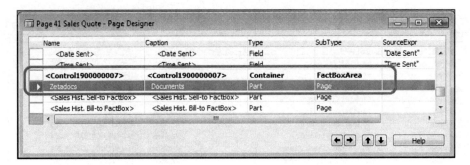

3. Select **Zetadocs Rel. Docs. Page Part (ID 9041209)** in the **PagePartID** property for the Zetadocs entry you have just created:

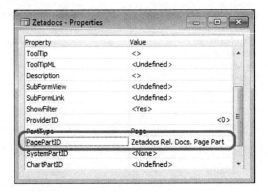

4. Create a new global variable named `RecRef` with **DataType** set to **RecordRef**. To do so, navigate to **View | C/AL Globals**.

5. Write the following code on the `OnAfterGetRecord()` trigger for the page:

```
RecRef.GETTABLE(Rec);
CurrPage.Zetadocs.PAGE.SetRecordID(RecRef.RECORDID);
```

6. Save and compile the page.

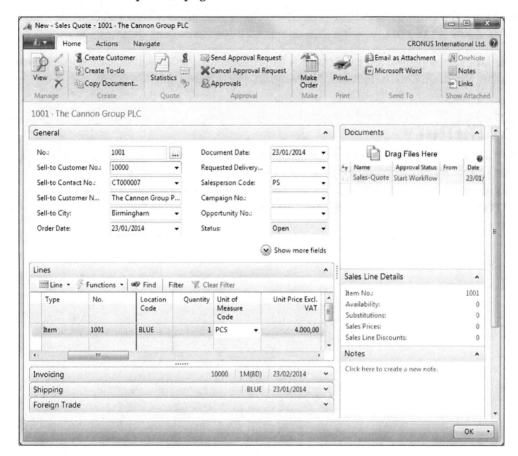

Configuring Zetadocs in Dynamics NAV

Run the **Zetadocs General Settings** page in Microsoft Dynamics to configure Zetadocs Express.

In this configuration page, you will have to enter the URL of your SharePoint online site.

You will also have to select the `Zetadocs Express Configuration.xml` file that you will find on the `Zetadocs` folder and click on **Import**.

Installing the Zetadocs help files

To install the Zetadocs help files so that it is available to Dynamics NAV users, copy the file `addin_a.hh` from the appropriate language folder in the `Zetadocs` folder to the appropriate language folder in your Dynamics NAV installation folder.

Copy the file from the location `\Zetadocs Express\Documentation\<language>\` to `Program Files\Microsoft Dynamics NAV\60\Service\<NAVLanguageCode>`.

The languages supported by Zetadocs Express are English, French, German, Danish, Italian, Spanish, Dutch, Finnish, Norwegian, Portuguese, and Swedish.

Summary

In this chapter we've seen two external applications included in Dynamics NAV that extend its functionality and are very useful to users and companies. When implementing new Dynamics NAV installations, take into account that they need to increase your customers' productivity and therefore their satisfaction with the product.

Index

Symbols

.NET interoperability, development
    environment 92

A

absence registration, human resources 54
accountancy, Financial Management
  about 13
  accounts 13
  credit amounts 13
  debit amounts 13
accounting balances 243, 253
accounting rules
  about 156, 157
  posting groups, creating 157, 158
account schedules, Analysis & Reporting
  section 413-416
account schedules, Financial Management
  15, 16
ACS 101
ADCS 95
Agile approach
  about 171
  digrammatic representation 171
Agile approach, Microsoft Dynamics Sure
  Step 177, 178
analysis by dimensions functionality 424
analysis views
  about 416
  analysis by dimensions functionality 424,
    425
  creating 420-422
  dimensions 416
  updating 423

  using 424
  using, as source for account schedules 425,
    426
analyst 182, 184
application changes
  about 63
  Windows client improvements 64
application code, upgrading
  about 280
  customizations, carrying out to new version
    281
  customized code, modifying 283
  customized code, revising 283
  data, upgrading 283
  forms, transforming to pages 282
  objects, converting to Dynamics NAV 2013
    format 281
  object versions, getting 280
  reports, transforming 282
application features
  about 72
  Assembly management 74
  CRM integration 80
  Financial Management 72
  inventory features 75
  jobs and project management features 78
  payment services 80
  RapidStart Services 79
  resources 79
  supply planning 77
  Warehouse management 75
Application Test Toolset
  about 84
  downloading 84
approval, Purchase 25

approval, Sales and Marketing
  about 22
  Approval Templates page 23
  limit type 23
Approval Templates page 23
ask others feature 313
aspects, methodology
  billing 166
  communication, with customer 168
  communication, with team 168
  development and testing 168
  developments, accepting 169
  documentation 169
  planning 167, 168
  purchases 168
  reporting and control 169
  time and cost, estimating 166, 167
assembly item 74
assembly management
  about 74
  assembly item 74
  assembly order 74
  business scenarios 74
assembly orders 74
assembly, Warehouse 30
Automated Data Capture System. *See* **ADCS**

B

bank entries
  about 243, 249
  migrating 249
basic object types, data model principles
  about 314
  Codeunit 315
  MenuSuite 315
  object elements 317-319
  page 315
  Query 315
  report 315
  table 314
  XMLport 315
basic options, Dynamics NAV 2013
    debugger
  Break On Error 447
  Break On Record Changes 447
  Skip Codeunit 1 447

bill of materials(BOM) 30, 34, 74
breakpoint
  about 447
  conditional breakpoint 450
  debugger breakpoint list 451
  placing 447
  placing, from Object Designer 448
  placing, in current statement of debugger
    449, 450
business consultants 180-184
Business Intelligence 70

C

C/AL 8
CalcFormula 154
C/AL code
  query, using 481-483
Calculate and Post VAT Settlement 17
calendars, for capacities
  machine centers availability 36
  shop calendar 35
  work center calendar 35
Call Stack FactBox 444, 457, 458
capacities, Manufacturing
  about 35
  machine centers 35
  Resource Capacities 36
  work centers 35
card pages 331-335
CardParts 341
cartera 312
Cartesian products 480
cash flow, Financial Management 72
cash management, Financial Management
  16, 17
Category Code 312
change management 206, 207
charts
  about 398
  adding, to role center page 400, 401
  building 399
  configuring 404
  creating 402
Check Availability page 343

Classic reports
  upgrading 290
ClickOnce 104
ClickOncedeployment 104
Code Coverage functionality
  about 461
  objects, importing 461
  use cases 466, 467
  using 461-465
coded data rules 161
Codeunit object 240, 315
Codeunit Web Services 60
Common Language Specification
    (CLS)-compliant 473
complexity
  adding, to query 476, 477
conditional breakpoint 450
configuration packages, RapidStart Services
  about 216
  applying 219
  creating 217, 218
  setup tables 216
Configuration Questionnaire, RapidStart
    Services
  about 228
  completing 229
  creating 228
configuration template, RapidStart Services
  about 226
  creating 226
  using 227
configuration wizard, RapidStart Services
    215, 216
configuration worksheet, RapidStart Ser-
    vices
  about 219
  data, migrating 223-225
  migration structure, creating 220-222
ConfirmationDialog pages 332, 343
considerations, Dynamics NAV
  accounting rules 156
  database 158
  data model 108
  data, navigating through 142
  no save button 127
  posting routines 130
  SIFT technology 152

consolidation, Financial Management 19
Continue option execution 455, 456
contracts, service 49
copy/paste rows 67
cost accounting, Financial Management 73
costing, Manufacturing 39
country localizations, human resources 54
credential mechanisms
  about 100
  AccessControlService 101
  NavUserPassword 101
  Username 101
  Windows 101
CRM integration 80
Cross Join, SQLJoinType 480
customer entries
  about 243
  creating 131
  migrating 243-248
Customer ledger Entry table 320
CustomerSource 313
customers, Sales and Marketing 21
Customer Statistics
  viewing 397, 398
customized code, Dynamics NAV
  alignment 350
  batch jobs 348
  C/AL statements 351, 352
  comments 351
  data, checking 348
  fields, validating 347
  language 350
  naming conventions 353
  small functions, using 355
  spacing 350
  text constants 351
  writing 347-350

D

data analysis and reporting
  about 391
  account schedules 413
  analysis views 416
  application reports 404
  charts 398
  Customer Statistics, viewing 397

data, extracting 426
filters and FlowFilters, using 392-395
report development 429
View, creating 395
database changes 103
data extraction
about 426
alternative ways 429
data, sending to Microsoft Excel 428, 429
data, sending to Microsoft Office
applications 427
data, sending to Microsoft Word 428
web services, used 429
DataItemLinkType property
about 478
Exclude Row If No Match option 478
options 478
SQL Advanced Options option 478
Use Default Values if No Match option 478
DataItemTableFilter property 473
data migration, Dynamics NAV 2013
about 211
go-live date, selecting 259
historical data 254
master data 242
old system data, converting 241
open documents 256
open entries 243
tools 212
data migration tools
about 503
custom tools, writing 240
limitations 504
RapidStart Services 212
XMLport 230
data model
about 108
documents 109-113
entries 118-120
journals 113-118
master data 108, 109
data model principles
about 314
basic objects 314-316
page structure 331
table structure 320
data navigating 142-144

dataports 230
dataset, report development
defining 431-433
data types, development environment
about 88
Binary 89
BLOB 88
Code 88
Text 89
debugger
Code area 444
Debugger page 444
Session List page 443
starting 442, 443
debugger breakpoint list 451
Debugger Break Rules page 446
debugging 441, 442
debugging, development environment 81
debugging, in Dynamics NAV 2013
about 442
breakpoints, placing 447
Break Rules page 446
Call Stack FactBox 457
debugger setup 446
debugger, starting 442-446
line-by-line execution 452
Watches FactBox 458
dedicated bins 75
deployment phase
about 192
configuration 193
data migration 194
end users training 195
go-live 195
software and hardware installation 193
user acceptance test 194
deprecated application features
about 105
Business Analytics 105
Business Notifications 105
Demand Planner 105
Microsoft Dynamics Mobile 105
Microsoft Dynamics NAV Employee Portal
105
Production Schedule (Gantt Chart) 105
Rapid Implementation Methodology
Toolkit 105

deprecated developer and IT features
about 105
C/FRONT and Communication Components 105
Client Monitor 106
Dataports 106
Dynamics NAV Classic Application Server (NAS) 105
Dynamics NAV Classic Client 105
Dynamics NAV Classic Database 105
Forms 106
Server-side COM 106
developer 182, 184
development changes
about 80
development environment 80, 81
standard C/AL code redesign 93
development considerations
about 311
customized code location 347
customized code, writing 349
data model principles 314
posting process 345
setup versus customization 311
development environment
about 61, 81
changed data types 88
changed functions 89
changed objects 92
changed properties 87
changed triggers 88
debugging 81
NET interoperability 92
page development 81
page testing 83
query development 85
report development 84, 85
RoleTailored client control add-ins enhancements 92
Start ID Offset 86
XMLport development 86
development phase 192
dimension entry storing
about 93
dimension set 94
dimension set entries 94
performance improvement 95

dimensions 205
dimensions, analysis views
about 416
accessing 418-420
categorizing 418
global dimensions 416
rest of the dimensions 417
setting up 417
shortcut dimensions 417
dimension set 94
dimension set entries 94
document pages 331
document report
about 411
report selection 411, 412
documents
about 109
manufacturing documents 109
purchase documents 109
sales documents 109
warehouse documents 109
document tables
about 320-326
Sales Header table 323
Sales Line table 323
Dynamics NAV
data model 108
development considerations 311
post 130
posting 112
upgrading, to Dynamics NAV 2013 263
Dynamics NAV 3.60 or 3.70
3.60 or 3.70 application code, upgrading to Dynamics NAV 2013 275, 276
3.60 or 3.70 data, upgrading to Dynamics NAV 2013 276-278
upgrading, to Dynamics NAV 2013 275
Dynamics NAV 4.0
4.0 application code, upgrading to Dynamics NAV 2013 272, 273
4.0 data, upgrading to Dynamics NAV 2013 273-275
upgrading, to Dynamics NAV 2013 272
Dynamics NAV 5.0
5.0 application code, upgrading to Dynamics NAV 2013 270

5.0 data, upgrading to Dynamics NAV 2013 271

upgrading, to Dynamics NAV 2013 269

Dynamics NAV 2009
2009 data, upgrading to Dynamics NAV 2013 268, 269

application code, upgrading to Dynamics NAV 2013 268

upgrading, to Dynamics NAV 2013 267

Dynamics NAV 2013
application features 72

Classic reports, upgrading 290

Code Coverage functionality 461

data migration 211

Hybrid reports, upgrading 289

implementation process 163

Toolkit, upgrading 285

upgrading, from 3.60 275

upgrading, from 4.0 272

upgrading, from 5.0 269

upgrading, from 2009 267

Dynamics NAV 2013 implementation
about 197

change management 206

endusers, involving 208

FAQs 200-202

goals, defining 198, 199

improvements, before automating 204

internal processes, defining 200

requirements 204, 205

testing 207

Dynamics NAV charts
query, using 483

Dynamics NAV database
about 158

coded data rules 161

TableRelation property 158

Dynamics NAV Development Environment 315

Dynamics NAV philosophy 107

Dynamics NAV Server Administration 96, 97

Dynamics NAV upgrade
about 263

application code, upgrading 280

database, testing 279

migrating, to SQL Server 278

philosophy, upgrading 264-266

prerequisites 278

process checklist, upgrading 266, 267

tools, upgrading 284

E

employees, human resources 53, 54
end user 183
Enterprise project type 175
Enterprise Resource Planning system. *See* ERP system
entries
about 118, 119

creating 119, 120

ledger entries, creating 120-126

entry tables
about 320, 328

Item Ledger Entry table 328

Item Register table 329

Value Entry table 328

ERP system 7
European Union (EU) companies 18
execution, Manufacturing 39

F

fault reporting, service 52
FieldClass 153
Financial Management
about 12, 72

accountancy 13

account schedules 15

cash flow 72

cash management 16

consolidation 19

cost accounting 73

Fixed assets 17

G/L budgets 14

intercompany transactions 18

Intrastat 18

multicurrency 19

VAT 17

VAT Rate Change Tool 73

VAT Reports 74

fixed asset entries
about 243, 251

migrating 251, 252

Fixed Asset functional area
    interacintg, with Financial Management
        361
Fixed Asset module 158
Fixed assets, Financial Management 17
FlowField 155, 498
FlowFilters
    about 498
    using 392-395
form transformation 288
Full Outer Join, SQLJoinType 480
functional areas, Dynamics NAV 2013
    about 8, 12
    Financial Management 12
    Human Resources 8, 52
    Job 8, 40
    Manufacturing 8, 33
    Purchase 8, 25
    Resource Planning 8, 45
    Sales & Marketing 8, 20
    Service 8, 47
    vertical and horizontal solutions 54
    Warehouse 8, 27
functional change implementation
    customized functionality, extending 379
    Fixed Assets implementation 375-377
    Item Tracking implementation 377, 378
    Requisition Worksheet implementation
        373-375
functional change, planning
    about 382, 383
    customized functionality, extending 388,
        389
    Fixed Assets 385
    Item Tracking 387, 388
    Requisition Worksheet 383, 385
functional changes, Dynamics NAV
    about 357, 358
    customized functionality, extending 360
    Fixed Asset functionality 359
    general guidelines 357, 358
    Item Tracking 359
    Requisition Worksheet 358
functions, development environment
    about 89
    BEEP 91
    CALCFIELDS 89

CALCSUM 89
CALCSUMS 89
COMMANDLINE 91
COUNT 89
COUNTAPPROX 91
CREATETOTALS 89
CURRENTEXECUTIONMODE 89
debugger functions 90
DELETE 90
ENVIRON 91
EXPORT 91
EXPORTOBJECTS 91
FormHandler 90
IMPORT 91
IMPORTOBJECTS 91
INSERT 90
ISSERVICETIER 90
LANGUAGE 91
ModalFormHandler 90
MODIFY 90
NEWPAGE 91
NEWPAGEPERRECORD 91
OBJECTID 91
OSVERSION 91
PAGENO 91
PAPERSOURCE 91
READCONSISTENCY 90
RECORDLEVELLOCKING 90
RENAME 90
SAVEASHTML 91
SAVEASXML 91
SETAUTOCALCFIELDS 89
SETCURRENTKEY 90
SETPERMISSIONFILTER 91
SHELL 91
SHOWOUTPUT 91
STARTSESSION 89
STOPSESSION 89
SYNCHRONIZEALLLOGINS 91
SYNCHRONIZESINGLELOGIN 91
TOTALSCAUSEDBY 92
URL 92
VARIABLEACTIVE 92
YIELD 92

G

General Ledger entries
  creating 131
general model combining 127
G/L budgets, Financial Management 14, 15
G/L Entry table locking redesign 93
global dimensions 416
goals
  defining 198, 199
go-live date
  beginning of fiscal year 259-261
  middle of fiscal year 261
  selecting 259
GridLayout 82

H

historical data
  migrating 254-256
human resources
  about 52
  absence registration 54
  country localizations 54
  employees 52-54
Hybrid reports
  upgrading 289

I

implementation 163
implementation process, Dynamics NAV 2013
  about 163, 165
  methodology 165
  phases 185
  roles 179
implementer 183, 184
improvements, before automating 204
Inner Join, SQLJoinType 479
installation
  Jet Reports Express 495
  Zetadocs Express 505
installation files, Jet Reports Express
  downloading 494
integration to service orders 75

interactions, with functionalities
  customized functionality, extending 371, 372
  Fixed Assets, with Financial Management 361
  Item Tracking, with functional areas 362, 363
  Requisition Worksheet, with Purchase functionality 360, 361
intercompany postings, Financial Management 18
internal processes
  defining 200
Intrastat, Financial Management 18
intrastat journal 18
inventory features
  about 75
  Item Availability by BOM Level 76
  Item Availability by Event 75
  Item Availability by Timeline 76
inventory movements 75
inventory, Warehouse 31, 32
invoice jobs, Job 44
IT changes
  about 95
  ClickOnce 104
  credential mechanisms 100
  database changes 103
  Dynamics NAV Server administration 96, 97
  installation 95
  NAS Services 101
  OData web services 102
  Portal Framework for SharePoint 2010 100
  Unicode support 103
  Web client 98-100
  Windows PowerShell 2.0 cmdlets 97, 98
Item Category table 322
item entries
  about 243, 249, 250
  creating 131
  migrating 249, 250
Item Journal Batches page 342
Item Journal posting routine 140
items, Warehouse 28
Item Tracking Code table 322

Item Tracking, interacting with functional areas
about 362, 363
item, creating 364
Item Tracking, enabling 368, 370
purchase order, creating 365
purchase order, posting 365, 367
sales order, creating 367
sales order, posting 368
Sales Shipment, undoing 371
Item Variant table 322

J

Jet Reports
creating 497-499
data, analysing 502, 503
filters, adding 500, 501
used, for retrieving data 503
Jet Reports community web page
URL 500
Jet Reports Express
about 493
configuring 497
data filtering 504
downloading 494
features 504
installation files, downloading 494
installing 495
installing, on client machines 495
installing, on Dynamics NAV 2013 495
Microsoft Dynamics NAV 2013 fob file, downloading 494
report, creating 497
table joining 504
Job
about 40
invoice jobs 44
Job card 41
phases and tasks 42
planning 42, 43
time sheet 44
Work in process (WIP) 44
Job card 41
job task 42
Job Usage Tracking 78

journals
about 113-116
Cash Receipt Journals 113
FA G/L Journals 113
FA Journals 113
FA Reclass. Journals 113
General Journals 113
IC General Journals 113
Insurance Journals 113
Intrastat Journals 113
Item Journals 114
Payments Journals 113
Purchase Journals 113
Recurring Fixed Asset Journals 113
Recurring General Journals 113
Sales Journals 113
journal tables 321, 329

K

key users 181, 184
kitting, assembly management 74
KPIs 71

L

ledger entries
creating 120-126
Left Outer Join, SQLJoinType 478
light manufacturing, assembly management 74
limit type, purchase approval system
request limits 26
limit types, Sales and Marketing approval system
approval limits 23
credit limits 23
no limit 23
line-by-line execution, debugging
about 452
Continue option 455, 456
options 452
Step Into option 452, 453
Step Out option 454, 455
Step Over option 454

list pages
about 331-337
item list page 336
Item Units of Measure page 338
Sales Order page 340
ListPart pages 331, 341
list report 410
locations, Warehouse 30
Lot Specific Tracking 362

M

machine centers availability 36
Manufacturing
about 33
capacities 35, 36
costing 39
execution 38
planning 37
Product design 33-35
subcontracting 40
manufacturing documents 109
marketing, Sales and Marketing 24
master data
about 242
migrating 242
migration plan 242
Master Planning Schedule (MPS) 37
master tables 320, 321
Material Requirements Planning (MRP) 37
Menusite object 315
MergeTool
about 268, 291
downloading 291
installing 291, 292
new base version, importing 298, 299
new custom version, exporting 309
new custom version, importing to
    Dynamics NAV 2013 database 309
old base and new base versions, comparing
    300, 302
old base version, importing 293, 294
old custom version, importing 295-297
URL 291
using 292, 293
versions, merging 303-308

methodology, Dynamics NAV
    implementation
about 165, 166
Agile approach 171
Microsoft Dynamics Sure Step 172
Waterfall approach 170
Microsoft Dynamics NAV 2013. *See also*
    Dynamics NAV 2013
Microsoft Dynamics NAV 2013
about 8, 63
application changes 63
client tier 9
data tier 9
debugging 441
deprecated features 105
development changes 80
features 8
functional areas 8
history 10, 11
IT changes 95
Jet Reports Express, installing 495, 496
limitations 9
query 469
Query Designer 470
query performance 489
server tier 9
single client access 55
three-tier architecture 9
Microsoft Dynamics NAV 2013 access
development environment 61
SharePoint client 59
Web client 57
Web Services 59
Windows client 55
Microsoft Dynamics NAV 2013 fob file, Jet
    Reports Express
downloading 494
Microsoft Dynamics NAV Server 9
Microsoft Dynamics Sure Step
about 172
Waterfall approach 173
Microsoft Excel
data, sending to 428, 429
Microsoft Office Excel
query, using 487, 488

Microsoft Report Viewer
reporting capabilities 430
Microsoft Word
data, sending to 428
multicurrency, Financial Management 19

N

naming convention, customized code
about 353
naming objects 353
naming objects, customized code naming convention
about 353
codeunit objects 354
page objects 353
report objects 353
table objects 353
tax field 354
user-defined functions 354
variables 354
NAS Services 101
Navigate functionality
about 142-144
data, finding by filtering 146-152
navigating ways 144, 145
NavigatePage pages 332, 343
NAV objects
importing, to Dynamics NAV 506
Zetadocs Express Interfaces 507
Zetadocs Express Objects 506
NAV Service Tier (NST) 158
NavUserPasswordcredentials 101
new keyboard shortcuts 70
no save button
about 127
advantages 128, 129
contra 130
data, checking 129

O

Object Designer 230 86
objects, Code Coverage
importing 461
objects, development environment
about 92
Dataports 92

Forms 92
Query object 92
RequestOptionsForm system variable 92
Test Pages 92
OData
about 102
URL 102
OData web services
about 60, 102
accessing 103
publishing 102, 103
query, using 485
OnDelete() trigger 161
OnRun function 140
OnValidate trigger 250
Open Data protocol
OData 102
open documents
migrating 256-259
open entries
accounting balances 243, 253
bank entries 243, 249
customer entries 243
fixed asset entries 243, 251
item entries 243, 249
posting 243
vendor entries 243
order modifiers 78
order processing, Purchase 25
order processing, Sales and Marketing 21, 22
Output Journal 118

P

Packt Publishing library 313
Page Designer 315
page development, development environment
about 81
Action and Activity button icon selection 82
default control names and captions 82
Page Field arrangement in a Grid 82
Page Preview in Page Designer 81
Page wizard 82

QuickEntry property 82
Standard Dialog page type 82
page object 315
Page Preview 81
page structure, data model principles
  about 331
  card pages 331, 333
  document pages 331, 340
  list pages 331-340
  role center pages 331, 332
Page testing, development environment 83
Page Web Services 60
PartnerSource 313
  URL 283
payment services 80
phases, Dynamics NAV implementation
  about 185
  deployment 192
  development 192
  prescales 185
  project requisites, getting 186, 188
  solution design 189
  support 195
philosophy
  upgrading 264, 265, 266
Phys. Inventory Journal 117
pick and put-away, Warehouse 31
planning line type, Job
  contract 43
  schedule 43
  schedule and contract 43
planning, Purchase 26, 27
planning system, Job
  about 42
  line type 43
planning system, Manufacturing
  about 37, 38
  MPS 37
  MRP 37
Portal Framework for SharePoint 2010 100
posted data cannot be modified
  about 141
  exceptions 141
posting 112
posting groups
  Bank Account Posting Group 157
  Customer Posting Group 157

FA Posting Group 157
General Posting Setup 157
Inventory Posting Setup 157
Job Posting Group 157
Service Contract Account Group 157
VAT Posting Setup 157
Vendor Posting Group 157
posting process
  about 130, 345
  checking, with example 131-133
  Codeunit structure, for general journal
    posting 346, 347
  Codeunit structure, for sales posting 345,
    346
  customer entries, creating 131
  General Ledger entries, creating 131
  item entries, creating 131
  steps, for sales invoice 134
  VAT entries, creating 131
posting report 410
posting routine, for sales invoice
  about 134
  confirmation question, asking to user 134
  Customer Ledger Entries, inserting 139
  data, checking 134
  document, releasing 135
  General Journal Line, posting 139
  General Journal Lines, creating 138
  G/L Entries, inserting 139
  Item Ledger Entries, inserting 137
  Item Ledger Entry, posting 137
  item-related information, updating 137
  Posted Invoice Header, inserting 136
  Posted Invoice Line, inserting 138
  Shipment Header, inserting 136
  Shipment Line, inserting 138
  Value Entries, inserting 137
  VAT amounts, calculating 136
  VAT entries, inserting 139
posting routines
  BOM posting routine 140
  Fixed Asset posting routine 141
  Job posting routine 141
  Purchase posting routine 140
  Resource posting routine 141
  Service posting routine 141
  Transfer Document posting routine 141

Warehouse posting routine 141
PowerPivot
  installing 487
  query, using 487
prescale phase 185
price management, service 49, 50
pricing, Purchase 26
pricing, Sales and Marketing 24
Printed documents 112
process checklist, Dynamics NAV upgrade
  about 266
  prerequisites 267
Product design, Manufacturing 33-35
Product Group table 322
project manager 180, 183, 184
Project Requirements Documents (PRD)
      180
project requirements, Dynamics NAV
      implementation 186
PromissoryNoteDelivered 312
properties, development environment
  about 87
  AutoReplace 87
  AutoSave 87
  AutoUpdate 87
  BottomMargin 88
  CardFormID 87
  DrillDownFormID 87
  LookupFormID 87
  PaperSourceDefaultPage 87
  PaperSourceFirstPage 87
  PaperSourceLastPage 87
  PaperSourceOtherPages 88
  RunFormLink 87
  RunFormOnRec 87
  RunFormView 88
  SaveTableView 88
  SubFormLink 88
  SubFormView 88
  TransactionType 88
  UseReqForm 88
Purchase
  about 25
  approvals 25
  order processing 25
  planning 26
  pricing 26

vendors 25
purchase approval system
  about 26
  limit type 26
purchase documents 109

Q

query
  about 469, 470
  complexity, adding 476, 477
  DataItemLinkType property 478
  defining 472-476
  features 470
  using, in C/AL code 481-483
  using, in Dynamics NAV charts 483
  using, in Microsoft Office Excel 487
  using, in web service 485, 486
Query Designer 470-472
Query development, development
      environment 85
QueryFunction() 489
Query object 315
query performance 489-491
Query Web Services 60
Quick Entry 67, 69
QuickEntryproperty 82

R

Rapid project type 173
RapidStart Services tool
  about 79, 212, 213
  components 213
  configuration packages 216
  Configuration Questionnaire 228
  configuration templates 226
  configuration wizard 215, 216
  configuration worksheet 219
  implementing 213-215
  location 212
  summary 230
read feature 313
register tables 321
report anatomy, report development 430
Report Dataset Designer 430
Report Definition Language Client-side
      (RDLC) report 429

report design guidelines 436-439
report development
about 429
dataset, defining 431-433
report design guidelines 436
reports anatomy 430
rules, for flattening data 435, 436
visual layout, defining 433, 434
report development, development
environment 84, 85
reporting capabilities, Microsoft Report
Viewer 430
Reporting Definition Language Client-side
(RDLC) 288
report items
chart 434
gauge 434
image 434
line 434
list 434
rectangle 434
table and matrix 434
textbox 434
report object 315
reports
about 404
Customer/Item Sales 412
document report 411
list reports 410
posting report 410
request pages 407
running 406, 407
searching 404-406
test report 410
transaction report 411
types 410
Vendor/Item Purchase 412
report transformation 288
request page, reports
Buttons section 408
Filter sections 408
Options section 407
requisites, Dynamics NAV 2013 204-206
Requisition Worksheet
interacting, with Purchase functionality
360, 361

research feature 313
Resource Capacities 36
resource card 46
resource planning
about 45
pricing 47
resource card 46
resources 79
rest of dimensions 417
ribbon 65
Right Outer Join, SQLJoinType 479
right time, for functional change
implementation,
customized functionality, extending 382
Fixed Assets 380, 381
Item Tracking 381, 382
Requisition Worksheet 380
selecting 380
role center pages 331, 332
roles, Dynamics NAV implementation
about 179
analyst 182
business consultants 180, 181
developer 182
end user 183
implementer 183
key user 181
project manager 180
salesperson 180
summarizing 183
RoleTailored client 64 55
RoleTailored client control add-ins enhancements
data types supported with database
binding 92
methods and properties, exposed to C/AL
code 92
resizing 93
RoleTailored clients 9
RoleTailored ERP 8
rules for flattening data, report development
about 435, 436
reports with indented data items 435
reports with multiple data items on the
same level 435
reports with one data item 435

S

Sales and Marketing
about 20
approvals 22, 23
customers 21
marketing 24
order processing 21, 22
pricing 24
sales documents 109
Sales Order document 109
salesperson 180
secondary or subsidiary tables 320, 322
select all 66
service
about 47
contracts 49
fault reporting 52
price management 49, 50
service item 48, 49
service orders 51
service quotes 51
service tasks 51
service item 48, 49
service orders
about 51
service header 51
service item lines 51
service lines 51
service tasks 51
Setup Best Practices 77, 78
setup tables 320, 322
setup versus customization 311, 312
SharePoint client 59
shop calendar 35
shortcut dimensions 417
SIFT
about 152, 153
Cust. Ledger Entry field, defining 153-156
SN Specific Tracking 362
SOAP Web Services 60
solution design phase
about 189
configurations 189, 191
data migration 192
new functionalities 192

standard Dynamics NAV functionality,
 modifying 191
SQLJoinType, DataItemLinkType property
about 478
Cross Join 480
Full Outer Join 480
Inner Join 479
Left Outer Join 478
Right Outer Join 479
SQL server 9
Standard C/AL code redesign
about 93
ADCS 95
dimension entry storing 93
G/L Entry table locking redesign 93
Standard Dialog page 82
Standard project type 174
standard software 165
Standard Solution 165
**Start ID Offset, development environment
 86**
Step Into execution 452, 453
Step Out execution 454, 455
Step Over execution 454
subcontracting , Manufacturing
about 40
subcontracting worksheet 40
subcontract work center 40
work center cost based on units or time 40
subcontracting worksheet 40
subcontract work center 40
Subform page 341
SumIndexField 155
SumIndexField calculations 156
Sum Index Field Technology. *See* **SIFT**
supply planning
about 77
order modifiers 78
planning parameters 77
setup best practices 78
**support phase, Dynamics NAV
 implementation**
about 195
data stabilization 196
issues, handling 195
old tasks from previous phases 195
system stabilization 196

T

Table Builder assistant 498
Table Designer 315
table object 314
TableRelation property 158-160
table structure, data model principles
  about 320
  document tables 320, 323
  entry tables 320, 328
  journal tables 321, 329
  master tables 320, 321
  register tables 321
  secondary or subsidiary tables 320, 322
  setup tables 320, 322
Tariff Number table 322
testing
  Dynamics NAV 2013 implementation 207
test report 410
text format upgrade 286
TextFormatUpgrade2013
  about 281, 286
  functioning 286
three-tier architecture 9
time sheet, Job 44
Time Sheets 79
Toolkit
  upgrading 285
tools, upgrading
  about 284
  form transformation 288
  MergeTool 291
  report transformation 288
  text format upgrade 286-288
  text tools, comparing 290
  Toolkit 285
transaction report 411
transfer orders, Warehouse 30
TransformationTool 288
triggers, development environment
  about 88
  OnAfterModifyRecord 88
  OnBeforeModifyRecord 88
  OnCreateHyperlink 88
  OnHyperlink 88
  OnPostSection 88
  OnPreSection 88

U

Unicode 103, 104
Universal Description and Discovery Information. *See* UDDI
Upgrade project type 176
Upgrade Report tool 289
use cases, Code Coverage 466, 467
user authenticating methods, Web client
  AccessControlService 58
  NavUserPassword 58
  Username 58
  Windows 58
user authenticating methods, Windows client
  NavUserPassword 56
  username 56
  Windows 56
user collaboration tools
  about 72
  Link Sharing 72
  OneNote Integration 72
username-password credentials 101
users 184

V

variables
  adding, to Watches FactBox 458
VAT entries
  creating 131
VAT, Financial Management 17
VAT Rate Change Tool 73
VAT Reports 74
VAT Statement definition 18
vendor entries
  about 243, 249
  migrating 249
vendors, Purchase 25
vertical and horizontal solutions 54
View
  creating 395, 396
visual layout, report development
  defining 433, 434
Visual Studio Report Designer 430
  features 433

W

Warehouse
about 27
assembly 30
inventory 31, 32
items 28
locations 30
pick and put-away 31
transfer orders 30
warehouse documents 109
Warehouse management
about 75
dedicated bins 75
integration to service orders 75
inventory movements 75
Watches FactBox
about 444, 458
variables, adding from code viewer 460
variables, adding from Debugger Variables
    List window 458, 459
Waterfall approach, Microsoft Dynamics
    Sure Step
about 173
Enterprise project type 175
Rapid project type 173
Standard project type 174
Upgrade project type 176
Waterfall model
about 170
digrammatic representation 170
Web client
about 57, 98, 100
features 57, 58
methods for authenticating users 58
Web Services
about 59
Codeunit Web Services 60
features 60
OData Web Services 60
Page Web Services 60
query, using 485, 486
Query Web Services 60
SOAP Web Services 60

Windows client
about 55
methods for authenticating users 56
Windows client improvements
about 64
Business Intelligence 70, 71
copy/paste rows 67
KPIs 71
new keyboard shortcuts 70
Quick Entry 67, 69
ribbon 65, 66
select all 66
user collaboration tools 72
Windows credentials 101
Windows PowerShell 2.0 cmdlets 98
WIP methods, Job
completed contract 45
cost of sales 45
cost value 45
percentage of completion 45
sales value 45
WMSCheckWarehouse function 161
work center calendar 35
work center cost based on units or time 40
work in process(WIP) 78
Work in process (WIP), Job
about 44
methods 44
worksheet pages 332
Worksheet pages 341, 342

X

XMLport
about 230
code, writing 234
creating 231
elements 232
running 233, 234
structure 232, 233
used, for migrating data 230
XMLport code
data not included in XML file,
    filing 236-238
data validation, preventing 239, 240
document structure 235, 236

XMLport Designer 230
XMLport development, development
    environment 86
XMLport object 315

Z

Zetadocs
    configuring, n Dynamics NAV 509
Zetadocs client
    installing 505
Zetadocs Express
    about 493, 504
    downloading 504
    features 504
    installing 505
    training video, URL 504

Zetadocs Express installation
    NAV objects, importing to Dynamics NAV
        506-509
    Zetadocs client, installing 505
    Zetadocs, configuring in Dynamics NAV
        509
    Zetadocs help files, installing 510
    Zetadocs SharePoint Extensions, adding
        505
**Zetadocs Express Interfaces (NAV7.00XX.
    fob) 507**
**Zetadocs Express Objects (NAV7.00.fob)
    506**
Zetadocs FactBox 508
Zetadocs help files
    installing 510
Zetadocs SharePoint Extensions
    adding 505

Thank you for buying
Implementing Microsoft Dynamics NAV 2013

About Packt Publishing

Packt, pronounced 'packed', published its first book "Mastering phpMyAdmin for Effective MySQL Management" in April 2004 and subsequently continued to specialize in publishing highly focused books on specific technologies and solutions.

Our books and publications share the experiences of your fellow IT professionals in adapting and customizing today's systems, applications, and frameworks. Our solution based books give you the knowledge and power to customize the software and technologies you're using to get the job done. Packt books are more specific and less general than the IT books you have seen in the past. Our unique business model allows us to bring you more focused information, giving you more of what you need to know, and less of what you don't.

Packt is a modern, yet unique publishing company, which focuses on producing quality, cutting-edge books for communities of developers, administrators, and newbies alike. For more information, please visit our website: www.packtpub.com.

About Packt Enterprise

In 2010, Packt launched two new brands, Packt Enterprise and Packt Open Source, in order to continue its focus on specialization. This book is part of the Packt Enterprise brand, home to books published on enterprise software – software created by major vendors, including (but not limited to) IBM, Microsoft and Oracle, often for use in other corporations. Its titles will offer information relevant to a range of users of this software, including administrators, developers, architects, and end users.

Writing for Packt

We welcome all inquiries from people who are interested in authoring. Book proposals should be sent to author@packtpub.com. If your book idea is still at an early stage and you would like to discuss it first before writing a formal book proposal, contact us; one of our commissioning editors will get in touch with you.

We're not just looking for published authors; if you have strong technical skills but no writing experience, our experienced editors can help you develop a writing career, or simply get some additional reward for your expertise.

Programming Microsoft Dynamics NAV 2013

ISBN: 978-1-849686-48-8   Paperback: 600 pages

A comprehensive guide to NAV 2013 development and design

1. A comprehensive reference for development in Microsoft Dynamics NAV 2013, with C/SIDE and C/AL

2. Brimming with detailed documentation that is additionally supplemented by fantastic examples

3. The perfect companion for experienced programmers, managers and consultants

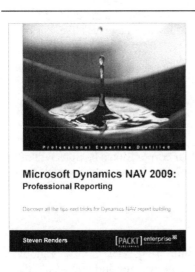

Microsoft Dynamics NAV 2009: Professional Reporting

ISBN: 978-1-849682-44-2   Paperback: 352 pages

Discover all the tips and tricks for Dynamics NAV report building

1. Get an overview of all the reporting possibilities, in and out of the box

2. Understand the new architecture and reporting features in Microsoft Dynamics NAV 2009 with this book and e-book

3. Full of illustrations, diagrams, and tips with clear step-by-step instructions and real-world examples

Please check **www.PacktPub.com** for information on our titles

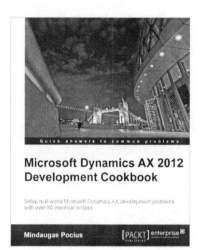

Microsoft Dynamics AX 2012 Development Cookbook

ISBN: 978-1-849684-64-4   Paperback: 372 pages

Solve real-world Microsoft Dynamics AX development problems with over 80 practical recipes

1. Develop powerful, successful Dynamics AX projects with efficient X++ code with this book and eBook

2. Proven recipes that can be reused in numerous successful Dynamics AX projects

3. Covers general ledger, accounts payable, accounts receivable, project modules and general functionality of Dynamics AX.

4. Step-by-step instructions and useful screenshots for easy learning.

Microsoft Dynamics CRM 2011: Dashboards Cookbook

ISBN: 978-1-849684-40-8   Paperback: 266 pages

Over 50 simple but incredibly effective recipes for creating, customizing, and interacting with rich dashboards and charts

1. Take advantage of all of the latest Dynamics CRM dashboard features for visualizing your most important data at a glance

2. Understand how iFrames, chart customizations, advanced WebResources and more can improve your dashboards in Dynamics CRM by using this book and eBook.

Please check **www.PacktPub.com** for information on our titles

Lightning Source UK Ltd.
Milton Keynes UK
UKOW02f0800050813

214827UK00005B/149/P